Intersectionality and

This collection addresses the present and the future of the concept of intersectionality within socio-legal studies. Intersectionality provides a metaphorical schema for understanding the interaction of different forms of disadvantage, including race, sexuality, and gender. But it also goes further to provide a particular model of how these aspects of social identity and location converge – whether at the level of subjectivity, everyday life, in culture or in the institutional practices of state and other bodies.

Including contributions from a range of international scholars, this book interrogates what has become a key organising concept across a range of disciplines, most particularly law, political theory, and cultural studies.

Emily Grabham is a Research Fellow at the AHRC Research Centre for Law, Gender and Sexuality at the University of Kent.

Davina Cooper is Professor of Law and Political Theory at the University of Kent, and Director of the AHRC Research Centre for Law, Gender and Sexuality.

Jane Krishnadas is a Lecturer in the Law School at Keele University and co-convenor of the Alternative Globalisations Forum.

Didi Herman is Professor of Law and Social Change at the University of Kent.

Social Justice

Series editors: Davina Cooper and Kate Bedford

University of Kent at Canterbury, UK

Social Justice is a new, theoretically engaged, interdisciplinary series exploring the changing values, politics and institutional forms through which claims for equality, democracy and liberation are expressed, manifested and fought over in the contemporary world. The series addresses a range of contexts from transnational political fora, to nation-state and regional controversies, to small-scale social experiments. At its heart is a concern, and inter-disciplinary engagement with, the present and future politics of power, as constituted through territory, gender, sexuality, ethnicity, economics, ecology and culture.

Foregrounding struggle, imagined alternatives and the embedding of new norms, Social Justice critically explores how change is wrought through law, governance and institutionalisation, everyday social and bodily practices, dissident knowledges, and movements for citizenship, belonging, and reinvented community.

Intersectionality and Beyond

Law, power and the politics of location

Edited by
Emily Grabham, Davina Cooper,
Jane Krishnadas and Didi Herman

Routledge·Cavendish
Taylor & Francis Group
a GlassHouse book

First published 2009
by Routledge-Cavendish
2 Park Square, Milton Park, Abingdon, Oxfordshire OX14 4RN

Simultaneously published in the USA and Canada
by Routledge-Cavendish
711 Third Avenue, New York, NY 10017

A GlassHouse Book

*Routledge-Cavendish is an imprint of the Taylor & Francis Group,
an informa business*

Typeset in Sabon by
HWA Text and Data Management, London

British Library Cataloguing in Publication Data
A catalogue record for this book is available from the British
Library

Library of Congress Cataloging-in-Publication Data
A catalog record has been requested for this title

ISBN 13: 978–0–415–43242–9 (hbk)
ISBN 10: 0–415–43242–1(hbk)

ISBN 13: 978–0–415–43243–6 (pbk)
ISBN 10: 0–415–43243–X(pbk)

ISBN 13: 978–0–203–89088–2 (ebk)
ISBN 10: 0–203–89088–4 (ebk)

This collection is dedicated to:

Sarah Witney for being such a wonderful mum

and

Eunice Mary Aubrey for her love of listening, learning and sharing ideas across the diversities of ages, abilities, languages, sexualties, religions, race and cultures in her family, the classroom and beyond.

Contents

Contributors

Lakshmi Arya has recently submitted a doctoral dissertation at the Centre for Historical Studies, Jawaharlal Nehru University, New Delhi, India. Her doctoral research on rape laws and trials in colonial times (British India and princely Mysore, 1860–1947) has engaged with the possibilities of historicizing discourses of rape and consent, rather than viewing them as ahistorical or natural essences, and with the questions of universal citizenship that a uniform law such as that of rape in post/colonial India raises. She was a Gender, Sexuality and Law Visiting Fellow at Keele University between March and May 2005. She has also assisted briefly in a research project on sex work, trafficking and migration coordinated by the Centre for Feminist Legal Research, New Delhi and the Global Alliance Against Trafficking in Women.

Doris Buss is an Associate Professor of Law at Carleton University, Canada. She teaches and researches in the areas of international law and human rights, feminist theory, violence against women, and global social movements. She is the co-author (with Didi Herman) of *Globalizing Family Values: The Christian Right in International Politics* (University of Minnesota, 2003) and the co-editor (with Ambreena Manji) of *International Law: Modern Feminist Approaches* (Hart, 2004). Her current research explores war crimes prosecutions and the production of ethnic and racial knowledge.

Joanne Conaghan is a Professor of Law at the University of Kent and a member of the AHRC Research Centre for Law, Gender and Sexuality. Her areas of research include labour law, tort law and feminist legal theory and she has published widely in all three fields. She is also Executive Editor of the international journal, *Feminist Legal Studies* and Co-Editor of the *New Oxford Companion to Law*.

Davina Cooper is Professor of Law and Political Theory at the University of Kent, and Director of the AHRC Research Centre for Law, Gender and Sexuality. She is the author of *Challenging Diversity: Rethinking Equality and the Value of Difference* (2004); *Governing Out of Order: Space,*

Law and the Politics of Belonging (1998); *Power in Struggle: Feminism, Sexuality and the State* (1995); and *Sexing the City: Lesbian and Gay Politics Within the Activist State* (1994). Her current project is on the power and practice of "everyday utopias".

Tracey De Simone is the Strategic Policy Officer with Legal Aid Queensland. After qualifying as a solicitor she worked for a criminal law practice in Brisbane, and for the Queensland State government on domestic violence law reform. She subsequently coordinated Legal Aid Queensland's Women's Legal Aid unit for six years, during the course of which she oversaw the production of the unit's annual *Gender Equity Report*, and co-authored the report on 'Women and Legal Aid: Identifying Disadvantage' with Rosemary Hunter and Louise Whitaker. She also acted for numerous women with a host of legal problems. She is currently undertaking an LLM at Griffith University.

Suzanne B. Goldberg is Clinical Professor of Law at Columbia Law School, New York. She directs Columbia's Sexuality and Gender Law Clinic and teaches civil procedure, lawyering, social change, and the movement for women's and gay, lesbian, bisexual, and transgender rights. She is the co-author of *Strangers to the Law: Gay People on Trial* (1998) and has published widely on constitutional law, civil rights, sexuality and the law, and social justice.

Emily Grabham is a Research Fellow at the AHRC Research Centre for Law, Gender and Sexuality. Her current research centres on how belonging is negotiated through the body. Her publications include 'Encountering Human Rights: Gender/Sexuality, Activism and the Promise of Law' Special Issue of *Feminist Legal Studies* (2008) (with Rosemary Hunter), 'Sexuality and the Citizen-Carer: The "Good Gay" and the Third Way' *Northern Ireland Legal Quarterly* (2007) (with Joanne Conaghan) and 'Citizen Bodies, Intersex Citizenship' in *Sexualities* (2007).

Didi Herman is Professor of Law and Social Change at the University of Kent and a member of the AHRC Research Centre for Law, Gender and Sexuality. Her key publications include *Globalizing Family Values: The Christian Right in International Politics* (with Doris Buss, University of Minnesota Press, 2003), *Sexuality in the Legal Arena* (co-edited with Carl Stychin, Athlone Press, 2000), *The Antigay Agenda: Orthodox Vision and the Christian Right* (University of Chicago, 1997), and *Rights of Passage: Struggles for Lesbian and Gay Legal Equality* (University of Toronto Press, 1994). She is currently writing *Jews and Jewishness in English Law* (forthcoming, Oxford University Press).

Rosemary Hunter is Professor of Law at the University of Kent, where she teaches family law and criminal law, and is a member of the AHRC

Research Centre for Law, Gender and Sexuality. She chairs the RCSL Working Group on Gender and Law, and is also the Academic Editor of *Feminist Legal Studies*. Her major research interest is in feminist legal scholarship, within which she has done work on family law, domestic violence, access to justice, women's employment (including women in the legal profession and women judges), anti-discrimination law and dispute resolution. She is particularly interested in the interface between law and society, and much of her work has taken an empirical approach, or has sought to build feminist legal theory from empirical data. She has recently edited (with Sharon Cowan) *Choice and Consent: Feminist Engagements with Law and Subjectivity* (RoutledgeCavendish, 2007).

Eunjung Kim received her PhD in disability studies at the University of Illinois at Chicago. She is a post-doctoral fellow of the Future of Minority Studies at University of Michigan at Ann Arbor working on a project of looking at representations of asexuality in relation to disability. Her previous research includes disabled women's life histories with a focus on job experiences and the history of disabled women's movements in South Korea. Her research interests include the sex industry, transnational feminist analysis on disability, disabled people's sexuality, intersectionality and conflicts among minority categories and disability in global representation.

Jane Krishnadas is a Lecturer in the Law School at Keele University and a member of the AHRC Research Centre for Law, Gender and Sexuality. Her main interests lie in the area of rights, gender and reconstruction. Her recent publications include 'Global De-valuing of Local Capacities to Care: From Rights of Redistribution to Revaluation in the Post-earthquake Reconstruction Process, Maharashtra', *Northern Ireland Legal Quarterly* (2008); 'Relocating the Master's Domain, Social and Legal Locations of Gender from Post-Disaster to Everyday Life', *Social and Legal Studies* (2007) and 'Identities in Reconstruction; From Rights of Recognition to Reflection in Post-disaster Reconstruction Processes', *Feminist Legal Studies* (2007).

Leslie McCall received her PhD in sociology from the University of Wisconsin in 1995. She is currently Associate Professor of Sociology at Northwestern University, Faculty Fellow at Northwestern's Institute for Policy Research, and Senior Fellow at Demos. Her work on how class, gender, and racial earnings inequality overlap and conflict with one other across labour markets in the United States has been published in a wide range of journals as well as in her book, *Complex Inequality: Gender, Class, and Race in the New Economy* (Routledge, 2001), which was the first runner-up for the C. Wright Mills Book Award. Her current research includes an ongoing study of rising economic inequality among women; an analysis of the impact of corporate restructuring (e.g., downsizing, subcontracting) on rising earnings inequality; and an investigation of the political consequences of rising inequality, in terms of awareness of and opposition to inequality and preferences for redistributive policies.

Siobhán Mullally is a Senior Lecturer and Co-Director of the Centre for Criminal Justice and Human Rights at the Faculty of Law, University College Cork. She has published widely in the fields of gender, human rights and migration law. Her book *Gender, Culture and Human Rights: Reclaiming Universalism* was published by Hart in 2006. She is Editor of the *Irish Yearbook of International Law* and is currently the Chairperson of the Irish Refugee Council. She is currently director of a three-year research project, funded by the Irish Research Council for the Humanities and Social Sciences, on gender, religious diversity and multiculturalism in contemporary Ireland.

Momin Rahman works in the Department of Sociology, Trent University, Canada. He is the author of *Sexuality and Democracy: Identities and Strategies in Lesbian and Gay Politics* (2000) and *A Sociological Introduction to Gender and Sexuality* (2008 with Stevi Jackson). He has published various articles on the politics of sexuality, identities and the materiality of these, including 'What Really Matters? The Concept of the Material in Feminist Thought' (2004 with Anne Witz) and 'The Shape of Equality: Discourses in the Section 28 Repeal Debate in Scotland' (2004).

Eilish Rooney teaches at the University of Ulster in the School of Sociology and Applied Social Studies. She is an Associate Researcher at the university's Transitional Justice Institute. Recent work has been published in *Feminist Legal Studies, International Journal of Law in Context*, and the *International Journal of Transitional Justice*. She contributed to the *Field Day Anthology of Irish Writing, Vol. V: Irish Women's Writing and Traditions*.

Toni Williams holds a law degree from Oxford University and a PhD in law and economics from the University of Newcastle upon Tyne. She is currently Professor of Law at the University of Kent, and a member of the AHRC Research Centre for Law, Gender and Sexuality. From 1992–1995, she served as one of six commissioners of the Commission on Systemic Racism in the Ontario Criminal Justice System, assuming primary responsibility for writing the commission's interim (1994) and final (1995) reports. In addition to her work on racial discrimination in the administration of criminal justice, Professor Williams has published in the areas of feminist legal theory, critical law and economics, and access to financial services for consumers and microentrepreneurs from marginalized populations. Her current research projects are in the areas of sentencing law, regulation of consumer financial services and economic justice.

Iris Marion Young was Professor of Political Science at the University of Chicago and was also affiliated with the Centre for Gender Studies there. Her research covered feminist theory, political theory, and social and public policy. Her books include *Justice and the Politics of Difference* (1990), *Throwing Like a Girl and Other Essays in Feminist Philosophy and Social Theory* (1990), *Intersecting Voices: Dilemmas of Gender, Political Philosophy, and Policy* (1997), and *Inclusion and Democracy* (2000).

Preface

The impetus for this collection emerged out of the conference *Theorising Intersectionality* held on the 21–22 May, 2005, at Keele University in Staffordshire, UK. The conference was the first major international event organised by the AHRC Research Centre for Law, Gender and Sexuality (CentreLGS) which opened on 1 June 2004, with five years funding from the UK's Arts and Humanities Research Council. CentreLGS is a partnership of three institutions: the Universities of Keele, Kent, and Westminster. CentreLGS aims to create an interdisciplinary, critical, theoretically oriented research environment to help advance the field of law, gender and sexuality, broadly conceived, through scholarship, academic networking events, graduate development, and policy engagement. Several Centre members, alongside other *Theorising Intersectionality* participants, have chapters in this book. Iris Marion Young was invited to give a plenary paper at the conference. Shortly before the conference, Iris wrote to us explaining that for reasons of ill-health she was unfortunately unable to attend. She did, generously, send us a copy of her talk, which we posted on our website. This paper is included, with minor revisions, in this collection. Iris Marion Young died on 1 August 2006. In common with many scholars in the field, this book and our work more generally owes an immense debt to Iris Young. The questions she posed about justice and inequality, her own crafted responses, and her tenacious pursuit of ever more complex ways of thinking about social difference and oppression, have, in multiple ways, indelibly shaped our work and how we approach these issues.

Acknowledgements

We would like to thank Mima Vicentijevic for her editorial assistance, and Colin Perrin and Kate Murphy at Routledge-Cavendish for all their work and support of this project. We are also grateful to the AHRC Research Centre for Law, Gender and Sexuality, and all our colleagues there, for their support and intellectual stimulation. Our greatest thanks go to our contributors for providing us with such outstanding work.

We would also like to acknowledge the following permissions:

Chapter 2 is reprinted from 'The Complexity of Intersectionality' *Signs: Journal of Women in Culture and Society* 30 (3): 1771–800.

Chapter 3 is a revised version of a public lecture published under the title: 'Punishing women: the promise and perils of contextualized sentencing for Aboriginal women in Canada' (2007) *Cleveland State Law Review* 55(3): 269–87.

Chapter 4: an earlier version of this chapter was published as: 'The Curious Visibility of Wartime Rape: Gender and Ethnicity in International Criminal Law' (2007) *Windsor Journal of Access to Justice* 25: 3–22.

Chapter 8: an earlier version of this chapter was published as: 'Intersectionality in Transition: Lessons from Northern Ireland' *Web Journal of Current Legal Issues* (2007) 5: 1–20.

Chapter 11: a revised version of this paper appears in Anthony Simon Laden and David Owen (eds) *Multiculturalism and Political Theory* Copyright Cambridge University Press 2007, pp. 60–88.

Chapter 13: an earlier version of this chapter was published as 'The Uniform Civil Code: The Politics of the Universal in Postcolonial India' (2006) *Feminist Legal Studies* 14(3): 293–328.

Introduction

Emily Grabham with Didi Herman,
Davina Cooper and Jane Krishnadas

Studies on intersectionality have proliferated in recent years. For some, this development, which began in the late 1980s, can be understood as one effect of the 'postmodern turn' in the academy: an attempt to trace and account for a supposed fragmentation of identities within political movements of the late twentieth century. For others, the focus on intersectionality provides tools for complicating our understanding of the systems and processes that define the social: intersectionality is thus a method for interrogating the institutional reproduction of inequality, whether at the level of the state, the family, or of legal structures more generally.

With some of its earliest applications in critical race studies, specifically critical race approaches in sociology (Anthias and Yuval-Davis, 1983) and law (see Crenshaw, 1989; Duclos, 1993), research engaging intersectionality can now be found in a wide range of contexts. A survey of recent journal articles indicates the currency of intersectionality in political geography (Valentine, 2007), political science (Hawkesworth, 2003), feminist approaches to economics (Brewer *et al.*, 2002), critical psychotherapy (Burman, 2004; Fernandes, 2004), sociology (Yuval-Davis, 2006), postcolonial studies (Arondeker, 2005), and socio-legal studies (Vakulenko, 2007; Deckha, 2004; Conaghan, 2007; Hannett, 2003; Grabham, 2006), to name only a few. This raises the question of why the concept of intersectionality, specifically, is being used, in such a ubiquitous way, to investigate social, political, and economic life. Certainly, the metaphor of the intersection appears to move beyond more static conceptions of inequality that focus on 'multiple' or 'compound' disadvantage. Apparently more fluid and responsive, intersectional approaches look to forms of inequality that are routed through one another, and which cannot be untangled to reveal a single cause. In this sense, intersectionality describes very well the coming together of forms of inequality through institutional and representational dynamics. It puts complexity centre-stage, and many scholars appear to find this approach refreshing and productive. At the same time, however, imagining social life through intersections inevitably directs the gaze away from the co-constitution of identities and inequalities to what, apparently, is not already intersected (Cooper, 2004: 48). Intersectionality requires vectors and identities that exist apart from each other. Acting like a fastener, or zip, intersectionality presumes the gaps that it attempts to close. This raises the question of whether there are, in fact, any areas of the social that exist apart from the meeting point, or overlap, that intersectionality describes.

Nevertheless, in drawing critical attention away from static conceptions of social life and experience, intersectionality continues to perform important conceptual work, and this work takes place on a number of registers. Intersectionality can be used to analyse law, in particular anti-discrimination law, to unpack the material and discursive effects of legal identity categories on socially constituted subjects. A cluster of arguments emerges here around the inadequate recognition of the complexly situated subject by various lawmaking or law-enforcing bodies or policy initiatives. The type of analysis then takes the following form: a subject might encounter the law, or the state, only to find that her experiences of inequality do not fit the dominant model. These analyses not only point to the repressive or coercive functions of top-down power, they also signal the exacerbation of hierarchical power relations through law's failure to recognise the subject's full identity, position, or the complexity or messiness of her experiences. From a liberal perspective, the law, or the state, therefore fails, and intersectionality can be presented as a way of showing this failure and asking for a better job to be done. From a radical perspective, the state has been successful in achieving its goals. As Joanne Conaghan points out in her contribution to this collection, (liberal) socio-legal narratives display a certain degree of confidence in legal or state apparatuses: the work of intersectionality is the work of improvement; it is optimistic about reform and representation. But they also take seriously concepts of state and nation as reified 'things': coherent, autonomous actors with institutional memory and the capacity for future planning. Explaining to the law its mistaken assumptions will lead the law/state to a consciousness of its omissions and to rational change.

At the same time, intersectionality has been deployed to indicate the inherent limits of law. Within these narratives, legal and policy interventions to tackle inequality are inevitably flawed. By their very nature, they can only ever work through fetishising categorical constructions of identity and experience that never respond to the material circumstances of subjects' lives. True subjectivity and experience are located 'outside' law and government: they will never be containable. Far from being a way of improving the functioning of legal or state apparatuses, intersectionality offers another argument against law reform. Intersectionality reveals how experience is incommensurable with the categorised representations of identity mobilised in human rights law and discourse, anti-discrimination law, and in government equality initiatives.

On another register, intersectionality can be used to investigate how inequalities are *produced* on the institutional scale, through structures, processes and techniques of governance. Within these frames, inequality is imagined at the level of the home, the workplace, the state, or the international 'community': complex inequalities are constituted through the operation of global capital, through international relations, monetary policies, domestic social policies, the employment relationship or the family. Deployments of intersectionality help to trace the complex material effects of these processes, and, in some respects, parallel earlier models such as dual systems theory, which focused on the relationship between patriarchy and class oppression. Intersectional approaches can also assist in investigating how social identities are formed as the congealed effects of power's workings rather than autonomous groups or identities (Cooper, 2004; Brown, 1995). Here, the analysis becomes less a question of finding the points at which inequalities meet and instead involves tracing the allocation and deployment of power in the organisation of social life.

With these perspectives in mind, our aim in this collection has been to take stock of intersectionality's significance after almost twenty years of discussion and analysis. Taken as a whole, the collection offers a critical picture of intersectionality's relevance within a range of disciplines – socio-legal studies, political and social theory, and history. We present situated work from a range of contexts, tracing productive tensions and resonances in the way that different scholars conceive intersectional analysis. Aiming for a cross-national debate, we have included papers that consider developments in Canada, Rwanda, the United States, India, the United Kingdom, Korea, Ireland and Australia. With some pieces drawn directly from empirical or other grounded research (including experiences of activism), the collection contains a range of analytical perspectives (postcolonial, feminist, critical race, disability studies) and troubles contemporary narratives and institutional dynamics ranging from international law constructions of wartime rape to community relations rhetoric in the 'transitional' setting of Northern Ireland. Many contributions engage gender and sexuality as organising principles of social life, but contributors also interrogate racialising and abilist dynamics, as well as the effects of class and colonialism.

We outline themes and disjunctures in more detail below, but if there is one theme to be found across this intentionally diverse collection, it is an endeavour to forge critical approaches to intersectionality that disembed or reframe received ways of thinking about complex inequalities. Our aim is to explore, and reflect critically on, how the concept of intersectionality has been used, and to address intersectionality's future. The book thus includes contributions from scholars who are committed to working with intersectionality as a concept, as well as others who suggest that alternative frameworks are better able to elucidate the relationship between different forms of inequality and identification. *Intersectionality and Beyond* addresses four key questions:

1 What are the implications of intersectionality analysis for how we understand relations of inequality, such as gender, race and sexuality?
2 How do state agencies, including the courts, constitute, understand and deploy the intersecting character of relations of inequality?
3 Can intersectional analysis illuminate the gendered, racialised and sexualised character of social structures?
4 How useful is intersectionality analysis for understanding the capacity of relations of inequality or difference to evolve and change? Do other frameworks offer better guides for understanding this?

The first part of the collection, *Mapping Intersectionalities*, provides an entry into these questions with two examples of how concepts of the social have been complicated by intersectional approaches. The consideration, or re-consideration, of intersectionality that Joanne Conaghan and Leslie McCall undertake is shaped by almost two decades of feminist work in the academy on intersectionality, and a much longer engagement with anti-essentialism more broadly. Conaghan and McCall both reject approaches to inequality based on identity politics and liberal conceptions of the individual, focusing instead on material structures and processes. Yet they differ in their assessment of intersectionality's continued use as a feminist tool of analysis. Conaghan argues that whilst intersectionality has been vitally important to feminist theory over the past twenty years, there is little more that it can now contribute. There are, as she argues, many reasons for this: intersectionality's roots in law; its 'mapping' function; the tendency to frame intersectionality as a problem of representation; its focus on the individual and identity. Conaghan recalls socialist and materialist feminist work which, embedded in historical analysis of social and political life, theorised the connections between sex and class based oppression and produced 'dual systems' theory. She traces significant critiques of this work by black feminist theorists, who pointed out the importance of bringing an account of race to an approach that was intended to provide a 'complete' picture of social relations. Comparing more recent work on intersectionality with earlier accounts of complex inequalities rooted in historical materialism, Conaghan highlights intersectionality's limits and the need for an analysis that connects experiences of inequality with structures, institutions and processes.

McCall is more positive about intersectionality's continued usefulness. This may be because she identifies different forms of intersectional research (anticategorical, intercategorical, and intracategorical analysis), thereby contributing a variegated picture of how the concept has been taken up. But it may also be because her account of intersectionality is deeply embedded in an understanding of social relations; that is to say, her working model of intersectionality already approximates Conaghan's 'social processes' model and she therefore may feel less restricted by intersectionality's legal roots. McCall's main concern is the methodology of intersectionality and the dearth of work on how to carry out intersectional enquiry. Her contribution, reprinted from *Signs*, is an attempt to pose methodology as a question in this area. What is impeding feminist research on intersectionality is not the 'narrowly disciplinary' subject matter under consideration in any particular instance but a reluctance to use a varied range of methodologies in response to substantive questions. Her own work on wage inequality in different regions of the US provides an example of an interdisciplinary methodological approach to intersectionality and the context-specific responses to inequality such enquiry suggests. The need for diverse methodologies is reflected in the contributions throughout this collection, many of which draw on interdisciplinary socio-legal analysis as a starting point and explore further methodologies in line with the demands of the subject matter.

Having set out some core questions around intersectionality in Part I, we explore in Part II – *Confronting law* – the ways in which law, and legal institutions, have engaged with intersectionality's challenge to essentialised concepts of identity and disadvantage. Legal practice may not always be best interrogated through the lens of intersectionality (Hunter and de Simone), and legal decision makers may ignore intersectionality in some circumstances (Buss) or implement intersectional perspectives with negative consequences for women in others (Williams). By criminalising Canadian Aboriginal women through 'risk' (Williams), or narrowly defining wartime rape in international law (Buss), law's appropriation of intersectionality frustrates its radical potential, whilst operationalising anti-essentialism may run into practical difficulties at the level of activism (Goldberg) or may require a focus on structural dynamics instead of apparently intersectional identity markers (Hunter and de Simone).

Toni Williams investigates how decision-makers receive feminist knowledges, including intersectionality. She focuses on a seemingly progressive legal provision: section 718.2(e) of the Canadian Criminal Code, which instructs criminal courts to take into account the specific circumstances of Aboriginal offenders, and she attempts to work out why, despite this provision, there has been an increase in the incarceration of Aboriginal women in Canada. Far from considering the impact of colonialism on Aboriginal peoples since European contact, decision-makers have assessed Aboriginal women as being at higher risk of re-offending due to their experiences of racialisation, community 'dysfunction', and economic vulnerability. In this way, as a form of feminist 'knowledge', the contextual assessment of Aboriginal women's 'intersectional' circumstances works in favour of their over-incarceration.

Doris Buss is similarly concerned with how intersectionality is constructed within legal decision-making regimes. Buss focuses on the prosecution of mass wartime rape as crimes against humanity by the Rwanda and Yugoslav Tribunals. She is particularly interested in how the Tribunals interpret large-scale gender-based violence and its role in the construction of ethnic identities. She analyses one decision of the Rwanda Tribunal in depth: the prosecution

DORIS BUSS

of Sylvestre Gacumbitsi for the rape and murder of Tutsi women in Rusumo, Eastern Rwanda in 1994. In this judgment, the Tribunal held that the rape of a Hutu woman married to a Tutsi man was an attack on the Tutsi community and therefore a crime against humanity, and in doing so it concluded that the rape targeted not her, but her husband. This decision, as Buss points out, depicted rape in a superficial manner, failing to address intersections of gender and ethnicity that enabled rape to take place, and disconnected it from everyday violence against women. Buss advocates instead an interpretation that acknowledges the structural basis of sexual violence within societies and the intersectional dynamics of oppression affecting racialised women in conflict situations. In turn, her contribution provides a nuanced route into the formations of ethnicity that are produced through state and institutional practices, specifically in relation to women and women's bodies.

The picture of intersectionality that emerges so far is of a method of analysis with radical roots, but which can be mobilised within legal structures either in inadequate ways, or in ways that undermine its foundational critical impulse. This is not to say that pursuing intersectional scholarship is destined to failure. Instead, what McCall shows is that, as an analytical framework, intersectionality has many different methodological routes and a number of potential outcomes. Heeding Conaghan's arguments, these routes should not overwhelmingly focus on subjective experiences and questions of identity but should instead account for material conditions and social practice. In juxtaposition with Williams's chapter, for example, Buss's suggested response to international law on mass rape arguably requires taking account of complex experiences and processes of inequality without further objectifying women in the legal process or classifying them through discourses of victimhood.

The next contribution, by Suzanne Goldberg, shifts the debate to the sphere of legal activism, and to the question of how intersectionality functions in not-for-profit organising. Goldberg focuses on identity based law reform organisations in the United States and their practices around intersectionality and other dimensions of inequality. She analyses two features in particular: the tendency for organisations to put themselves forward as advocating on behalf of a single identity or inequality, and their practice of filing *amicus curiae* briefs to support the legal struggles of other groups. With regard to the former, Goldberg's question is why, when the insights of intersectionality have been important to activists for so long, the not-for-profit field in the United States remains stratified by single identity groups. Using the mission statements of these groups as a starting point, she then considers a number of pragmatic reasons: infrastructural set ups that make it easier to incorporate intersectional practice into existing institutional arrangements rather than coming up with new structures; the necessity of defining the organisation's target group clearly in order to access funding; and the single-identity structure of antidiscrimination law. But if organisations are single-dimensional, why

[Handwritten margin notes:]

Looking @ Rape in Rwanda ignoring the intersect of ♀ & ethnic in order to avoid Rape as an everyday issue.

intersect is not about subj exper But rather makes sense of social practice

→ ♀ as people not as victims

AMICUS CURIAE

the way in which not-for-profit set for exacerbates & proliferation of society do they support other identity organisations? When filing an *amicus curiae* brief in favour of another organisation, a group may take into consideration their interdependence with the legal struggles of other groups; their wish to create an environment 'friendly' to civil rights claims; or their wish to contribute their authority to the struggle of a more marginalized group. In Goldberg's opinion, the filing of supportive *amicus curiae* briefs indicates that intersectional approaches exist within the US legal activist field, but that they do not primarily take an organised form. What Goldberg's contribution adds to the analysis so far is an appreciation of the subtle and contingent techniques through which alliances are formed within activism, leading to practices of intersectionality that undermine the apparently stratified and single identity structure of many large not-for-profit organisations.

[handwritten margin note: not-for-profit field relied on single ID for funding]

Accessing the law, this time in the context of legal aid decisions, is also the concern of Rosemary Hunter and Tracey de Simone. Hunter and de Simone discuss findings from a recent research project that aimed to identify barriers to women being granted legal aid in Queensland, Australia. Hunter and de Simone's project took as its basis an environment of financial cut backs: it focused on scarce distribution of legal aid to women, and, heeding the intersectionality literature, they were interested in the potentially greater impact of this enforced scarcity on marginalised women in particular. What they found, however, was that despite some differences in women's experiences by target group (Indigenous women, for example, had more trouble finding funds to pay for legal advice after being refused legal aid; older women were more likely to be refused legal aid due to the means test), there was a more significant association between refusals of legal aid, the matter that formed the basis for the application (for example, residence applications or anti-discrimination claims), and the conditions facing individual offices at particular moments. They conclude that disadvantage in applying for legal aid was shaped by the institutional context of the Queensland legal aid system and did not significantly correlate with pre-existing identity markers. In their view, analysing inequalities through identity categories is, in this context therefore, less productive than concentrating on context and structural dynamics such as institutional practices, access to adequate legal representation, and geographical location, for example.

Hunter and De Simone's conclusion echoes Conaghan's argument that focusing on identity and experience should be balanced with an analysis of systems and processes of inequality, and it resonates with the careful approach to intersectionality evidenced in all of the contributions in this collection. It also raises the additional question of how to account for materially significant differences of circumstance beyond the usual ways that the social has been imagined. This question takes a different trajectory to questions around 'doing' intersectionality or intersectional scholarship. It challenges intersectionality's relevance to socio-legal analysis (as opposed to its effectiveness or how it is interpreted in law), especially where intersectionality is defined as the study of complex identities.

A further critical angle on intersectionality, although from a different perspective, can be found in Emily Grabham's contribution. Grabham draws on her experience of working as a discrimination lawyer to investigate problems with mobilising intersectional equality claims through employment tribunal claims in the UK. Engaging Wendy Brown's analysis of rights claims in *States of Injury,* Grabham argues that intersectional approaches to rights claims cannot challenge law's disciplinary constructions of identity and that they in fact function as 'anatomies of detail' which support law's propensity to classify. Moving away from the regulatory effects of intersectionality within law, Grabham aims to reframe her understanding of the liberal subject's experience of inequalities. She connects questions of justice with emotional and physical encounters through the cultural functions of trauma and the role of impressions (drawing on the work of Ann Cvetkovich and Sara Ahmed). Viewing discrimination claims as expressions/impressions of trauma, she argues, may yield new ways of viewing complex inequalities, shifting the focus of intersectionality away from disciplinary identity categories and towards the cultural circulation of emotions. In reframing the cultural significance of experiences beyond the individual, this approach arguably responds to Conaghan's suggestion that we move beyond the identity model of intersectionality. What remains here is a question about what to do with the law. Like many of the contributions in this collection, Grabham is sceptical about how to envisage an effective, anti-essentialist encounter with law as an institution, and her focus on intersectionality's potential for cooption resonates with Williams's critique of technologies of risk-management in Canadian criminal law.

Part III shifts the analysis to the level of the state. The contributions in this section – *Power relations and the state* – address critically how law and the state imagine and deploy single and multi-dimensional understandings of inequality. They highlight how not only gendered but racialised and other processes are at work in the constitution and reproduction of state power (Mullally). They explore from an intersectional and post-intersectional perspective the state's deployment of one-dimensional figures: the trope for instance of woman is seemingly uncontaminated, yet inevitably saturated by other relations of power (Rooney). And they critically rebut any claim that relations of inequality work together neatly and symmetrically, to investigate how particular inequalities can be rendered invisible, overwhelmed or deployed instrumentally and culturally in the service of each other (Kim).

Eilish Rooney's focus is the policy discourse, and considerable academic literature, that has arisen in relation to Northern Ireland. Policy narratives spotlight the concept of 'sectarian' opposition between Catholic and Protestant men, leading to a 'community relations' rhetoric that leaves women's experiences out of the picture. Likewise, the thriving field of academic work around the conflict leaves women, particularly working-class women, invisible, thereby erasing important dynamics of gender and class in the construction of the Northern Irish political scene, both during and post conflict. The impetus for Rooney's analysis is a recognition of how state discourses impact on low-income women in Northern Ireland through government social policy initiatives, research, and legislation. For her, intersectionality has a great deal of promise as a tool that enables scholars to focus on the material contours of women's lives and on the intersections of gender, class and sect that generate poverty over time. Rooney's work thus taps into an important theme in the intersectionality literature: that of highlighting erasures in dominant discourses and bringing into view what would otherwise be obscured. The role of intersectionality analysis in revealing the partiality of legal frameworks and government rhetoric is a vitally important one which, for all of intersectionality's potential pitfalls, should not be discarded without careful thought.

Eunjung Kim also addresses state policy initiatives in her chapter *Minority politics in Korea: disability, interraciality, and gender*. She investigates the recently created Republic of Korea National Action Plan for the Promotion and Protection of Human Rights, which sets out eleven categories of vulnerable social groups. Kim's analysis specifically points to the importance of maintaining a critical attitude to the type of intersectionality that is imagined in anti-essentialist scholarship. She focuses on the paradoxes raised by two clusters of intersections in Korean law: disabled women or female disabled persons, and interracial bodies, disability and nationality. Despite the rise of disabled women's activism in Korea, a 1994 provision that imposes harsher sentences for those raping disabled women has led to Korean law constructing disabled women as unable to consent to sexual intercourse, and to a definition of rape as requiring the use of force. Furthermore, the historic construction of bi-ethnic children of Korean mothers and US fathers (from the military occupation) as disabled has lent the concept of disability a great degree of flexibility in Korean society but has failed adequately to connect this construction with other social categories such as disabled people and mothers engaged in sex work. Kim concludes that the most useful model of intersectionality to apply in this context is one based on the interdependent construction of categories. Theorising intersectionality through separate axes, she contends, leaves essentialism intact. Kim's grounded analysis poses a challenge to forms of anti-essentialist thinking that, as we have seen, require categories to be intact before imagining how they merge.

Siobhán Mullally's focus is the treatment of migrant women in Ireland. Mullally traces in particular the many ways in which the Irish state has recently deployed the intersectional figure of the (fertile) asylum-seeking woman to shore up the boundaries of the nation state. Non-Irish women claiming rights to family life under the European Convention on Human Rights in order to stay with children born in Ireland have provided a pretext for the Irish government's renewed focus on women's bodies and sexual roles, linking racialised notions of citizenship and belonging to gender and reproduction. Citizenship for the children of migrant parents, having been based on geographical location (being born within the boundaries of Ireland, or, more emotively 'on Irish soil'), shifted in 2004 after a government referendum to being based on lawful residence of the parents within the state for three years or more. Alarmist media coverage of 'pregnant asylum-seekers' moving to Ireland to claim health care and Irish citizenship and 'asylum seekers ... breeding like rabbits' contributed to a set of public discourses that connected racialised others with the spectres of overpopulation and citizenship tourism. Mullally juxtaposes these developments with the difficulties Irish women faced in accessing safe abortions. The fact that many Irish women obtain abortions in the UK every year highlights disjunctures in the ways that migration and reproduction are constructed, depending on the direction of, and reason for, travel. Mullally concludes that intersectional analysis provides tools for understanding how citizenship excludes migrant women in Ireland in specific ways, but she is more sceptical about its potential for providing a feminist praxis around migration, gender and reproduction.

In the context of the state, intersectionality plays the useful role of challenging nationalised, racialised and sexualised versions of belonging, whether this belonging is linked to citizenship status (Mullally), legal protection against discrimination (Kim), or social policy initiatives (Rooney). In this sense, intersectionality teases out what is at stake in decision-making processes, how these processes construct norms across multiple sites of power and identity, and the distributive consequences of complicated norms. Yet the question of how these different flows of inequality exert pressure on each other remains difficult to answer. In many senses, intersectionality as a method of analysis can raise more questions than it answers.

With this in mind, Part IV – *Alternative pathways* – addresses different springboards for theoretical and interpretive analysis in law, political theory, critical race studies and feminist theory. The contributions in this section engage with questions of how to imagine the projects of equality and social justice and how such an imagining changes our approaches to intersectionality. Thinking through the politics of difference yields a range of approaches to questions of structure, culture, and social relations, which in turn affect how we visualise the building blocks, flows of power, and axes through which intersectionality is usually theorised. If the aim of anti-essentialism has been to challenge the erasures inherent within the dominant paradigm of liberal universalism, can universalism be reconfigured outside the liberal model? How does our conception of social justice affect the work that we want intersectionality to do?

The focus of Iris Young's contribution is the problems that ensue when a politics of cultural difference fails adequately to take account of structures of power and their role in constituting the 'normal'. Young begins by setting

fear of "aliens"

linking fem things (repro) to fear

intersect of citizenship (migrants) + gender (fem) and how it intersect is the point intersect that

politics of difference

Iris Young

RAINBOW loom as a means of exclusion
- string just need the string
- loom-elastics & plastic thing   Introduction   11

out two different but related ways in which the politics of difference has
been framed in recent political thought: the politics of positional difference
and the politics of cultural difference. These, she argues, have often been
read together, erasing in the process important definitional distinctions and
issues of justice. The politics of positional difference focuses on dominating
structural axes in Western societies, such as the social division of labour,
and Young examines three groups – women, people with disabilities, and
racialised people – in order to discuss the structural features of inequality
that affect each one.

The politics of cultural difference, following largely from the work of
Will Kymlicka, focuses on groups defined by 'societal culture', that is to
say, cultural difference coalesces in these literatures only through ethnicity
and nation. Young argues that the politics of cultural difference underplays
structural analysis of certain inequalities, for example racism; it attaches
itself to liberal theorising that promotes a focus on individuals and groups to
the detriment of social relations; and it normalises dominant power relations
through an uncritical discourse of tolerance. Her aim in drawing attention to
these theoretical lacunae is to put structural dynamics of power back on the
agenda for political theorists as they contemplate issues of ethnicity, nation,
and religious difference.

The next chapter, *Intersectional travel through everyday utopias: the
difference sexual and economic dynamics make*, maintains a similar focus on
the stakes involved in different ways of framing questions of injustice and
inequalities. Davina Cooper looks behind debates around intersectionality
to the ways that we think about 'inequality's conceptual building blocks'.
She uses the concept of social dynamics – in this chapter the economic and
the sexual (although previous work has looked at the intimate/impersonal)
– to navigate away from visualising the social through groups, axes or
vectors of inequality, systems, or gendering and racialising processes. The
social dynamics approach provides a perspective on social life that focuses
on the 'how' and the 'what' of inequality. In this way, studying the social
dynamics of the economic (here, generation–access–use) and the sexual
(desire–intimacy–embodiment) enables us to trace the shifting ways in which
relations of inequality become attached to aspects of social life, and Cooper
uses two prefigurative social sites – the Toronto Women's Bathhouse and UK
Local Exchange and Trading Schemes – to examine how this works.

The pieces in the first section of this Part, therefore, return to the task of
re-thinking theoretical models to respond to questions of injustice. Young's
intervention, in particular, should be understood in the post 9/11 climate
as an injunction to remain critical about who 'we' are when theorising
difference. Young reminds us of the significance of structure in analysing
what are traditionally viewed as 'cultural' forms of inequality, thereby
challenging deterministic readings of social configurations. For her part,
Cooper uses the lens of counter-normative social sites to challenge the

Cooper uses counter cult societies to exemp the way dif social rules are not "normal"

coupling of predetermined social groups with overarching systems of power. Her analysis opens up a fluid understanding of how power, structure, and systems fold into each other in the constitution of social inequalities. The significance, for intersectionality, of the approaches that both Young and Cooper advocate (albeit in different ways) is that they broaden analysis of inequalities away from the archetypal multidimensional subject towards an open-ended, dynamic account that reflects the evolving interactions between inequalities and social structures.

Working with similar concerns, albeit in a different register, Lakshmi Arya uses a case study of the Universal Civil Code debate in India to consider whether it is possible to construct an alternative understanding of universalism from a postcolonial perspective. The Universal Civil Code debate – the proposal for a common civil code for India instead of civil laws stratified by religion – raises many issues that are pertinent to this study: whether such a development would be beneficial for women and consequently who is the subject of Indian feminism; and whether, recognising the problems with universalist Western discourses, this initiative should be welcomed in any case from a postcolonial, poststructuralist standpoint. Arya contrasts these debates with discussions around an earlier piece of uniform civil legislation, the Child Marriage Restraint Act 1929, within which subjects did not limit themselves to speaking from Dalit, or Hindu, or Muslim perspectives. Arya's aim is to retrieve an understanding of intersectional subaltern resistances within the anti-colonial movement, which challenged the categorisation of identities in the colonial state. Undertaking this exercise, she concludes, makes it possible to delineate an empowering, non-Western discourse of the universal. This challenges the presumed problem that intersectionality intends to address, that of the universal subject being essentially the hegemonic subject.

Challenge the categorization of identities

universal subject vs. hegemonic subject

Momin Rahman similarly focuses on universalism, but Rahman's project aims to theorise intersectionality through an understanding of materiality. There are considerable dilemmas involved in thinking through the specificities of lived experience alongside, or through, structural and systemic oppression. Rahman's approach retains a focus on identities, but destabilises the apparent fixity of identity markers by addressing how they are materially constructed through intersections of social processes and structures. Such a materialist interpretation of intersectionality works against a liberal, universal conception of equality and requires instead a social ontology in which widely varying social locations and experiences require a radically differentiated set of equality demands. As Rahman indicates, resonating with Toni Williams's concerns, moving away from the liberal universal also presents a challenge to liberalism's technologies: the abstract citizen, rights discourse, the conception of equality as a mainly legal endeavour. Contesting liberal technologies in this way, he advocates approaching inequalities through lived experience, but with an understanding of how this ontology is

Black & hood is not a shared experience over cultures & locations

materially structured through social processes of oppression. This focus on 'effective materiality' provides one alternative to viewing intersectionality through discrete categories of oppression, which, as he argues, has not provided us with the tools to challenge universalising essentialism within identity politics.

Having provided a brief outline of the collection, we would like to conclude by raising some ongoing questions regarding intersectional scholarship, many of which have been inspired by our engagement with the contributors and with colleagues. It seems that there are a number of concerns with the present use of intersectionality within socio-legal analysis and within connected fields. One preliminary question concerns intersectionality's role or function. In this introduction, we have been referring to intersectionality as a type of analysis, implying an overarching theoretical or ideological framework (such as Marxist analysis or feminist analysis, for example, although these terms also require complication). Yet intersectionality does not assume any particular ideological stance. Without ignoring its strong connection to Black feminist thought, intersectionality has been, and is, mobilised from a number of different standpoints and in conjunction with a number of different intellectual frameworks. It has no particular conceptual home, apart from the imperative to de-essentialise categories and complicate our understanding of social dynamics of inequality. In some institutional or legal settings, as we have seen, this intersectional endeavour need not even be particularly critical or used to improve the lives of targeted groups. With this in mind, what are the implications of referring to intersectionality as a methodology? Does this capture the political development of the term and its current use within the academy? If it is a methodology, or a methodological *orientation*, then McCall has highlighted very clearly the range of techniques that it spans (see also Yuval-Davis, 2006). Furthermore, if it is a methodology, this implies that it can be applied alongside a range of different frameworks of thought. Are we happy to assign intersectionality such an instrumental role? In doing so, do we risk making a false distinction between conceptual framework and methodology itself?

If the role of intersectionality is difficult to discern, this is probably because of its fundamentally challenging nature; yet there is a concern that intersectionality can be used rhetorically, as a way of performing apparently situated analysis without changing prevailing structures of thought. This is typified by work that contains a sentence along the lines of: 'and it is also important to recognise the gendered/sexualised dynamics of this process', where the significance of an intersectional viewpoint to a particular project has not been explained. A connected issue is the use of intersectionality to criticise work that does not appear, to some, to be sufficiently complex. Here, the injunction is to 'take account of race/class/gender/age in this analysis' in such a way that intersectional analysis may appear to require a number of disciplining add-ons.[1]

It would be easy to criticise such mobilisations of intersectionality as lazy or unfinished, or, in the latter instance, overzealous, yet taking them seriously requires us to ask questions of intersectionality itself. Some unease remains within the academy about how to 'do' intersectional research, and it may even be that we are expecting too much of it. This is perhaps the motivation behind a recent effort within literatures on intersectionality to find more appropriate metaphors or terms for complicating relations of inequality: 'geometries', 'taxonomies', 'symbiosis', 'hybridity', and 'multisectionality' are a few examples. In the US context, in particular, discussion in the *University of Missouri-Kansas Law Review* recently turned to the question of how specifically to capture the ways that different forms of oppression and privilege combine and work against each other within individuals and communities (see Ehrenreich, 2002–2003 and associated discussion from Chang and Culp, Cooper, Marcosson, Valdes, Arriola, Westley, Levit, Hutchinson, Razack and Williams). Within these discussions, the concept of 'post-intersectionality' has gained currency (Chang and Culp, 2002–2003). Whilst we would suggest that intersectionality is not yet 'post' due to the many dissonant and productive ways that it is currently articulated, the metaphor of the 'intersection' itself may lead to formulaic analysis. With the image of the intersection, we could see a potentially unlimited number of criss-crossing paths. Productive in some respects, by increasing the potential scope of analysis it thereby increases the likelihood that any particular piece of work can be read as too narrow. It also performs a levelling function, with the roads or routes implying a flat journey from A to B, and this contributes to perceptions that it cannot adequately describe or explain social processes. In particular, the term 'intersection' implies stasis rather than movement. It does not help us to visualise the construction of the social in an active sense, through sexualising, gendering and racialising dynamics. In raising these limitations, there is little room for arguing that intersectionality has not greatly advanced how we think about social injustice. Yet what alternative or supplementary approaches exist to describe the constitution of the social through multiple simultaneous processes?

As many contributors to this collection have argued, intersectionality is still useful as an anti-essentialist approach as long as it is used in conjunction with a clear focus on institutions, structural dynamics, and power. It helps us to account for the formation and evolution of identities not just as discursive effects of legal argument, but also through social, economic and political practices as the effects of material policies (Krishnadas, 2007). It also reminds us how important it is to remain aware of how we think about the social: whose perspectives form the background for the social stories we tell and which experiences and deployments of power are obscured as a result. Intersectionality is not the only way of doing this work, especially when we bear in mind both developments outside law and approaches that pre-date intersectionality. And if it is sometimes deployed in ways that frustrate its radical imperative, then maybe this is less to do with the concept itself and more to do with how feminist knowledge claims are received and neutralised both institutionally and culturally. Perhaps the question is not so much how to 'do intersectionality well' but more how to acknowledge the distance we have travelled with this conceptual framework whilst remaining aware of what we might lose if we move away from it without careful thought. On these terms, the choice is not whether to give it up or not. Instead, recognising its problems and the ways that it can be appropriated within law and policy, we can continue to use intersectionality in the way that it was first developed: as a powerful and relevant method of social analysis.

Acknowledgments

This discussion, and our work on the collection as a whole, were greatly advanced by the input of colleagues at the AHRC Research Centre for Law, Gender and Sexuality at a meeting specifically dedicated to 'thinking through' intersectionality on 17 October 2007. Many thanks to Suhraiya Jivraj, Toni Williams, Sarah Lamble, Sarah Keenan, Brinda Bose (visiting from Nehru Memorial Museum and Library, India), Kate Bedford, and Rosemary Hunter.

Note

1   Thank you to Sarah Lamble for useful discussions on this point.

References

Anthias, Floya and Nira Yuval-Davis (1983) 'Beyond Feminism and Multiculturalism: Locating Difference and the Politics of Location' *Women's Studies International Forum* 25(3): 275–86.

Arondeker, Anjali (2005) 'Border/Line Sex: Queer Postcolonialities, or How Race Matters Outside the United States' *Interventions: International Journal of Postcolonial Studies* 7(2): 236–50.

Arriola, Elvia (2002-2003) 'Staying Empowered by Recognizing our Common Grounds: A Reply to Subordination and Symbiosis: Mechanisms of Mutual Support Between Subordinating Systems by Nancy Ehrenreich' *UMKC Law Review* 71: 447–58.

Brewer, Rose M., Cecilia A. Conrad and Mary C. King (2002) 'The Complexities and Potential of Theorizing Gender, Caste, Race, and Class' *Feminist Economics* 8(2): 3–18.

Brown, Wendy (1995) *States of Injury: Power and Freedom in Late Modernity* Princeton University Press.

Burman, Erica (2004) 'From Difference to Intersectionality: Challenges and Resources' *European Journal of Psychotherapy, Counselling & Health* 6(4): 293–308.

Cho, Sumi (2002–2003) 'Understanding White Women's Ambivalence towards Affirmative Action: Theorizing Political Accountability in Coalitions' *UMKC Law Review* 71: 399–418.

Conaghan, Joanne (2007) 'Intersectionality and UK Equality Initiatives' *South African Journal of Human Rights* 23(2): 317–54.

Cooper, Davina (2004) *Challenging Diversity: Rethinking Equality and the Value of Difference* Cambridge University Press.

Cooper, Frank (2002–2003) 'Understanding "Depolicing": Symbiosis Theory and Critical Cultural Theory' *UMKC Law Review* 71: 355–76.

Crenshaw, Kimberlé (1989) 'Demarginalising the Intersection of Race and Sex: A Black Feminist Critique of Antidiscrimination Doctrine, Feminist Theory and Antiracist Politics' *The University of Chicago Legal Forum* 89: 139–67.

Deckha, Maneesha (2004) 'Is Culture Taboo? Feminism, Intersectionality, and Culture Talk in Law' *Canadian Journal of Women and the Law* 16: 14–53.

Duclos, Nitya (1993) 'Disappearing Women: Racial Minority Women in Human Rights Cases' *Canadian Journal of Women and the Law* 6: 25–51.

Ehrenreich, Nancy (2002–2003) 'Subordination and Symbiosis: Mechanisms of Mutual Support Between Subordinating Systems' *UMKC Law Review* 71: 251–324.

Fernandes, Fátima (2003) 'A Response to Erica Burman' *European Journal of Psychotherapy, Counselling & Health* 6(4): 309–16.

Grabham, Emily (2006) 'Taxonomies of Inequality: Lawyers, Maps, and the Challenge of Hybridity' *Social and Legal Studies* 15(1): 5–23.

Hannett, Sarah (2003) 'Equality at the Intersections: The Legislative and Judicial Failure to Tackle Multiple Discrimination' *Oxford Journal of Legal Studies* 23: 65–86.

Hawkesworth, Mary (2003) 'Congressional Enactments of Race-Gender: Toward a Theory of Raced-Gendered Institutions' *American Political Science Review* 97(4): 529–50.

Hutchinson, Darren (2002–2003) 'New Complexity Theories: From Theoretical Innovation to Doctrinal Reform' *UMKC Law Review* 71: 431–45.

Krishnadas, Jane (2007) 'Identities in Reconstruction: From Rights of Recognition to Reflection in Post-Disaster Reconstruction Processes' *Feminist Legal Studies* 15: 137–65.

Kwan, Peter (2002–2003) 'The Metaphysics of Metaphors: Symbiosis and the Quest for Meaning' *UMKC Law Review* 71: 325–30.

Levit, Nancy (2002–2003) 'Theorizing the Connections Among Systems of Subordination' *UMKC Law Review* 71: 227–50.

Marcosson, Samuel (2002–2003) 'Multiplicities of Subordination: The Challenge of Real Inter-Group Conflicts of Interest' *UMKC Law Review* 71: 459–83.

Razack, Sherene (2002–2003) ' "Outwhiting the White Guys:" Men of Colour and Peacekeeping Violence' *UMKC Law Review* 71: 331–53.

Vakulenko, Anastasia (2007) ' "Islamic Headscarves" and the European Convention on Human Rights: An Intersectional Perspective' *Social and Legal Studies* 16(2): 183–99.

Valdes, Francisco (2002–2003) 'Identity Maneuvers in Law and Society: Vignettes of a Euro-American Heteropatriarchy' *UMKC Law Review* 71: 377–98.

Valentine, Gill (2007) 'Theorizing and Researching Intersectionality: A Challenge for Feminist Geography' *The Professional Geographer* 59(1): 10–21.

Westley, Robert (2002–2003) 'Reparations and Symbiosis: Reclaiming the Remedial Focus' *UMKC Law Review* 71: 419–30.

Williams, Joan (2002–2003) 'Fretting in the Force Fields: Why the Distribution of Social Power has Proved so Hard to Change' *UMKC Law Review* 71: 493–505.

Yuval-Davis (2006) 'Intersectionality and Feminist Politics' *European Journal of Women's Studies* 13(3): 193–209.

Part I
Mapping intersectionalities

Chapter 1

Intersectionality and the feminist project in law

Joanne Conaghan

Introduction

In recent years, the focus of feminist studies has shifted away from the concept of gender as an isolated category of analysis towards a concern with the way in which gender intersects with other categories of identity for purposes of understanding and combating inequality. This shift is in large part spawned by rejection within feminism of 'essentialist' invocations of sex and gender and the corresponding collapse of the category 'woman' as a core unit of feminist engagement and critique. As such, it may properly be welcomed in its promise to provide more effective ways of tackling the complex and diverse manifestations of inequality which women experience. At the same time, it is arguable that the conceptual and analytical framework generated by 'intersectional' approaches has not proved adequate to this challenge and has been dogged by difficulties of application and delivery in the context of feminist theory and strategy.

The object of this chapter is to explore the implications of intersectionality for the feminist project in law. By 'project' I do not mean to suggest that feminist engagement with law is reducible to a fixed set of objectives and strategies. Rather, I use the term in the sense articulated by Duncan Kennedy: 'a project is a continuous goal-oriented practical activity based on an analysis of some kind ... but the goals and analysis are not necessarily internally coherent or consistent over time' (Kennedy 1997: 6). While undoubtedly characterised by divergence in normative, theoretical and strategic approach, feminist legal engagement is, broadly speaking, a practical activity designed to engender, directly or indirectly, socially transformative processes and effects. It follows that part of the value (or otherwise) of intersectionality lies in the possibilities for and effects of its practical deployment. I want to suggest that although intersectionality has been an important dimension of feminist theory and strategy in recent years, it has now reached the limits of its potential. There is nothing more that it can do to advance the feminist project, whether in law, or more broadly. This is not an uncontroversial assertion and it should be emphasised at the outset that it does not imply

[margin note: interpret fails to unravel the complexities of the ID statuses]

any rejection of the view that inequality is complex and multifaceted. It is however to suggest that intersectionality does not adequately get at that complex multiplicity; it cannot unpick or unravel the many ways in which inequality is produced and sustained. Part of the problem lies in the fact that, as a frame of reference, intersectionality has its roots in law. Therefore, the limits of law and legal engagement infuse and constrain intersectional approaches. If we are truly to get to grips with the problem of inequality we need to develop more effective analytical and strategic tools. This requires consideration of other perspectives which have engaged with and sought to account for unequal social relations, including approaches which have been overlooked or rendered theoretically 'suspect'.

The first part of this chapter traces the evolution of intersectionality analysis as a response to perceived limits in feminist theory and politics, highlighting its legal derivation – which accounts in large part for the grid-like aesthetic to which it adheres – and evaluating its deployment as a feminist theoretical tool beyond the narrow confines of legal doctrine. The second part of the chapter excavates earlier efforts to theorise interrelations of gender, race and class within the context of encounters between Marxism and feminism. The section explores the character and contours of materialist feminist debate on gender, race and class to exemplify how intellectual, theoretical and political context can shape the way in which problems are conceived and understood. The chapter concludes with an emphasis on the importance of recognising the contingency of our conceptual and analytical frameworks, arguing that a failure to do so may impede a broader understanding of the issues we address. A focus on alternative ways of thinking about and theorising unequal social relations helps to highlight the limitations of intersectionality as a way of making sense of (gendered) inequality while at the same time providing additional analytical tools in the context of strategic engagements with law.

Intersectionality: a feminist legal story

Origins

[margin note: 1980s anti-essentialism as a part of fem theory]

The modern roots of intersectionality lie in anti-essentialism although the issues to which intersectionality gives rise have been the focus of feminist theorising for much longer. Anti-essentialism emerged in feminist theory in the late 1980s, producing a cluster of texts which were to become seminal in the feminist legal canon (Fuss 1989; Harris 1990; Spelman 1988). Much of the critique was driven by the concerns of women of colour who argued that mainstream feminist discourse was predicated upon and thereby privileged the experiences of white women. Just as women's experiences were overlooked through the 'universalisation' of men's, so also were the experiences of women of colour eclipsed by feminist attendance to white women's interests and concerns: the 'woman' of feminism was, for most *the problem w/ akheela & the Bee is that it paints the Black experience as one that is about skin color & economic class. The social aspects/realities are not rep.*

purposes, white; whiteness was part of the 'essence' of womanhood which feminism represented.

& were excd b/c of univer of & exper & Black & were exclude b/c of ~~what~~ the univ of white & experience

The critique of essentialism activated a series of separate but related political and theoretical concerns (Hunter 1996; Conaghan 2000). There emerged a growing recognition of the need to broaden the representational base of feminism to take better account, substantively and strategically, of differences between women. There was also detectable a new willingness among feminists to interrogate their own theories and methodologies, in particular, to problematise the invocation of women's individual and shared experience as the epistemological base of feminist theoretical knowledge. Finally, there arose a keen suspicion of categories – of categories in general and of the category 'woman' in particular (Butler 1990). This was in part because of a desire to avoid importing undesirable essences into feminist theory; but, increasingly also, it entailed the rejection of the idea of essence itself, the eschewal of any notion that categories possessed a pure, incontestable core independent of discursive context. It followed that gender categories had no 'authentic' content nor was there a gendered reality which feminist theory could represent. Feminism was without a subject.[1]

shared exper cannot be the base of theoretical knowledge

In some ways, intersectionality constituted a response to the concerns to which anti-essentialism gave expression. In other ways, it was a restatement of those concerns but one perceived to have the potential to move debate beyond the theoretical and political stalemate to which anti-essentialism seemed inexorably to lead. As Rebecca Johnson observes: 'The point was, as intersectionality theorists reminded, that anti-essentialism for its own purpose was a weak insight ... To have any political value, the critique had to be combined with a strategy of anti-subordination. Intersectional theory attempts to do just that' (2005: 29).

anti-essential is not good enough – there needs to be something to make it active – anti-subord

In 1989, in an article by Kimberlé Crenshaw, intersectionality received its inauguration. Speaking about black women's experience of discrimination, Crenshaw commented:

> Consider an analogy to traffic in an intersection, coming and going in all four directions. Discrimination, like traffic through an intersection, may flow in one direction and it may flow in another. If an accident happens at an intersection, it can be caused by cars travelling from any number of directions and, sometimes, from all of them. Similarly, if a black woman is harmed because she is in the intersection, her injury could result from sex discrimination or race discrimination.
>
> (Crenshaw 1989: 149)

Crenshaw argued that black women were located at the intersection of racism and sexism. Their experiences were thus the product of both and equivalence of neither. The reliance of anti-discrimination law on a 'single-axis framework' (Crenshaw 1989: 139) in which separate claims could be made on the basis of race or sex but not in combination, deprived black women of a legal remedy in relation to their particular experience of discrimination as black women.[2] At the same time, precisely because that experience was perceived by the courts to be a 'hybrid' rather than 'pure' form of race or sex discrimination, it rendered black women ineligible class representatives of women or black people for anti-discrimination law purposes,[3] their intersectional identity being seen to overwhelm the assumed single identities of anti-discrimination complainants. In these somewhat contradictory ways (Crenshaw 1989: 148–50) black women's multidimensional experience of discrimination became theoretically and practically erased from the doctrinal framework.

It is worth pausing for a moment to consider the imagery that Crenshaw deploys to support her claims in this context: it is the imagery of lines and planes, crossings, and coordinates. Mathematical and cartographic references are not infrequently deployed in anti-discrimination law discourse. Indeed, it is common legal parlance to talk in terms of 'axes' or 'vectors' of discrimination while, in the application of equality norms, lawyers make frequent recourse to 'equations' of similarity and difference (Stafford 2001: 30). Emily Grabham, among others, argues that cartographic methods are widely deployed in legal discourse, infusing processes of legal categorisation and functioning as techniques for reducing the messiness of people's' lives into 'intelligible legal frameworks' (Grabham 2006: 7). Similarly, Pierre Schlag, in his analysis of the role of aesthetics in shaping our perception and apprehension of law, highlights the continued grip of what he calls the 'grid aesthetic' in legal thought: 'In the grid aesthetic, law is framed as a field, as a territory, a two-dimensional space that can be mapped and charted' (Schlag 2002: 1047). While acknowledging the early twentieth century to be the historical high point of this particular aesthetic, manifest in formalist/ 'scientific' approaches to law (ibid: 1053), the grid, Schlag insists, continues to leave its mark on modern jurisprudence, encouraging the demarcation of law into bounded legal spaces whose proximity and interrelation can be comprehensively charted and explored.

Intersectionality[4] is a concept closely entwined with mapping processes, locating points of crossing and charting their significance within a broader legal and theoretical topography. Cartographic imagery therefore cannot help but infuse our thinking around the cluster of issues of which intersectionality discourse is comprised. However, the correspondence with mapping is more than metaphorical. By framing it in this particular way, the problem of intersectionality is 'brought into being' (Schlag 2002: 1053) *as a problem of representation*. Thus, it is no surprise that a primary concern of intersectionality analysis is with how law represents women's experiences. Indeed, much of the work on intersectionality can be understood as a critique of the 'map' of gender inequality offered by law and legal feminism, accompanied by calls for a better representation, a richer topography of women's lives. This becomes apparent when we consider the development and application of intersectionality discourse by feminist legal scholars.

Development

An immediate concern for Crenshaw was to identify remedial gaps in relation to black women's experiences of discrimination. This theme has continued to inform doctrinal engagements with intersectionality with a number of scholars taking up and developing Crenshaw's critique in their own jurisdictions.[5] However, the problem for Crenshaw went beyond the doctrinal boundaries of anti-discrimination law. The real difficulty, she argued, lay in 'the tendency to treat race and gender as mutually exclusive categories of experience and analysis' (Crenshaw 1989: 139). This tendency underpinned anti-discrimination law but also infused feminist theory and politics more generally. By failing to develop an analytical framework which recognised and/or took account of experiences at the intersection, feminism was both conceptually limited and politically distorted. It privileged the concerns of white women, adopted a 'top-down' model of subordination (in which the experiences of the least subordinated in the subordinated group – white women – became the measure of subordination overall) and thereby failed to get to grips with the complex ways in which racism and sexism worked through one another to produce forms of subordination with which feminism – and anti-racism – unwittingly conspired.[6]

In a second article, Crenshaw (1991) further developed her critique, focusing on the relationship between intersectionality and identity politics. Noting a tension between negative and positive deployment of identity categories – on the one hand, as a source of powerlessness and subordination, on the other, as a route to social and political empowerment – Crenshaw argued that identity-based political engagement was similarly hampered by a single-axis framework:

> The problem with identity politics is not that it fails to transcend difference, as some critics charge, but rather the opposite – that it frequently conflates or ignores intragroup differences.
> (Crenshaw 1991: 357)

[handwritten margin note: intragroup diff]

Crenshaw called for 'recogni[tion] that identity politics take place at the site where categories intersect' (ibid: 377) and sought to adapt the framework of identity politics to take better account of experiences which were the product of intersecting identities. She placed this argument in the context of violence against women, showing how intersecting patterns of sex and race-based subordination shaped and informed women's experiences of violence in ways rarely recognised by the gendered experiential norm (ibid: 359). Crenshaw also highlighted the risk of political conflict between identity groups if intersectional issues were not adequately addressed (ibid: 367–74). The overall thrust of her critique was not the abandonment of categories such as race and sex, nor the rejection of identity politics; rather, her purpose was to develop a theoretical and political framework which was attentive to intersections of subordination, which 'mapp[ed] the margins' of identity. Her work was strongly embedded in the practical application of feminist theory and politics and her primary concern was to facilitate more effective strategic engagement with law.

Crenshaw's deployment of the language of intersectionality soon caught the attention of other feminist scholars. Alongside direct engagement with anti-discrimination regimes, scholars began to test the theoretical potential of intersectionality other than at the race/gender interface and in relation to categories beyond the conventional reach of anti-discrimination law, for example, sexuality (Eaton 1994; Arriola 1994) and class (Hutchinson 2001). A central theme in much of this analysis is the failure of law to capture the complexity and fluidity of identity and the implications of this failure for progressive theory and politics. Thus, the work is illustrative and elaborative of precisely the kind of tensions between the positive and negative deployment of identity categories that Crenshaw signalled (1991). At the same time, one can detect a gradual shift away from practical questions of legal and political strategy (exemplified in Crenshaw's work) towards more abstract consideration of the nature of identity and its (mis)representation in legal discourse.

This is particularly evident in Trina Grillo's much-cited article published in 1995. For Grillo, intersectionality is deeply bound up with identity which law renders separate and fragmented: 'a fragmenting entirely at odds with the concrete life of [a] woman' (Grillo 1995: 17). In this, Grillo's analysis coheres more or less with Crenshaw's. However, for Grillo, the power of intersectionality lies in its potential to give voice to the individual, multidimensional subject who finds herself 'unable to speak' within paradigms of thought which posit identity as singular and one-dimensional:

> Each of us ... sits at the intersection of many categories. She is Latina, woman, short, mother, lesbian, daughter, brown-eyed, long-haired, quick-witted, short-tempered, worker, stubborn. At any one moment in time and space some of these categories are central to her being ... Some categories, such as race, gender, class and sexual orientation, are important most of the time. Others are rarely important ... yet, if we turn the traditional tools of legal analysis upon this woman, we find she is someone entirely different. She is fragmented, capable of being only one thing at a time.

(ibid)

Identity is Based on others (not to Be confused w/ The "other") and This is The problem. Identities take agency from the indiv & put power in the hands of others to define & marginal as such.

Intersectionality and the feminist project in law 27

I Identities are not neutral They are Biased.

The thrust of this analysis is to posit identity as forever fluid and multifaceted, possessing a dynamic, unstable quality stifled by the application of unidimensional, hierarchically-conceived group classifications. The repressive results are individually and distinctly experienced by those who struggle to 'fit' core identity paradigms. Intersectionality is thus a way of making sense of a world which appears constantly at odds with our concrete lived experiences. These experiences include the confusion and discomfort we feel when 'official' versions of truth do not correspond with our own perceptions or the sense of ruptured despair arising when parts of ourselves – our ethnicity and sexuality perhaps – are pitted against each other. At the same time, intersectionality places limits on the significance and reach of individual experience, our very complexity providing us with a unique but inevitably 'limited view of the world' (ibid: 22), an authentic view but not, in any fundamental sense, a privileged one.

Grillo's analysis is highly resonant of multiple inequality experiences. However, the political implications are somewhat troubling. Her focus on the particularity of individual experience might be said to leave little room for organised, collaborative initiatives; her analysis certainly stands as an account of why collective identity-building initiatives are so difficult to accomplish. What then is her political strategy? In so far as a strategic dimension can be gleaned, it focuses on combating the silencing effects of mainstream identity discourses, discourses rendered legitimate, *inter alia*, by their deployment in law:

> In the end, the anti-essentialism and intersectionality critiques ask only this: that we define complex experiences as closely to their full complexity as possible and that we do not ignore voices at the margin.
> (Grillo 1995: 20)

where does stereotype & other perception play in this. The issue is btw the percieved Reality of one – the way that

Intersectionality thus emerges as a theoretical and political response to individual, experiential complexity and to the essentialising tendencies of law with respect to it. In addition, intersectionality offers the possibility of resisting the repressive effects of such essentialism by directing us to a discursive space in which representing complexity – particularly with regard to subject/identity formation – becomes a key theoretical and political object.

Applications

Grillo's analysis signalled an increasing preoccupation within legal feminism with representations of individual experience, in particular, with the lack of correspondence between legal accounts of the social world and the 'real experiences' of 'real people' (Pothier 2001). While recognising that this is a general problem deriving from law's tendency to 'compartmentalise' – that is, to require experience to fit within 'prefabricated' legal categories (Iyer 1993) – feminists contend it is of particular concern in an intersectional context because the 'problem' of intersectionality appears to flow directly from the limits of the relevant categorical structure. This not only problematises encounters with law, leaving individual claimants 'with a sense that they have been "disauthenticated"' by the legal process (Grabham 2006: 7), it also highlights the extent to which our expectations of law are linked to a particular understanding of the relationship between law and life. To a significant extent, law derives legitimacy from belief in its capacity to govern the messy complexities of everyday existence. This presupposes that law accurately captures and reflects those complexities; that they are, in some sense, within the sphere of law's operation.

Such an understanding confers upon law considerable authority as a purveyor of 'truth'. Law's representations are perceived to be 'authentic', its narratives assumed to bear some correspondence to social occurrences and phenomena. At the same time, where such correspondence is absent or difficult to glean, law may be criticised for its failure adequately to represent the real. In this way, law becomes both a source of truth as well as a site for contesting its production, drawing feminists and other progressive activists into legal engagement, not just as a remedial strategy but also as a forum for the discursive reconstruction of meaning and understanding.

This approach characterises Lise Gotell's (2002) evaluation of the litigation strategy of the Women's Legal Action and Education Fund (LEAF) in relation to the Canadian Charter of Rights and Freedoms. Gotell notes a shift in LEAF's approach during the 1990s from singular to more complex presentations of women's experience which she welcomes, not only for providing an opportunity within law for articulating accounts capable of displacing the limited and repressive categorical ordering currently governing understandings of inequality, but also for their potential to call into question law's foundationalism through a discursive emphasis on complexity and contingency. Implicit in Gotell's stance is an acknowledgement of the *performative* dimensions of law, the way in which law and legal categories work to confer meaning and to shape (and limit) understanding, contributing to processes of social identity formation which repress or deny intersectional experiences.[7] Intersectionality analysis thus becomes located within a particular critical and theoretical approach which posits law as a discourse with active, constitutive effects in relation to meaning and understanding, identity and subjectivity, inequality and subordination with much of the current legal scholarship on intersectionality falling within this frame.[8]

There is nothing wrong with this approach; it highlights a particular and important aspect of law's implication in unequal social relations and offers strategic possibilities for countering law's repressive, inegalitarian effects. However, as an analytical tool, intersectionality has limited theoretical and strategic purchase in this context, serving as little more than an *exhortation* to take account of complexity in considering processes of social identity formation. Thus, for example, Maneesha Deckha characterises intersectionality as a feminist norm which requires us to 'pay attention to how multiple social forces, such as race, class, gender, age... shape our experiences' (2004: 16). Rebecca Johnson asserts that it compels a 'focus on the very specific ways that gender intersects with ... other dimensions in women's lives' (Johnson 2005: 29). Johnson goes on to assert that 'the point of this focus has not simply been to document difference... the point ... is to see whether or not the experiences of those located at the intersections can provide insights crucial to the construction of better theories' (ibid). And therein lies the challenge: *does* intersectionality produce better theories? And better theories of what?

In my view, intersectionality is rather limited in its theory-producing power. In particular, while it acts as an aid to the excavation of inequality experiences at a local level, it tells us little about the wider context in which such experiences are produced, mediated and expressed. Experiences of inequality are much more diverse and complex than the relations and processes from which they derive; yet intersectionality does not engage in any sustained way with these relations and processes. Moreover, it tends to discourage any serious efforts to relate experiences on the ground with broader consideration of the social and legal context in which they occur, the focus on the local acting as an injunction against what Kathi Weeks describes as 'the aspiration to totality', understood in a minimal sense as 'the methodological mandate to relate and connect', which Weeks asserts to be a positive, indeed necessary, aspect of theoretical enquiry (1998: 71). In sum, intersectionality is far too modest in its theoretical ambitions, it is unduly circumscribed in its perception of what theoretical work may entail. Thus, it is as likely to close off enquiry as to open it up, particularly where it involves consideration of gender or race not as aspects of identity but as core structural components of a regulatory framework such as law.

Indeed, I would argue that intersectionality has become too bound up with notions of identity and identity formation. Within feminist legal scholarship in particular, intersectionality has taken a strong 'identity turn' (see e.g. analyses of Grillo 1995; Wing 2000). While undoubtedly an important dimension of inequality analysis, issues of identity are but an aspect, not a substitute for, fuller investigation into the operation of gender and race within inequality regimes within which identities are formed, navigated and resisted. In addition, the concept of identity is less suited to certain kinds of analysis. Take, for example, the uneasy status of class in intersectionality discourse. At best, class functions rather crudely in intersectionality analysis as an unexplored signifier of socio-economic inequality. Notwithstanding efforts by some intersectionality scholars to incorporate it more deeply into their analyses (Hutchinson 2001), the literature as a whole fails to do so. This is in part because class is a concept which predates identity politics but it is also because class does not typically function as an identity category.[9] Traditionally, and particularly in a Marxist context, class has been understood in *relational* rather than *locational* terms, that is, as an expression of 'objective' relational structures rather than 'subjective' located experiences. While this does not preclude acknowledgment of the role of experience in shaping the formation of class identity – in Marxist terms, 'consciousness' – this process must be understood in close association with the operation and effects of social relations of production (Meiksins Wood 1998: Chapter 3). While identity analyses tend to highlight experiences of inequality and law's characterisation of and response to those experiences, class discourse tends to focus on the structured processes and relations which produce and mediate experience. These tendencies are by no means fixed or absolute and it is perfectly possible (and not unusual) to engage with processes and relations in the context of enquiries into identity formation. However, because law is embedded in a liberal individualist paradigm it is not an ideal site for this kind of interrogation. Hence the difficulties with according class any kind of legal significance.

For similar reasons, identity discourse also limits the reach of gender inequality analysis. In a politics of identity framework, gender is positioned within a model of social relations in which different groups clamour for recognition and access to political power. As a result, the specificities of gender disadvantage, for example, the centrality of labour in structuring patterns of gender relations, is at risk of being overlooked or marginalised. Moreover a strong political emphasis on issues of recognition can lead to a neglect of economic and distributive issues – which remain a crucial dimension of gender inequality – as well as a failure fully to explore the interrelation of recognition and redistribution concerns (Fraser and Honneth 2003). Finally, and particularly in a legal context, the focus of identity engagement is overwhelmingly rights-oriented with all the attendant limitations of rights discourse as an emancipatory strategy.[10] This includes the emergence of seemingly irresolvable rights 'conflicts', for example, between the equality rights of religious groups and those of gays and lesbians, conflicts which intersectionality cannot easily resolve precisely because of the reliance of rights discourse on the *identification* of rights-bearers (Conaghan 2007).

Thus, although intersectionality purports to be a critique of identity politics, the concept of identity for the most part retains its centrality as a core unit of analysis, with gender, race and other inequality 'grounds' being repositioned as 'dimensions' of identity which law fails adequately to capture and reflect. This prompts calls for further delineation of identity categories. For example, Adrien Katherine Wing, in elaborating a notion of 'multiplicative identity', argues:

> To assist women of colour we need to delineate their multiple identities, examine how those identities intersect to privilege or lead them to face

discrimination, and then design multidimensional programs that would enhance their life situations.

(Wing 2000: 8)

This seems a project of limitless scope and limited promise. Not only does it preclude the deployment of equality categories in other ways, for example, to explain or elaborate structures, relations and/or processes of inequality, it ensures that the focus of intellectual, political and legal energy is directed towards the infinite elaboration of inequality subgroups, engendering a slow but steady march towards conceptual fragmentation and, ultimately, dissolution. In the meantime, other ways of thinking about and theorising the problem are lost from view.

Materialism feminism: reports on women's subordination

The tradition of historical materialism

In 1975, Gayle Rubin commented: 'There is no theory which accounts for women's oppression with anything like the explanatory power of the Marxist theory of class oppression' (Rubin 1997: 29). In so pronouncing, Rubin offers an account of why feminists were attracted to Marxist theory notwithstanding the relative lack of attention which Marx himself paid to women's situation. Marx's analysis of class oppression had enormous theoretical and political purchase. By offering a way of thinking about social organisation and structures, it challenged the view that social hierarchies were natural and pre-ordained. Moreover, it provided effective tools for engaging in sweeping, yet contextually detailed, historical analyses of the genesis and development of relations of subordination, the focus on class highlighting the lack of a similar developed analysis in relation to sex/gender.

During the 1960s and 1970s, class-based initiatives formed the core of organised resistance to the social and political order. In a period in which, in the USA and the UK, left-wing activism was enjoying a resurgence, it is hardly surprising that the burgeoning Women's Liberation Movement should find its feet in the course of a 'critical dialogue with a broader left movement fighting for a more egalitarian world' (Segal 1999: 4) or that second-wave feminist theory should be so closely aligned to the anti-capitalist struggle. Even liberal feminist approaches, with their emphasis on state-initiated reform, relied significantly for support on trade unions and other class-based organisational forms, with many feminists choosing to pursue the somewhat schizophrenic path of simultaneous revolution and reform. Lynn Segal captures the spirit of feminist politics at the time, observing:

Women's liberation was a *theory and practice of social transformation*, full of all the embroiled and messy actions, hostilities and compromises of collective political engagement. For the most part it manoeuvred within a broader culture of the left: refusing to separate women off from wider struggles against inequality and subordination, but fighting the perpetual marginalisation or neglect of what were often women's most specific interests and concerns.

(Segal 1999: 15)

In this sense, second-wave feminism was, to a significant extent, an intersectional project, one which sought to explore and delineate, with a view to offering a theoretical synthesis of, the complex interconnections between class and sex-based oppression, primarily – although by no means exclusively – through engagement with historical materialism, at that time the prevailing social theoretical tradition.

In 1980 Iris Marion Young describes a materialist account 'as one that considers phenomena of "consciousness" – e.g. intellectual production, broad social attitudes and beliefs, cultural myths, symbols, images, etc – as rooted in real social relationships' (Young 1997: 105). In this, Young aligns herself with a philosophical tradition which understands mind to derive from matter, that is, <u>views ideas as consequential upon social relations rather than social relations</u> resulting from ideas, a perspective also <u>underpinning</u> Marx's critique of Hegelian idealism in *The German Ideology*:

views as consequence to social relations

Men are the producers of their conceptions, ideas etc – real, active men, as they are conditioned by a definitive development of their productive forces and of the intercourse corresponding to these ... Consciousness can never be anything else than conscious existence, and the existence of men is their actual life-process.

(Marx 1983: 169)[11]

For Marx, a focus on the 'life-process' entailed engaging with 'real individuals, their activity and the material conditions in which they live' (ibid: 163), specifically with those activities and relations necessary to ensure the production of the means of subsistence. It is in this context that labour – and the structures and processes surrounding labouring activity – emerged as a primary object of analysis, including, Marx argued, in relation to historical enquiry:

The first historical act is ... the production of the means to satisfy [men's basic] needs, the production of material life itself... The first necessity therefore in any theory of history is to observe this fundamental fact in all its significance and all its implication and to accord it due importance.

(ibid: 171).

From these beginnings came historical materialism, a theory of history which not only sought to explain the world but also, as Marx famously remarked in his *Theses on Feurbach*, 'to change it' (Marx 1983: 158). Thus, historical materialism was an ethical and political practice, an engagement with history which viewed class struggle – and, in particular, the political organisation of the working class – as the means by which social transformation could be achieved.[12] While perhaps aspiring to offer a 'total' theoretical account of historical and social change (although see Weeks, at 29 above), the merits of historical materialism lay in its emphasis on historicity and contingency from which capitalism emerged not as a set of universal relations but as a specific mode of production and exchange. Historical materialism was not a tradition which forsook detail and context in favour of abstract postulates and pronouncements; rather it entailed the careful analysis of 'historically constructed social and political life with all its complexity, multiplicity of tensions and lack of linearity' (Rupert and Smith 2002: 3). Thus was the theoretical stage set when feminism intervened.

Historical Materialism

Materialist feminism

Early second-wave feminism comprised at least two theoretical moves. The first was to offer an account of women's oppression which cohered with Marxist analyses of capitalist social relations. Taking their cue from the theoretical terrain in which they found themselves, many feminists sought to expand the parameters of materialism to encompass issues of women's subordination. The second[13] was to devise a distinct explanatory framework, for example, accounting for women's oppression in terms of 'patriarchy' (Hartmann 1997) or 'the sex/gender system' (Rubin 1997), although even in these contexts the theoretical approach tended to mirror Marxism, whether in terms of form, substance, or both. Radical feminism was perhaps the theoretical stance most distant from Marxism, focusing on psycho/sexual factors rather than labouring practices and engaging less with the question of how class and gender oppression interrelated (Mitchell 1975; Firestone 1974; Millett 1977).[14] At the same time, most radical feminists were sympathetic to and certainly conversant with class analysis and in this sense the distinction between 'socialist' and 'radical' feminists was far from clear-cut.[15] What is apparent is that virtually all feminist theoretical engagement took a form which mirrored historical materialism and, in that context, the theoretical work most closely attentive to what we might now understand as intersectional issues was socialist and/or materialist feminism as it addressed directly the relation between class and gender in a theoretical and political context.[16]

An early but significant intervention came from Mariarosa Dalla Costa and Selma James in 1972. Dalla Costa and James (1997 rep.) argued that women's unpaid domestic labour, by reproducing labour power, contributed directly to the production of surplus value.[17] They thus identified a material dimension to women's oppression in the capitalist production process and offered a political rationale for a feminist–anti-capitalist alliance. However, Dalla Costa and James did not offer an account of women's oppression outside a capitalist framework; nor did their theory explain why it was *women* who engaged in the necessary reproductive work (Rubin 1997: 30–1). The logic of their argument, in terms of political strategy, was to equate women's liberation with the overthrow of capitalism, while theoretically it allowed for the subsumption of feminist concerns within a Marxist framework. This left little room for the development of an autonomous feminist political or theoretical stance.

A number of feminists responded to these deficiencies by offering a separate account of women's subordination. Rubin, for example, drew upon anthropological studies to develop an account of the 'sex/gender system' which she described as 'a set of arrangements by which society transforms biological sexuality into products of human activity, and in which those transformed sexual needs are satisfied' (ibid: 28). According to Rubin, sex/gender systems were a feature of all societies although, as social and cultural products,[18] they varied significantly. However, because sex was closely related to basic human needs they did need to fulfil certain minimum functions: 'A human group must ... reproduce itself from generation to generation. The needs of sexuality and procreation must be satisfied as much as the need to eat' (ibid: 32). In this way Rubin could assert that sexual relations were as materially based as class relations, at the same time locating women's subordination in the development of specific relational forms emerging in response to a reproductive imperative.[19]

The idea that women's oppression stemmed from a separate system of subordination – which co-existed with but did not derive from capitalism – crystallised in the notion of 'patriarchy'.[20] This 'dual systems' approach was highly resonant of Marxism and drew directly from Marxist concepts and methodology. Christine Delphy, for example, deployed the Marxist concept of class to analyse women's position in terms of men's expropriation of women's domestic labour. She argued that the family formed the site of women's exploitation by men within the context of a domestic mode of production which was analytically distinct from capitalism (Delphy 1984). An important feature of Delphy's analysis was to situate working-class men in both the exploited and exploiting class depending on the mode of production. By the same token, working-class women were revealed to be doubly exploited, by capitalism and patriarchy simultaneously.[21]

Heidi Hartmann, writing in 1981, is perhaps the best-known exponent of a dual systems approach (Hartmann 1997). Hartmann's work focused on elaborating the interrelations of patriarchy and capitalism within the context of a theoretical tradition which had, for the most part, been blind to them: 'The marriage of Marxism and feminism has been like the marriage of husband and wife depicted at common law: Marxism and feminism are one and that one is Marxism' (ibid: 97). Like Delphy, she posited patriarchy as a distinct system of social relations with a material base in men's control over women's labour (ibid: 101). Moreover it was a system which predated capitalism but now worked largely in partnership with it, although – Hartmann made clear – there was nothing inevitable about this partnership and many potential tensions between the two systems. Hartmann grounded her argument in a close study of the development of the family wage which, she contended, emerged as a means of resolving the conflict between capitalist and patriarchal interests in the context of industrialisation (ibid: 104–6). The overall thrust of her approach was to insist on theoretical recognition of and engagement with patriarchy as distinct system of social relations, maintaining that a failure to do so was a failure also to attend to crucial aspects of the operation of capitalism in a patriarchal society.[22]

Black feminist analysis

Given the theoretical tradition in which they found themselves, it was crucial for feminists to assert the analytical distinctiveness of gender to prevent its absorption within a framework which privileged class and submerged women's interests in those of men. Dual systems theory was thus an attempt to problematise prevailing understandings of oppression as unidimensional and exclusively class-based. The development of a dual systems approach also facilitated recognition of working class women's 'intersectional' location while, by challenging the primacy of class (and, with it, the capacity of Marxism fully to account for relations of exploitation), it created space for theoretical engagement beyond the class/gender interface.

Thus, for example, Gloria Joseph (1997) responded to Hartmann by indicting both Marxism and feminism for their failure to address race: 'if one cannot claim that Marxism is complete without a consideration of feminism, it is certainly true that neither is complete without a consideration of race issues' (Joseph 1997: 107). Joseph's intervention demonstrates an understanding of theory as offering – or at least striving to offer – a *complete* account of social relations. At the same time, the nature of her critique was to call into serious question the viability – and desirability – of such an account. Thus, on the one hand, she talks of 'white supremacy' in systemic terms, suggesting the need for a 'tri-systems' analysis of relations of domination. On the other hand, by so doing, she highlights the enormity and sheer complexity of such a totalising project. In other ways too, Joseph's critique moves away from strict adherence to materialist theoretical form, most significantly by challenging the centrality of economic exploitation in Marxist and feminist theorising: 'the virulent suppression of one race by another does not appear reducible to purely economic considerations' (ibid) and by highlighting the obvious difficulties which cross-cutting forms of oppression posed for the emancipatory struggle:

> Black women have to be considered one of those groups with special interests. Just as women cannot trust men to 'liberate' them, Black women cannot trust white women to 'liberate' them during or 'after the revolution' … White feminists have to learn to deal adequately with the fact that by virtue of their whiteness, they are oppressors as well as oppressed persons.
>
> (ibid: 108)

Thus, Joseph's intervention was representative of a critical move rendering problematic the materialist project of social transformation by raising serious questions of political agency: *who* were the agents of *what* change in a context in which the oppressed were simultaneously oppressors? How could one develop a theory and practice of emancipation in such circumstances?

The eventual conclusion of Young (1997) and other feminist scholars (for example, Eisenstein 1979) was to move towards theoretical and political synthesis, but not one which privileged class over gender or other forms of social domination.[23] In fact, this was early recognised by those whose intersectional position had already alerted them to the inadequacies of a separate systems approach. The Combahee River Collective, for example, called for a political and analytical stance which encompassed feminism, socialism, racism and heterosexism simultaneously:

> The most general statement of our politics … would be that we are actively committed to struggling against racial, sexual, heterosexual and class oppression and see as our particular task the development of an integrated analysis and practice based upon the fact that the major systems of oppression are interlocking. The synthesis of these oppressions creates the conditions of our lives.
>
> (Combahee River Collective 1997)

The idea of 'interlocking' oppressions was quickly taken up by other black feminists, most notably, Patricia Hill Collins (1990) who argued against additive approaches to oppression:

> Instead of starting with gender and then adding in other variables such as age, sexual orientation, race, social class, and religion, Black feminist thought sees these distinctive systems of oppression as being part of one overarching structure of domination.
>
> (Hill Collins 1990: 222)

Hill Collins characterised this structure as a 'matrix of domination' (ibid: 224). There are various ways in which the idea of a matrix can be understood in this context. One could, for example, draw upon a computing analogy to view a matrix as 'a gridlike array of interconnected circuit elements' (*Concise Oxford English Dictionary* 1991), thus resonating not only with popular associations derived from the film, *The Matrix*, but also with Crenshaw's conjuring of the gridlike image of an intersection to account for black women's position in anti-discrimination law. However, there is another notion of a matrix, etymologically derived from the French *matrice* and the Latin *matrix*, meaning 'womb' (Barnhart 1988: 641) which coheres with Hill Collins' insistence on an understanding of relations of domination in which sex, race, and other 'axes of oppression' work *together* to produce diverse experiences of domination – depending on the social location and particular relational configuration – within a structured *whole*. This is quite incompatible with an analytical focus which views relations of domination engendered by sex, race and class as separate and distinct. The evocation of matrix as womb also gets at another dimension of Collins' analysis, that is, the dynamic and shifting character of relations of domination, the way in which they evolve and develop over time, space and socio-economic location.[24] This makes them difficult to *map* in any comprehensive sense but it does invite an analytical approach which places weight on the kind of detailed historical exploration which materialism championed. At the same time, the emphasis on a single 'overarching structure' serves as a constant reminder of the need to relate the local to the global, the part to the whole. Hill Collins was not advocating a retreat from the 'aspiration to totality' (Weeks 1998: 71); rather, she was suggesting how it might be effectively retained, that is, through the reconceptualisation of relations of domination in terms of interlocking rather than separate systems of oppression:

> Viewing relations of domination ... as being structured via a system of interlocking race, class and gender oppression expands the focus of analysis from merely describing the similarities and differences distinguishing these systems of oppression and focuses greater attention on how they interconnect. *Assuming that each system needs the other in order to function* creates a distinct theoretical stance that stimulates the rethinking of basic social science concepts.
>
> (Hill Collins 1990: 223, my emphasis)

An important consequence of Hill Collins' analysis, like Joseph's, is that it enabled a better theoretical understanding of intersectional locations, highlighting, for example, how forms of resistance by white women to white men's domination could simultaneously operate as modes of domination in relation to black women and men.

This posited the possibility of multiple standpoints in the context of political agency but, as Hill Collins went on to elaborate, it also conferred upon black women the dubious 'privilege' of occupying a distinct social location of triple oppression in the context of interlocking systems of race, gender and class oppression.

Hill Collins did not contend that black women's standpoint was epistemologically privileged: 'No one group' she observed 'has a clear angle of vision' (Hill Collins 1990: 236). However, she did emphasise the importance of attending to those standpoints most likely to be suppressed:

> A black women's standpoint may provide a preferred stance from which to view the matrix of domination because, in principle, Black feminist thought as specialized thought is less likely than the specialized knowledge produced by dominant groups to deny the connection between ideas and the vested interests of their creators.
>
> (Hill Collins 1990: 234).

Although in many ways echoing Marx's account of the distinct vantage point of the working class in the context of capitalism, such an acknowledgement of multiple standpoints inevitably rendered unstable a theoretical commitment to providing a 'total' account of relations of domination. Moreover, by bringing to the fore epistemological questions about how knowledge of oppression was (to be) attained, Hill Collins' analysis cohered with growing attention within feminism and critical race theory to the excavation of forms of subjugated knowledge as well as with the greater general emphasis on questions of subjectivity, identity and experience which emerged in the 1990s and shaped intersectionality theory. In the end and notwithstanding the best efforts of many feminist and critical race scholars to hold on to core aspects of the theoretical tradition from which they came, the difficulties and uncertainties engendered by their own critiques could not, it seemed, co-exist with a continued commitment to the tenets of historical materialism.

Conclusion: a tale of two theories

Just as feminist efforts to address issues of intersectionality in a social theoretical context were contributing to the dissolution of the dominant theoretical tradition, feminist legal scholars were becoming alert to the possibilities of law not just as a tool to pursue reform-oriented political ends but also as a way of thinking about and theorising gender relations. Carol Smart's *Feminism and the Power of Law* (1989), emphasising law's role as a hegemonic discourse, was particularly influential here, shifting the focus of legal feminism away from instrumental analyses of law towards an exploration of its constitutive effects on women's apprehension of themselves (Chunn and Lacombe 2000). Similarly, Judith Butler's theory of performativity has played a crucial role in directing feminist analysis toward questions of legal subjectivity (Butler 1990; 1993). It is largely within the context of such engagements with law – as a performative process of subjectivity formation – that 'modern' intersectionality theory has taken shape.

As a result, there are striking differences between the approaches of past and present efforts to theorise intersectionality, particularly with regard to the way in which issues are framed and the kinds of questions generated by theoretical enquiry. One striking contrast is the relative lack of historical attention in contemporary intersectionality analyses, echoing what Lynn Segal suggests has become a broader tendency in feminist theory (Segal 1999: 14). In addition, modern intersectionality scholarship is much less concerned with tracing the root causes of inequality manifestations. It is more a discourse of representation than origins, one which sees the possibilities for future transformation in interpretations of the present rather than interrogations of the past.

Current intersectionality theory is also more distanced from collective political activism; certainly the politics of collective action is much less evident in modern analyses. In this sense, materialist feminism (and second-wave feminism in general) was characterised by a very different notion of political agency in which some form of collective organisation was viewed as a necessary condition of any strategy of emancipation and individual acts of resistance were recognised as such only in so far as they contributed to the development of a collective consciousness. The perceived enormity of the enterprise, entailing wholesale economic, political and social restructuring, simply did not produce the kind of focus on individual subjectivity which characterises current analyses.

This theoretical retreat from collective political agency coincides, in radical thinking, with a decline in attention to economic considerations, what is sometimes characterised as the 'cultural turn' in left politics. This shift is clearly detectable in feminist legal theory (Conaghan 2000) and a striking feature of much intersectionality analysis, notwithstanding gestures of acknowledgement in the direction of class inequality. Part of the difficulty here is the absence of an adequate framework for thinking conceptually about the economic. Once the materialist project of economic transformation was abandoned, so also were ways of thinking about economic issues outside a materialist frame. When the importance of attention to distributive considerations reasserted itself in the neo-liberal context of growing socio-economic inequalities worldwide, it was a simple move to annex class to existing conceptions of identity, to locate the economic in the cultural, to adopt a frame in which 'the material' (those 'life processes' to which Marx referred) was repositioned as textual product which could be resisted and reconfigured through discursive contestation.

Kathi Weeks highlights the problem with such a perspective from the point of view of political transformation:

> In the absence of some sense of the whole, some conception of the complex social formations that constitute and constrain subjects, we end up with an impoverished model of the subject, that overestimates its capacities for self-creation and self-transformation, as well as a very limited understanding of the forces we must subvert in order to make possible the construction of alternative subjects.
>
> (Weeks 1998: 4)

In other words, even within the context of a focus on subjectivity, current feminist theoretical models do not deliver because they fail to produce an effective agent of political change. Indeed, the absence of sustained historical engagement in much contemporary theorising makes the idea of change conceptually problematic; in a sense, there is only the present to be confronted and only what is before us to map and represent.

What then are the implications of the above analysis for the feminist project in law? I began by asserting that feminist legal engagement is a practical activity designed to engender, directly or indirectly, socially transformative processes and effects. In this, it may be understood as part of broader feminist commitment to 'praxis', that is, to the convergence of theory and practice, a productive coming together of thought and action, ideas and strategies, scholarship and politics. It is, I would contend, against this standard that the value of intersectionality, as a theoretical and strategic approach, should be measured.

Comparing present efforts to unravel issues of intersectionality with those of past theoretical traditions is instructive for a number of reasons. First, it draws to our attention the extent to which our conceptual tools are the product of broader frameworks of thinking which, at any given time, may be beyond the scope of critical scrutiny precisely because they *are* frames *within which* theoretical engagement is taking place. A second virtue of such a comparative approach is that it introduces a necessary historical dimension by which such an insight may be gleaned. Revisiting the past allows us to draw connections between our current theoretical agendas and broader intellectual and political developments. Not only does it facilitate Weeks' practices of 'relating and connecting' (1998: 5), in a very real sense, it compels them.

Finally, the act of comparison serves as a means of highlighting particular limitations in intersectionality analysis. Chief among them is the preoccupation with law's representational role. It is not difficult to understand why feminist scholars should seek to 'map the margins' of inequality (Crenshaw 1991) or to address its failure, substantively and strategically, to recognise and represent experience at the intersection. However, it must be remembered that a map is merely a surface representation; topographical techniques notwithstanding, it cannot adequately denote either depth or dimension. Nor can it capture or evoke movement or change through time. Moreover, it is always to scale, depicting proportion not size and producing spatial representations whose correspondence with the real is partial and sometimes misleading.

If we are truly to get to grips with the issues intersectionality raises, we need a theoretical framework which is genuinely *multidimensional*, possessing breadth, depth and, most importantly, mobility. We must not allow our conception of the problems – and solutions – to become caught within a narrow legal aesthetic. Moreover, if we are serious about equality, we cannot continue to sidestep economic issues. The theoretical framework we adopt must not only confront and accommodate problems of distribution; it must acknowledge their centrality in any equality-seeking project. This must entail more than simply tracking and addressing 'random' disparities.[25] Intersectionality can chart and map a range of disparities with relative ease. It can generate a rich stock of data, for example, about how categories of women are differently situated in relation to education, the family, the labour market, and the political system. However, intersectionality is less able to capture the processes through which these disparities are produced or the relations of subordination of which they are expressive. We need to look at ways in which we can theorise these relations and processes. We need a language to 'relate and connect' diverse experiences of inequality with the structures, processes, practices and institutions in which they occur. And we need to consider the role and potential of law in this context.

This is not to insist that we return wholesale to the tenets of historical materialism or that we take up the project of systems-synthesis urged by Young, Hill Collins and others. However, it is to suggest that we turn again to some aspects of that earlier engagement, in particular, that we take seriously the idea 'that what we do can have consequences for who we are and how we think' (Weeks 1998: 5) and that we attend more closely to what we do, e.g., labouring activities, and the regulatory regimes in which we do them.

The notion of a regime is a useful one, eliciting a softer, less determinative image of ordering processes than is implied by the idea of a system. Regimes can be navigated, negotiated, resisted, undermined and overcome, yet still remain meaningfully operative. They are not dependent, as Duncan Kennedy observes, on any structural coherence or system logic (1993: ix). Regimes engender tendencies but they may also meet with counter-tendencies. They may be more or less stable, more or less controlling but they do not rely on an understanding of their operation which requires them to be determinative or overriding. Duncan Kennedy characterises patriarchy as a regime. In fact he describes 'social life in the West today' as '... in a rough way a capitalist, patriarchal, white supremacist "regime"' (ibid). (One might add heteronormative but the approach remains a compelling one.) Another scholar making use of the notion of a regime is Joan Acker (2006) who invokes the idea of 'inequality regimes' to conceptualise issues of intersectionality. She describes inequality regimes as 'loosely interrelated practices, processes, actions and meanings that result in and maintain class, gender and racial inequalities within particular organisations' (Acker 2006: 443).[26]

Inequality regimes may vary in terms of the type and degree of inequality they produce, the organising processes producing inequality and the opportunities for resistance. However, what is important is that they operate within and across organisations: any organisational form is likely to generate an inequality regime which will operate on top of and against the background of existing regimes. This makes the business of mapping inequalities, whether at the intersections or otherwise, more or less impossible: regimes are always acting upon and intersecting with other regimes so that the inequalities they yield, while the product of ordering processes, are nevertheless fluid and to a degree unpredictable. To put it another way, *all* inequalities are intersectional; moreover they must be understood in relation to dynamic processes of social ordering, both at the 'local' and the 'global' level. Such an approach requires retention of a focus on the specificity of inequality experiences but within a framework which endeavours to relate and connect those experiences to multiply interlocking ordering processes.

This should not imply the abandonment of categories of race, gender, sexuality or class in favour of the complex elaboration of inequality subgroups. On the contrary, such categories are meaningful because they signal forms of ordering commonly found within and across organisations.[27] The point is that they don't operate in isolation from each other and that makes the business of challenging their operation all the more complicated.

The role of law in this equality-seeking process should be to facilitate egalitarian change in inequality regimes. This may or may not require anti-discrimination law as we currently understand it; and it may or may not be aided by the development of a constitutional equality guarantee. However, what is clear is that law's equality-seeking strategies should flow directly from an analysis of the (inter)operation of inequality regimes, including but not restricted to the ordering effects of law itself. This is not incompatible with much of what currently passes as intersectionality analysis in a legal context but it does help to identify its limitations. Law cannot be the starting point of inequality analysis and we should resist the lure of its particular aesthetic in our engagements with it.

Acknowledgements

My grateful thanks to Davina Cooper and Didi Herman for their helpful comments on an earlier version of this chapter, and to my colleagues at the

AHRC Research Centre for Law, Gender and Sexuality for providing me with endless opportunities to discuss intersectionality analysis with them. Thanks too to Kathi Weeks for her support and inspiration.

Bibliography

Acker, J. (2006) 'Inequality Regimes: Gender, Class and Race in Organizations', *Gender & Society*, 20: 441–64.

Arriola, E. (1994) 'Gendered Inequality: Lesbians, Gays and Feminist Legal Theory', *Berkeley Women's Law Journal*, 9: 103.

Ashiagbor, D. (1999) 'The Intersection between Gender and "Race" in the Labour Market: Lessons for Anti-Discrimination Law' in A. Morris and T. O'Donnell (eds), *Feminist Perspectives on Employment Law*, London: Cavendish.

Barnhart, R.K. (ed.) (1988) *Chambers Dictionary of Etymology*, Edinburgh: Chambers Harrap Publishers.

Barrett, M. and McIntosh, M. (1979) 'Christine Delphy? Towards a Materialist Feminism?', *Feminist Review*, (January): 95–106.

Benston, M. (1969) 'The Political Economy of Women's Liberation', *Monthly Review*, (September) 21: 13–25.

Butler, J. (1990) *Gender Trouble: Feminism and the Subversion of Identity*, New York: Routledge.

Butler, J. (1993) *Bodies that Matter: On the Discursive Limits of Sex*, New York: Routledge.

Chunn, D. and Lacombe, D. (2000) *Law as A Gendering Practice*, Oxford: OUP.

Combahee River Collective (1997) 'A Black Feminist Statement' in L. Nicholson (ed.), *The Second Wave: A Reader in Feminist Theory*, New York: Routledge

Conaghan, J. (2000) 'Reassessing the Feminist Theoretical Project in Law', *Journal of Law and Society*, 27: 351–85.

Conaghan, J. (2007) 'Intersectionality and UK Equality Initiatives', *South African Journal of Human Rights*, 23/2: 317–34.

Concise Oxford English Dictionary (1991), Oxford: OUP.

Cooper, D. (2004) *Challenging Diversity: Rethinking Equality and the Value of Difference*, Cambridge: Cambridge University Press.

Crenshaw, K. (1989) 'Demarginalizing the Intersection between Race and Sex: A Black Feminist Critique of Anti-Discrimination Doctrine, Feminist theory and Anti-Racist Politics', *University of Chicago Legal Forum*, 139–67.

Crenshaw, K. (1991) 'Mapping the Margins: Identity Politics, Intersectionality and Violence against Women', *Stanford Law Review*, 43: 1241-79.

Dalla Costa, M. and James, S. (1997) 'Women and the Subversion of Community' in R. Hennessy and C. Ingraham (eds), *Materialist Feminism: A Reader in Class, Difference and Women's Lives*, New York: Routledge.

Deckha, M. (2004) 'Is Culture Taboo? Feminism, Intersectionality and Culture Talk in Law', *Canadian Journal of Women and Law*, 16: 14–53.

Delphy, C. (1984) *Close to Home: A Materialist Analysis of Women's Oppression*, London: Hutchinson.

Duclos, N. (1993) 'Disappearing Women: Racial Minority Women in Human Rights Cases', *Canadian Journal of Women and Law*, 6: 25–51.

Eaton, M. (1994) 'At the Intersection of Gender and Sexual Orientation: Towards a Lesbian Jurisprudence', *Southern California Review of Law and Women's Studies*, 3: 183.

Eisenstein, Z. (1979) *Capitalist Patriarchy and the Case for Socialist Feminism*, New York: Monthly Review Press.

Firestone, S. (1974) *The Dialectic of Sex*, London: Bantam Books.

Fraser, N. and Honneth, A. (2003) *Redistribution or Recognition: A Political-Philosophical Exchange*, London: Verso.

Fuss, D. (1989) *Essentially Speaking: Feminism, Nature and Difference*, New York: Routledge.

Gotell, L. (2002) 'Towards a Democratic Practice of Feminist Litigation: LEAF's Changing Approach to Charter Equality' in R. Jhappan (ed.), *Women's Legal Strategies in Canada*, Toronto: University of Toronto Press.

Grabham, E. (2006) 'Taxonomies of Equality: Lawyers, Maps and the Challenge of Hybridity', *Social & Legal Studies*, 15: 5–23.

Grillo, T. (1995) 'Anti-Essentialism and Intersectionality: Tools to Dismantle the Master's House', *Berkeley Women's Law Journal*, 10: 16–30.

Hannett, S. (2003) 'Equality at the Intersection: The Legislative and Judicial Failure to Tackle Multiple Discrimination', *Oxford Journal of Legal Studies*, 23: 65–86.

Harris, A. (1990) 'Race and Essentialism in Feminist Legal Theory', *Stanford Law Review*, 42: 581.

Hartmann, H. (1997) 'The Unhappy Marriage of Marxism and Feminism: Towards a More Progressive Union' in L. Nicholson (ed.), *The Second Wave: A Reader in Feminist Theory*, New York: Routledge.

Hartsock, N. (1985) *Money, Sex and Power: Towards a Feminist Historical Materialism*, Boston, MA: Northeastern University Press.

Hennessy, R. (2000) *Profit and Pleasure: Sexual Identities in Late Capitalism*, New York: Routledge.

Hill Collins, P. (1990) *Black Feminist Thought: Knowledge, Consciousness and the Politics of the Women's Movement*, Boston, MA: Unwin Hyman.

Hunter, R. (1996) 'Deconstructing the Subjects of Feminism: the Essentialist Debate in Feminist Theory and Practice', *Australian Feminist Law Journal*, 6: 135–62.

Hutchinson, D. (2001) 'Identity Crisis: "Intersectionality", "Multidimensionality" and the Development of an Adequate Theory of Subordination', *Michigan Journal of Race and Law*, 6: 285–316.

Iyer, N. (1993) 'Categorical Denials: Equality Rights and the Shaping of Social Identity', *Queens Law Journal*, 19: 179–207.

Johnson, R. (2005) 'Gender, Class and Sexual Orientation: Theorizing the Intersections' in G. MacDonald, R.L. Osborne and C.C. Smith (eds), *Feminism, Law and Inclusion: Intersectionality in Action*, Toronto: Sumach Press.

Joseph, G. (1997) 'The Incompatible Menage à Trois: Marxism, Feminism and Racism' in R. Hennessy and C. Ingraham (eds), *Materialist Feminism: A Reader in Class, Difference and Women's Lives*, New York: Routledge.

Kennedy, D. (1993) *Sexy Dressing etc: Essays on the Politics and Power of Cultural Identity*, Cambridge, MA: Harvard University Press.

Kennedy, D. (1997) *A Critique of Adjudication: Fin de Siècle*, Cambridge, MA.: Harvard University Press.

McColgan, A. (2007) 'Reconfiguring Discrimination Law', *Public Law*, 74–94.

MacDonald, G., Osborne R.L. and Smith, C.C. (2005) *Feminism, Law and Inclusion: Intersectionality in Action*, Toronto: Sumach Press.

Marx, K. (1983) *The Portable Karl Marx*, edited by Eugene Kamenka, Harmondsworth: Penguin Books.

Meiksins Wood, E. (1995) *Democracy against Capitalism*, Cambridge: Cambridge University Press.

Millett, K. (1977) *Sexual Politics*, London: Virago.

Mitchell, J. (1975) *Psychoanalysis and Feminism*, Harmondsworth: Penguin Books.

Pothier, D. (2001) 'Connecting Grounds of Discrimination to Real People's Real Experiences', *Canadian Journal of Women and Law*, 13: 37–73.

Razack, S. (1999) *Looking White People in the Eye*, Toronto: University of Toronto Press.

Rubin, G. (1997) 'The Traffic in Women: Notes on the "Political Economy" of Sex' in L. Nicholson (ed.), *The Second Wave: A Reader in Feminist Theory*, New York: Routledge.

Rupert, M. and Smith, H. (2002) *Historical Materialism and Globalization*, London: Routledge.

Schiek, D. (2005) 'Broadening the Scope and Norms of EU Gender Equality Law: Towards a Multidimensional Conception of Equality Law', *Maastricht Journal of European and Comparative Law*, 12: 427–66.

Schlag, P. (2002) 'The Aesthetics of American Law', *Harvard Law Review*, 115: 1047–118.

Segal, L. (1999) *Why Feminism?*, Cambridge: Polity Press.

Shoben, E.W. (1980) 'Compound Discrimination: The Interaction of Race and Sex in Employment Discrimination', *New York University Law Review*, 55: 793–836.

Skeggs, B. (1997) *Formations of Class and Gender: Becoming Respectable*, London: Sage Publications.

Smart, C. (1989) *Feminism and the Power of Law*, London: Routledge.

Spelman, E. (1988) *Inessential Woman: Problems of Exclusion in Feminist Thought*, Boston, MA: Beacon Press.

Stafford, B. (2001) *Visual Analogy: Consciousness as the Art of Connecting*, London: MIT.

Thompson, E.P. (1978) *The Poverty of Theory and Other Essays*, London: Merlin.

Walby, S. (1990) *Theorising Patriarchy*, Oxford: Blackwell.

Weeks, K. (1998) *Constituting Feminist Subjects*, Ithaca, NY: Cornell University Press.

Wing, A.K. (2000) *Global Critical Race Feminism: An International Reader*, New York: New York University Press.

Young, I.M. (1997) 'Socialist Feminism and the Limits of Dual Systems Theory' in R. Hennessy and C. Ingraham (eds), *Materialist Feminism: A Reader in Class, Difference and Women's Lives*, New York: Routledge.

Notes

1 I use this term in a dual sense to denote the actor/speaker/agent of feminist discourse and the object/field/area of study. Anti-essentialism addressed and problematised both.

2 See Crenshaw's analysis of *De Graffenreid v General Motors* 413 F Supp 142 (E D Mo 1976) (Crenshaw 1989: 141–3).

3 See Crenshaw's analysis (1989) of *Moore v Hughes Helicoptor* 708 F2d 475 (9th Cir 1983) and *Payne v Travenol* 673 F2d 798 (5th Cir 1982) at 143–50.

4 The term 'intersect' comes from the Latin *intersecare*, 'to cut between'. It has been used in English to denote a place of crossing or passing through since at least the sixteenth century. The application of the term to the place where streets cross is first recorded in the mid-nineteenth century in the writing of Nathanial Hawthorne (Barnhart 1988: 539). Crenshaw is not the first scholar to use the idea of an intersection in equality analysis; however, she is generally credited with having launched it as an analytical framework, particularly within law.

5 See e.g., Duclos (1993), Iyer (1993), Pothier (2001) (Canada); Ashiagbor (1999), Hannett (2003), McColgan (2007) (UK); and Schiek (2005) (Europe). See also Shoben (1980) for an early engagement with the problem of 'compound discrimination' (note the mathematical terminology) from which Crenshaw draws. Strikingly, nearly two decades later, the conceptual and remedial deficiencies which Crenshaw highlighted remain a problematic feature of most anti-discrimination regimes (Conaghan 2007).

6 Crenshaw's example here is feminist engagement with 'separate spheres' ideology which, she argues, has limited purchase when applied to the lives of black men and women, particularly against a historical background of slavery, failing to tease out way in which gender norms cross-cut and reinforce race-based subordination (1989: 155–6).

7 Of course, this repression or denial is rarely absolute. After all, law 'performs' alongside/in combination/in conflict with other performative processes in the context of social relations in which one's intersectional location is often likely to be of material significance. What is important is the legitimacy accorded to legal truths, contributing to a lack of official recognition of particular aspects or experiences of inequality.

8 See e.g., the essays in Chunn and Lacombe (2000) and MacDonald *et al.* (2005).

9 This is not to suggest that class cannot function as signifier of identity (see e.g., Skeggs 1997) but it is to acknowledge particular difficulties which derive from the context in which class emerged as a social theoretical category (see further below).

10 See e.g., Razack (1999) highlighting the ways in which rights discourse can disguise forms of domination.

11 A central preoccupation of postmodernism was to challenge what was viewed as the over-determinism of materialism by highlighting the role of the discursive realm in constituting 'real relations'. However, in so doing, many postmodernist theorists lost sight of the possibility that the relationship between mind and matter may be two-way. As a result, our theoretical access to the 'material' world is now dominated by a focus on the cultural production of meaning, and a fuller understanding of the inter-relation (dare I say 'intersection') of cultural and material production has been slow in emerging. Ironically, within the tradition of historical materialism, a two-way relationship has long been acknowledged, as for example, in E.P. Thompson's characterisation of 'social being' and 'social consciousness' as in 'dialogue' (1978: 9).

12 This analysis provides the origin of standpoint theory which feminists subsequently took up and developed in a gender context (Hartsock 1985).

13 There was also a third 'move', i.e., to analyse women's situation within traditional liberalism, e.g., by asserting their equal status as autonomous individuals in an

atomised society. Most feminist legal engagement took this form but it produced little in the way of sustained theoretical engagement.

14 Although Firestone's analysis of reproductive labour practices highlights the difficulties of drawing strict lines between materialist and radical feminism (see further below).

15 See e.g., the 1977 statement of the Combahee River Collective, a group of black lesbian feminists, discussed below.

16 The tendency to equate 'socialist' and 'materialist' perspectives in much of the theoretical literature (itself a product of Marx's appropriation and deployment of the concept of the material) does not preclude recognition of the *materiality* of sex (Hennessy 2000). In practice though, it did contribute to the development of a theoretical frame in which sexuality was located in the 'cultural' rather than in the 'material' domain (Weeks 1998).

17 Dalla Costa's analysis differed from previous analyses of housework because it posited a *direct* link between women's domestic labour and the production of surplus value. While prior analyses acknowledged a relationship between housework and processes of production, they nevertheless placed it outside the realm of capitalist relations of production (Benston 1969).

18 'Sex as we know it – gender identity, sexual desire and fantasy ... is itself a social product' (Rubin 1997: 32).

19 Rubin argued that women's subordination derived from kinship practices which facilitated the exchange of women: 'The exchange of women does not necessarily imply that women are objectified in the modern sense... but it does imply a distinction between gift and giver. If women are the gifts, then it is men who are the exchange partners. And it is the partners, not the presents, upon whom reciprocal exchange confers its quasi-mystical power of social linkage. The relations of such a system are such that women are in no position to realise the benefits of their own circulation' (ibid: 37).

20 Understandings of 'patriarchy' vary from text to text but Sylvia Walby catches the general gist of it: 'patriarchy [is] a system of social structures and practices in which men dominate, oppress and exploit women' (1990: 20).

21 Delphy was criticised by Marxist-feminists for misusing Marxist concepts, e.g., class (Barrett and McIntosh 1979). It was also argued that women's social and economic position varied too much for them to fall within the same (exploited) class. However, this was to misunderstand the notion of class as Delphy – drawing on Marx – applied it, i.e., not as a concept of group identity but rather as a structural *relation* within a particular *system* of production (Delphy 1984: 25–7).

22 Dual systems theory was subject to a sustained critique by Iris Marion Young in 1980 who argued that it had failed to challenge the primacy of a Marxist model or to deliver a viable structure for the analysis of patriarchy and capitalism as separate systems of oppression. Efforts to do so, she argued, had led to the 'ghettoization' of women's oppression within the family and the neglect of gender issues outside that context (1997: 101). Young argued for a unified theory which acknowledged gender 'as a basic axis of social structuration' and placed it at the centre of any analysis of social relations of domination: 'we need not merely a synthesis of feminism with traditional Marxism, but also a thoroughly feminist historical materialism which regards the social relations of a particular historical formation as one system in which gender differentiation is a core attribute' (ibid: 102). See further below.

23 Young did commit herself to the development of a 'truly materialist theory', which she described as 'a methodological priority to concrete social institutions and practices, along with the material conditions in which they take place' (1997:

105). She also argued for the retention of a Marxist focus on 'the structure of labouring activity and the relations arising from labouring activity... as a crucial determinant of social phenomena' (ibid).

24 A matrix can also mean 'an environment or substance in which a thing is developed' (*Concise Oxford English Dictionary* 1991).

25 This is the kind of approach which underpins, for example, the recent Equalities Review (2007).

26 Inequalities here are understood in terms of 'systematic disparities between participants' whether in relation to access to power, resources, opportunities pleasures and other rewards (ibid).

27 What Davina Cooper has described as 'ordering principles' (2004: 51).

Chapter 2

The complexity of intersectionality

Leslie McCall

Introduction

Since critics first alleged that feminism claimed to speak universally for all women, feminist researchers have been acutely aware of the limitations of gender as a single analytical category. In fact, feminists are perhaps alone in the academy in the extent to which they have embraced intersectionality – the relationships among multiple dimensions and modalities of social relations and subject formations – as itself a central category of analysis. One could even say that intersectionality is the most important theoretical contribution that women's studies, in conjunction with related fields, has made so far.[1]

Yet despite the emergence of intersectionality as a major paradigm of research in women's studies and elsewhere, there has been little discussion of how to study intersectionality, that is, of its methodology. This would not be worrisome if studies of intersectionality were already wide ranging in terms of methodology or if the methodological issues were fairly straightforward and consistent with past practice. I suggest, however, that intersectionality has introduced new methodological problems and, partly as an unintended consequence, has limited the range of methodological approaches used to study intersectionality. Further, both developments can be traced to what arguably has been a defining characteristic of research in this area: the complexity that arises when the subject of analysis expands to include multiple dimensions of social life and categories of analysis.[2] In a nutshell, research practice mirrors the complexity of social life, calling up unique methodological demands. Such demands are challenging, as anyone who has undertaken the study of intersectionality can attest. Not surprisingly, researchers favor methodologies that more naturally lend themselves to the study of complexity and reject methodologies that are considered too simplistic or reductionist. This in turn restricts the scope of knowledge that can be produced on intersectionality, assuming that different methodologies produce different kinds of knowledge. Note that this is equally a problem outside and inside women's studies, though I mainly address the field of women's studies here in order to simplify the argument.

But are these assumptions about the capacity of different methodologies to handle complexity warranted? Scholars have not left a clear record on which to base a reply to this question. Feminists have written widely on methodology but have either tended to focus on a particular methodology (e.g., ethnography, deconstruction, genealogy, ethnomethodology) or have failed to pinpoint the particular issue of complexity. Although it is impossible to be exhaustive, my intention is to delineate a wide range of methodological approaches to the study of multiple, intersecting, and complex social relations and to clarify and critically engage certain features of the most common approaches. In total, I describe three approaches. All three attempt to satisfy the demand for complexity and, as a result, face the need to manage complexity, if for no other reason than to attain intelligibility. For each approach, I describe how scholars manage complexity and what they achieve and sacrifice in the process.

The three approaches, in brief, are defined principally in terms of their stance toward categories, that is, how they understand and use analytical categories to explore the complexity of intersectionality in social life. The first approach is called *anticategorical complexity* because it is based on a methodology that deconstructs analytical categories. Social life is considered too irreducibly complex – overflowing with multiple and fluid determinations of both subjects and structures – to make fixed categories anything but simplifying social fictions that produce inequalities in the process of producing differences. Of the three approaches, this approach appears to have been the most successful in satisfying the demand for complexity, judging by the fact that there is now great scepticism about the possibility of using categories in anything but a simplistic way. The association of the anticategorical approach with the kind of complexity introduced by studies of intersectionality may have also resulted from the tendency to conflate this approach with the second one, which I will discuss momentarily, despite the fact that the two have distinct methodologies, origins, and implications for research on intersectionality.

Jumping to the other end of the continuum next, the third approach is neither widely known nor widely used, making its introduction a key purpose of this chapter. This approach, *intercategorical complexity*, requires that scholars provisionally adopt existing analytical categories to document relationships of inequality among social groups and changing configurations of inequality along multiple and conflicting dimensions. I describe my own research methodology as an example of the intercategorical approach. Because it is the lesser known of the three approaches, I spend more time discussing an example of this type of research than I do the other two approaches. I also identify examples of research by other social scientists working with similar methodologies, though my aim is to be illustrative rather than exhaustive.

Finally, although the approach I call *intracategorical complexity* inaugurated the study of intersectionality, I discuss it as the second approach because it falls conceptually in the middle of the continuum between the first approach, which rejects categories, and the third approach, which uses them strategically. Like the first approach, it interrogates the boundary-making and boundary-defining process itself, though that is not its *raison d'être*. Like the third approach, it acknowledges the stable and even durable relationships that social categories represent at any given point in time, though it also maintains a critical stance toward categories. This approach is called *intracategorical complexity* because authors working in this vein tend to focus on particular social groups at neglected points of intersection – "people whose identity crosses the boundaries of traditionally constructed groups" (Dill 2002: 5) – in order to reveal the complexity of lived experience within such groups. Since the second approach is sometimes associated (erroneously) with the anticategorical approach, I discuss these two approaches in the same section.

Before proceeding, I must raise four caveats. First, not all research on intersectionality can be classified into one of the three approaches. Second, some research crosses the boundaries of the continuum, belonging partly to one approach and partly to another. Third, I have no doubt misunderstood and misclassified some pieces of research and some researchers, for which I issue an apology up front. Fourth, I do not claim that all research cited in the same category is the same on all counts – only roughly the same on the count that concerns me, which is the researcher's stance toward categorical complexity. For example, there is no seamless overlap between feminist poststructuralists and anticategoricalists. All this being said, the three approaches can be considered broadly representative of current approaches to the study of intersectionality and together illustrate a central element of my argument: that different methodologies produce different kinds of substantive knowledge and that a wider range of methodologies is needed to fully engage with the set of issues and topics falling broadly under the rubric of intersectionality.

Since my primary goal is a substantive one – to expand research on intersectionality – all other philosophical and methods-related issues are important only to the extent that they impede or facilitate this goal. As philosophical and methods-related issues *have* played a large role in the development of feminist research, they must be considered here as well. To that end, I adopt a fairly expansive view of what a methodology is. Ideally, a methodology is a coherent set of ideas about the philosophy, methods, and data that underlie the research process and the production of knowledge. As is clear from this definition, I am not concerned solely with methods but with the philosophical underpinnings of methods and the kinds of substantive knowledge that are produced in the application of methods. My focus is on the connections among these elements of the research process rather than on identifying any particular philosophy or method as feminist, as some feminist writings on methodology do.[3] Indeed, I consider all three approaches to be consistent with feminist research.

Given that, my aim is to understand how methodological issues have had a hand in drawing the nebulous line within feminist research between interdisciplinary and disciplinary scholarship. This distinction is extremely consequential, for research that falls on the interdisciplinary side of the line is more likely to constitute the core of women's studies as a new inter/ disciplinary field and thus spark new feminist research in women's studies proper as well as in the disciplines. In the end, it is my hope that dispelling at least some of the philosophical and methods-related concerns that have been raised about the interdisciplinary status of the intercategorical approach in particular may help to expand the scope of research on intersectionality.

Anticategorical and intracategorical complexity

I begin with a very brief and stylized chronology of the development of the field of women's studies. Many overviews and critiques of the stages of development of feminist studies have covered the same ground, so that is not my objective (see, e.g., Sandoval 1991). My emphasis instead is on the convergence of several interrelated but analytically separate developments that led to the current mode of research on intersectionality.

One of the first developments in the emergent field of women's studies was a critique of existing fields for not incorporating women as subjects of research.[4] This critique was substantive in nature, and the solution was equally substantive: women should be added to the leading research agendas across the full range of disciplines. Women's distinctive experiences became important ingredients in the attempt to set the record straight. However, mounting evidence of the pervasiveness of male bias led to a critique that became primarily theoretical in nature; consequently, the simple addition of women to the research process no longer seemed adequate. The introduction of gender as an analytical category, feminism as a theoretical perspective, and male dominance as a major social institution all became necessary to counter the tendency toward neglecting and misrepresenting women's experiences (Scott 1986).

But feminist scholars also took their critique to a much deeper level. They began to question the very edifice of modern society – its founding philosophies, disciplines, categories, and concepts. All of the valued categories that fraternized on the male side of the modern male/female binary opposition became suspect for symbolizing and enacting the exclusion of women and femininity.[5] In particular, the philosophical critique of modernity included a disciplinary critique of modern science and a methodological critique of the scientific method, its claims to objectivity and truth belied by the actual practice of science (see, e.g., Keller 1985; Harding 1986). Finally, these critiques dovetailed with two separate but highly influential developments:

first, the postmodernist and poststructuralist critiques of modern Western philosophy, history, and language (see, e.g., Foucault 1972; Derrida 1974), and second, critiques by feminists of color of white feminists' use of *women* and *gender* as unitary and homogeneous categories reflecting the common essence of all women.[6]

The methodology of anticategorical complexity was born in this moment of critique, in which hegemonic feminist theorists, poststructuralists, and antiracist theorists almost simultaneously launched assaults on the validity of modern analytical categories in the 1980s, though, as I said, often from differing perspectives and with different consequences for the course of feminist theory's intellectual trajectory. I will return to these differences in a moment, but for now it is important to recognize that some similarities in the positions of all three groups compounded and reinforced the conflation of the anticategorical and intracategorical approaches into a single widely received approach. More specifically, writings by feminists of color, which were more oriented toward the intracategorical approach, were often assimilated into and then associated with the writings of feminist poststructuralists, which were more oriented toward the anticategorical approach.[7]

At least initially, the emphasis for both groups was on the socially constructed nature of gender and other categories and the fact that a wide range of different experiences, identities, and social locations fail to fit neatly into any single "master" category. Indeed, the premise of this approach is that nothing fits neatly except as a result of imposing a stable and homogenizing order on a more unstable and heterogeneous social reality. Moreover, the deconstruction of master categories is understood as part and parcel of the deconstruction of inequality itself. That is, since symbolic violence and material inequalities are rooted in relationships that are defined by race, class, sexuality, and gender, the project of deconstructing the normative assumptions of these categories contributes to the possibility of positive social change. Whether this research does in fact contribute to social change is irrelevant. The point is that many feminist researchers employ this type of analysis because of their belief in its radical potential to alter social practices – to free individuals and social groups from the normative fix of a hegemonic order and to enable a politics that is at once more complex and inclusive. Feminist researchers take this stance even with the acknowledgment that it is impossible to fully escape the normalizing confines of language because new relations of power/knowledge are continuously reinscribed in new systems of classification, and yet it is impossible to avoid using categories strategically for political purposes.[8]

The primary philosophical consequence of this approach has been to render the use of categories suspect because they have no foundation in reality: language (in the broader social or discursive sense) creates categorical reality rather than the other way around. The methodological consequence is to render suspect both the process of categorization itself and any research that is based on such categorization, because it inevitably leads to demarcation, and demarcation to exclusion, and exclusion to inequality. At the anticategorical end of the continuum I have developed, these philosophical and methodological consequences have been fully embraced.

How, then, are intersectionality and the complex social relations it embodies analyzed substantively in an anticategorical framework? Methodologies for the study of anticategorical complexity crosscut the disciplinary divide between the social sciences and the humanities. The artificiality of social categories can be illuminated in history with the method of genealogy, in literature with deconstruction, and in anthropology with the new ethnography. In each case, the completeness of the set of groups that constitutes a category is challenged. For example, the category of gender was first understood as constituted by men and women, but questions of what distinguishes a man from a woman — is it biological sex, and if so what is biologically male and female? — led to the definition of "new" social groups, new in the sense of being named but also perhaps in the sense of being created. There are no longer two genders but countless ones, no longer two sexes but five (Fausto-Sterling 2000). Other examples abound. In a remarkably short period of time, bisexual, transgendered, queer, and questioning individuals have been added to the original divide between gay and straight sexuality groups, and the social groups that constitute the category of race are widely believed to be fundamentally indefinable because of multiracialism (see, e.g., Fuss 1991; Omi and Winant 1994). And, theoretically, eventually all groups will be challenged and fractured in turn. As these examples make clear, this approach has been enormously effective in challenging the singularity, separateness, and wholeness of a wide range of social categories.

As stated in the anticategorical approach above, these vexing questions about *how* to constitute the social groups of a given social category, which have often arisen in the context of empirical research, have inevitably resulted in questions about *whether* to categorize and separate at all.[9] But we can still go a step further. In psychoanalytic versions of the anticategorical approach, complexity is contained within the subject and therefore the very notion of identity on which categories are based is fully rejected:

> Locating difference *outside* identity, in the spaces *between* identities, [ignores] the radicality of the poststructualist view which locates differences *within* identity. In the end, I would argue, theories of 'multiple identities' fail to challenge effectively the traditional metaphysical understanding of identity as unity.
>
> (Fuss 1989: 103)

Given theories of the "irreducible heterogeneity of the other" (and self), even single individuals, let alone social collectivities, cannot be given voice as they had been in the days of "'innocent' ethnographic realism" (Lather 2001: 222, 215).

Thus new practices of ethnographic representation have been developed to allow feminist research to proceed while the authenticity of both the subject and the researcher – as if either had a single, transparent voice – is questioned.[10] Ruth Behar's *Translated Woman* (1993) is a well-known example of this new style of research in which the complexity of a single individual's life and the complicated nature of the researcher's relationship to the individual/subject are the central themes of the book. Another example is given by Patti Lather and Chris Smithies (1997), who self-consciously split their book on women with HIV/AIDS into three separate panels, first for their analysis and interpretation as researchers and authors, second for the voices of the subjects, and third for other relevant issues such as information and facts about HIV/AIDS. Not surprisingly, these authors are careful to resist claims of having transcended the crisis of representation that they see as essentially irresolvable in epistemological terms (Visweswaran 1994).

While broadly influential in feminist studies, these methodological interventions follow directly only from the anticategorical critiques of categorization and not from many of the critiques of categorization by feminists of color. It is probably more appropriate to describe much of the literature emerging from the latter group as critical of broad and sweeping acts of categorization rather than as critical of categorization per se. Certainly feminists of color have been critical of a certain version of essentialism that has defined women as a single group, but virtually all feminists now share this criticism. Feminists of color have also rejected the individualistic project of a politics based on identification and opposition, as have poststructuralists.[11] But while taking such positions, many feminists of color have also realized that such a critique does not necessitate a total rejection of the social reality of categorization.[12] In other words, one cannot easily lump these critics in with either deconstructionists, on the one hand, or multiculturalists and proponents of identity politics, on the other, which Nancy Fraser and others have distinguished as the two main and opposing perspectives on the conceptual and political status of excluded groups (Fraser 1998). Whereas the multicultural and identity-politics perspective tends to maintain group boundaries uncritically in order to revalue them and the deconstructive perspective seeks to eliminate them, the alternative perspective described here seeks to complicate and use them in a more critical way. Feminists of color have steered a middle course, consistently engaging in both theoretical and empirical studies of intersectionality using finer intersections of categories. It is these studies that inaugurated the study of intersectionality and what I call the intracategorical approach to complexity. They and their intellectual descendents are the primary focus of the remainder of this section.

Interest in intersectionality arose out of a critique of gender-based and race-based research for failing to account for lived experience at neglected points of intersection – ones that tended to reflect multiple subordinate locations as opposed to dominant or mixed locations. It was not possible, for example, to understand a black woman's experience from previous studies of gender combined with previous studies of race because the former focused on white women and the latter on black men. Something new was needed because of the distinct and frequently conflicting dynamics that shaped the lived experience of subjects in these social locations. To take just one example from the earliest explorations, black women seemed to achieve greater equality with men of their race relative to white women because the conditions of slavery and white supremacy forced them to work on par with black men, yet black women also were more vulnerable to sexual violence because whites did not consider them worth protecting "as women" (see, for example, Davis 1981). The potential for both multiple and conflicting experiences of subordination and power required a more wide-ranging and complex terrain of analysis. How was this to be achieved? The primary subject of analysis was typically either a single social group at a neglected point of intersection of multiple master categories or a particular social setting or ideological construction, or both. To illustrate, I discuss only the first of these approaches, which I also take to be the most common of the three, particularly in earlier writings.[13]

This prototypical approach was set out in the early narrative essays that defined the field of intersectionality.[14] Narratives take as their subject an individual or an individual's experience and extrapolate illustratively to the broader social location embodied by the individual. Often such groups are "new" groups in the sense of having been named, defined, or elaborated upon in the process of deconstructing the original dimensions of the master category. A key way that complexity is managed in such narratives is by focusing on the single group represented by the individual. How does this minimize complexity? Individuals usually share the characteristics of only one group or dimension of each category defining their social position. The intersection of identities takes place through the articulation of a single dimension of each category. That is, the "multiple" in these intersectional analyses refers not to dimensions within categories but to dimensions across categories. Thus, an Arab American, middle-class, heterosexual woman is placed at the intersection of multiple categories (race-ethnicity, class, gender, and sexual) but only reflects a single dimension of each. Personal narratives may aspire to situate subjects within the full network of relationships that define their social locations, but usually it is only possible to situate them from the partial perspective of the particular social group under study (i.e., if an Arab woman is the subject of analysis, then issues of race and nationality are more fully examined from the perspective of Arab women than from the perspective of Arab men).

In personal narratives and single-group analyses, then, complexity derives from the analysis of a social location at the intersection of single dimensions of multiple categories, rather than at the intersection of the full range of dimensions of a full range of categories, and that is how complexity is managed. Personal narratives and single-group studies derive their strength from the partial crystallization of social relations in the identities of particular social groups. Whether the narrative is literary, historical, discursive, ideological, or autobiographical, it begins somewhere, and that beginning represents only one of many sides of a set of intersecting social relations, not social relations in their entirety, so to speak.

The intracategorical approach to complexity can also be extended to include more recent studies. In particular, there are similarities between those narrative and theoretical interventions that essentially created the study of intersectionality and a longer tradition of social scientific research that focuses on the intensive study of single groups, or "cases." Case studies are in-depth studies of a single group, culture or site and have long been associated with the more qualitative side of the divide between qualitative and quantitative methods in the social sciences. Case studies and qualitative research more generally have always been distinguished by their ability to delve into the complexities of social life – to reveal diversity, variation, and heterogeneity where quantitative researchers see singularity, sameness, and homogeneity (Ragin 2000). As is well known, anthropologists are the exemplary practitioners of multivocal, interpretive, and qualitative research, with their method of ethnography or "thick description" (Geertz 1994), which explains the popularity and widespread influence of anthropology in women's studies.

Many feminists who are trained in social science methods and who are interested in intersectionality use the case-study method to identify a new or invisible group – at the intersection of multiple categories – and proceed to uncover the differences and complexities of experience embodied in that location. Traditional categories are used initially to name previously unstudied groups at various points of intersection, but the researcher is equally interested in revealing – and indeed cannot avoid – the range of diversity and difference *within* the group. Although broad racial, national, class, and gender structures of inequality have an impact and must be discussed, they do not determine the complex texture of day-to-day life for individual members of the social group under study, no matter how detailed the level of disaggregation.[15]

In this incarnation of the study of intersectionality, which can be considered an intellectual descendent of narrative studies, categories have an ambivalent status. Once again, such studies tend not to fall strictly into either the anticategorical or the intercategorical approach. On the one hand, some feminist scholars explicitly use categories to define the subjects of analysis and to articulate the broader structural dynamics that are present in the lives of the subjects. In addition, although a single social group is the focus of intensive study, it is often shown to be different and therefore of interest through an extended comparison with the more standard groups that have been the subject of previous studies. This strategy is evident in the comparison of working-class women to working-class men (Freeman 2000), the black middle class to the white middle class (Pattillo-McCoy 1999), Latina domestic workers to an earlier generation of African American domestic workers (Hondagneu-Sotelo 2001), and black female victims of domestic violence to white female victims of domestic violence (Crenshaw 1991). In each of these studies the former group is the focus of study and the latter group the source of background comparison and contrast.

On the other hand, scholars also see categories as misleading constructs that do not readily allow for the diversity and heterogeneity of experience to be represented. While the standard groups are homogenized as a point of contrast, the social group that is the subject of analysis is presented in all its detail and complexity, even though in the end some generalizations about the group must be made. These studies, then, avoid the fully deconstructive rejection of all categorization, yet they remain deeply skeptical of the homogenizing generalizations that go with the territory of classification and categorization. The point is not to deny the importance – both material and discursive – of categories but to focus on the process by which they are produced, experienced, reproduced, and resisted in everyday life (Fernandes 1997; Glenn 2002).

These, then, are the two main methodologies that have led the study of intersectionality. In addition to delineating these methodologies, it is important to take a moment to reflect on how the trajectory of their development has had an impact on the production of knowledge about intersectionality. To begin with, the social construction of all new knowledge tends to have a particular structure to it.[16] In this structure the development of a new field is celebrated on the tomb of the old. Since the new field cannot possibly supersede immediately the expansive terrain of its predecessors, it advances in some directions but not in all. Where it lags behind may be due to several different factors: either those areas were buried willfully or were more intransigent or were undeveloped and unclaimed. Where it advances and where it lags might be considered the starting conditions for the new field's eventual structuring. These starting conditions perpetuate gaps in reciprocal directions, where the old fields fall relatively farther behind new intellectual trends and the new field itself grows more impervious to new issues arising in the established disciplines. Ironically, one measure of how far feminism has come might be the distance between it and its most distant disciplinary cousins, which may be greater now than ever. Importantly, this has as much to do with research on new and timely subjects in the older disciplines as it does with the growth and sophistication of feminist studies itself. In other words, the older fields have not been standing still.

Interdisciplinary progress is deeply structured by these developments and so therefore are substantive fields of research (e.g., intersectionality) because substantive topics are often given shape in the disciplines. Judith A. Allen and Sally L. Kitch put it well: "When disciplinarity is the only institutional framework, progress is made one discipline at a time; and uncertainty, unevenness, and time lags are inevitable. Thus the field of women's studies grows increasingly fragmented" and ends up being more multidisciplinary than interdisciplinary (Allen and Kitch 1998: 286). I have tried to make the dynamics of this process more explicit – at least for the topic of intersectionality – as a way to help lessen that fragmentation, or at least some of the unintended consequences of it. With that in mind, I offer a third approach to the problem of complexity in the study of intersectionality, one that permits an examination of substantive issues that are far less prominent in women's studies than they are in the social science disciplines and in contemporary society more generally.

Intercategorical complexity

The intercategorical approach (also referred to as the *categorical approach*) begins with the observation that there are relationships of inequality among already constituted social groups, as imperfect and ever changing as they are, and takes those relationships as the center of analysis. The main task of the categorical approach is to explicate those relationships, and doing so requires the provisional use of categories. As Evelyn Nakano Glenn writes, in advocating for a greater emphasis on relationality in studies of intersectionality, scholars can treat race and gender categories as "'anchor' points – though these points are not static" (2002: 14). The concern is with the nature of the relationships among social groups and, importantly, how they are changing, rather than with the definition or representation of such groups per se, though some scholars like Glenn (2002) engage in both practices to great effect.[17] Finally, the type of categorical approach I am developing here goes further in exploring whether meaningful inequalities among groups even exist in the first place. Perhaps inequalities were once large but now they are small, or in one place they are large but in another they are small. This perspective leaves open the possibility that broad social groupings more or less reflect the empirical realities of more detailed social groupings, thus minimizing the extent of complexity. In the formulation of Irene Browne, whether there are complex differences and inequalities between groups is treated as a hypothesis.[18]

Some may counter that an interest in relationships among groups underlies the first two approaches as well. How is it possible to deconstruct definitions of social groups without reference to the relational dynamics underlying them? What is more, in terms of the emphasis on change, the reason why categories and the social relations they articulate can be deconstructed in the anticategorical approach is precisely because they can be shown to change across cultural and historical boundaries, that is, to have no underlying essence. Is the categorical approach's emphasis on relationships and change really all that different from the emphasis of the other two approaches?

I would contend that each approach shares the premise that relationships among social groups are containers of definable and indeed measurable inequalities. However, to empirically chart the changing relationships among multiple social groups defines the goal, rather than the premise only, of the categorical approach. Relationships of inequality among social groups do not enter as background or contextual or discursive or ideological factors, as they often do in the other two approaches, but as the focus of the analysis itself.[19] If structural relationships are the focus of analysis, rather than the underlying assumption or context of the analysis, categorization is inevitable. The only question is whether such an approach can adequately respond to legitimate, and often quite fatal, critiques of the homogenizing and simplifying dangers of category-based research. In short, can the categorical approach respect the demand for complexity?

The categorical approach focuses on the complexity of relationships among multiple social groups within and across analytical categories and not on complexities within single social groups, single categories, or both. The subject is multigroup, and the method is systematically comparative.[20] What is the source of complexity in such designs? The categorical space can become very complicated with the addition of any one analytical category to the analysis because it requires an investigation of the multiple groups that constitute the category. For example, the incorporation of gender as an analytical category into such an analysis assumes that two groups will be compared systematically – men and women. If the category of class is incorporated, then gender must be cross-classified with class, which is composed (for simplicity) of three categories (working, middle, and upper), thus creating six groups. If race-ethnicity is incorporated into the analysis, and it consists of only two groups, then the number of groups expands to twelve. And this example makes use of only the most simplistic definitions. If researchers want to examine more detailed ethnic groups within racial groups – say, Cubans, Mexicans, and Puerto Ricans within the broader category of Latino/as – it becomes necessary to limit other dimensions of the analysis, such as the gender or class dimensions, for the sake of comprehension. In this respect, intercategorical researchers face some of the same trade-offs between scale and coherence or difference and sameness that intracategorical researchers face in determining the appropriate level of detail for their studies.

Unlike single-group studies, which analyze the intersection of a subset of dimensions of multiple categories, however, multigroup studies analyze the intersection of the full set of dimensions of multiple categories and thus examine both advantage and disadvantage explicitly and simultaneously.[21] It is not the intersection of race, class, and gender in a single social group that is of interest but the relationships among the social groups defined by the entire set of groups constituting each category. The categorical approach formally compares – say, in terms of income or education – each of the groups constituting a category: men and women, blacks and whites, working and middle classes, and so on. Moreover, the categorical approach takes as its point of departure that these categories form more detailed social groups: white women and black women, working- and middle-class men, and so on.

The comparative and multigroup characteristics of such designs create a form of complexity that differs significantly from the anticategorical and intracategorical forms. Complexity is managed in comparative, multigroup studies of this kind by what at first appears to be a reductionist process – reducing the analysis to one or two between-group relationships at a time – but what in the end is a synthetic and holistic process that brings the various pieces of the analysis together. Whereas the intracategorical approach begins with a unified intersectional core – a single social group, event, or concept – and works its way outward to analytically unravel one by one the influences of gender, race, class, and so on, the categorical approach begins with an analysis of the elements first because each of these is a sizable project in its own right.

In fact, the size and significance of each element is perhaps why current quantitative social scientific research is divided, regrettably, into separate specialties on gender, race, and class, with little overlap among them. It is also why it is nearly impossible to publish grandly intersectional studies in top peer-reviewed journals using the categorical approach: the size and complexity of such a project is too great to contain in a single article. Indeed, there is much hostility toward such complexity; most journals are devoted to additive linear models and incremental improvements in already well-developed bodies of research. In the language of statistics, the analysis of intersectionality usually requires the use of "interaction effects" – or "multilevel," "hierarchical," "ecological," or "contextual" modeling – all of which introduce more complexity in estimation and interpretation than the additive linear model. Such models ask not simply about the effect of race on income but how that effect differs for men versus women, or for highly educated men versus poorly educated men, and so forth.[22]

My own research provides a concrete example of how the methodology of categorical complexity is informed by feminist work on intersectionality and yet applicable in other interdisciplinary sites (McCall 2000, 2001a, 2001b).[23] In terms of subject matter, I took the emphasis on differences among women as a call to examine structural inequalities among women, especially among different classes of women, since much less attention is devoted to class than to race in the new literature on intersectionality.[24] At the same time, a major new social issue was becoming the subject of intense research and political debate. Beginning in the late 1970s, earnings inequality between the rich and poor, and also between the college-educated and non-college-educated, rose significantly (see, for example, Wilson 1997). Since gender inequality was virtually the only type of inequality to have declined during the same period, men were often seen as the primary victims of the new economy and women as the beneficiaries. Since the new inequality was seen as afflicting mainly white men, there was a revolt against gender-based and race-based forms of redistribution (Kahlenberg 1996).

In such an environment, there was a clear need to supplement the focus on inequality among men with a detailed analysis of the changing structure of class and racial inequality among women. Were *all* women better off and *all* men worse off in the new economy? What was happening to class inequality among women? Was it as high and growing as much as it was among men? Had greater equality between men and women come at the price of greater inequality among women? Were the causes and thus solutions the same for rising class inequality among women and among men? If the causes were the same, did this mean that gender and racial differences were no longer important? Not only were the answers to these questions unknown, but this line of inquiry had natural affinities with the emphasis in women's studies on differences among women. Such an inquiry would also answer criticisms of feminist and multicultural scholarship for seeming to valorize differences among women without interrogating systemic inequalities among women, while at the same time intervening in an arena of political and public policy importance.

In keeping with the multigroup and comparative nature of the categorical approach, and to add a further contextual component, my analysis examined the roots of several different dimensions of wage inequality in regional economies in the United States. I examined each dimension of inequality first (between men and women; between the college-educated and non-college-educated; among blacks, Asians, Latino/as, and whites; and among intersections of these groups) and then synthesized this information into a configuration of inequality – a set of relationships among multiple forms of inequality, the underlying economic structure that fosters them, and the anti-inequality politics that would make most sense under such conditions. Four different configurations of inequality emerged from the analysis and are summarized in Table 2.1. The main finding to note is that patterns of racial, gender, and class inequality are not the same across the configurations. For example, heavily unionized blue-collar cities with a recent history of deindustrialization such as Detroit exhibit relatively modest class and racial wage inequality among employed men but elevated gender wage inequality and class inequality among employed women (relative to average levels of wage inequality in the United States as a whole). In contrast, a postindustrial city such as Dallas exhibits the opposite structure of inequality – it is marked more by class and racial inequality than gender inequality.

If we dig a little deeper into the complexity of these configurations, we find that the average levels of gender inequality that I just reported are somewhat misleading. If gender inequality is broken down by class, we find that it is higher among the college-educated and lower among the non-college-educated in Dallas, and vice versa in Detroit. This indicates that the same economic environment creates advantage for some groups of women

Table 2.1 Wage inequality by gender, class, and race in four cities relative to the national average for urban areas, 1989

Type of wage inequality	St. Louis (High-tech manufacturing)	Miami (Immigrant)	Dallas (Post-industrial)	Detroit (Industrial)
Class inequality among men	Lower	Higher	Higher	Lower
Class inequality among women	Lower	Higher	Lower	Higher
Racial inequality among men	Higher	Higher	Higher	Lower
Racial inequality among women	Higher	Higher	Higher	Lower
Gender inequality (average level)	Higher	Lower	Lower	Higher
Gender inequality among college-educated	Higher	Lower	Higher	Lower
Gender inequality among non college-educated	Higher	Lower	Lower	Higher

and disadvantage for other groups of women relative to similarly situated men. This conclusion can also be reached by looking at the configuration of inequality in immigrant-rich cities such as Miami, where gender inequality is lower for both college-educated and non-college-educated groups, but racial and class inequality among both men and women is much higher. Based on such systematic comparisons of levels of gender, racial, and class wage inequality across hundreds of cities, these configurations suggest that deindustrialized regions are ripe for comparable worth and affirmative action approaches to reducing earnings inequality, whereas in postindustrial and immigrant-rich regions, more universal or non-gender-specific strategies (e.g., minimum- and living-wage campaigns) may be more appropriate.

Although configurations of inequality illustrate how the sources and structures of economic inequality are multiple and conflicting, I would not want to go so far as to say that the resulting complexity is inherent to the subject, unless one takes the social ontological position that social relations are always by nature complex, or that gender inequalities always conflict with class inequalities and with racial inequalities. Rather, the complexity derives from the fact that different contexts reveal different configurations of inequality in this particular social formation. The point is not to assume this outcome a priori but to explore the nature and extent of such differences and inequalities. In short, having used traditional analytical categories as a starting point, classified individuals into those categories, and examined relationships of wage inequality among such groups of individuals, I arrived at the complex outcome that no single dimension of overall inequality can adequately describe the full structure of multiple, intersecting, and conflicting dimensions of inequality. Indeed, in the spirit of the anticategorical approach,

I question whether so-called general indicators of inequality, such as family income inequality and male earnings inequality, can be used as the standard indicators of the new inequality. My findings suggest not only that no single form of inequality can represent the rest but that some forms of inequality seem to arise from the same conditions that might reduce other forms, including, potentially, a conflict between reducing gender inequality and reducing inequality among women.

If the underlying contributions of feminist scholarship to this project are (I hope) obvious by now, then the question remains: why is this methodology not the primary one in the study of intersectionality in women's studies? Since this type of research falls outside the core of current feminist theory and research practice in women's studies, it can be used to explore many of the more general issues involved in the establishment of any new intellectual field that I raised at the end of the first section; hopefully, it can also diffuse at least some of the reasons why women's studies has not embraced this type of approach to the study of intersectionality.

First, the substantive issue of rising economic inequality between the rich and poor is a new trend, one that gained widespread recognition only in the early 1990s, well after the establishment of women's studies. This raises perhaps the most important question: What happens when new social issues of potential interest to the new field arise in older fields far (and moving farther) from the new field's center? Second, almost all of the research on this subject uses advanced quantitative techniques and large data sets from impersonally administered survey questionnaires. These are data and methods that many in the anticategorical and even intracategorical camps associate negatively with the legacies of positivism, or empiricism, or both when the two are collapsed in the three-category typology of feminist epistemologies (i.e., postmodern, standpoint, and empiricist) formulated by Sandra Harding (1986). This raises the question: what happens when particular methods, appropriate to the subject at hand and unlikely to change dramatically, become conflated with particular philosophies of science and potentially prevent freer flows of knowledge across disciplines and among members of the new field as a consequence? This limits knowledge in all relevant disciplines but is especially a problem for new fields such as women's studies, which aspires to be interdisciplinary. And, finally, the new feminist theories themselves (e.g., those based on anticategorical approaches to complexity) were not necessarily developed to address these issues. This should not be taken as a unique critique of women's studies; most social theories are not universal theories. I treat feminist theory as I would any other social theory and judge it based on the adequacy of its rendering of social life (in this case the new social inequality). What happens, then, when vanguard theories are not universal theories capable of fully covering the territories they hoped to supersede?

I have already responded to the first concern – about the substantive disconnect between new and old fields when new issues arise in the old fields – by describing a way (i.e., the categorical approach to complexity) to better integrate insights from women's studies on complex intersectionality, on the one hand, with the study of inequality in the social sciences, on the other. More generally, this kind of ongoing interaction between feminist theory and new issues arising in the disciplines needs to occur with greater regularity and consistency across disciplines. In terms of the methods-related, philosophical, and theoretical issues that inform the broader methodology of categorical complexity, my aim, given the range of issues covered and limited space, is simply to introduce alternative perspectives that many feminists have overlooked rather than to provide a comprehensive definition and defense of them.

In my research, I began with the subject matter of changing and intersecting forms of structural inequality and selected the methods and data that were most appropriate to it. However, these choices did not necessitate a positivist stance, which feminists and others have rightly criticized for setting unbiased empirical observation as the only valid basis for the construction of true scientific knowledge.[25] In my research and that of many social scientists, a postpositivist stance is often taken for granted.[26] In addition to feminist epistemologies, though, other postpositivist epistemologies are just as relevant. The one I will discuss is critical realism, which steers a middle course between positivism and postmodernism (Bhaskar 1989). As a philosophy of science and social science, critical realism is particularly apropos here because some realists have tried to integrate recent advances in complexity and chaos theory into it.

What is critical realism, and how does it differ from positivism, empiricism, and postmodernism? There are many different variants of realism (as there are of positivism), but what binds them together is a predilection for ontological over epistemological concerns and a critique of both positivism and postmodernism for being overly concerned with epistemological issues and overly pessimistic about what can be known about the world in the absence of unmediated access to it (Outhwaite 1987; Alcoff 1996). In contrast to other philosophies, realism does not subordinate knowledge of the natural and social worlds only to that which can be derived from the application of value-free observation and deductive logic, as in positivism. Nor does it subordinate knowledge of the world only to that which can be derived from direct sensory perception, as in empiricism. Nor does it pronounce ontology dead because all knowledge of the real world requires human interpretation and the truth claims of one human interpretation cannot be distinguished from those of another, as in postmodernism.

Rather, realism's basic premise is that the real world puts limits on knowledge so that not all interpretations are equally plausible.[27] Furthermore, in positing that some scientific explanations are more plausible than others, and yet maintaining that the real world is not knowable in any absolute sense because of the role of human interaction and interpretation, realism maintains a prominent place for the development of theoretical knowledge about unobservable phenomena. This position on theoretical knowledge is in contrast to both positivism and empiricism, which are skeptical at best of theoretical knowledge. In fact, because many fields of science are either highly theoretical or rely on sophisticated methods to mediate and interpret evidence about the real world, realism is frequently put forward as the best account of actually existing scientific practice (see, e.g., Barad 1996).

Some realists have gone even further in their argument against positivism, asserting that the lawlike, linear, reductionist, and predictable world that positivism describes does not offer a plausible account of the real natural or social world, which is actually more contingent, nonlinear, organic/holistic, chaotic, and, in a word, complex than the positivists assume.[28] However, as N. Katherine Hayles (1991) has been at pains to emphasize in her writings on chaos theory and literature, abandoning such hallmarks of positivism as predictability and linear explanation does not mean that anything goes: reality is complexly patterned but patterned nonetheless. We can determine the source of the complexity, we can describe it, and we can theorize it. In this view, changes in patterns of inequality and in the underlying structural conditions of society are dynamic, complex, and contingent but also amenable to explanation.

This is not the place to advance a philosophical defense of a strong social ontology of this kind, but it is important to highlight these efforts at developing a scientific and social scientific practice that is postpositivist and consistent with feminist theories of intersectionality in their emphasis on complexity.[29] Just as methods must fit the substantive question, so this philosophy seems to fit the project of analyzing complex and intersecting social relations. Even though many of the central concepts, modes of explanation, methods, and philosophies of science and social science may develop and evolve in welcome ways (e.g., critical realism), many of their core features nevertheless remain rooted in particular disciplines. This is because the disciplines have been and continue to be well suited to the study of particular subject matters, not because they are stuck in an antiquated era (i.e., of positivism). In order to be wide-ranging and effective, feminist analysis requires "extensive knowledge in aspects of a person's home discipline that appear to have little to do with women," and this is as true of deconstruction as it is of statistics (Friedman 1998: 314–15).

Conclusion: a first step in defining interdisciplinarity

Both the new and old fields are inadequate to the task of studying inter-sectionality in all its complexity. Older fields in the social sciences, from which I have been drawing examples throughout this article, have yet to deal fully with the complexity inherent in intersectional studies, while women's studies has yet to fully open up to the kinds of complex intersectionalities that are so much a part of systemic inequality in contemporary society. There is a disconnect between theory and social reality in both fields, with current theories unable to fully grasp the current context of complex inequality. Each field (i.e., the old and new) has changed and developed without insights from the other, and the upshot is that little feminist or mainstream work is being done on new and important topics at the intersection of both fields. In my mind, both fields suffer from not being interdisciplinary enough, even though women's studies is the only one of the two that makes strong claims to interdisciplinarity. It is appropriate, then, to hold women's studies to a higher standard.

This brings us back to the nebulous line between disciplinary and interdisciplinary feminist research (the latter representing the core of women's studies as an inter/disciplinary site). Where does the categorical approach fall? Is the subject matter – intersections of structural inequality – narrowly disciplinary? Not in broad terms, but perhaps in terms of the particular way in which it is studied in the social sciences, an important distinction to which I shall return in a moment. Is the underlying philosophy of science – realism – narrowly disciplinary? No. Are the underlying theoretical motivations of the project – feminist theories of intersectionality – narrowly disciplinary? No. Is the method – quantitative and large scale – narrowly disciplinary? Perhaps yes. Hence, what is restricting feminist research on intersectionality comes down primarily to methods – not substance, theory, or philosophy. Substance is the only other possible candidate. But if one were to dismiss structural inequality as being primarily of disciplinary interest, one would have to argue that there is no room for the particular kind of structural analysis described under the categorical approach. To advance this argument, one also would have to defend the central place of alternative forms of structural inequality in women's studies (e.g., discursive regimes). In other words, why should women's studies favor one over the other a priori?

The pressing issue then is to overcome the disciplinary boundaries based on the use of different methods in order to embrace multiple approaches to the study of intersectionality. Just because parts of a methodology are more akin to one discipline than to another does not mean that the methodology as a whole is not part of an interdisciplinary program. The overall methodology is feminist and interdisciplinary in orientation, but the methods and specific subject matters will be, to a certain extent, shaped by the disciplines – because of the division of substance that the disciplines support and because particular methods are appropriate to particular subject matters. There is nothing wrong with this; in fact, it is a much more expansive and radical notion of what interdisciplinarity means since it is not limited by default to those disciplines that have methods that travel easily (or, according to their practitioners, do not have a method at all). Feminism's development as a new field has been partial, perhaps unintentionally so, but this is a matter of course in the development of any new field and something that the new field must continually resist.

Acknowledgements

I am grateful for comments from participants at the 2001 American Sociological Association meetings in Anaheim, California, especially Judith Howard and Lisa Brush; the Institute for Research on Women at Rutgers University, especially Dorothy Sue Cobble and Averil Clarke; and the Northwestern University Gender Workshop in the Department of Sociology, especially Ann Orloff and Jeff Manza; as well as from Vilna Bashi, Maria Cancian, Vivek Chibber, and Charles Ragin. The graduate students in my seminar on intersectionality provided invaluable feedback on an earlier version of this article, and their insights are woven throughout this version. I have also benefited enormously from conversations with Leela Fernandes and Irene Browne as well as from the reviewers' comments. For financial support during the initial writing of this article, I thank the Russell Sage Foundation visiting scholars program. I alone bear responsibility for all errors and omissions.

Bibliography

Abbott, Andrew. 2001. *Chaos of Disciplines*. Chicago, IL: University of Chicago Press.

Alarcón, Norma. 1990. "The Theoretical Subject(s) of *This Bridge Called My Back* and Anglo-American Feminism." In Gloria Anzaldúa (ed.) *Haciendo Caras: Making Face, Making Soul: Creative and Critical Perspectives by Feminists of Color*. San Francisco, CA: Aunt Lute Books.

Alcoff, Linda Martín. 1996. *Real Knowing: New Versions of the Coherence Theory*. Ithaca, NY: Cornell University Press.

Alexander, M. Jacqui and Chandra Talpade Mohanty. 1997. "Introduction: Genealogies, Legacies, Movements." In M. Jacqui Alexander and Chandra Talpade Mohanty (eds) *Feminist Genealogies, Colonial Legacies, Democratic Futures*. New York: Routledge.

Allen, Judith A., and Sally L. Kitch. 1998. "Disciplined by Disciplines? The Need for an *Interdisciplinary* Research Mission for Women's Studies." *FS: Feminist Studies* 24(2): 275–300.

Anzaldúa, Gloria. 1987. *La Frontera/Borderlands: The New Mestiza*. San Francisco, CA: Aunt Lute Books.

Anzaldúa, Gloria. 1990. *Haciendo Caras: Making Face, Making Soul: Creative and Critical Perspectives by Feminists of Color*. San Francisco, CA: Aunt Lute Books.

Armatage, Kay. 1998. "Collaborating on Women's Studies: The University of Toronto Model." *FS: Feminist Studies* 24(2): 347–55.

Baker, Pamela, Bonnie Shulman, and Elizabeth H. Tobin. 2001. "Difficult Crossings: Stories from Building Two-Way Streets." In Maralee Mayberry, Banu Subramaniam, and Lisa Weasel (eds) *Feminist Science Studies: A New Generation*. New York: Routledge.

Barad, Karen. 1996. "Meeting the Universe Halfway: Realism and Social Constructivism without Contradiction." In Lynn Hankinson Nelson and Jack Nelson (eds) *Feminism, Science, and the Philosophy of Science*. Dordrecht: Kluwer.

Behar, Ruth. 1993. *Translated Woman: Crossing the Border with Esperanza's Story*. Boston, MA: Beacon.

Bhaskar, Roy. 1989. *Reclaiming Reality: A Critical Introduction to Contemporary Philosophy*. New York: Verso.

Blum, Linda M. 1999. *At the Breast: Ideologies of Breastfeeding and Motherhood in the Contemporary United States*. Boston, MA: Beacon.

Bourdieu, Pierre. 1988. *Homo Academicus*. (trans. Peter Collier). Stanford, CA: Stanford University Press.

Brown, Wendy. 1997. "The Impossibility of Women's Studies." *Differences: A Journal of Feminist Cultural Studies* 9(3): 79–101.

Browne, Irene. 1999. *Latinas and African American Women at Work: Race, Gender, and Economic Inequality*. New York: Russell Sage.

Browne, Irene, and Joya Misra. 2003. "The Intersection of Race and Gender in the Labor Market." *Annual Review of Sociology* 29(1): 487–514.

Butler, Judith. 1990. *Gender Trouble: Feminism and the Subversion of Identity*. New York: Routledge.

Butler, Judith. 1995. "Subjection, Resistance, Resignification: Between Freud and Foucault." In John Rajchman (ed.) *The Identity in Question*. New York: Routledge.

Byrne, David. 1998. *Complexity Theory and the Social Sciences: An Introduction*. New York: Routledge.

Collins, Patricia Hill. 2000. "It's All in the Family: Intersections of Gender, Race, and Nation." In Uma Narayan and Sandra Harding (eds) *Decentering the Center: Philosophy for a Multicultural, Postcolonial, and Feminist World*. Bloomington, IN: Indiana University Press.

Crenshaw, Kimberlé. 1989. "Demarginalizing the Intersection of Race and Sex: A Black Feminist Critique of Antidiscrimination Doctrine, Feminist Theory, and Antiracist Politics." *University of Chicago Legal Forum* 1989:139–67.

Crenshaw, Kimberlé. 1991. "Mapping the Margins: Intersectionality, Identity Politics, and Violence against Women of Color." *Stanford Law Review* 43(6): 1241–79.

Davis, Angela Y. 1981. *Women, Race, and Class*. New York: Random House.

Derrida, Jacques. 1974. *Of Grammatology* (trans. Gayatri Chakravorty Spivak). Baltimore, MD: Johns Hopkins University Press.

Dill, Bonnie Thornton. 2002. "Work at the Intersections of Race, Gender, Ethnicity, and Other Dimensions of Difference in Higher Education." *Connections: Newsletter of the Consortium on Race, Gender, and Ethnicity* (Fall): 5–7. Available online at http://www.crge.umd.edu/publications/news.pdf.

Fausto-Sterling, Anne. 2000. *Sexing the Body: Gender Politics and the Construction of Sexuality*. New York: Basic Books.

Fernandes, Leela. 1997. *Producing Workers: The Politics of Gender, Class, and Culture in the Calcutta Jute Mills*. Philadelphia, PA: University of Pennsylvania Press.

Foster, Johanna. 2000. "Feminist Theory and the Politics of Ambiguity: A Comparative Analysis of the Multiracial Movement, the Intersex Movement, and the Disability Rights Movement as Contemporary Struggles over Social Classification in the United States." PhD dissertation, Rutgers University.

Foucault, Michel. 1972. *The Archaeology of Knowledge and the Discourse on Language*. New York: Random House.

Fraser, Nancy. 1989. *Unruly Practices: Power, Discourse, and Gender in Contemporary Social Theory*. Minneapolis, MN: University of Minnesota Press.

Fraser, Nancy. 1998. "From Redistribution to Recognition? Dilemmas of Justice in a 'Postsocialist' Age." In Nancy Frase (ed.) *Justice Interruptus: Critical Reflections on the "Postsocialist" Condition*. New York: Routledge.

Fraser, Nancy, and Linda Gordon. 1998. "A Genealogy of 'Dependency': Tracing a Keyword of the U.S. Welfare State." In Nancy Fraser (ed.) *Justice Interruptus: Critical Reflections on the "Postsocialist" Condition*, New York: Routledge.

Freeman, Carla. 2000. *High Tech and High Heels in the Global Economy: Women, Work, and Pink-Collar Identities in the Caribbean*. Durham, NC: Duke University Press.

Friedman, Susan Stanford. 1998. "(Inter)Disciplinarity and the Question of the Women's Studies Ph.D." *FS: Feminist Studies* 24(2): 301–25.

Fuss, Diana. 1989. *Essentially Speaking: Feminism, Nature, and Difference*. New York: Routledge.

Fuss, Diana. 1991. *Inside/Out: Lesbian Theories, Gay Theories*. New York: Routledge.

Gamson, Joshua. 1996. "Must Identity Movements Self-Destruct? A Queer Dilemma." In Steven Seidman (ed.) *Queer Theory/Sociology*. Cambridge, MA: Blackwell.

Geertz, Clifford. 1994. "Thick Description: Toward an Interpretive Theory of Culture." In Michael Martin and Lee C. McIntyre (eds) *Readings in the Philosophy of Social Science*. Cambridge, MA: MIT Press.

Glenn, Evelyn Nakano. 1985. "Racial Ethnic Women's Labor: The Intersection of Race, Gender and Class Oppression." *Review of Radical Political Economics* 17(3): 86–108.

Glenn, Evelyn Nakano. 1992. "From Servitude to Service Work: Historical Continuities in the Racial Division of Paid Reproductive Labor." *Signs: Journal of Women in Culture and Society* 18(1): 1–43.

Glenn, Evelyn Nakano. 2002. *Unequal Freedom: How Race and Gender Shaped American Freedom and Labor*. Cambridge, MA: Harvard University Press.

Haraway, Donna. 1989. *Primate Visions: Gender, Race, and Nature in the World of Modern Science*. New York: Routledge.

Harding, Sandra. 1986. *The Science Question in Feminism*. Ithaca, NY: Cornell University Press.

Hayles, N. Katherine. 1991. *Chaos and Order: Complex Dynamics in Literature and Science*. Chicago, IL: University of Chicago Press.

Hondagneu-Sotelo, Pierrette. 1994. *Gendered Transitions: Mexican Experiences of Immigration*. Berkeley, CA: University of California Press.

Hondagneu-Sotelo, Pierrette. 2001. *Domestica: Immigrant Workers Cleaning and Caring in the Shadows of Affluence*. Berkeley, CA: University of California Press.

hooks, bell. 1984. *Feminist Theory: From Margin to Center*. Cambridge, MA: South End Press.

Kahlenberg, Richard D. 1996. *The Remedy: Class, Race, and Affirmative Action*. New York: Basic Books.

Keat, Russell, and John Urry. 1975. *Social Theory as Science*. Boston, MA: Routledge & Kegan Paul.

Keller, Evelyn Fox. 1985. *Reflections on Gender and Science*. New Haven, CT: Yale University Press.

King, Deborah. 1988. "Multiple Jeopardy, Multiple Consciousness: The Context of a Black Feminist Ideology." *Signs* 14(1): 42–72.

Lamont, Michèle. 2000. *The Dignity of Working Men: Morality and the Boundaries of Race, Class, and Immigration*. New York: Russell Sage.

Lather, Patti. 2001. "Postbook: Working the Ruins of Feminist Ethnography." *Signs* 27(1): 199–227.

Lather, Patti and Chris Smithies. 1997. *Troubling the Angels: Women Living with HIV/AIDS*. Boulder, CO: Westview/HarperCollins.

Lieberson, Stanley and Freda B. Lynn. 2002. "Barking Up the Wrong Branch: Scientific Alternatives to the Current Model of Sociological Science." *Annual Review of Sociology* 28(1): 1–19.

Manza, Jeff and Clem Brooks. 1999. *Social Cleavages and Political Change: Voter Alignments and U.S. Party Coalitions*. New York: Oxford University Press.

McCall, Leslie. 2000. "Explaining Levels of Within-Group Wage Inequality in U.S. Labor Markets." *Demography* 37(4): 415–30.

McCall, Leslie. 2001a. *Complex Inequality: Gender, Class, and Race in the New Economy*. New York: Routledge.

McCall, Leslie. 2001b. "Sources of Racial Wage Inequality in Metropolitan Labor Markets: Racial, Ethnic, and Gender Differences." *American Sociological Review* 66(4): 520–42.

Mink, Gwendolyn. 1995. *The Wages of Motherhood: Inequality in the Welfare State, 1917–1942*. Ithaca, NY: Cornell University Press.

Mohanty, Chandra Talpade. 1988. "Under Western Eyes: Feminist Scholarship and Colonial Discourses." *Feminist Review* 30 (Autumn): 61–88.

Moraga, Cherríe. 1983. *Loving in the War Years*. Cambridge, MA: South End Press.

Moraga, Cherríe, and Gloria Anzaldúa. 1984. *This Bridge Called My Back: Writings by Radical Women of Color*. 2nd edn. New York: Kitchen Table Press.

Moya, Paula. 1997. "Postmodernism, 'Realism,' and the Politics of Identity: Cherríe Moraga and Chicana Feminism." In M. Jaqui Alexander and Chandra Talpade Mohanty (eds) *Feminist Genealogies, Colonial Legacies, Democratic Futures*. New York: Routledge.

Offe, Claus. 1998. "'Homogeneity' and Constitutional Democracy: Coping with Identity Conflicts through Group Rights." *Journal of Political Philosophy* 6(2): 113–41.

Omi, Michael and Howard Winant. 1994. *Racial Formation in the United States: From the 1960s to the 1990s*. New York: Routledge.

Outhwaite, William. 1987. *New Philosophies of Social Science: Realism, Hermeneutics, and Critical Theory*. New York: St. Martin's Press.

Pardo, Mary S. 1998. *Mexican American Women Activists: Identity and Resistance in Two Los Angeles Communities*. Philadelphia, PA: Temple University Press.

Pateman, Carole. 1988. *The Sexual Contract*. Stanford, CA: Stanford University Press.

Pattillo-McCoy, Mary. 1999. *Black Picket Fences: Privilege and Peril among the Black Middle Class*. Chicago, IL: University of Chicago Press.

Platt, Jennifer. 1996. *A History of Sociological Research Methods in America, 1920–1960*. New York: Cambridge University Press.

Ragin, Charles C. 2000. *Fuzzy-Set Social Science*. Chicago, IL: University of Chicago Press.

Reed, Michael and David Harvey. 1991. "The New Science and the Old: Complexity and Realism in the Social Sciences." *Journal for the Theory of Social Behaviour* 22(4): 353–80.

Riley, Denise. 1988. *"Am I That Name?" Feminism and the Category of "Women" in History*. Minneapolis, MN: University of Minnesota Press.

Sandoval, Chela. 1991. "U.S. Third World Feminism: The Theory and Method of Oppositional Consciousness in the Postmodern World." *Genders* 10 (Spring): 1–24.

Scott, Joan Wallach. 1986. "Gender: A Useful Category of Historical Analysis." *American Historical Review* 91(5): 1053–75.

Scott, Joan Wallach. 1988. *Gender and the Politics of History*. New York: Columbia University Press.

Smith, Barbara. 1983. *Home Girls: A Black Feminist Anthology*. New York: Kitchen Table/Women of Color Press.

Spelman, Elizabeth V. 1988. *Inessential Woman: Problems of Exclusion in Feminist Thought*. Boston, MA: Beacon.

Steinmetz, George. 1998. "Critical Realism and Historical Sociology: A Review Article." *Comparative Studies in Society and History* 40(1): 170–86.

Twine, France Winddance, and Jonathan W. Warren. 2000. *Racing Research, Researching Race: Methodological Dilemmas in Critical Race Studies*. New York: New York University Press.

Visweswaran, Kamala. 1994. *Fictions of Feminist Ethnography*. Minneapolis, MN: University of Minnesota Press.

Wilson, William Julius. 1997. "The New Social Inequality and Affirmative Opportunity." In Stanley B. Greenberg and Theda Skocpol (eds) *The New Majority: Toward a Popular Progressive*. New Haven, CT: Yale University Press.

Notes

1 A crucial note on terminology: it is impossible to find a term that is both recognizable and merely descriptive of the kind of work that is the focus of this article. Many scholars will not regard *intersectionality* as a neutral term, for it immediately suggests a particular theoretical paradigm based in identity categories (see, for example, Brown 1997). This is not the only sense in which I use the term here; rather, I intend for it to encompass perspectives that completely reject the separability of analytical and identity categories. As for the origins of the term itself, it was probably first highlighted by Kimberlé Crenshaw (1989, 1991). Many other key texts introduced the conceptual framework and offered similar terms: see Davis 1981; Moraga 1983; Smith 1983; hooks 1984;

Moraga and Anzaldúa 1984; Glenn 1985; Anzaldúa 1987, 1990; King 1988; Mohanty 1988; Spelman 1988; Sandoval 1991.

2 The terms *complex*, *complexity*, and *complexities* appear frequently and are central in key texts on intersectionality, although no text focuses on complexity as such. A representative early statement, for example, is from the back cover of bell hooks's *Feminist Theory: From Margin to Center* (1984): "Feminists have not succeeded in creating a mass movement against sexual oppression because the very foundation of women's liberation has, until now, not accounted for the complexity and diversity of female experience." Similarly, but from a different theoretical perspective, Wendy Brown writes: "We are not simply oppressed but *produced* through these discourses, a production that is historically complex, contingent, and occurs through formations that do not honor analytically distinct identity categories" (1997: 87). A more recent example appears in the short description of the Consortium on Race, Gender, and Ethnicity at the University of Maryland, which, according to its website, is "a university-wide initiative promoting research, scholarship, and faculty development that examines intersections of race, gender, ethnicity, and other dimensions of difference as they shape the construction and representation of identities, behavior, and complex social relations." For more information, see http://www.umd.edu/crge.

3 In particular, the distinction between qualitative and quantitative methods, which has characterized much feminist writing on this subject, is severely underdeterminative of the philosophical and substantive issues involved in any study of intersectionality.

4 I will use the term *subject* throughout this article in two quite different ways. First, I will use it to refer to the actual topic of research or the actual individuals or groups who are being studied in any particular research project, as in "the subjects of analysis." Second, I will use it to refer to the more theoretical notion of an implied collective author or speaker or agent, as in "the theoretical subject of feminism."

5 See, e.g., Pateman 1988; Scott 1988; Fraser 1989; Fuss 1989.

6 Although I use *feminists of color* to refer to the authors of this perspective, not all feminists of color adhere to the same theoretical position or this position, and not all feminists writing from this perspective are feminists of color.

7 It is impossible to prove this point, but others have made it. See especially Moya 1997 for specific examples of conflation. In terms of the hegemony of the deconstructive position, Nancy Fraser (1998) implies it, as does Kay Armatage in speaking about institutionalizing women's studies as a department: "The transformative, self-critical nature of women's studies, combined with the emphasis on postcolonial and poststructural approaches that ceaselessly question the established canons and canonicity itself, is seen as the check against retrograde institutional tendencies" (Armatage 1998: 315).

8 See, e.g., Riley 1988; Fuss 1989; Butler 1990, 1995; Gamson 1996. See also Fraser 1998 for a cogent, if controversial, summary of this position and its dominance in feminist studies.

9 Interestingly, as part of their critique of multiculturalism, universalists have also seized on the problems of defining social groups (see, for example, Offe 1998).

10 For a recent methodological discussion of the complicated relationship between the identity of researchers and subjects that does not reject categories as a basis for research and is oriented toward the other two approaches, see Twine and Warren 2000.

11 Norma Alarcón, building on Gloria Anzaldúa's writings, argues that "consciousness as a site of multiple voicings is the theoretical subject, par excellence, of [*This*]

Bridge [*Called My Back*]. ... Indeed, the multiple-voiced subjectivity is lived in resistance to competing notions for one's allegiance or self-identification. It is a process of disidentification with prevalent formulations of the most forcefully theoretical subject of feminism. ... Thus, current political practices in the United States make it almost impossible to go beyond an oppositional theory of the subject, which is the prevailing feminist strategy and that of others; however, it is not the theory that will help us grasp the subjectivity of women of color" (1990). For an insightful analysis of how the "politics of ambiguity" plays out in several different types of social movements, see Foster 2000.

12 Crenshaw writes, for example, "Recognizing that identity politics takes place at the site of where categories intersect thus seems more fruitful than challenging the possibility of talking about categories at all" (1991: 377). Similarly, M. Jacqui Alexander and Chandra Talpade Mohanty argue that "postmodernist discourse attempts to move beyond essentialism by pluralizing and dissolving the stability and analytic utility of the categories of race, class, gender, and sexuality ... but the relations of domination and subordination that are named and articulated through the processes of racism and racialization still exist, and they still require analytic and political specification and engagement" (1997: xvii).

13 Authors who provide excellent examples of the second approach are Patricia Hill Collins (2000), who traces "the family" as a site of intersectionality; Nancy Fraser and Linda Gordon (1998), who trace historically the various dimensions of the concept "dependency"; and Leela Fernandes (1997), who examines the "politics of categories" – the political production and mutual constitution in everyday practice of the categories of class, gender, caste, and community. See also Haraway 1989; Mink 1995; and the contributions to Alexander and Mohanty 1997.

14 Though narrative, these writings ushered in a theoretical revolution in women's studies and therefore should be considered central texts in feminist theory.

15 For example, in writing about migration patterns between Mexico and the United States, Pierette Hondagneu-Sotelo argues that "macrostructural factors alone do not explain how people respond to new opportunities and pressures ... political and economic transformations may set the stage for migration, but they do not write the script" (1994: 187). Writing from a different methodological perspective, one that is more genealogical, Alexander and Mohanty express a similar sentiment, even though they too highlight the importance of structural transformations: "Analytic centrality [is] given to the experiences, consciousness, and histories of Third-World women" (1997: xxx).

16 In this section I develop a line of argument that both draws and deviates from the work of Andrew Abbott (2001), Pierre Bourdieu (1988), and others on the social construction and structure of academic fields and disciplines. The deviations stem from my interpretation of what has happened in women's studies in particular, rather than what has happened in other fields. For example, Abbott (2001) argues that new fields attempt to take over old fields in their entirety, whereas I argue that women's studies has been selective in its appropriation.

17 I want to be clear, however, that both relational and representational forms of inquiry have empirical aspects, so that is not the relevant distinction. Changes in representation can be documented in empirical terms just as well as changes in relationships of inequality can be.

18 Personal correspondence, May 15, 2002.

19 For example, Alexander and Mohanty describe a key set of studies that arguably fall in the intracategorical approach: "Central to our theorization of feminism is a comparative analysis of feminist *organizing, criticism, and self-reflection*; also

crucial is deep contextual knowledge about the nature and contours of the present political economic crisis. Individual analyses are grounded in the contemporary crisis of global capitalism, suggesting that these particular contexts are the ones which throw up very specific analytic and political challenges for organizations" (1997: xx; emphasis added). Though very much informed by macrostructural processes, and defined as "comparative and relational" (ibid: xvi), the primary empirical subject of analysis tends to be located at a more micro level (i.e., a single group or organization).

20 In contrast, one could say that the method of the intracategorical approach is single case intensive rather than comparative.

21 In practice, the number of social groups within categories can also be limited by the available data. As new racial and ethnic categories have become available in the US census, researchers have incorporated increasing numbers and combinations of racial, ethnic, and national groups in their analyses.

22 It is very common for discussions of quantitative research to point to these types of models as the proper vehicle for introducing complexity into the analysis (Byrne 1998; Ragin 2000; Abbott 2001), but there may be more promising alternatives on the horizon (see, e.g., Lieberson and Lynn 2002).

23 I focus on my research for two reasons: first, because the burden of proof (to satisfy the demand for complexity) is presumably higher with quantitative data than with qualitative data; and second, because I can share firsthand knowledge of trying to publish research that was widely regarded as "too complex." For qualitative examples, see Glenn (1992, 2002), who analyzes how relationships among different class and racial-ethnic groups of women and men have varied historically across different regions and racial-ethnic groups in the United States; Michèle Lamont (2000), who compares beliefs about work and morality for working-class white men and working-class black men, and compares these in turn with the beliefs of middle-class men in the United States vs. in France; Linda M. Blum (1999), who compares beliefs about and practices surrounding breast-feeding for black working-class women and white working-class women; and Mary S. Pardo (1998), who compares community activism among Mexican American women in working- and middle-class communities. Quantitative work that aims at unraveling the multiple and conflicting effects of race, class, and gender is still rare, but for an excellent set of studies, see Browne 1999, and for an excellent review, see Browne and Misra 2003. See also Manza and Brooks 1999.

24 The recent literature on rising wage inequality focuses on disparities between college- and non-college-educated workers. For the sake of consistency, I use education as a marker of class distinctions.

25 Positivism has other defining characteristics besides the possibility and primacy of unbiased observation, including rules for the correspondence of regularities of observation with universal generalizations and laws and the predictability of human and natural behavior based on such laws (see, e.g., Keat and Urry 1975).

26 In fact, as Jennifer Platt (1996) argues, the social scientists who first developed or extensively used survey-based methods did so without any knowledge of or allegiance to positivist philosophies.

27 This fundamental point is consistent with much of what feminists from various perspectives have repeatedly argued about the need to reject the opposition between nature and culture because both are at work (see, for example, Baker et al. 2001).

28 See, e.g., Reed and Harvey 1991; Byrne 1998; Steinmetz 1998. See also Stanley Lieberson and Freda B. Lynn (2002), who favor evolutionary models because of their greater complexity.
29 See also Ragin 2000 for a comprehensive methodological (as opposed to philosophical) discussion of how to incorporate complexity into the practice of social science research.

Part II
Confronting law

Chapter 3

Intersectionality analysis in the sentencing of Aboriginal women in Canada

What difference does it make?

Toni Williams

Introduction

Long overlooked in studies of crime and punishment, the woman 'in conflict with the law' arrived on scholarly and policy agenda toward the end of the twentieth century, a period of contradictory developments that position this era among the best of times for feminist scholarship and the worst of times for many women's lives. As feminist theory consolidated its place in universities and as references to women's equality started to appear in policy discourses and decision-making fora of national and international institutions, changes associated with neo-liberal economic restructuring began to make the conditions of life for most women harder and less secure (Cossman and Fudge 2002; Balfour and Comack 2006; Luxton and Bezanson 2006).

This juxtaposition of enhanced capacity to produce more – and more sophisticated – critique of inequalities in women's lives with deterioration in many women's circumstances suggests that important aspects of feminist knowledges do not reach or do not persuade decision makers. Persistent gender inequality in access to means of influence such as money, power and social capital may lend credence to such suggestions; but an array of policy measures of the last thirty years featuring feminist, or at least women-centred, discourses seems to belie them. Studies of reforms intended to empower women and girls have sometimes noted a complicated process of interactions between feminist and non-feminist knowledges. Analysing the fate of such reforms, Snider contends that factors that influence the reception of feminist and other critical knowledges may impede progressive change through law as much as the more frequently discussed obstacles to knowledge production and circulation. Better understanding of the potential and limitations of law reform as a strategy to improve women's lives therefore requires investigation of how decision makers receive feminist knowledges; that is, how they 'hear' claims, interpret critique of their practices, and act on proposals for change (Snider 2003).

The development of the intersectionality construct as a foundation for descriptive and normative claims about women from racialized populations provides an opportunity to explore how decision-makers receive critical feminist knowledges about women, race and crime. While much of the literature on intersectionality and law enforcement features the experiences of racialized women as complainants, this chapter is about one aspect of how law responds to racialized women as defendants. Focusing on the penalization of Aboriginal women in Canada, the chapter investigates the effects of a sentencing reform that purports to reduce the over-incarceration of Aboriginal people.

Part II briefly sketches the development of the intersectionality construct, highlighting some of the difficulties that may arise when attempting to use it instrumentally to shield women against criminal law. Part III describes relevant elements of the 1996 changes in Canadian sentencing law, including s.718.2(e) of the Criminal Code. This remedial section, which is intended to address over-representation of Aboriginal people in Canadian prisons, states that in imposing a sentence, a court should take into consideration all sanctions other than imprisonment that are 'reasonable in the circumstances... with particular attention to the circumstances of aboriginal offenders'. I outline the policy context of the reforms, the rationales for change, and R. v. Gladue (1999), the first Supreme Court of Canada case on the new sentencing regime, which sets out how judges should apply s.718.2(e). Part IV investigates the incarceration of Aboriginal women ten years after the reforms. After summarizing some of the changes in Canadian incarceration rates since 1996, this part turns to judges' reasons for sentence in a sample of recent cases to explore to what extent and to what effect intersectionality analysis features in courts' decisions about the penalization of Aboriginal women. Finding that the over-incarceration of Aboriginal women has worsened during the last ten years, this part shows that intersectionality analysis may not remedy the problem because sentencing courts that receive this form of knowledge may act on it in ways that blunt its critical edge. Specifically, the discussion suggests that intersectionality analysis interacts with new conceptions of the salience of risk to penalization in ways that may tend to strengthen rather than weaken faith in imprisonment as the appropriate response to offences committed by Aboriginal women.

Development of the intersectionality construct: from anti-essentialist theory to strategic sentencing practice

Much has changed since Crenshaw coined the term 'intersectionality' for the claim that black women encounter discriminatory social practices differently from white women and black men (e.g., Crenshaw 1989). By showing that the organization of equality rights along 'single axes' of discrimination masks complex interactions among subordinating social relations – specifically race and sex – and that such interactions structure daily experiences of inequality,

Crenshaw inserted into feminist legal analysis critical insights from the work of Black activists and scholars about how to theorize – and how to resist – women's oppression (Lorde 1984; hooks 1984). Born of struggles to confront the implications of black/white racialization for feminist praxis and of male/female relations for Black civil rights activism, intersectionality analysis has mushroomed during the last twenty years, in Canada as well as the United States. Although a substantial share of early research involved (re)framing the identities and (re)claiming the experiences of black women of the global North, recent scholarship encompasses a larger set of hierarchical social relations, including sexuality-gender, disability, culture and age, as well as class and different manifestations of race/racialization (e.g., Kline 1993; Rosenblum 1994; Andrews 2000; Pothier 2001; Deckha 2004; Gamson and Moon 2004; Hoyes 2004).

Alongside theoretical critique of essentialist representations of gendered and racialized identities, an overtly instrumental stream of policy research has developed, which purports to use intersectionality strategically to change how law and social policy affect members of marginalized groups. As with so many other strategies to reform legal or administrative practice, this analysis proceeds by exposing gaps between institutional commitments to equal provision of services and benefits and the lived experiences of discrimination, barriers and exclusions of those located at particular intersectionalized margins, and then formulating legal rights to substantively equal enjoyment of social goods and protection against social harms. Proponents may employ an intersectionality construct to locate or identify subordinated populations, in demands for the recognition of such populations and their entry into places from which they have been excluded, and to craft (re)distributional claims to services and benefits (Fraser 1997).

Repressive legal processes such as criminalization offer more complex settings for the application of instrumental models of intersectionality. Unlike areas of social policy such as health, education or income security, law enforcement or criminalization is not in itself a desirable social good or service, but at best a means to the end of a more peaceful society (Snider 1994). However widely shared that objective, conflicts persist about the role of criminalization in advancing it. Application of state discipline to some people ostensibly to protect others implicitly assumes the possibility of slotting individuals into discrete categories of 'the good' and 'the bad', the 'dangerous' and their 'innocent' victims. This binary division breaks down, however, when individuals at once embody victimized and victimizer, as do so many female lawbreakers (Comack 1996). In a domain where surveillance, discipline and control of marginalized populations are the tasks of law, the capacity of instrumental intersectionality analysis to protect marginalized women against harsh treatment in legal processes is open to question.

Nonetheless, some scholars advocate the insertion of an intersectionality construct into key decision-making processes such as sentencing, arguing that it should have the beneficial effect of reducing the high incarceration rates of poor women from racialized groups. Richie's finding (1996) that intersections among subordinating relations of gender, race and class combine to create a form of 'gender entrapment' that coerces battered black women into crime persuaded her that courts should consider this harsh social context as a reason to mitigate sentence (see also Tinto 2001). Writing from a very different perspective, Stenning and Roberts (2001, 2002) propose enactment of a general statutory mitigating factor that takes account of a defendant's social context and in particular her or his 'social/cultural disadvantage'. Although not explicitly informed by intersectionality analysis, this proposal nevertheless relies on the notion that a defendant's particular 'social/cultural disadvantage' generally stems from intersections of class, race, gender and other subordinating social relations (ibid).

By contrast, Lawrence and Williams (2006) question the progressive potential of resorting to social contextualization at sentencing by pointing to the variable and unstable ways that courts have employed intersectionalized constructions of black female defendants convicted of importing drugs. In their view, the deployment of such constructions in sentencing decisions about drug couriers offers another example of the appropriation of progressive feminist knowledge to legitimate oppressive practices. Reluctant to concede that such knowledge never serves to advance women's interests, the authors called for further research on the reception of feminist and critical race theoretic work at sentencing and in other judicial settings (ibid: 332). With its exploration of the penalization of Aboriginal women after reforms that purported to reduce incarceration, this chapter offers insights into the reception of instrumental intersectionality analysis in a setting where law explicitly authorizes judicial decision makers to take account of the social context of an Aboriginal defendant's life.

Sentencing reform

The policy context of sentencing reform

Reforms to Canada's sentencing laws occurred during a turbulent era in criminal justice policy, a period when many jurisdictions sought radically to restructure fundamental aspects of their criminalization and penalization practices. Neoliberal restructuring exerted pressure on states to reduce public expenditures on social security and protection at the same time as it created conditions that destabilized communities and exacerbated inequality, conditions conducive to increased conflict and rates of 'crime' (Carlen 1988; Comack 2000; Balfour & Comack 2006). Although very real differences separated states in terms of the particular interactions among political, fiscal and managerial factors that shaped their reforms (Tonry and Hamilton 1997; Tonry and Frase 2001), observers have noted common themes indicative of the emergence of a risk-based model of law enforcement (Feeley and Simon 1992). This forward-looking, predictive model directs criminalization processes towards management of populations perceived as problematic rather than simply responding to individual wrongdoing. It relies on actuarial methods of defining risk pools and criminological risk factors to populate the pools; it emphasizes individual responsibilization more than penal welfare; and, in the United States in particular, it helped to justify the extraordinary late-twentieth century growth in incarceration and the expansion of the privately operated prison as container of risk (Schicor 1995; Downes 2001).

Canada has not relied on the prison to incapacitate and contain as heavily as the United States nor does it appear to have wholeheartedly embraced actuarialism.[1] Incarceration and the threat of incarceration before and after conviction feature in its technologies of risk-based governance, however, including technologies that incorporate aspects of feminist and other critical knowledges (Hannah-Moffat 2000). Research on the Correctional Services Canada (CSC) has found, for example, that as it developed a mandate to promote 'women-centred corrections' (TFFSW and Canada 1990), the CSC transformed feminist findings about the needs of criminalized women into indicia of risks that such women allegedly pose to others. Since the late 1990s, this notion of risk/need has become an important justification for the CSC's rehabilitative and responsibilizing interventions into the lives of women prisoners and the notion also has infused its routine practices of prisoner classification and assessment (Campbell 2004; Hannah-Moffat and Shaw 2001; Hannah-Moffat 2005; Webster and Doob 2004).

Although risk has subsequently influenced policy and practice in relation to female (federal) prisoners, it did not figure prominently in the formulation of the rationales for the 1996 amendments to the Criminal Code, which responded to other persistent concerns of that time, notably, general over-use of incarceration as a penal sanction and the disproportionate representation of Aboriginal people in Canadian prisons.[2] Penal managers had begun to sound the alarm about the over-use of imprisonment during the early 1990s when Canada reported high incarceration rates relative to those of other Western democratic states (Solicitor-General Canada 1997). As one, often-repeated, statistic indicates, a 1995 imprisonment rate of 132 per 100,000 of the adult population ranked Canada as the third most punitive nation among a group of 15 comparator states (PSEPC 2005). More troubling than a data point from a single year, was the growth in the prison population during the early 1990s, a growth that seemed inconsistent with falling rates of police-recorded crime and a declining number of criminally-charged adults.[3] Absent plausible evidence that harsh sentencing had caused the crime rate to fall, the coupling of less crime with more severe punishment challenged the Canadian state in two ways. Symbolically, the large and growing prison population conflicted with Canada's sense of itself and its place in the world as a beacon of progressive social policy (e.g., *R. v Gladue*: para 52). More pragmatically, by the mid-1990s, correctional administrators and political elites had begun to view imprisonment as an expensive and ineffective form of crime control (Solicitor-General Canada 1997).

Consistent with this view, Canada did not substantially expand its prisons for men – although it did significantly increase its much smaller number of prison places for federally incarcerated women. Because men constitute more than 80 per cent of defendants in criminal proceedings, managerial anxieties about incarceration rates invariably centre on them and on the threat of protest against deterioration in the living conditions of prisoners and the working environments of staff. Moreover, a large and growing prison population housed in overcrowded conditions exposed prison officials to the risks of litigation, especially in the wake of changes in rights consciousness after adoption of the Charter of Rights and Freedoms in 1982 and enactment of statutory minimum standards of penal practice in 1992 (Corrections and Conditional Release Act 1992). In an era of tight fiscal restraint, reducing reliance on a costly, ineffective institution such as imprisonment presented itself as a rational political choice (Solicitor-General Canada 1997).

Even more entrenched than the general problem of over-reliance on incarceration was Canada's record of incarcerating Aboriginal people at excessive rates, a record that by the mid-1990s was well documented and incontrovertible. One influential late 1980s study reported, for example, that Aboriginal people, then about two per cent of the national population, constituted about ten per cent of the federal prison population; in western Canada, which has a relatively large Aboriginal population, the over-representation was much worse (Jackson 1988–9). Referring specifically to the over-representation of Aboriginal women among prisoners, one 1990s study showed that at only three per cent of the national Canadian population, Aboriginal women accounted for one in ten federally incarcerated women, and 'nearly half' of the women admitted to provincial prisons (LaPrairie 1996).

A new sentencing methodology: the rise of section 718.2(e)

The 1996 amendments sought to reduce incarceration by expanding the sanctioning options available to judges and by reforming their decision-making procedures. Parliament enacted new powers to divert adult defendants from the criminal sanction; it modified the procedures for imposing the fine to reduce imprisonment for default; and it created a new penalty, the conditional sentence of imprisonment, which suspends execution of a prison sentence of less than two years and serves as the main mechanism for implementing the decarceration goals of the reforms (*R. v Proulx* 2000). Courts have constructed the conditional sentence as primarily a punitive sanction for giving effect to penal purposes such as denunciation and deterrence rather than duplicating the more rehabilitative aims of probation. As such it promotes decarceration not by repudiating the idea of punishment, but by relocating 'imprisonment' from the dedicated institutions to the defendant's community. Thus a conditional sentence may specify a lengthy period of penal control, likely longer than the custody term that the judge would have imposed; it ought to be served under house arrest and other stringent, punitive restrictions on liberty for at least part of the term; and there is a presumption of incarceration if the defendant breaches any of the conditions (ibid).

As well as providing new penal options, Parliament sought to assert its authority over sentencing policy and to make decision-making more transparent (Doob 1997). Some changes essentially codify common-law norms, but others reinforce the new priority given to parsimonious use of the prison. Perhaps the most controversial provision, and certainly the most innovative, is s.718.2(e), which, as already mentioned, states that: 'all available sanctions other than imprisonment that are reasonable in the circumstances should be considered for all offenders, with particular attention to the circumstances of aboriginal offenders'. Three years after its enactment, the Supreme Court of Canada considered s.718.2(e) in the Court's first decision on the 1996 sentencing reforms. *R. v Gladue* (1999) concerns an appeal of a three-year prison term imposed on a young Aboriginal woman convicted of manslaughter for killing an emotionally – and sometimes physically – abusive common-law spouse. Although the Court did not change Ms Gladue's sentence, it took the opportunity to elaborate on the purpose of s.718.2(e) and how judges should apply it.

Three aspects of the Court's decision seem to open up space for the sentencing process to receive critical knowledge claims, such as those of instrumental intersectionality analysis. First, the decision charges judges with the responsibility to 'remedy injustice against aboriginal peoples in Canada' (ibid: para 65), in so far as they can do so within the parameters of the sentencing process (ibid: para 64). Judges bear this responsibility even though the Court does not regard discriminatory sentencing as a significant cause of over-representation, a problem that it attributes instead to the economic and social consequences for Aboriginal individuals and communities of the 'dislocation' and 'economic [under-]development' of Aboriginal society (ibid: para 67). This positioning of judges as activists authorizes them to employ creative methods to reduce the population of Aboriginal prisoners and as such it opens up sentencing as a site at which to engage with claims such as those derived from intersectionality analysis.

Second, the decision instructs judges to take into account 'the unique systemic or background factors which may have played a part in bringing the particular offender before the courts' (ibid: para 66) when deciding which sanction to impose on an Aboriginal defendant. 'Unique systemic and background factors' refers to the history and contemporary social context of Aboriginal people's lives and to how the effects of that context may have contributed to the defendant's offending. The Court classifies knowledge of the general consequences for Aboriginal persons and communities of Canada's colonial history as within the realm of judicial notice,[4] but requires specific evidence of the links between those consequences and the defendant's appearance before the court; evidence, in other words, of the defendant's experiences of abuse and victimization at home, school or in the wider society, discrimination, poverty, unemployment, substance abuse, family dysfunction, community fragmentation and so on. By endorsing these aspects of social context as relevant to sentencing decisions about Aboriginal defendants, the *Gladue* analysis gives legitimacy to knowledge claims that connect individuals' identities to their experiences of occupying locations constituted by subordinating social relations. The Court thus presents its conception of the distinctive methodology of s.718.2(e) in a manner that seems highly conducive to instrumental intersectionality analysis.

Third, the *Gladue* decision offers judges robust reasons to reject incarceration as a fit penal sanction for Aboriginal defendants. Noting that many Aboriginal societies construct violence and other harms as wounds to the community that require healing rather than as crimes deserving of individualized punishment, the Court holds that this difference in worldview may prevent imprisonment from performing its designated function of communicating deterrence and denunciation to an Aboriginal defendant and her community (ibid: para 69). It finds also that Canadian prisons have failed dismally to bring about rehabilitation of Aboriginal prisoners; that prison conditions are 'often culturally inappropriate'; and that 'discrimination ... is so often rampant in penal institutions' (ibid: para 68). In this third element of the judgment, the Court's claims about the perversity, ineffectiveness and cruelty of the prison for Aboriginal persons conforms to the familiar analytic move of highlighting the distinctively harmful impact of social institutions and practices on identities forged at the intersections of subordinating social relations.

With its recognition of the particular histories of Aboriginal Peoples in Canada, its endorsement of the relevance of social context to determination of a fit sanction, and its acknowledgement of the often harmful nature of the prison environment for Aboriginal prisoners, *Gladue*'s elaboration of s.718.2(e) seems receptive to the instrumental deployment of intersectionality analysis as a means of reducing the imprisonment of Aboriginal women. A closer look at the decision, however, raises questions about this intuition: for *Gladue* rests on liberal legalism's assumptions about the innocence of law (Fitzpatrick 1987) and on erasure of crucial knowledges about the structures and social relations that shape the context of Aboriginal women's lives. Judges need not consider how sentencing practices may be complicit in producing over-representation and they should not talk about Canada's colonial history – or its not-quite-post-colonial present.[5] Even the failures of imprisonment, such as its purported inability to speak to Aboriginal persons, may be disregarded in the far from unusual circumstance of a judge sentencing an Aboriginal person who has been convicted of a 'more serious' offence (*Gladue*: paras 33, 78–9, see also *R.* v *Wells* 2000).

Such erasures and omissions communicate ambivalence about the substantive equality project of sentencing Aboriginal people differently. More concretely, the Court's favoured method of scrutinizing the defendant's experience of disadvantage and trauma at home, in the family and the community to explain her offence as well as to justify non-carceral sanctions, forges a link between her contextualized intersectional identity and lawbreaking. This move not only masks the unequal relations inside and outside the criminal justice system that structure the defendant's experience but it also revives and reinforces stereotypes about Aboriginal criminality. In focusing on the performance of the 1996 reforms, the next section of the chapter considers the implications of *Gladue's* ambivalence and its individualizing method for the reception of intersectionality analysis in sentencing courts.

Implementation of the reforms

Findings from the quantitative data

Some commentators welcomed the new methodology of s.718.2(e), embracing its promise to adapt the sentencing process to the lives of Aboriginal defendants (e.g., Turpel Lafond 1999; Rudin and Roach 2002). Others expressed scepticism about its viability (e.g., Haslip 2000) or criticized Parliament and the Supreme Court for making faulty assumptions about the causes of aboriginal over-representation and for adopting a 'reverse discrimination' methodology that favours Aboriginal defendants (Stenning and Roberts 2001, 2002). Despite their very different evaluations of the desirability of s.718.2(e) as a response to the over-incarceration of Aboriginal persons, detractors and supporters alike tend to assume that the provision has the intended effects of reducing the incarceration of Aboriginal defendants relative to past levels and rates of incarceration and relative to the incarceration of non-Aboriginal persons.

Data on the use of imprisonment in the last ten years do not support this assumption as the following comparison of changes in Canada's total imprisonment rates with changes in the incarceration of Aboriginal women illustrates. From a 1995 high of 132 prisoners per 100,000 adults, Canada dropped its incarceration rate to 108 per 100,000 in 2003, a fall of almost twenty per cent (PSEPC 2006: table A3). This finding indicates that changes in sentencing policy and practice may have had the intended effect on the size of the prison population, a noteworthy achievement when most comparator states have increased their incarceration rates and prison populations (ibid).[6]

By contrast, the number of Aboriginal women – and men – in prisons has increased. This increase reflects three developments, two of which directly implicate sentencing decisions while the third does so indirectly. First, the last ten years has witnessed a much larger rise in the number of federally incarcerated Aboriginal women than non-Aboriginal women.[7] Specifically, the Aboriginal female population of the federal prisons has doubled (from 64 in 1996 to 128 Aboriginal women in 2006) since the enactment of s.718.2(e), whereas the non-Aboriginal female population of federal prisons has increased by fourteen per cent (from 244 to 280 non-Aboriginal women). As a result of this difference, Aboriginal women represent close to one in three (31 per cent) federal female prisoners in 2006, up from one in five (21 per cent) in 1996.[8]

Second, the number of Aboriginal women admitted to sentenced custody in provincial/territorial prisons has not declined to the same extent as has the number of non-Aboriginal women. In 1994/95, the 2,447 sentenced Aboriginal women admitted to provincial and territorial prisons accounted for about one in five (21 per cent) of all female admissions while the 2,123 Aboriginal women admitted in 2003/04 represented more than one in four (29 per cent) female admissions to sentenced custody in provincial/territorial prisons.[9]

Third, remand imprisonment has increased substantially in Canada since the mid-990s. Once again Aboriginal women have fared badly, with almost twice as many admitted to remand custody (2,751) in 2003/04 as in 1995/96 (1,403). By 2003/04, Aboriginal women represented 23 per cent of adult female admissions to remand custody, up from 14 per cent in 1995/96 (Brzozowski *et al.* 2006).[10]

With regard to all three developments, the differences between Aboriginal and non-Aboriginal women exceed the differences between Aboriginal and non-Aboriginal men. Thus ten years after enactment of s.718.2(e), there are more Aboriginal women in federal and provincial/territorial prisons (including remand prisons) than before the reforms; Aboriginal women represent a much higher proportion of women prisoners than before the changes; and they are significantly more over-represented in Canadian prisons than are Aboriginal men.

Since sentencing practice is but one of several factors that influence who goes to prison and for how long, these findings about the imprisonment rates of Aboriginal women could simply reflect the limited capacity of sentencing reforms to bring about change in the face of policy, discretionary and administrative decisions taken elsewhere in the criminal justice system.[11] The drop in Canada's overall incarceration rate since 1995, however, indicates that changes to the sentencing regime have had a discernible impact on prisoner numbers and suggests that a more specific process may be at work in the penalization of Aboriginal women. This contradiction between a declining total incarceration rate and increasing imprisonment of Aboriginal women thus points to the need to examine more closely how judges apply *Gladue*'s remedial interpretation of s.718.2(e) and to consider what role if any the intersectionality construct may play in decisions about Aboriginal female defendants.

Findings from judges' reasons for sentence

The sample

Exploration of the reasons judges cite for the sanctions they select when sentencing Aboriginal women defendants illuminates links between the new sentencing methodology and the increase in Aboriginal women's imprisonment and permits reflection on the potential for instrumental intersectionality analysis to bring about change. For the purposes of this discussion I retrieved from one of the major electronic databases eighteen first instance cases decided in 2005 and 2006 in which a Canadian court sentenced an adult Aboriginal woman. Not all sentencing decisions are published in the database, thus the cases are presented as illustrative of themes rather than representative of sentencing decisions about Aboriginal women.[12]

Judges imposed a carceral sanction in eight cases, a conditional sentence – the prison term served in the community – in nine cases, and a stand-alone probation order on top of time already served on two female defendants in the remaining case (see Table 3.1). Of the eight prison terms, three are provincial/territorial custody terms, ranging from six months for dangerous driving and possession of a stolen vehicle (*Armstrong* 2006) to eighteen months for aggravated assault (*Gladue* 2006). The shortest discretionary term[13] of federal incarceration is two and a half years (*Schoenthal* 2006); the longest is five years (*C.M.A.* 2005), reduced to three years after taking account of pre-sentence custody.[14]

One notable characteristic of the sample is the similarity between the offences of women receiving conditional sentences and federal prison terms.[15] Each of the five federally sentenced women had killed someone, and so had five of nine women who received a conditional sentence. Of these ten cases: two women convicted of manslaughter received federal sentences (*C.M.A.*; *W.L.Q.* 2005) and two conditional sentences (*Byrd* 2006; *Kahypeasewat* 2006); one federally sentenced (*Schoenthal*)[16] and one conditionally sentenced (*S.O.S.* 2006) woman had killed her child; and one federally sentenced (*Pépabano* 2005) and two conditionally sentenced women (*Bone* 2005; *Spence* 2006) had been convicted of impaired driving causing death. Two other conditionally sentenced women were convicted of a serious violent offence (*Diamond* 2006; *Pawis* 2006), as were the two women who received probation terms on top of time served (*Heavenfire*

Table 3.1 2005 and 2006 sentencing decisions about Aboriginal women

Case	Most serious offence	Sanction
R. v *Spence* 2006 (Manitoba)	Impaired driving causing death	Conditional sentence – 24 months less 1 day (maximum term)
R. v *S.O.S.* 2006 (Manitoba)	Infanticide	Conditional sentence – 18 months
R. v *Schoenthal* 2006 (Saskatchewan	Criminal negligence causing death (23-month-old son)	Federal prison term – 30 months
R. v *Pawis* 2006 (Ontario)	Aggravated assault (on 9-month-old son)	Conditional sentence – 24 months less 1 day (maximum term); probation – 36 months
R. v *Kahypeasewat* 2006 (Saskatchewan)	Manslaughter	Conditional sentence – 24 months less 1 day (maximum term); probation – 24 months
R. v *Heavenfire* 2006 (Alberta)	Uttering threats and forcible entry (home invasion with three co-defendants)	Remand custody (time served) – 8 months; provincial prison term – 1 day; probation – 12 months.
R. v *Lisa Gladue* 2006 (Alberta)	Aggravated assault	Provincial prison term – 18 months
R. c *Diamond* 2006 (Québec)	Aggravated assault	Remand custody – 6 months equivalent; conditional sentence – 18 months
R. v *Byrd* 2006 (Manitoba)	Manslaughter	Conditional sentence – 24 months less 1 day; probation – 24 months
R. v *W.L.Q.* 2005 (Saskatchewan)	Manslaughter	Remand custody (time served) – 12 months equivalent; federal prison term – 36 months
R. c *Pépabano* 2005 (Québec)	Impaired causing death	Federal prison term – 42 months
R. v *Goodstoney* 2005 (Alberta)	Second-degree murder	Mandatory life imprisonment – 15-year parole ineligibility period
R. v *C.M.A.* 2005 (Yukon)	Manslaughter	Remand custody – 24 months equivalent; federal prison term – 36 months
R. v *Bone* 2005 (Manitoba)	Impaired causing death	Conditional sentence – 2 years less 1 day
R. c *Happyjack* 2005 (Québec)	Fraud	Provincial prison term – 8 months; probation – 18 months
R. v *Armstrong* 2006 (Alberta)	Dangerous driving	Remand custody – 6 months equivalent; provincial prison term – 6 months; probation – 24 months
R. v *Chouinard* 2005 (Ontario)	Accessory to manslaughter	Remand custody – 14 months equivalent; conditional sentence – 22 months; probation – 24 months
R. v *S.A.P.* 2005 (Saskatchewan)	Trafficking	Conditional sentence – 18 months

Source: Canadian judgments database, Quicklaw Lexis-Nexis

2006). None of the women sentenced to a post-conviction custody term of less than two years was responsible for another person's death and only one had been convicted of a serious violent offence (*Lisa Gladue* 2006).

All of the defendants convicted of homicides and assaults knew the victims, as did at least two of the three impaired drivers (*Pépabano*; *Bone*). Almost all of the victims of violence were spouses (former or current) or children, a finding consistent with numerous studies showing that women's violence tends to be inflicted on family members (e.g., Comack 1996; Dekeseredy 2000; Brzozowski *et al.* 2006). In some decisions the relationship of the defendant to the victim, as spouse or parent, was specifically cited as an aggravating factor as per the policy to intensify punishment of familial violence offences now enshrined in the Criminal Code (s.718.2(a)(ii) & 718.2(a)(ii).1).

Reasons for sentence: application of the Gladue methodology

That judges sometimes justify non-carceral sanctions when an offence has resulted in death or serious injury and sometimes impose the longest prison terms on defendants convicted of such offences raises the question of how the new sentencing methodology of s.718.2(e) influences decisions. Consistent with the *Gladue* proposition that judges should take 'judicial notice' of the history of Aboriginal societies since European contact, and thus need not explicitly consider it, the decisions do not usually discuss that history or the contemporary discrimination and unequal treatment that Aboriginal persons continue to experience in Canada.[17] In case after case, by contrast, the judges describe the defendant's experiences of sexual and other physical violence in childhood, substance dependency, educational disadvantage, under- or unemployment, dislocation, parental abandonment and family dysfunction as factors that had shaped her identity, stunted the development of essential coping skills and led her to reproduce toxic and dangerous relationships in adulthood. As well as cataloguing those aspects of the defendant's life that *Gladue* characterizes as 'unique systemic and background factors',[18] judges usually commented on parenting by Aboriginal women, noting early-age pregnancies, the number of children a defendant has birthed, how many remain under her care and other indicia of her performance of the maternal role (*W.L.Q*; *Heavenfire*; *Pépabano*; *Schoenthal*; *S.O.S.*; *Diamond*; *S.A.P.* 2005; *Pawis*; *Chouinard* 2005; *Kahypeasewat*; *Spence*; *Happyjack* 2006; *Lisa Gladue*).[19]

Many judges specifically included Aboriginal heritage or identity among the litany of factors they referenced to explain the defendant's appearance before the court, but others minimized its significance. Minimization usually occurred when the judge considered the offence to be so serious that an Aboriginal defendant should receive a similar sanction to a non-Aboriginal defendant convicted of the same offence; in these instances it served in effect to nullify s.718.2(e) (e.g., *Armstrong; Spence*). The judge in *Chouinard*, by contrast, sought to apply the parsimony principle even as she attempted to uncouple the defendant's Aboriginal ancestry from the extreme physical and sexual violence of the defendant's childhood and youth. Perhaps concerned to avoid the stereotypical association of Aboriginality and law breaking that the *Gladue* methodology potentially may produce, the judge chose to explain the defendant's appearance before the court as a consequence of alcohol abuse (Ms Chouinard's and that of both parents) rather than racialized identity (para 20).

Through their accounts of defendants' identities and circumstances, judges connect Aboriginal women's appearances before the courts to lives lived at the economic margins of society and to subordinated locations at intersections of relations of gender, racialization and disability. With regard to these aspects of the defendants' contexts and identities, judges seemed to have little difficulty applying the *Gladue* methodology that asks for the particular circumstances of the individual Aboriginal defendant to be specifically adduced and linked to the offence. According to the judge who sentenced Ms S.O.S., for example, a young Aboriginal woman who was already successfully parenting two children, the 'monstrosity of the defendant's circumstances' drove her to commit 'the monstrous act' of killing her newborn baby and then concealing its body.[20]

More challenging for the courts than procedural dimensions of *Gladue* is the extent to which the 'unique background and systemic factors' also represent aspects of identity and circumstances that penal practitioners classify as sources of criminogenic risk or needs (Hannah-Moffat and Shaw 2001; Hannah-Moffat 2006). As '*Gladue* factors', these considerations function as a reason not to incarcerate Aboriginal women, but as risk/needs they operate as justifications for prison terms to contain the threat the defendant poses and custodial correctional programming to reduce it.

Cases in which judges imposed a non-carceral sanction illustrate two main strategies for resolving the conflicting demands of actuarial decision-making based on levels of risk/need and the imperative to try to avoid imprisonment because of the defendant's experience of life located at the intersections of multiple subordinating relations. One strategy relied on constructions of the sanction as a healing rather than a primarily punitive intervention in the defendant's life. Judges deciding these cases attempted to fashion conditional sentences that would facilitate the defendant's (re)integration into the community, thereby reducing the risk that she poses and enhancing safety (*Chouinard; Diamond, S.O.S.*). They did not impose punitive restrictions on liberty and they formulated discretionary conditions requiring the defendant to participate in programmes that the judges regarded as conducive to rehabilitation of the defendant in the community. The defendant's circumstances in these cases may have been assessed as equating her identity with substantial levels of risk/need, but the judges concluded that restorative/rehabilitative sanctions offered a better fit with this identity. Thus Ms S.O.S., convicted of the 'monstrous' infanticide, scored as a medium risk on the criminological risk/need scales, a level that could have justified a prison sentence.[21] Attributing the score 'largely [to] external factors beyond Ms S.O.S.'s control related to her situation and upbringing' (S.O.S., para 12), the judge chose to focus instead on Ms S.O.S.'s capacity to benefit from counselling and psychotherapy offered in the community.

The second strategy draws on the capacity of the non-carceral sanction to punish, rather than its potential to heal. Judges in these cases tend to focus more specifically on whether the community would be able to contain the risk the defendant's intersectionalized identity reputedly posed. They sometimes constructed the defendant as less dangerous than the risk factors seemed to suggest, deciding that her behaviour did not mark her as a serious threat to society regardless of her rating on criminogenic risk/need scales (Byrd). In support of such conclusions judges noted the absence of a criminal record, or the aged or minor character of the defendant's record (e.g., Spence, Pawis, Bone) and they found ways to treat the offence as situational and an aberration, often linking it to an unhealthy, dangerous relationship (Kahypeasewat; Byrd; Heavenfire).

When passing sentence on defendants whom they constructed as presenting a 'containable' risk, judges usually characterized the non-carceral sanction as meeting punitive objectives of deterrence and denunciation and then reinforced the punitive dimension through long terms and the imposition of highly restrictive punitive conditions, such as long periods of home confinement. Thus, seven of the nine conditional sentences in the sample are initially maximum terms of two years less a day, (with two somewhat reduced because of time served on remand) and two are eighteen-month terms (S.A.P; S.O.S.) and all of the punitive conditional sentences include periods of home confinement and similar restrictions. While lengthy conditional sentences served under punitive conditions may initially contribute to lower incarceration rates, this effect may be somewhat fragile because such sentences expose defendants to non-trivial risks of a substantial period of incarceration if they breach a condition early in the term.[22] Moreover, judges often supplement the punitive conditional sentence with a significant period of probation extending the defendant's period of subjection to state supervision for several years, usually far longer than if she had received a provincial prison term, and likely for more time than if she had been sentenced to federal custody.

Unsurprisingly, criminogenic risks and punitive objectives tend to feature prominently in cases where the defendant received a custodial term rather than a conditional sentence. Sometimes judges seemed to minimize the defendant's identity as an Aboriginal woman (Armstrong; Schoenthal). In other cases, the very same background factors that constituted the defendant's identity as an Aboriginal woman and explained her appearance before the court also rendered her risky and needy (*Lisa Gladue* 2006).[23]

Rather more interesting than the conventional response of incarcerating the defendant to denounce and deter her and to keep society safe (*Schoenthal*; *Pépabano; Happyjack*) are decisions in which judges give significant weight to reintegration and restorative justice objectives in their reasons for responding to the defendant's criminogenic/risk needs with a lengthy carceral term (e.g., *W.L.Q.*; *C.M.A.*). Thus, Ms C.M.A., a 27-year-old First Nations woman, received a three-year (post-conviction) prison term for manslaughter of her common-law spouse, not only to denounce and deter 'domestic violence', but also to 'help her change what has become a very entrenched, destructive lifestyle' (para 16). The judge who sentenced Ms W.L.Q. was more explicit about the prison as a space of stability and support, when he explained that three years of post-conviction custody for spousal manslaughter would enable the defendant to: 'obtain the help that she needs...'; 'reflect upon the harm she has done...; and 'accept responsibility' for her actions and behaviour (paras 35–36). With this positioning of custody as a vehicle for achieving the 'restorative' sentencing objectives of the defendant acknowledging harm, achieving rehabilitation and accepting responsibility, these cases construct the prison at least to some extent as a therapeutic environment, a place of safety, healing and growth for a defendant whose life in the community marks her as both victimizer and victimized.

Discussion and analysis

This thematic analysis of 18 sentencing cases does not conclusively answer the question of why Aboriginal women have fared so badly in the new sentencing regime. Nor does it establish that social context or intersectionality analysis never steers judges away from choosing prison sentences; after all, half of the women in the sample received non-custodial sentences, most for serious violent offences. But the cases do suggest that intersectionalized constructions of Aboriginal women may not reliably shield them from imprisonment in part because of how courts have integrated intersectionality claims into decision-making processes that are organized around controlling risk.

Taken as a whole, the reasons for sentences show that the judges generally attempted to work with the *Gladue* methodology for applying s.718.2(e) and that when doing so they tended to characterize the Aboriginal female bodies before them as distinctively marked by emotional trauma, familial failings and community dysfunction. This contextualization of the defendant and her offence fashions an intersectionalized identity of sorts from these failings and inadequacies in that it constructs the defendant's gender as racialized and her race as gendered through her vulnerability to male violence, her parental responsibilities and her economic deprivation. Repeated reference to this construct in sentencing decisions seems to signal receptivity to intersectionality analysis and it serves as a reminder of commonalities among Aboriginal women and the distinctiveness of their experiences. It may also have the more troubling effect, however, of representing lawbreaking by Aboriginal women as over-determined by ancestry, identity and circumstances, exactly the type of representation of compromised moral agency that feeds stereotypes about criminality.

Far from creating a site for contesting conventional accounts of women's oppression and opening up a space in which to tell more complicated stories about how women experience inequality (Gotell 2002), sentencing courts respond to intersectionality claims about Aboriginal women with a simple narrative that constructs Aboriginal families as incubators of risk, Aboriginal communities as containers of risk and the prison as a potential source of healing intervention in the defendant's life. With law's gaze intently fixed on family and community, broader dimensions of societal discrimination and exclusion and concerns about the role of criminalization in exacerbating the problems of Aboriginal communities fade from view. The social and economic relations and the legal regimes that maintain the subordination of Aboriginal Peoples in Canada are no more than the faintest of backdrops in the decisions. None of the cases mentions the 'rampant' discrimination against Aboriginal persons in prisons cited in *Gladue* (supra), nor do they refer to the extensive evidence of the discrimination and harmful treatment that women in general and Aboriginal women in particular have received – and continue to suffer – in Canadian prisons (Arbour and Canada 1996; Monture-Angus 2000; CHRC 2003; CAEFS 2006; Horii *et al.* 2006).

Finally, the association of the 'unique systemic and background factors' of the *Gladue* methodology with the criminogenic risk/needs of contemporary penal practice complicates the task of employing an intersectionality construct instrumentally to reduce the incarceration of Aboriginal women. When faced with an Aboriginal woman who embodies what the criminalization process deems to be criminogenic risk/needs, the sentencing judge is asked to justify a non-carceral sanction in terms of those same aspects of the defendant's intersectionalised identity that point to incarceration as necessary to contain and manage her risk of re-offending. While intersectionality claims may lend support to decisions that seek to contain the defendant's risk/needs in the community, now reconfigured to serve punitive ends, similar claims may appear also in justifications for assigning the defendant to carceral space.

Conclusion

Feminists have successfully employed intersectionality analysis to identify differences among women in their exposure to the burdens of criminalization and in the forms of control to which they are subjected. Whether intersectionality analysis may be deployed more strategically to remedy the substantively unequal effects of criminalization is a more complicated question. Evidence that the incarceration of Aboriginal women has increased substantially since the enactment of the 1996 reforms shows that the new sentencing model of s.718.2(e) has failed to achieve its remedial objective. While judicial incorporation of intersectionality constructs into their reasons for sentence may not be responsible for this failure, it does not seem to have significantly assisted Aboriginal women defendants to avoid imprisonment.

The conclusion that aspects of criminalization processes may receive feminist knowledge in ways that do not help and potentially may harm women is not new. In this setting, as elsewhere, however, this conclusion challenges some of the ways that feminists have sought to deploy our knowledge claims through law. Specifically with regard to the imprisonment of Aboriginal women, the findings reported in this chapter suggest a need to shift away from strategies that purport to adjust how judges exercise discretion and towards more direct means of preventing incarceration of Aboriginal women. This shift may require revisiting debates about how to penalise those offences that expose Aboriginal women to the greatest risk of prison terms: violent offences committed in familial settings. To re-orient a substantial share of feminist knowledge work on penalization toward the abolitionist project is likely to be a difficult, contentious and slow process because so many women, Aboriginal and non-Aboriginal, have fought long and hard to intensify the criminalization of family violence and to secure harsher penalties for these offences.[24] To reject abolitionism outright when tinkering with discretion has failed Aboriginal female lawbreakers so abjectly, however, is to ignore how intersecting hierarchical relations privilege certain actors, knowledges and perspectives just as they subordinate others. Though feminist knowledge may be unable to avoid complicity in how the state regulates lawbreaking women, it may at least exercise its relative privilege to refuse to support sentencing practices that perpetuate the over-incarceration of Aboriginal women.

Acknowledgements

I wish to thank Jarvis Hétu, LLB class of 2008, Osgoode Hall Law School, for his excellent research assistance on this project, the editors and Iain Ramsay for very useful comments on earlier drafts. This chapter developed out of my collaboration with Sonia Lawrence on research into the sentencing of black women convicted of importing drugs and I would like to thank Sonia for stimulating me to think in different ways about race/racialization, culture and intersectionality. Aspects of the framework of this chapter were presented at the conference on 'Theorizing Intersectionality' hosted by the Research Centre for Law, Gender and Sexuality, Keele University, UK, 22 May 2005 and as a public lecture at Cleveland-Marshall Law School, Cleveland State University, on 14 November 2006, subsequently published in volume 55(3) of the Cleveland State Law Review 269–87. Thanks for the very many helpful comments and suggestions I received at those venues. All remaining errors and omissions are mine.

Bibliography

Andrews, P.E. (2000). 'Globalization, Human Rights and Critical Race Feminism: Voices from the Margins'. *The Journal of Gender, Race & Justice* 3: 373.

Arbour L. and Canada (1996). *Commission of Inquiry into Certain Events at the Prison for Women in Kingston*. Ottawa: Public Works and Government Services Canada:

Balfour, G. and Comack, E. (2006) (eds). *Criminalizing Women: Gender and (in) Justice in Neo-Liberal Times*. Black Point, NS: Fernwood.

Beattie, K. (2006) 'Adult Correctional Services in Canada, 2004/2005'. *Juristat* 26(5): 1–34.

Brzozowski, J.-A., Taylor-Butts, A. and Johnson, S. (2006). 'Victimization and Offending among the Aboriginal Population in Canada'. *Juristat* 26(3): 1–31.

Bunting, A. (2004). 'Complicating Culture in Child Placement Decisions'. *Canadian Journal of Women and the Law*. 16: 137–64.

CAEFS (Canadian Association of Elizabeth Fry Societies) (2006). Tenth Anniversary of the Arbour Commission Report. Ottawa, CAEFS. http://www.elizabethfry.ca/arbr10e.pdf (accessed 1 March 2007).

Campbell, A (2004). *Punishment Through Exclusion: Maximum Security in the Creating Choices Era*. M.A. Thesis, Simon Fraser University, Vancouver, BC.

Canadian Panel on Violence Against Women (1993). *Changing the Landscape: Ending Violence Achieving Equality: Final Report of the Canadian Panel on Violence Against Women*. Ottawa: Supply and Services Canada.

Carlen, P. (1988). *Women, Crime and Poverty*. Milton Keynes: Open University Press.

Cheliotis, L.K. (2006). 'How Iron Is the Iron Cage of New Penology?: The Role of Human Agency in the Implementation of Criminal Justice Policy'. *Punishment & Society* 8(3): 313–40.

CHRC (Canadian Human Rights Commission) (2003). *Protecting Their Rights: A Systemic Review of Human Rights in Correctional Services for Federally Sentenced Women*. Ottawa: Canadian Human Rights Commission.

Comack, E. (1996). *Women in Trouble: Connecting Women's Law Violations to Their Histories of Abuse*. Halifax, NS, Fernwood.

Comack, E. (2000). 'The Prisoning of Women: Meeting Women's Needs', in K. Hannah-Moffat, and M. Shaw (eds) *The Ideal Prison: Critical Essays on Women's Imprisonment in Canada*. Halifax, NS: Fernwood

Commission on Systemic Racism and Ontario (1995). Report of the Commission on Systemic Racism in the Ontario Criminal Justice System. Toronto: Queen's Printer.

Cossman, B.and Fudge, J. (2002). *Privatization, Law, and the Challenge to Feminism*. Toronto: University of Toronto Press.

Crenshaw, K. (1989). 'Demarginalizing the Intersection of Race and Sex: A Black Feminist Critique of Antidiscrimination Doctrine, Feminist Theory, and Antiracist Politics'. *University of Chicago Legal Forum*: 139–68.

Daubney, D. and Parry, G. (1999). 'An Overview of Bill C-41 (the Sentencing Reform Act)', in J.V. Roberts and D.P. Cole (eds) *Making Sense of Sentencing*. Toronto: University of Toronto Press.

Deckha, M. (2004). 'Is Culture Taboo? Feminism, Intersectionality, and Culture Talk in Law'. *Canadian Journal of Women and the Law*. 16: 14–53.

Dekeseredy, W.S. (2000). *Women, Crime and the Canadian Criminal Justice System*. Cincinnati, OH: Anderson Publishing.

Doob, A.N. (1997). 'Sentencing Reform in Canada', in M. Tonry and K. Hatlestad (eds) *Sentencing Reform in Overcrowded Times: A Comparative Perspective*. New York: Oxford University Press.

Doob, A.N. and Webster, C.M. (2006). 'Countering Punitiveness: Understanding Stability in Canada's Imprisonment Rate'. *Law and Society Review* 40(2): 325–68.

Downes, D.M. (2001). 'The Macho Penal Economy: Mass Incarceration in the United States – A European Perspective', *Punishment & Society* 3: 61–80.

Feeley, M.M. and Simon, J. (1992). 'The New Penology: Notes on the Emerging Strategy of Corrections and Its Implications'. *Criminology* 30(4): 449–74.

Fitzpatrick, P. (1987) 'Racism and the Innocence of Law'. *Journal of Law and Society* 14(1): 119–32.

Fraser, N. (1997). *Justice Interruptus: Critical Reflections on The "Postsocialist" Condition*. New York: Routledge.

Gamson, J. and Moon, D. (2004). 'The Sociology of Sexualities: Queer and Beyond'. *Annual Review of Sociology* 30: 47–64.

Goel, R. (2000). 'No Women at the Center: The Use of the Canadian Sentencing Circle in Domestic Violence Cases'. *Wisconsin Women's Law Journal* 15: 293.

Gotell, L., (2002). 'Toward a Democratic Practice of Feminist Litigation? LEAF's Changing Approach to *Charter* Equality', in R. Jhappan (ed.) *Women's Legal Strategies in Canada*. Toronto: University of Toronto Press.

Hannah-Moffat, K. (2000). 'Prisons That Empower: Neo-Liberal Governance in Canadian Women's Prisons'. *British Journal of Crimonology* 40: 510–31.

Hannah-Moffat, K. (2005). 'Criminogenic Needs and the Transformative Risk Subject: Hybridizations of Risk/Need in Penality'. *Punishment & Society* 7(1): 29–51.

Hannah-Moffat, K. (2006). 'Empowering Risk: The Nature of Gender-Responsive Strategies', in G. Balfour and E. Comack (eds) *Criminalizing Women: Gender and (in)Justice in Neo-Liberal Times*. Halifax, NS: Fernwood.

Hannah-Moffat, K. and Shaw, M. (2001). *Taking Risks: Incorporating Gender and Culture into the Classification and Assessment of Federally Sentenced Women in Canada*. Ottawa: Status of Women Canada.

Haslip, S. (2000) 'Aboriginal Sentencing Reform in Canada – Prospects for Success: Standing Tall with Both Feet Planted Firmly in the Air'. *Murdoch University Electronic Journal of Law* 7, http://www.murdoch.edu.au/elaw/issues/v7n1/haslip71_text.html#Restorative%20versus%20Retributive%20Elements_T (accessed 21 October 2006).

Hooks, b. (1984). *Feminist Theory from Margin to Center*. Boston, MA: South End Press.

Horii, G., Parkes, D., and Pate, K. (2006). 'Are Women's Rights Worth the Paper They're Written On? Collaborating to Enforce the Human Rights of Criminalized

Women', in G. Balfour and E. Comack (eds) *Criminalizing Women*. Halifax, NS: Fernwood.

Hoyes, C. (2004). 'Here Comes the Brides' March: Cultural Appropriation and Latina Activism'. *Columbia Journal of Gender and Law* 13: 328.

Jackson, M. (1988–89). 'Locking up Natives in Canada', *University of British Columbia Law Review* 23: 215.

Kempf-Leonard, K. and Peterson, E.S.L. (2000). 'Expanding Realms of the New Penology: The Advent of Actuarial Justice for Juveniles', *Punishment Society* 2(1): 66–97.

Kline, M. (1993). 'Complicating the Ideology of Motherhood: Child Welfare Law and First Nation Women'. *Queen's Law Journal* 18: 306.

Koshan, J. (1998). 'Aboriginal Women, Justice and the Charter: Bridging the Divide?' *U.B.C. Law Review* 32: 23.

LaPrairie, C. (1996). *Examining Aboriginal Corrections in Canada*. Aboriginal Peoples Series. Ottawa: Ministry of Supply and Services.

Lawrence, S. and Williams, T. (2006). 'Swallowed Up: Drug Couriers at the Borders of Canadian Sentencing'. *University of Toronto Law Journal* 56(4): 285–332.

Lorde, A. (1984). *Sister Outsider: Essays and Speeches*. Trumansburg, NY: Crossing Press.

Luxton, M. and Bezanson, K. (2006). *Social Reproduction: Feminist Political Economy Challenges Neo-Liberalism*. Montreal: McGill-Queen's University Press.

McGillivray, A and Comaskey, B. (1999). *Black Eyes all of the Time: Intimate Violence, Aboriginal Women and the Justice System*. Toronto: University of Toronto Press

Monture-Angus, P. (1999). 'Women and Risk: Aboriginal Women, Colonialism, and Correctional Practice', *Canadian Women's Studies Journal* 19: 24.

Monture-Angus, P. (2000). 'Aboriginal Women and Correctional Practice: Reflections on the Task Force on Federally Sentenced Women', in K. Hannah-Moffat and M. Shaw (eds) *An Ideal Prison? Critical Essays on Women's Imprisonment in Canada*. Halifax, NS: Fernwood.

O'Malley, P. (2002). 'Globalizing Risk?: Distinguishing Styles of "Neo-Liberal" Criminal Justice in Australia and the USA'. *Criminal Justice* 2(2): 205–22.

Ontario Native Women's Association (1989). *Breaking Free: A Proposal for Change to Aboriginal Family Violence*. Thunder Bay: Ontario Native Women's Association.

Pothier, D. (2001). 'Connecting Grounds of Discrimination to Real People's Real Experiences'. *Canadian Journal of Women and the Law* 13: 37.

PSEPC (2005). *Corrections and Conditional Release Statistical Overview: 2005*. Ottawa: Public Safety and Emergency Preparedness Canada.

PSEPC (2006). *Corrections and Conditional Release Statistical Overview: 2006*. Ottawa: Public Safety and Emergency Preparedness Canada.

Richie, B. (1996). *Compelled to Crime: The Gender Entrapment of Battered Black Women*. London: Routledge.

Rosenblum, D. (1994). 'Queer Intersectionality and the Failure of Recent Lesbian and Gay "Victories"'. *Law & Sexuality* 4: 83.

Royal Commission on Aboriginal Peoples (1996). *Bridging the Cultural Divide*. Ottawa: Ministry of Supply and Services.

Rudin, J. and Roach, K.W. (2002). 'Broken Promises: A Response to Stenning and Roberts' "Empty Promises"'. *Saskatchewan Law Review* 65(1): 3–34.

Shaw, M. and Hannah-Moffat, K. (2000). *An Ideal Prison?: Critical Essays on Women's Imprisonment in Canada*. Halifax, NS: Fernwood.

Shichor, D. (1995). *Punishment For Profit: Private Prisons/Public Concerns*. Thousand Oaks, CA: Sage.

Sinclair, R.L. and Boe, R., (2002). *Canadian Federal Women Offender Profiles: Trends from 1981–2002 (Revised)*. Ottawa: Correctional Service of Canada.

Snider, L. (1994). 'Feminism, Punishment and the Potential of Empowerment', *Canadian Journal of Law and Society* 9(2): 75–104.

Snider, L. (2003). 'Constituting the Punishable Woman. Atavistic Man Incarcerates Postmodern Woman'. *British Journal of Criminology* 43(2): 354–78.

Solicitor-General Canada, (1997). *Corrections Population Growth: First Report on Progress for Federal/Provincial/Territorial Ministers Responsible for Justice*. Fredricton: Solicitor-General Canada.

Stenning, P. and Roberts, J.V. (2001). ' Empty Promises: Parliament, the Supreme Court, and the Sentencing of Aboriginal Offenders'. *Saskatchewan Law Review* 64(1): 137–68.

Stenning, P. and Roberts, J.V. (2002). 'The Sentencing of Aboriginal Offenders in Canada: A Rejoinder'. *Saskatchewan Law Review* 65: 75–95.

Sugar, F. and Fox, L. (1989/1990). 'Nistum peyako séht'wawin iskwewak: breaking chains'. *Canadian Journal of Women and the Law* 3 (2): 465–82.

TFFSW and Canada (1990). *Report of the Task Force on Federally Sentenced Women: Creating Choices*. Ottawa: Ministry of the Solicitor General.

Tinto, E.K. 'The Role of Gender and Relationship in Reforming the Rockefeller Drug Laws'. *New York University Law Review* 76 (2001): 906.

Tonry, M.H. and Frase, R.S. (2001). *Sentencing and Sanctions in Western Countries*. Oxford: Oxford University Press.

Tonry, M.H. and Hamilton, K. (1997). *Sentencing Reform in Overcrowded Times : A Comparative Perspective*. New York: Oxford University Press.

Turpel Lafond, M.E. (1999). 'Sentencing within a Restorative Justice Paradigm: Procedural Implications of *R. v Gladue*'. *The Criminal Law Quarterly* 43(1): 34–50.

Webster, C.M. and Doob, AN. (2004). 'Classification Without Validity or Equity: An Empirical Examination of the Custody Rating Scale for Federally Sentenced Women Offenders in Canada'. *Canadian Journal of Criminology and Criminal Justice* 46(4): 395–422.

Legislation

Canadian Charter of Rights and Freedoms, enacted as Part I
of the *Constitution Act* 1982.   84
Corrections and Conditional Release Act S.C. 1992, c. 20   84
Criminal Code of Canada R.S.C. 1985, c-46   80, 83, 91

Table of cases

Supreme Court of Canada and Court of Appeal authorities

Reasons for sentence sample

Notes

1 (O'Malley 2002). There are debates about whether actuarialism has been wholly embraced even in the United States, whether it replaces or co-exists with the mid-twentieth-century model of penal welfare and about whether it is new; see, for example (Cheliotis 2006), (Kempf-Leonard and Peterson 2000).
2 Sentencing law in Canada had historically shown considerable deference to sentencing judges, offering them virtually no guidance and demanding little by way of accountability. A pincer movement of the mid-1990s matched political demands for more accountability in sentencing with technocratic critique of the failings of Canada's criminal justice system. This movement exposed the lack of transparency and inconsistent decision-making of Canadian courts, paving the way for reforms that purported to establish a consistent framework of sentencing policy and practice, enhance democratic accountability and improve public access to sentencing law (Doob 1997; Daubney and Parry 1999).

3 As the police-recorded crime rate dropped by 13 per cent, and the number of adults charged fell by 15 per cent, admissions to federal and provincial prisons *grew* by 15 per cent and the incarceration rate of charged persons increased by 36 per cent (PSEPC 2006).

4 The Court does not use the term colonialism.

5 The Report of the Royal Commission on Aboriginal Peoples declares that 'we live in a post-colonial world' but at the same time asserts that: 'The social pathology, economic deprivation and political instability that prevail in many Aboriginal communities cannot be overcome until we address the fundamental contradiction of continuing colonialism in this country', RCAP, *Part Three: Building the Foundations of a Renewed Relationship*, Chapter 14. The Turning Point, available at http://www.ainc-inac.gc.ca/ch/rcap/sg/cg14_e.pdf, (accessed 15 August 2007). For analysis of the significance of colonialism to relationships between Aboriginal Peoples and the criminal justice system in Canada, see Sugar and Fox 1989; Monture-Angus 1999.

6 A recent analysis of the use of imprisonment in Canada since the 1960s suggests a need for caution when making claims about changes in incarceration rates. Doob and Webster (2006) argue that the data essentially show stability in the use of incarceration during the past forty years, which somewhat belies the urgent need for change expressed by correctional administrators during the early to mid-1990s. They also identify a dramatic shift away from sentenced towards remand custody more recently. Thus a drop in the use of imprisonment post-conviction may indicate that more defendants are receiving non-custodial sanctions at sentencing simply because they have already served their prison terms on remand.

7 Prison terms of at least two years are served in federal prisons operated by the Correctional Service of Canada, shorter terms up to a maximum of 'two years less a day' are served in prisons operated by provincial and territorial governments.

8 There are small discrepancies among the various data sources. The numbers for 1991 and 1996 are from Sinclair and Boe's *Canadian Federal Women Offender Profiles: Trends from 1981–2002 (Revised)* (2002). The numbers for 2006 are from PSEPC (2006). Federal imprisonment of Aboriginal men also has increased since the 1996 reforms although not to the same extent: PSEPC (2006).

9 More specifically, the data show that the number of Aboriginal women admitted to sentenced custody in Canada's provinces and territories dropped during the first few years after the 1996 reforms, (from 2,447 in 1994–95 to 1,894 in 2000–01, a 23 per cent decline), but then started to climb in 2001–02, shortly after the *Gladue* decision, reaching 2,123 in 2003–04, an increase of 12 per cent (Brzozowski *et al.* 2006). Aboriginal men are 21 per cent of admissions to sentenced custody in the provinces and Territories (Beattie 2006).

10 Remand decision-making is not based on the same factors as sentencing and in theory, detention before sentencing ought to reduce the likelihood or the length of carceral sentences. Empirical studies have shown, however, that individuals incarcerated before trial are more likely to receive prison sentences than those convicted of the same offences but released on bail (Commission on Systemic Racism and Ontario 1995). The quantitative data presented here do not show interactions between imprisonment decisions taken at different stages, but the high levels of both remand and sentenced incarceration of Aboriginal women indicates that other factors conducive to incarceration at sentencing tend to outweigh the discount that courts apply for time served.

11 Other contributing factors include political decisions about which behaviours and interactions qualify as criminal offences, policy decisions about enforcement

priorities, and discretionary decisions to charge, detain before trial, and prosecute or alternatively to divert individuals from criminal proceedings. Post sanction decisions related to the release of prisoners also affect the size of the prison population, especially among the population of longer-term prisoners. We know that prison authorities tend to classify Aboriginal women as higher risk than non-Aboriginal women partly because of the very same criminogenic risk/needs that feature in the *Gladue* methodology for justifying non-carceral sentences (Hannah-Moffat and Shaw 2001; Campbell 2004; Webster and Doob 2004) and we know that higher classification may affect access to prison programming and impair a prisoner's prospects of being assessed as 'ready' for release at the very earliest possible date. Parole decision-making relies on similar risk/need factors and again, within the carceral environment, they tend to militate in favour of the prison rather than against it (Hannah-Moffat 2005).

12 It seems that databases typically publish all of the cases they receive from first-instance courts and they may also receive decisions from lawyers or court reporters, but judges, courts, lawyers and court reporters do not send every case decided to the database (e-mails on file with author). The search looked for cases in 2005 and 2006 in which appeared the terms '718.2' and 'Aboriginal' and 'words beginning "senten"'. This search retrieved 148 cases in 2006 and 146 in 2005. After eliminating cases about men and one case about a female Aboriginal youth, the sample consisted of 36 cases, 23 in 2006, and 13 in 2005. I then reviewed these cases to select only those decided at first instance where the defendant is Aboriginal, which yielded 11 cases in 2006 and 7 in 2005.

13 *R. v Goodstoney* 2005 involves a mandatory life imprisonment term imposed on a defendant convicted of second-degree murder, thus the only decision to be made at sentencing concerned the minimum time the defendant had to serve before becoming eligible for parole consideration.

14 In *R. v W.L.Q.* (2005) the defendant was sentenced to a total term of four years and credited with a total of one year for pre-sentence custody and liberty restrictions; in *R. v Pépabano* 2005, she received a sentence of 42 months. I have indicated the full terms that judges imposed even when the actual time to be served is reduced by pre-sentence custody because my focus here is the normative judgment about the severity of the sanction, rather than the empirical questions about how much time is in fact served. Moreover, given the conditional release regime it is impossible to know how much of a carceral sentence is spent in custody.

15 In this sample the nature of the offence and the seriousness of its consequences do not seem closely related to the sanctions that judges imposed, nor for that matter does criminal history. But the sample does reveal one intriguing pattern that deserves fuller treatment in future research: namely the differences between jurisdictions and consistencies within them. Comparison of the province of Manitoba with its western neighbours is particularly noteworthy. Each of the four Manitoban defendants had killed another person and all received conditional sentences. By contrast none of the three Alberta defendants was convicted of a homicide offence and each served at least some time in provincial custody. Sentencing in the Saskatchewan cases was more varied. Three of four defendants were convicted of a homicide offence; one received a conditional sentence, two received federal prison terms (the fourth Saskatchewan defendant, S.A.P., received an 18-month term for drug trafficking).

16 The court does not treat Ms Schoenthal as an Aboriginal defendant, although it notes that Ms Schoenthal's father is Métis, one of the groups classified as Aboriginal in Canada.

17 (Royal Commission on Aboriginal Peoples 1996). Ironically, in the one case that references this history and contemporary experience, by extensive reference to *Gladue* 1999, the judge states that he is describing those realities to communicate the rationale for s.718.2(e) to the local Aboriginal community affected by the offence (*Diamond* 2006).

18 Recent sentencing appeals suggest that compliance with the *Gladue* sentencing methodology is still not universal, see e.g., *R. v Kakekagamick* 2006.

19 For insightful analysis and critique of judicial ideology about parenting by Aboriginal women, see Kline (1993); see also Bunting (2004).

20 These circumstances included a childhood spend in 'an abusive, dysfunctional, alcoholic home marked by violence and instability', surviving sexual abuse by her grandfather from age four until his death eight years later, a succession of abusive relationships during her teens and early adulthood and living with a partner who scared her so much that she felt forced to conceal the unwanted pregnancy and birth that resulted from a sexual assault.

21 Compare the three-year post-conviction term imposed on Ms C.M.A. who was assessed as 'moderate risk' (*C.M.A.* para 17).

22 Conditional sentences such as these potentially result in more incarceration than the custodial terms they replace because judges often will lengthen the period of a sentence served conditionally as well as imposing punitive restrictions on liberty. The longer the sentence and the more stringent the conditions, the greater the opportunity for breach and the more likely it is that breach will occur. Custody does not automatically follow from breach but it is the presumed sanction and courts have held that defendants incarcerated for breach of a conditional sentence should serve the entire remaining term in custody without the benefit of parole or remission.

23 When sentencing Lisa Gladue, convicted of aggravated assault after stabbing the man with whom she had shared a 'turbulent', alcohol-fuelled relationship, the judge noted that the defendant had suffered sexual and physical abuse as a child but that Ms Gladue 'had not been involved with her Native Community as a status Native for some time' (para 259). The judge nonetheless concluded that the 'systemic problems' identified by the Supreme Court of Canada may have contributed to Ms Gladue's appearance before the court (para 259). Despite the facts that the defendant had no criminal record, participated in the paid workforce and was successfully sole parenting her eight-year-old son, the judge regarded the 18-month custody term as necessary because 'the risk of repetition of these offences and the consequences of a repetition are sufficiently grave' (para 295).

24 For obvious reasons, most of the voluminous legal and policy literature on family violence in Aboriginal societies focuses on male batterers and aggressors, (e.g., Ontario Native Women's Association 1989; Canadian Panel on Violence against Women 1993; Koshan 1998; McGillivray and Comaskey 1999; Goel 2000). Studies by Sugar and Fox (1989/1990), Comack (1996) and Dekeseredy (2000) analyse violence by Aboriginal women in family settings and show the futility of carceral responses to such violence.

Chapter 4

Sexual violence, ethnicity, and intersectionality in international criminal law

Doris Buss

Introduction

Since the early 1990s and the wars in Yugoslavia, wartime rape has become, arguably as a matter of necessity, a feminist preoccupation. In the face of increasingly stark reports of extreme sexual violence against women in armed conflicts across the globe, feminists and other human rights activists have been working to secure greater international condemnation and prevention of violence against women. But, as Cynthia Enloe (2000) notes, sometimes making rape visible as a matter of political concern can be 'dangerously easy'.[1] Narratives of wartime rape engage a myriad of discourses and interests that shape and constrain how the rapes of 'our' women – or the enemies' women – materialize. Not only is rape often refracted through the prism of nationalism – rape as an attack on the home front – but, as the recent wars in Afghanistan remind us, the suffering of women can be an all too visible and malleable justification for militarization.

At the same time, rape and violence against 'third world' women has been a recurrent Western preoccupation, shaping and justifying Western colonial intervention (Loomba (1993 [2003]; Sen 2002), and, more recently, focusing and coalescing international human rights campaigns (Kapur 2005; Merry 2006). Legal and political efforts to address rape, sexual violence, and gender inequality, have become crucial sites for the (re)constitution – and contestation – of international order (Kapur 2005; Buss 2004; Chesterman 1997).

Feminist activists and lawyers have entered into the fray of these competing narratives mobilizing international criminal mechanisms to prosecute large-scale sexual violence occurring in conflict situations. That activism has focused, largely but not exclusively, on the prosecution of war crimes by the Rwanda and Yugoslav tribunals. These tribunals represent a significant advance, often through the hard work of feminists, in making visible and condemning as criminal, sexual violence against women as an instrument of armed conflict. And, in engaging in this legal and political work, feminists have sought to disentangle the different narratives through which wartime rape has been minimized, privatized and militarized.

It is this effort at 'disentangling' that interests me in this chapter. In both Rwanda and Yugoslavia the mass rapes of women took place within conflicts variously described as 'nationalist' (in the Yugoslav context) and/or 'ethnic' (for both Yugoslavia and Rwanda)[2] in which sexual violence was depicted as a way for one group to harm the other. That is, particular groups of women were subject to mass sexual violence because of their deemed ethnic identity. But unraveling the intersection of gender and nationalism or, more often, ethnicity was not straightforward. In the early stages of the Yugoslav conflict, feminist legal activists and scholars highlighted concerns with how and if to bring an intersectional understanding of mass rape to international legal action on mass rape. Would the emphasis on the ethnic context of the conflicts minimize the seriousness of the gender inequality that made sexual violence possible in the first place? Would an approach to wartime rape emphasizing its intersection with other social processes serve to dilute the gender markings of this crime?

The subsequent decisions from the Rwanda and Yugoslav tribunals have gone a long way in establishing rape as a serious crime, condemned by the international community and attracting heavy penalties for the perpetrators. And yet, I want to suggest in this chapter that despite these ostensible successes in prosecuting wartime rape, the earlier feminist concerns about how to strategize around the intersectional harms of large-scale sexual violence still have currency.

In this chapter I am interested in how the phenomenon of mass rape against women, particularly in Rwanda, is narrated by the tribunal in its decisions. In particular, I want to consider how the tribunal describes the relationship between sexual violence against women and ethnic conflict. I argue here that the tribunal's approach to the confluence of gender and ethnicity minimizes rather than opens up the complexity of large-scale sexual violence. To explore how this happens, I provide a reading of one decision from the Rwanda Tribunal: *Prosecutor* v. *Gacumbitsi*.

My discussion of *Gacumbitsi* maps the maneuvers by which the complex political, economic and social contexts within which sexual violence against women took place are omitted from the tribunal's decisions. In focusing on just one decision I am not suggesting this is the landmark case by which a particular understanding of wartime rape emerges. I focus on *Gacumbitsi* because it is an 'ordinary' decision within the war crimes context, in which the extreme and structurally complex phenomena of wartime rape becomes lost within the intricacies of judicial decision making focused on the ethnic contours of the conflict.

The tribunal's disappointing analysis of the intersection of gender and ethnicity raises for me not just questions about the limits of international criminal law in addressing violence against women. It highlights some of the difficulties encountered when unraveling the complexity of wartime rape. In my reading of *Gacumbitsi*, I argue that a major difficulty in the tribunal's reasoning is its failure to consider sexual violence as part of the process by which ethnic identities are constituted. That is, in characterizing the conflict as inter-ethnic, the tribunal shifts the focus to ethnicities as established entities rather than exploring the processes – including sexual violence – by which identities resonate and cohere at particular times and circumstances.

While the tribunals do not engage in intersectional analysis of the kind preferred by feminist scholars and activists, I suggest in this chapter that the decision in *Gacumbitsi* highlights some of the difficulties in doing intersectional analysis. The genocide in Rwanda, and its international criminal prosecution, involve a context in which the identities said to be in conflict were in fact unstable and needed to be mobilized in the name of the conflict. This was a case where the intersecting axes – here gender and ethnicity – were neither inevitable nor uncontested. In the final part of this chapter, I consider some of the implications both for international criminal prosecutions, and feminist advocacy, of an approach to intersectionality that considers the multiple ways in which gender violence is constitutive of, rather than simply resulting from, group identities. How does law narrate and understand 'ethnic' violence without, at the same time, treating social distinctions, such as the ethnic group 'as an empirical reality' (Eltringham 2004: 29)? How do feminists tell the stories of women's suffering through the lens of ethnic cleansing without accepting as truths and reproducing the very logic of the ethnic contours of the conflict? How do we, in effect, account for the instability, fluidity and contested nature of the social groupings that we see as intersecting and co-constituting?

Wartime rape and the perils of intersectionality

In 1993 and 1994, the conflicts in Yugoslavia took a horrifying turn in the eyes of the Western world as reports (e.g., Gutman 1993) emerged of mass atrocities including concentration camps, all done in the name of 'ethnic cleansing'.[3] Among the reported atrocities were the mass rapes of women in Bosnia Herzegovina and the establishment of *de facto* 'rape camps' where (primarily Croatian and Muslim) women were held for periods of time and subjected to rape and other abuses.

In 1993 the United Nations Security Council authorized the establishment of the International Criminal Tribunal for the Former Yugoslavia,[4] followed a year later by the establishment of a tribunal to prosecute perpetrators of the Rwanda genocide. Activists, particularly legal activists, turned their attention to the tribunals' statutory framework and field of operation (see e.g., Kohn 1994; Chinkin 1994). The existing international legal provisions on war crimes and crimes against humanity largely failed to treat wartime rape as a serious violation. And, where rape was recognized, it was defined narrowly as an attack on a 'woman's honour' (Askin 2003). For feminists, the weak legal provisions in place raised the possibility that rape would be either treated as a minimal crime or, as was the case in the two world wars, completely overlooked once the initial public outcry and condemnation receded (Stephens 1994; Tompkins 1995).

These concerns were eventually laid to rest, though not without substantial feminist lobbying (Copelon 2000; Hagan 2003). Both the Rwandan and Yugoslav tribunals issued early judgments ruling that, in the case of Rwanda, rape could constitute genocide (*Prosecutor* v. *Akayesu*), and in Yugoslavia (*Prosecutor* v. *Delalić* 2001), that rape would be effectively 'read in' to provisions where it was not specifically listed, such as grave breaches of the Geneva Conventions and war crimes.

The legal maneuvers by which rape was eventually brought into these international criminal law categories is not my focus (for further discussion, see Askin 2003; 2005). I am interested in the feminist debates that took place against the backdrop of the mass rapes in Bosnia. While feminist responses to the atrocities in Bosnia argued for the need to recognize the link between gender violence and nationalism (Mertus 1994; Buss 1998), this link was neither clear nor uncontroversial. The rape camps in the early 1990s were run primarily by Serbs in which non-Serb women were held and raped, the vast majority of whom were Muslim women (*Prosecutor* v. *Kunarac* 2001). While some journalists reported the Serb involvement in committing these and other mass atrocities (e.g., Gutman 1993), other media tended to characterize the conflict as 'ancient ethnic rivalry' in which all sides were culpable of egregious acts (for a discussion, see Alvarez 1999; Gagnon 2004).

At the same time, perpetrators themselves engaged in a series of narratives about ethnic difference and the place of sexual violence in demonstrating that difference. Decisions of the tribunals reveal that in both conflicts the sexuality of certain categories of women was particularly targeted as part of the ethnic campaigns. Rapes in the former Yugoslavia, for example, were accompanied by explicit ethnic epithets, while the Rwanda genocide was encouraged by a media campaign that relentlessly focused on the deemed lascivious and duplicitous sexuality of Tutsi women (discussed below).

In the mid-1990s and before the tribunals began their work, feminist lawyers and scholars were concerned with how best to characterize the intersectional harm of mass rape within a weak and unreliable international legal system.[5] The debates from this period raised two strategic questions: would the prosecution of *mass* rape erase the continuities between 'everyday' violence against women and its egregious wartime form (Chinkin 1994; Copelon 1994); and was it possible to characterize mass rapes as the product of both gender and ethnic violence without one identity erasing the other (MacKinnon 1993a; 1993b; Gibson 1993)?

At the time these debates were unfolding, feminist legal literature was beginning to grapple with critiques of feminist analysis as privileging white, middle-class women. By focusing on a single axis of oppression – gender – feminist analysis was overlooking and minimizing other forms of oppression (see e.g., hooks 1984; Mohanty 1991). For scholars and activists committed to a more inclusive feminism, the question then became how could feminist analysis account for the ways different forms of oppression, together with gender, combine to disadvantage different categories of women?

Intersectionality offered a method for examining how individuals and groups were positioned within matrices of domination (Collins 2000: 227). Kimberlé Crenshaw's work (see, for example, Crenshaw 1991) examined the intersection of gender and race in US legal responses to violence against women. She traced how the convergence of gender and race produced particular notions of black and white, male and female sexuality in the context of US history. The dangerous black male rapist, for example, materializes against the vulnerable white female complainant; black women's sexuality, culturally understood as lascivious, marks the black woman as always an illegitimate rape victim against the idealized, white female victim (Crenshaw 1991). And feminist legal interventions – whether through changes to the criminal rape trial, or the attempted politicization of 'domestic' violence – sometimes had harmful, racialized consequences (ibid. 1259–64 1269–71). Intersectionality, for Crenshaw, offered a way to unravel how gender and race within the context of sexual violence, positioned individuals and groups in particular ways that could not be understood without seeing gender *in relation to* race, and vice versa.

For feminists working to mobilize international legal action on the mass rape of women, a focus on intersecting forms of oppression had clear resonance. But characterizing rape as an international crime with intersecting forms of harm presented a challenge. Would it be possible for feminists to advocate for a complex picture of wartime rape in which the violence done to women was systemic, structural, but also, in this instance, shaped by the peculiar situation of ethnic conflict?

For Catharine MacKinnon, complexity was just one of several devices used by 'feminists' and others to 'obscure' the Serbian policy of genocide and particularly rape as genocide. A focus on mass rape in Bosnia-Herzegovina as a 'gender' crime risked minimizing its genocidal components, she argued (1993a, 1993b). To avoid erasing the orchestrated dimensions of mass rape, which shared many similarities with the Holocaust (MacKinnon 2006: Chapters 17, 22), MacKinnon argued for a clear identification of the conflict as perpetrated by the Serbs against Muslims and Croats. In her approach, there was no room for 'complexity' in feminist accounts.

[T]he analysis I have offered is not 'indeterminate'. It is not 'tentative'. It is not characterized by 'ephemerality', 'discontinuity', or 'fragmentation'.

How much 'constant rethinking' does the fact of genocide need? The
theory I have presented has not exemplified the luxury of withholding
commitment, a refusal to be pinned down, nor can it rest on the margin
of anything. Is this a problem? Do we want 'chaotic' war crimes trials?

(1993b: 91)

In MacKinnon's analysis, the mass rape of Bosnian women was best
understood in terms of layers: Muslim and Croatian women faced 'twice as
many rapists with twice as many excuses, two layers of men on top of them'
(1993a: 89). The concept 'ethnic rape' as a tool of genocide offered the best
formulation of a crime that recognized the orchestrated nature of mass rapes
committed as part of what she saw as a genocidal campaign waged by Serbs
against Bosnian Muslims and Croats.

For other feminists, such as Rhonda Copelon (1994), focusing on
'genocidal rape' was limiting and risked erasing the everyday-ness of rape.
She suggested that emphasizing the genocidal character of the rapes in Bosnia-
Herzegovina was 'factually dubious' (1994: 198), and created a hierarchy in
which the deemed 'uniqueness' of genocidal rape would obscure 'normal'
rape (1994: 205). Genocidal rape, she argued, further diminished violence
against women by characterizing rape as criminal only in the context where
it was a vehicle for another form of persecution, here ethnic genocide.
Rather than pushing for a headline grabbing, but potentially short-lived label
like 'genocidal rape', Copelon argued for 'gender justice', the recognition
that persecution based on gender was a crime in its own right (1994: 208).
Croatian and other regionally based feminists (see e.g., Kesic 1994; for a
discussion, see Philips 2002) added to this critique and specifically objected
to MacKinnon's writings as overplaying and misconstruing the ethnic
character of the wars.

While only Copelon was explicitly concerned with intersectionality, both
scholars appear to share an unease with what the Yugoslav, and later Rwanda,
war crimes tribunals might do when faced with a crime that is both gendered
and 'raced'. For MacKinnon, emphasizing the complex interrelationship
between mass rape and 'everyday rape' as gendered crimes risked minimizing
the orchestrated nature of the sexual violence campaign against certain
categories of women, in this case, Bosnian Muslim and Croatian women.
Copelon, in contrast, was concerned that without situating rape within
the structures of gender and ethnicity more broadly, the tribunals might
minimize sexual violence or other forms of wartime violence as crimes in
their own right.

International war crimes prosecutions

Since the early–mid 1990s and the publication of feminist writing on the
possibilities and limits of prosecuting rape as a war crime, the Yugolsav and

Rwanda tribunals have become established international courts, generating a body of jurisprudence that now forms a key component in an emerging field of international criminal law. Stemming from the political momentum created by these tribunals, a permanent International Criminal Court (ICC) has also been established. While the ICC's statute is broader, it concentrates on the same four categories of crimes that are the focus of the two tribunals: laws of war (what armies can and cannot do in the waging of armed conflict); egregious violations of the Geneva Conventions (an abbreviated list of severe acts – killing, torture, extensive destruction, etc. – contravening the obligation to protect civilians caught up in war); crimes against humanity, and genocide (both explained below).

Both tribunals are focused on prosecuting crimes committed in the context of a campaign primarily targeting large groups of people for extermination or abuse and removal from geographic areas. The early stages of each tribunal involved extensive evidence of the political and social history of the regions, mapping how identities – Bosnian Muslim or Serb; Rwanda Hutu or Tutsi – emerged and came into conflict (see, e.g., *Prosecutor v. Akayesu*, paras. 78–129; *Prosecutor v. Tadic*, paras. 53–126). Having established this framework, both tribunals now prosecute the crimes against a backdrop of the conflicts depicted in terms of a history of inter-ethnic tension.

And both tribunals (*Prosecutor v. Akayesu; Prosecutor v. Tadic*, para. 166) have ruled that each conflict was characterized by a deliberate strategy to target a population based largely on their ethnic identification. That is, Bosnian Serbs attacked Bosnian Muslims; Rwandan Hutu attacked Rwandan Tutsi, and so on, and they did so on a widespread basis to achieve certain objectives, principally ethnic cleansing and genocide. Thus, identity and ethnicity in particular have become central to the work of the tribunals.

Finally, both tribunals have issued a number of decisions which, broadly and with some exceptions, are seen by many to be positive developments in an international criminal codification of violence against women (Askin 2005; 2003; but see Engle 2005; Nowrojee 2005). As set out above, the tribunals ruled that rape and related sexual violence constitute not only war crimes, but also the more grave offences of crimes against humanity and genocide. The decisions also note that in the context of ethnic conflict, particular categories of women were targeted for abuse because of their deemed ethnic community (*Prosecutor v. Nahimana* 2003; *Prosecutor v. Kunarac* 2001). And finally, the gendered nature of war crimes, and the seriousness of sexual violence, is recognized throughout the statute of the new International Criminal Court, in effect mainstreaming gender in the unfolding area of international criminal law. Against the backdrop of these successes, feminist debates about how best to strategize around wartime sexual violence seem to have dropped away from the literature (but see Engle 2005; Nowrojee 2005).

While there is much to celebrate in the tribunals' work, I argue that the concerns about intersectionality raised by feminists in the early 1990s still have currency, though perhaps not in the same way initially anticipated. The tribunal decisions forefront the ethnic context of the conflicts and consider how specific harms, such as sexual violence, are exacerbated as a result. In this approach to understanding multiple forms of oppression, the tribunal decisions, I suggest, throw into relief a difficulty in doing intersectial analysis.

Intersectionality

Intersectional scholarship considers the ways in which oppressions converge to position individuals or groups at unique points of disadvantage. For example, in Kimberlé Crenshaw's analysis, as outlined above, race and gender, as distinct axes of oppression, converge to enact a particular form of oppression that cannot be primarily attributable to either race or gender. The black female rape victim and the black male accused who encounter the criminal justice system are enmeshed in a web of intersecting oppressions. Gender and race structure the social disadvantage of the black female rape victim, or the black male accused, at the point of their intersection. But in this analysis, gender and race emerge as already existing and constituted axes of oppression located within the historical context of the United States. What about situations in which one of those axes is unstable and contested, where claims to the very existence of the group or the mechanisms by which group membership is determined are neither established nor agreed upon? How does intersectionality account for the ongoing constitution – and contestation – of group identity?

The prosecution of mass sexual violence against women in the conflicts in Yugoslavia and Rwanda, I suggest, raises just this sort of a problem. In the following section, I explore one decision from the Rwandan tribunal: *Prosecutor* v. *Gacumbitsi*. This decision is neither headline grabbing nor definitive of sexual violence prosecutions. It is, in effect, a seemingly unremarkable decision, but one that reveals the limitations of the tribunal's prosecution of sexual violence against women within the framework of 'ethnic conflict'.

Gacumbitsi

Sylvestre Gacumbitsi, former mayor of Rusumo in Eastern Rwanda, was convicted in June 2004 by the Rwandan tribunal of genocide and crimes against humanity for his role in orchestrating and participating in murder, rape, and extermination in the Rusumo commune, April, May and June 1994 (*Prosecutor* v. *Gacumbtsi*, upheld on appeal 7 July 2006). The Rwandan tribunal's first decision in *Akayesu* had already established the judicial framework in which the Rwandan genocide was understood: this was a genocide overwhelming committed by those identified as Hutu against those seen to be Tutsi. Hutu deemed to be sympathetic to Tutsi were also targeted (des Forges 1999). A significant part of the attacks by Hutu against Tutsi was the rape and sexual abuse of Tutsi women, often ending in the murder of the women (des Forges 1999; HRW 1996).

In *Gacumbitsi* the tribunal considered charges relating both to the defendant's role as an authority figure orchestrating murder, rape and genocide, and his own role in individual acts of rape and murder. A crucial part of the evidence is a speech the defendant gave on 17 April 1994, in which he enjoined the men of Rusumo to have sex with 'Tutsi girls' and, should the women refuse, to kill them 'in an atrocious manner'.[6]

There are two separate difficulties for the tribunal in Gacumbitsi's incitement to rape I want to highlight here. The first is his responsibility for rapes that occurred around the time of his speech, but for which the tribunal cannot find sufficient evidence to link to his incitement. These are the rape charges involving witnesses TAO, TAS, TAP and TAP's mother, for which the defendant is ultimately acquitted. The second relates to the rape of one of these women: a Hutu woman, witness TAS.

Witness TAS, married to a Tutsi man, was raped while seeking a place to hide. Her Hutu attacker told her he 'just wanted to rape her and not kill her'. Another male Hutu attacker intervened saying that 'no decision [on raping] had yet been taken concerning Hutu women who were married to Tutsi'. But both men raped witness TAS anyhow. The tribunal notes that witness TAS 'thought that she was raped because she was married to a Tutsi' (para. 209). Witness TAS's ethnicity becomes relevant because the tribunal is considering her rape as a crime against humanity.

Crimes against humanity are defined as specific criminal acts – murder, torture, rape, and so on – that are committed as part of a larger attack against a population. Thus, the underlying offence – rape, for example – is itself a crime, but when it is committed as part of a larger targeting of a group of people – defined as such on national, political, ethnic, racial or religious grounds – it becomes a different type of crime, a crime against humanity (Mettraux 2005; Schabas 2006). This different category of international crime – as with the crime of genocide – is aimed at condemning the orchestrated, broad-based context in which individual crimes sometimes take place.

To prove the rape of witness TAS was a crime against humanity, the prosecutor's office lead evidence of the rape itself, and that the rape of this Hutu woman was part of an 'attack' against the Tutsi community. Witness TAS's ethnicity is a problem given that as a Hutu she is not formally part of the population – Tutsi – under attack. To resolve this difficulty, the tribunal rules that, 'through the woman, it was her husband, a Tutsi civilian, who was the target. Thus, the rape was part of the widespread attacks against Tutsi civilians' (para. 222).

There are a number of self-evident problems here, foremost of which is the tribunal's characterization of witness TAS's rape as a crime against her husband. Part of the reason the tribunal does this is because of the legal requirements of a crime against humanity outlined earlier; that the individual criminal act, here rape, must be shown to be part of a larger attack, the targeting of Tutsi civilians. In this case, the tribunal is recognizing that rape occurred in Rusumo commune, that it included the rape of Hutu women, and that, taken together, these rapes were part of the larger attack against the Tutsi population. In a strict legal reading, then, the tribunal's characterization of TAS's rape as a crime against *her husband* may not appear that strange. However, this legal maneuver, placed in the context of the decision as a whole, is disturbing.

The tribunal concludes that while it accepts TAS's evidence she was raped, it discounts her evidence she was told by her attackers they were acting under orders. The tribunal concludes, then, that the defendant is *not* responsible for TAS's rape because there was 'no evidence' linking Gacumbitsi's utterances to the rape of TAS and three others (para. 329). Hence, there is no conviction for a crime committed against TAS herself; her rape is recognized only as a crime against the Tutsi population (through TAS's husband). The tribunal did find that other rapes – of witness TAQ and seven other women and girls – resulted from Gacumbitsi's speech because they happened 'immediately after' his speech (para. 328).

The decision in *Gacumbitsi* is unsettling. While sexual violence against women *is* prosecuted in this case, and the defendant is ultimately held responsible for eight rapes, sexual violence against women is, at the same time, depicted in a strangely superficial manner. In this respect, *Gacumbitsi* appears to realize some of the feminist concerns outlined earlier: that the egregious mass rape of women in Yugoslavia (and later Rwanda) would be seen as disconnected from 'everyday' violence against women, and, an understanding of sexual violence at the intersection of ethnicity and gender minimizes the gendered phenomenon of violence against women in wartime.

The bulk of the trial chamber's reasoning on the rapes of witness TAS and three others is focused on the reliability of individual witnesses alleging rape. The doctrinal rules of individual responsibility shift the focus from rape as a widespread phenomena, recognized by the tribunal in other decisions (see e.g., *Prosecutor* v. *Akayesu; Prosecutor* v. *Nahimana)*, to rape in a few individual cases, for which there is insufficient evidence to hold the defendant entirely accountable. In the end result, the defendant is found guilty of only eight rapes.

When read in its entirety, the *Gacumbitsi* decision maps the ways in which gender violence, when placed in the frame of ethnic conflict, becomes difficult to see as a complex social problem. The tribunal's analysis could be read as an over-determination of the ethnic contours of the conflict so that all violence is understood within a framework of inter-group conflict in which Rwanda Hutu seek to annihilate Rwandan Tutsi. And any violence, including sexual violence, that does not fit this framework, such as the rape of witness TAS, a Hutu woman, slips out of focus. The same is true for other identity factors, such as region, occupation, and class (Pottier 2002; Newbury 1998; Jefremovas 2002, 1997; Twagilimana 2003) that greatly impacted the ways in which the violence in Rwanda unfolded but which are, for the most part, ignored in dominant legal and popular understandings of the genocide (Eltringham 2004; Pottier 2002).

But there is a related and, I argue, more serious distortion at play in the tribunal's reasoning, and that is its failure to consider how the violence, and sexual violence in particular, was used to *mobilize* and give meaning to the categories of Hutu and Tutsi at that particular time. The history of ethnic categorization in Rwanda has been thoroughly documented elsewhere (Twagilimana 2003; Jefremovas 2002; des Forges 1999; Prunier 1995; Newbury 1988), and it is clear that Hutu, Tutsi and Twa ethnic groups were established and hierarchically ordered in Rwandan society. However, many of these same scholars also note that these ethnic identities were neither static nor necessarily socially, politically or economically determinative in pre-genocide Rwanda (see, e.g., Twagilimana 2003; Jefremovas 1997). Further, a number of scholars have noted that other identities – class, occupation and region – were increasingly important in structuring political and economic life (Twagilimana 2003; Jefremovas 2002).

In the following discussion, I argue that widespread violence against women, particularly when placed against the background of the political economy of Rwandan society in the early 1990s, was part of the process by which the labels 'Hutu' and 'Tutsi' were made to cohere. My objective is not to present an alternative version of the 'causes' of the Rwanda genocide to displace the ethnic focus of the tribunal. Rather, in exploring some components of the economic, political and social upheaval preceding and accompanying the genocide, I want to consider how 'ethnicity' took shape as an identity category in and through the genocide. If ethnicity is understood as produced through, rather than just leading to the genocide, then the phenomenon of sexual violence, and its role in 'ethnic conflict' becomes more complex. This, in turn, raises questions about how – and by whom – meaning is ascribed to wartime sexual violence, and how law may reproduce as a given particular narratives of violence.

The political economy of rape

In *Gacumbitsi*, the tribunal finds that much of Sylvestre Gacumbitsi's responsibility for crimes committed in Rusumo commune relate to his speech on 17 April 1994, in which he specifically called upon Hutu men to rape 'Tutsi girls' and to kill them 'in an atrocious manner'. Gacumbitsi went further to specify that Hutu youth should be called upon to rape 'young girls' who 'had refused to marry' (2004: para. 215). The tribunal decision in *Gacumbitsi* recounts the evidence of several raped women and girls whose attackers specifically stated the rapes were motivated by revenge for the women's refusal to marry the men.[7]

This focus on marriage and rape as a form of revenge against Tutsi women is unaddressed by the tribunal in this or other decisions (see, e.g., *Akayesu* 1998: para. 431). And yet, it is these references to marriage that provide an important insight into the overall sexual economy in Rwanda that helped to produce the conditions both for the genocide and the resulting mass sexual violence.

In the sexual economy that accompanied ethnic stratification in Rwanda (Newbury 1998; Taylor 1999; Turshen 2001), Tutsi women, at least symbolically, were idolized and highly sexualized. Having a Tutsi mistress or secretary was seen as a sign of social capital for Hutu men (Taylor 1999). In Christopher Taylor's account (1999), the propaganda accompanying the build up to and conduct of the genocide particularly targeted Tutsi women's sexuality. Images of duplicitous and conniving Tutsi mistresses and secretaries were used to vilify the Tutsi population, and to convince the Hutu majority the Tutsi were on the brink of overthrowing and massacring the Hutu (see also, *Prosecutor* v. *Nahimana, Barayagwiza and Ngeze* 2003; Twagilimana 2003).

The tribunal decisions are replete with testimony about the extreme sexual abuse and torture committed against (primarily) Tutsi women during the genocide. But, Hutu women were also raped and not always because of their affiliation or deemed sympathy with Tutsi. Meredeth Turshen (2001) argues that the rape of women in Rwanda needs to be seen as implicated in men's access to women's assets. Turshen notes that sometimes the rapes were called 'marriages', the purpose of which, among other things, was to gain access to land and farming (2001: 62–3). These marriages and the targeting of women's assets continued after the genocide ended (see also Newbury 1998: 92).

Other scholars of Rwanda and the Great Lakes region (Uvin 2001; Pottier 2002; Eltringham 2004) have noted that the period leading up to the genocide was characterized by, among other things, an extreme crisis in access to arable land. The consequent poverty was exacerbated in the period prior to the genocide by the collapse of coffee prices together with the imposed structural adjustment policies of the International Monetary Fund/World Bank, among other international institutions (Pottier 2002: 21–2; Jefremovas 1997). One of the consequences of this sharp deterioration in the economy was the social displacement of large numbers of young men whose prospects for marriage were reduced while land shortages remained acute (Newbury 1998: 91–2). At the same time, the war initiated by the Tutsi-dominated Rwandan Patriotic Force (RPF) and resulting Arusha peace negotiations, at which Western powers pressured the Rwandan government to engage in political reform and power-sharing (des Forges 1999; Magnarella 2005), were contributing to the rise of an active opposition movement, some organized along ethnic lines, others along regional or class interests (Twagilimana 2003).

Taken together, these changes in Rwandan society contributed to a state of social crisis in which ethnicity was not necessarily the defining feature. However, through a relentless campaign demonizing the Tutsi, the Hutu-power movement was able to channel what otherwise might have been regional, economic, political, and class grievances into conflicts over 'ethnicity' (Jefremovas 1997). This was true also for the propaganda that focused on Tutsi women, which was part of a campaign to orchestrate the displacement of regional and class differences onto the Tutsi and Hutu binary. And while this particular aspect of the propaganda resulted in extreme violence directed at Tutsi women, it came out of the political and economic upheaval that had implications for gender relations in general, not just those between Tutsi and Hutu (Newbury 1998: 92). The resulting mass sexual violence against Tutsi women was part of the process by which Tutsi and Hutu identities were made to cohere, at the same time as it was a particularly gendered form of violence, with implications beyond the deemed inter-ethnic nature of the genocide.

There are unexplored questions around this intersection of gender and ethnicity. Witness TAS is an example of a woman whose identity does not fit neatly into either Hutu or Tutsi groups. She is a different identity – a Hutu woman married to a Tutsi man – that disrupts, however partially, the bifurcation of ethnic identity that frames the tribunal's analysis of this conflict. Is it possible, I wonder, to fully appreciate the rape of witness TAS in isolation from the sexualization of women and Tutsi women in particular? What was the impact on *Hutu* women of the sexualized violence and imagery of Tutsi women? How did the sexualization of Tutsi women impact upon the position of Hutu women in the sexual hierarchy of race *before* the genocide? How did that sexual hierarchy facilitate and enable the patterns of sexual violence against *all* women?

Wartime sexual violence and the limits of law

I began this chapter by outlining some of the feminist legal debates that accompanied early reports and legal developments on mass rapes in the former Yugoslavia. I suggested those debates, read through the lens of intersectionality, reveal a concern that international war crimes prosecutions would be unable to fully address the complexity of wartime sexual violence that takes place within the conditions of genocide/ethnic cleansing. In some respects, the resulting jurisprudence from the Yugoslav and Rwanda tribunals appear to have laid to rest some of those earlier concerns. Both have found that rape was a specific policy of ethnic cleansing/genocide, both ruled that rape constituted a crime against humanity in each conflict and the Rwanda tribunal has gone further to find that rape was conducted as part of a genocide.

In other respects, however, the concerns expressed in those early debates about the visibility of rape as a systemic social problem remain pertinent. The tribunals, as Copelon and MacKinnon both speculated, provide a limited assessment of how ethnicity and gender converge in the production of genocide and crimes against humanity. In my discussion of *Gacumbitsi*, I argued the tribunals see rape only as an added layer to ethnic conflict, and that an overdetermination of ethnicity constrains the types of sexual violence – and victims – the tribunals are able to see.

But I want to suggest that the problems *Gacumbitsi* reveals are not just about the limits of law in addressing the complexity of social ills, like violence against women. Rather, *Gacumbitsi* is important in demonstrating how, in this case, legal decisions presume rather than interrogate the processes by which conflict is deemed to be ethnic, and violence becomes sexual. The Rwanda tribunal offers a narrative in which sexual violence is depicted as almost the inevitable outcome of ethnic conflict, rather than considering the mechanisms by which a genocide might be enacted through particular modalities of violence, and particular types of sexual violence.

Why is this distinction important? First, a more nuanced approach to genocide that challenges the inevitability of certain forms of violence allows for a sustained consideration of the structural dimensions of everyday life that form the bases for violent confrontation. Mass sexual violence is not a feature of all conflicts and we need to question why and in what circumstances violence takes certain forms (Wood 2006). Second, challenging the inevitability of sexual violence opens up consideration of the work that certain narratives of sexual violence do, including legal narratives, in justifying forms of (international) governance. And finally, exploring rather then presuming the operation of identity categories like 'ethnicity', may avoid the problem of legal decisions reproducing the narratives of ethnic conflict used – and orchestrated – by the perpetrators themselves.

Are there lessons to be learned from the work of the tribunals for feminist analyses of intersectionality? Just as the tribunals are faced with the problem of how to assess conflict without reproducing the very narratives of ethnic grievance used to mobilize the conflicts in the first place, feminists confront similar difficulties in exploring the intersection of gender and ethnicity without treating either as fixed. How might our analysis of large-scale wartime rape be different if we considered the conditions of possibility necessary for, and enabled by, both the mass sexual violence against women *and* its representation in international arenas? And, is there a way the intersection of different axes – here gender and ethnicity – could be examined without treating either as inevitable or with settled meaning?

One place to start such an analysis would be to consider the different levels or social fields within which these identities are mobilized and given meaning (Yuval-Davis 2006: 200). This would mean distinguishing between identities as they are framed within ethnic propaganda, within different socio-political and economic spheres, and finally, identities as they were engaged – or not – in the ensuing acts of violence. For feminist activists, such a distinction would also have implications. It would call for a more nuanced and historically rooted consideration of which forms of violence against women are visible, in what contexts, and to what end. How does violence against women, and representations of violence against women, enable a particular understanding of conflicts, their causes and consequences? And, how do those understandings, in turn, enable particular forms of law and legal intervention?

Acknowledgements

Earlier versions of this chapter were presented at the AHRC workshop 'Theorizing Intersectionality', Keele University, UK, and at the Feminist Legal Theory 'New Scholars' workshop at the Faculty of Law, University of British Columbia (sponsored also by the *Canadian Journal of Women and the Law*). My thanks to the conference participants who provided useful comments and feedback. My thanks also to Valerie Oosterveld, Christiane Wilke, the members of Carleton Law Department's feminist theory reading group (FRIG), and the editors of this volume for their detailed and thoughtful comments. This chapter developed out of an early paper (Buss 2007) examining the operation of ethnicity in decisions from both tribunals and the implications for legal analysis of sexual violence and women's inequality.

Bibliography

Alvarez, J. (1999) 'Crimes of State/Crimes of Hate: Lessons from Rwanda', *Yale Journal of International Law*, 24: 365–483.
Askin, K.D. (2005) 'Gender Crimes Jurisprudence in the ICTR: Positive Developments'. *Journal of International Criminal Justice*, 3: 1007–18.
— (2003) 'Prosecuting Wartime Rapes and other Gender-Related Crimes under International Law: Extraordinary Advances, Enduring Obstacles', *Berkeley Journal of International Law*, 21: 288–349.
Buss, D. (2007) 'The Curious Visibility of Wartime Rape: Gender and Ethnicity in International Criminal Law', *Windsor Yearbook of Access to Justice*, 25: 3–22.
— (2004) 'Finding the Homosexual in Women's Rights: The Christian Right in International Politics', *International Feminist Journal of Politics*, 6 (2), 259–86.
— (1998) 'Women at the Borders: Rape and Nationalism in International Law', *Feminist Legal Studies*, 6(2): 171–203.

Chesterman, S. (1997) 'Never Again ... and Again: Law, Order, and the Gender of War Crimes in Bosnia and Beyond', *Yale Journal of International Law,* 22: 299–343.

Chinkin, C. (1994) 'Rape and Sexual Abuse of Women in International Law', *European Journal of International Law,* 5: 326.

Collins, P. H. (2000) *Feminist Thought: Knowledge, Consciousness, and Politics of Empowerment,* 2nd edn, New York: Routledge.

Copelon, R. (1994) 'Surfacing Gender: Reconceptualizing Crimes against Women in Time of War', in A. Stiglmayer (ed.) *Mass Rape: The War against Women in Bosnia-Herzegovina,* Lincoln, NB: University of Nebraska Press.

— (2000) 'Integrating Crimes against Women into International Criminal Law', *McGill Law Journal,* 46: 217–40.

Crenshaw, K. (1991) 'Mapping the Margins: Intersectionality, Identity Politics and Violence against Women of Color', *Stanford Law Review,* 43: 1241–79.

des Forges, A. (1999) *Leave None to Tell the Story: Genocide in Rwanda,* New York: Human Rights Watch; Paris: International Federation of Human Rights.

Eltringham, N. (2004) *Accounting for Horror: Post-Genocide Debates in Rwanda,* London: Pluto.

Engle, K. (2005) 'Feminism and its (Dis)contents: Criminalizing Wartime Rape in Bosnia and Herzegovina' *American Journal of International Law* 99(4): 778–816.

Enloe, C. (2000) *Maneuvers: The International Politics of Militarizing Women's Lives,* Berkeley, CA: University of California Press.

— (2004) *The Curious Feminist: Searching for Women in a New Age of Empire,* Berkeley, CA: University of California Press.

Gagnon, V.P. (2004) *The Myth of Ethnic War,* Ithaca, NY: Cornell University Press.

Gibson, Suzanne. (1993) 'The Discourse of Sex/War: Thoughts on Catharine MacKinnon's 1993 Oxford Amnesty Lecture', *Feminist Legal Studies* 1(2): 179.

Gutman, R. (1993) *A Witness to Genocide,* New York: Macmillan.

Hagan, J. (2003) *Justice in the Balkans: Prosecuting War Crimes in the Hague Tribunal,* Chicago, IL: University of Chicago Press.

hooks, b. (1984) *From Margin to Center,* Boston, MA: Southend Books.

HRW (Human Rights Watch) (1996) *Shattered Lives: Sexual Violence During the Rwandan Genocide and its Aftermath,* New York: Human Rights Watch.

Jefremovas, V. (2002) *Brickyards to Graveyards: From Production to Genocide in Rwanda,* Albany, NY: State University of New York Press.

— (1997) 'Contested Identities: Power and the Factions of Ethnicity, Ethnography and History in Rwanda', *Anthropologica* 39: 91.

Kapur, R. (2005) *Erotic Justice: Law and the New Politics of Postcolonialism,* London: Glasshouse Press.

Kesic, V. (1994) 'A Response to Catharine MacKinnon's Article, "Turning Rape into Pornography: Post Modern Genocide"', *Hastings Women's Law Journal,* 5(2): 267.

Kohn, E. (1994) 'Rape as a Weapon of War: Women's Human Rights During the Dissolution of Yugoslavia', *Golden Gate University Law Review,* 24: 199.

Loomba, A. (1993) 'Dead Women Tell No Tales: Issues of Female Subjectivity, Subaltern Agency and Tradition in Colonial and Postcolonial Writings on Widow Immolation in India', *History Workshop Journal,* 36: 209–27; reprinted in R.

Lewis and S. Mills (eds) (2003) *Feminist Postcolonial Theory: A Reader*, Edinburgh: University of Edinburgh Press.

MacKinnon, Catharine A. (1993a) 'Crimes of War, Crimes of Peace', in S. Shute and S. Hurley (eds) *On Human Rights: The Oxford Amnesty Lectures 1993*, New York: Basic Books.

— (1993b) 'Comment: Theory is Not a Luxury', in D. G. Dallmeyer (ed.), *Reconceiving Reality: Women and International Law*, Washington, DC: American Society of International Law.

— (2006) *Are Women Human? And Other International Dialogues*, Cambridge, MA: Harvard University Press.

Magnarella, P (2005) 'The Background and Causes of the Genocide in Rwanda', *Law Journal of International Criminal Justice*, 3: 801–22.

Merry, S.E. (2006) *Human Rights and Gender Violence: Translating International Law into Local Justice*, Chicago, IL: University of Chicago Press.

Mertus, J. (1994) ' "Women" in the Service of National Identity', *Hastings Women's Law Journal*, 5: 5–23.

Mettraux, G. (2005) *International Crimes and the* Ad Hoc *Tribunals*, Oxford: Oxford University Press.

Mohanty, C.T. (1991) 'Under Western Eyes: Feminist Scholarship and Colonial Discourses' in C.T. Mohanty (ed.) *Third World Women and the Politics of Feminism*, Bloomington, IN: University of Indiana Press.

Newbury, D. (1998) 'Understanding Genocide', *African Studies Review*, 41: 73–97.

Newbury, C. (1988) *The Cohesion of Oppression: Clientship and Ethnicity in Rwanda (1860–1960)*, New York: Columbia University Press.

Nowrojee, B. (2005) ' "Your Justice is Too Slow": Will the ICTR Fail Rwanda's Rape Victims?', Occasional Paper 10, United Nations Institute for Social Development.

Philips, R. B. (2002) 'Too Close to Home? International Criminal Law, War Crimes and Family Violence', *Thomas Jefferson Law Review*, 24: 229–38.

Pottier, J. (2002) *Re-Imagining Rwanda: Conflict, Survival and Disinformation in the Late Twentieth Century*, Cambridge: University of Cambridge Press.

Prunier, G. (1995) *The Rwanda Crisis: History of a Genocide*, New York: Columbia University Press.

Schabas, W. (2006) *The UN International Criminal Tribunals: The Former Yugoslavia, Rwanda and Sierra Leone*, Cambridge: Cambridge University Press.

Sen, S. (2002) 'Century India', *Journal of Women's History*, 14(2): 53–79.

Stephens, B. (1994) 'The Civil Lawsuit as a Remedy for International Human Rights Violations Against Women', *Hastings Women's Law Journal*, 5(2): 143.

Taylor, C. (1999) *Sacrifice as Terror: The Rwandan Genocide of 1994*, London: Berg.

Tompkins, T. (2005). 'Prosecuting Rape as a War Crime: Speaking the Unspeakable', *Notre Dame Law Review* 70: 845–90.

Turshen, M. (2001) ' The Political Economy of Rape: An Analysis of Systematic Rape and Sexual Abuse of Women during Armed Conflict in Africa', in C. Moser and F. Clark (eds) *Victims, Perpetrators or Actors? Gender, Armed Conflict and Political Violence*, London: Zed Books.

Twagilimana, A. (2003) The Debris of Ham: Ethnicity, Regionalism, and the 1994 Rwandan Genocide, Lanham, CO: University Press of America.

Uvin, P. (2001) 'Reading the Rwanda Genocide', *International Studies Review*, 3: 75–99.

Wood, E. (2006) 'Variations in Sexual Violence during War', *Politics & Society*, 34(3): 307–41.

Yuval-Davis, N. (2006) 'Intersectionality and Feminist Politics', *European Journal of Women's Studies*, 13(3): 193–209.

Table of cases

Notes

1 In a related paper (Buss 2007) I take up the question of visibility more directly, exploring the limits of making violence against women visible as an international criminal law issue.

2 Attaching labels to the conflicts in Yugoslavia and Rwanda, as I demonstrate later in this chapter, is not straightforward. The social groupings identified as 'ethnic' may be more accurately defined as racial, economic, regional, religious,

occupational and so on. In this chapter, I use 'ethnicity' because this is the term the tribunals use to categorize group difference. The larger question of how 'ethnicity' comes to be constructed in and through the tribunal decisions is beyond the scope of this chapter.

3 *Report of the Secretary-General Pursuant to Paragraph 2 of the Security Council Resolution 808 (1993)*, S/25704 (May 3, 1993); Helsinki Watch, *War Crimes in Bosnia-Hercegovina*, vol I (New York, Washington, Los Angeles and London, Human Rights Watch, 1992); Gutman 1993.

4 For a discussion of the events leading to these SC decisions, see Schabas 2006, Hagan 2003.

5 Karen Engle (2005) offers a slightly different reading of these feminist debates. She characterizes them as disagreeing over whether and how specifically to label Serbians as the aggressors, particularly in the war in Bosnia.

6 *Gacumbitsi*, Trial Chamber, para. 215. At least one woman, Chantal, died after 'her genitals had been impaled with a stick' (para. 214). This manner of torturing and killing women during the genocide was widespread. See HRW 1996.

7 Witness TAQ, who was raped while heavily pregnant, testified that her attacker said he wanted to 'take revenge on the witness's sister who had refused to marry him' (para. 203). Witness TAP testified that her 'attackers were saying that in the past Tutsi women and girls hated Hutu men and refused to marry them, but that now they were going to abuse the Tutsi girls and women freely' (para. 208).

Chapter 5

Intersectionality in theory and practice

Suzanne B. Goldberg

Intersectionality theory, an important elaboration of the relationship between law and identity that emerged in legal scholarship in the early 1990s, has run into some difficulty. Its core insight – that analysis of discrimination based on a single identity trait does not adequately account for intersecting aspects of identity, such as race or sex (Crenshaw 1989: 139; Crenshaw 1991: 1241) – has been widely embraced. But as theorists have pressed further, examining the multiple, shifting dimensions of identity (Hutchinson 2002: 431; Levit 2002: 227; Wing 2000),[1] the project of understanding identity and its relationship to law has become more challenging. Concerns about "false coherence – ignoring the differences within identity categories that constitute the true variety of human experiences" – have emerged (Levit 2002: 227),[2] as have the challenges of ever-more complex identity combinations. Together, these have led to what Nancy Ehrenreich has described as the "infinite regress problem: the tendency of all identity groups to split into ever-smaller subgroups, until there seems to be no hope of any coherent category other than the individual" (Ehrenreich 2002: 267).[3] In the search for new theoretical directions, some scholars have shifted the analytic frame away from further refinements of identity categories and toward common "systems of oppression" that support identity-based subordination (Ehrenreich 2002: 272; Williams 2002: 493), while others remain pessimistic about the possibilities for successfully managing the complexity.[4]

At this pivotal moment for intersectionality theory, this chapter looks to practice – specifically, to the ways in which identity-based law reform organizations in the United States work within and across identity boundaries – as an alternate venue for analyzing and theorizing about the relationship between law and identity. Although meshing theory and practice is often challenging (Gilmore 1977: 17),[5] at first glance this particular juxtaposition may seem especially puzzling. As if in deliberate contrast to theoretical insights regarding the multidimensionality of identity, the predominant American advocacy groups present themselves as each serving a unitary, rather than complex, identity category. Separate law reform groups represent, among others, the interests of African Americans; Asian Americans; Latinos; Native

Americans;[6] women; lesbians, gay men, bisexuals, and transgender (LGBT) people;[7] and people with mental or physical disabilities.[8] Yet, in practice, the groups turn out not to be as isolationist as their missions might suggest.[9] Indeed, they work with some regularity across identity boundaries by joining together in political coalitions, engaging in public education efforts, and, of particular interest here, filing *amicus* briefs[10] in each other's cases.

This chapter pursues two questions about conceptualizing the identity/ law relationship that grows out of law reform practice. The first concerns the organizational landscape, asking why the predominant advocacy organizations align according to single identity categories. In flagging and analyzing the apparent differences and possible bridges between theory and practice in this area, the point is not that organizations should abandon their single-identity focus or that theorists should give up their commitment to complexity. Instead, the aim is to draw out possible benefits to each from the other's analytic frame. I begin this inquiry with a methodological discussion about the particular value law reform organizations bring to the study of intersectionality. The chapter then describes the contemporary organizational landscape and analyzes why single identity groups remain the dominant home for identity-related advocacy despite intersectionality theory's well-accepted insights regarding the complexity of identity.

Second, the chapter questions how single-identity organizations respond to the intersections of identity categories. In particular, I look at the organizations' practice of filing *amicus* briefs across identity categories as, for example, when a race-focused group files a brief to support a case being litigated by a women's rights organization, or a women's rights group files in support of a gay rights case. This part of the chapter identifies four major interests that shape the filing of cross-identity *amicus* briefs: 1) legitimation of claims by marginalized groups; 2) support for a civil-rights-friendly environment; 3) protection of mutual interests in antidiscrimination law, policies and procedures; and 4) security for identity-based protections where identity categories overlap. This discussion also highlights the distinct ways in which each interest shapes the treatment of relationships among and across identity categories.

Of course, any anti-essentialist or social constructionist would quickly point out the instability of the identity categories that I rely on for this discussion (Ehrenreich 2002: 267; Levit 2002: 227). Even when members of an identity group treat a category as stable, defining the category's precise contours can be a daunting, if not impossible, task. The category of "race," for example, which is commonly treated as unitary, is itself broken down by multiple organizations that focus on different racial and ethnic groups. Likewise, the question of who falls in or outside of the category "woman" depends on whether one defines "woman" by chromosomal makeup, anatomy, self-identification, or various other means (Currah 2006: 32).[11] Because the law reform organizations themselves treat the categories as meaningful and stable, however, I do the same for the specific purpose of carrying forward the analysis of cross-identity practice.

Before turning in depth to the chapter's first point, it bears noting that the concerns of intersectionality theory do not map precisely onto cross-identity practice as I have described it here. In part, this is because the theory itself has multiple strands (see this volume).[12] One dominant version of intersectionality theory has focused on law's response to intersecting identity categories within an individual. Other theorists focus less on the interaction of identities within the individual and more on the intersection of social or political structures that privilege or subordinate particular aspects of identity. Indeed, the very question of what constitutes identity – whether it is an individual's sense of self or an individual's social location or some combination of the two – is itself contested. The project here involves yet another approach. The intersections that occur when an advocacy group files a brief in support of another identity-based organization's case are neither the inevitable, embodied multidimensional experience of an individual person nor the necessary product of particular social location. Instead, by contrast, they are both deliberate and contingent, in that the organizations choose whether to file *and* how to characterize the cross-identity relationship when they do file. Thus, the analysis here cannot offer a full escape from some of the traps that have stymied the theory as is, but, by expanding the frame of inquiry, it aims to create new openings for continued study.

It turns out that cross-identity advocacy has little inclination for multidimensionality, at least in the way theorists tend to deploy the concept – perhaps not surprisingly, given the generally instrumental orientation of litigation. Although advocates share with theorists a desire for a world free of identity-based harms, the bulk of their work, including their cross-identity projects, treats identity categories as stable and embraces widely recognized distinctions among them rather than attempting to destabilize their boundaries. When viewed through the theorists' vision, advocates' aims seem far less transformative and radical than they might otherwise appear.

At the same time, however, advocates work with these purportedly stable categories in litigation in strategic, instrumental, and dynamic ways, suggesting that the variable and contingent *use* of identity categories may be as important to our understanding of identity as the content of the categories themselves. More specifically, concentrating on the multiple roles and functions of identity categories may be a useful move for new theorizing about how the meaning and boundaries of identity categories take shape. The remainder of this chapter begins to explore what we might learn from practice about the ways in which identity categories and their intersections are and could be used.

Why study intersectionality through the practice of law reform organizations?: a methodological note

This chapter focuses on the work of identity-based law reform organizations in the United States, by which I mean organizations that work primarily through American litigation fora to address systematic problems or issues important to their constituent identity groups.[13] Although almost all identity-based organizations – including those focused on political change, social networks, social or legal services, or law reform – work across identity categories at times, the intersectional practice of law reform groups adds distinct value to the analysis here. In particular, the law reform organizations' cross-identity *amicus* briefs that I examine below provide a unique window into the organizations' conceptualization of identity.

The value of law reform organizations for this study comes in part from their organizational missions,[14] which lead them to be explicitly preoccupied with questions of identity. In deciding what cases to bring and how to pursue them, groups must invariably address the questions of how best to conceive of the constituent identity group and advocate on its behalf.[15] To maximize impact, cases must bring an important group issue to the fore rather than simply raising a claim that might resolve a problem unique to an identity group member. This process of considering which issues are important to the group requires, in turn, a sophisticated and thoughtful conceptualization of the group itself. For example, if a woman of color brings her discrimination case to a race-focused organization, that organization will gauge whether the case is likely to advance the group's race-focused mission sufficiently to merit dedication of organizational resources. A women's rights group doing the same intake will likely find salient different aspects of the proposed case as it makes its own evaluation. (On this point, intersectionality theorists might observe that the separation of the racial and gender dimensions of the same person's claim is precisely the problem with the current set of advocacy groups, in that the single-identity organizational framework forces individuals to pull apart their interrelated claims and subordinate their complexity. I address this observation below.)

Neither service providers nor political organizations face the same degree of pressure to repeatedly revisit and reconceptualize their own identity category and its relation to other identities. For legal and social service providers who assist with housing, health care, and public benefits for identity group members, there is, of course, a need to decide who is eligible for services. But the day-to-day work focuses less on elaborating identity and more on providing access to resources. If the same woman of color just discussed brought her claim to a service-oriented organization, the provider would consider her race and sex only as factors to determine qualification for service. Once deemed eligible, she would presumably be served in the same fashion by either organization, whose aim would be to provide access to resources or resolve the client's immediate problems rather than establish broad identity-based protections.

For political organizations, the conceptualization of identity is a more constant question – as it is for law reform groups – because the ever-shifting political landscape requires groups regularly to reevaluate their priorities and strategies. The constraints of the political process, however, especially including the need to build coalitions, can make it difficult to determine exactly what meaning the group attributes to its constituent identity category. Legislative advocates for minority groups *must* work with others outside their immediate identity group for the simple reason that bills do not pass without majority support. Hence the success of cross-identity umbrella organizations in politics, like the Leadership Conference on Civil Rights (LCCR), which describes itself as having "coordinated the national legislative campaign on behalf of every major civil rights law [in the United States] since 1957" (Leadership Conference on Civil Rights). The organization's members include nearly 200 organizations that represent "persons of color, women, children, labor unions, individuals with disabilities, older Americans, major religious groups, gays and lesbians and civil liberties and human rights groups" (ibid).

In litigation, by contrast, the targeted decision-maker is either a jury or a judge, neither of which requires a show of majoritarian support before deciding a claim. A group bringing a women's rights case, for example, need not work with other identity groups to achieve its aims in court. While these sorts of coalitions are sometimes desirable, they are not required for success and, consequently, they are undertaken deliberately rather than by default. Thus, although political groups arguably spend as much time as the law reform organizations conceptualizing and strategizing about their own identity concerns, the intense, constant pressure to work in coalition with other identity groups makes it more difficult than in litigation to identify the motive for intersectional practice at any given moment. An organization working with other identity groups to help pass an initiative seemingly unrelated to its constituents' immediate concerns might have deep theoretical connections in mind but, just as easily and more likely, could simply be going along with the coalition that will support its own initiatives in the future.

The organizational landscape: on the dominance of single identity-based advocacy groups

This section first offers a selective sketch of the United States law reform landscape through the mission statements of leading national groups. From this foundation, it asks why unitary identity groups have remained so dominant given intersectionality theory's lessons about complexity and then considers the effects of this dominance on possibilities for more nuanced advocacy in the future.

The iconic identity-based legal organization, the NAACP Legal Defense and Educational Fund, is the nation's oldest and largest. LDF, as the organization is known colloquially, "pursues racial justice," and describes itself as "America's legal counsel on race" (NAACP LDF). LDF is not, however, the sole law reform organization in the country dedicated to racial justice, which underscores, for our purposes, the inescapable complexity residing within the superficially unitary category of race, as well as the complex relationship between the categories of race and ethnicity. At the Asian American Legal Defense and Education Fund, for example, advocates work to "protect ... and promote ... the civil rights of Asian Americans" (AALDEF). The Puerto Rican Legal Defense and Education Fund works to "protect ... opportunities for all Latinos" (PRLDEF), as does the Mexican American Legal Defense and Educational Fund, which works "to protect and promote the civil rights of the more than 40 million Latinos living in the United States" (MALDEF).

Organizations focused on women, sexuality, and gender are also powerful advocacy groups with organizational models and missions similar to LDF's. The women's rights litigation group known as Legal Momentum (formerly NOW Legal Defense and Education Fund) states, for example, that it works to "advance ... the rights of women and girls" (Legal Momentum). Lambda Legal Defense and Education Fund, which is "committed to achieving full recognition of the civil rights of lesbians, gay men, bisexuals, transgender people and those with HIV" (Lambda Legal), is the largest of several organizations with similar missions. The National Center for Lesbian Rights likewise works to "advance the legal and human rights of LGBT people and their families" (NCLR). The Transgender Legal Defense and Education Fund is "committed to ending discrimination based upon gender identity and expression and to achieving equality for transgender people" (Transgender LDEF).

Not every law reform group has such a unitary mission, however. The American Civil Liberties Union, for example, at first seems to be a major exception to the norm. It is one of the country's largest and most comprehensive civil rights and civil liberties advocacy organizations dedicated to protecting individual rights. Yet even within this broad-ranging organization, fields are divided by identity, so that someone wanting to work on lesbian issues would most likely go to the organization's Lesbian Gay Bisexual Transgender and AIDS Project, on women's issues to the Women's Rights Project, and on race issues to the Racial Justice Project.[16]

Numerous plausible and mutually reinforcing theories might explain why legal advocates hew to single-identity organizations when we know, both from intersectionality theory's insights and ordinary life experience, that identity is complex. The most obvious, perhaps, is simply that the identities that mobilized the creation of these organizations remain salient for people today (Putnam 2006: 152). Even though no single identity fully describes any individual, single identity categories are deployed regularly and broadly, usually informed by stereotypes, to categorize people, distribute benefits, and impose disadvantages. Individuals may also prefer, or at least derive special enjoyment from, associations with others who fall into the same identity category, whether as a result of this externally imposed categorization or for other reasons. If these categories lost their social salience tomorrow, it is difficult to imagine how the advocacy organizations would retain their current structure.

Yet the salience of the single-identity categories is insufficient to account for the organizations' single-identity focus. Just as single identities are salient markers, so too are many complex identities (such as woman of color or gay African American man, among many other examples). Nonetheless, while an array of social, political, and service-oriented groups respond to identity combinations, virtually no complex identity category has spawned its own law reform organization.

Path dependency theory (Pierson 2000: 251), which holds that current practices are shaped by past as well as current conditions, may more powerfully explain the existing arrangement. Under this theory, the existing organizations' longevity and history of capital investment not only describe the past but also account for the endurance into the future of the single-identity framework. Indeed, just as intersectionality can be understood as the theoretical legacy of the civil rights movement (Levit 2002: 227), the identity-based litigation groups can be seen as a part of the civil rights movement's structural legacy. Apart from LDF, which was founded in 1940, most of these organizations emerged in the 1970s or 1980s, at a time when identity-based movements were ascendant in the United States. They modeled themselves on the legal defense and education fund format pioneered by LDF (Stone 1992: 200), with some organizations literally copying others' applications for not-for-profit status (In re Thom 1973: 613). By the time identity-based social movements began to grapple seriously with the diversity that roiled beneath their superficial unity, single-identity advocacy organizations were already firmly in place in terms of both reputation and infrastructure. To preserve their status and continue their growth, these groups have strong incentives to integrate intersectionality theory's insights into the existing organizational format rather than under the radical structural transformations the theory might suggest.

This explanation dovetails with other resource-related points. While current thought regarding identity might produce a different array of organizations if the slate were wiped clean (or it might not, for other reasons discussed in this section and below),[17] the existing slate is quite full. As a practical matter, then, the contemporary landscape's division into single-identity units makes it nearly impossible for a newcomer to amalgamate sufficient resources and supporters to spur a paradigm shift in identity-based advocacy. Instead, to gain a foothold, new law reform organizations have to work around the others already occupying the field. An upstart group will likely face overwhelming obstacles to survival if it does not foreground one aspect of its focal identity, whatever its commitments to intersectionality. The Sylvia Rivera Law Project (SRLP), for example, is a law reform organization that self-consciously focuses on the intersection of gender identity, race, and class. By foregrounding the issue of gender identity, which is a relatively underserved identity category, even as it remains attentive to other dimensions of its constituents' lives, it has been able to mount a successful campaign for survival in a field already crowded with other groups that center their concerns on either race or low-income individuals. Had it not done so, it is difficult to imagine that SRLP would have survived. Yet, because law reform organizations that foreground transgender individuals are relatively new to the organizational landscape, it will be interesting to see how SRLP fares in the future, especially given the increased advocacy role played by transgender groups whose missions are less explicitly intersectional.

Single-identity organizations also have efficiency advantages for outreach and fundraising that may contribute to their sustainability. Put most simply, while many people may share one trait and all people have many traits, fewer people share the same combination of multiple traits. Consequently, an organization that focuses on a single trait has, numerically anyway, a larger 'natural' pool of likely adherents and supporters than an organization devoted to a more complex combination of identities.[18] By focusing broadly on race, for example, the NAACP Legal Defense and Educational Fund taps a larger potential constituency than it would if it focused more specifically on the rights of lesbians of color or even the larger subset of women of color.

To be sure, identity-based advocacy organizations draw support from more than just their presumptive constituents. Men support women's rights organizations, whites support organizations focused on securing rights for people of color, and heterosexuals support LGBT advocacy groups. Still, the more refined the identity group becomes, the smaller the presumptive constituency and pool of other supporters whose friends, family, or political views will influence them to prioritize support for this group over another.

One might argue, however, that this efficiency claim overstates the willingness of individuals to support single-identity organizations that do not represent their more complex selves. Indeed, individuals who prize their multidimensional identities might not only decline to support the single-identity organization but also be more vigilant objectors to the organization's single-identity focus than those fully outside and therefore less invested in the group's work (Yoshikawa 1998: 41).[19] But, given the survival rates of single-identity focused groups and the relative absence of complex counterparts, the current landscape seems largely invulnerable.

The efficiency explanation also sheds light on why single-identity groups are likely to be more successful at fundraising than their complex counterparts. Because men earn more than women and whites earn more than people of color (U.S. Dept. of Labor 2005: 4, 5, 76,)[20] an organization that includes either whites or men among its primary constituents can tap into a wealthier potential donor base. When the core constituency is neither white nor male, it is less likely to have abundant resources, which in turn makes fundraising more difficult and, often, less successful in terms of total volume.[21]

The legal context may shape the landscape as well. Antidiscrimination law itself has a single-identity focus. Although laws identify multiple categories for legal protection, they list categories sequentially and do not ordinarily address intersectional or multidimensional discrimination explicitly. The Equal Employment Opportunity Commission, for example, which is the governmental agency charged with enforcing federal antidiscrimination law, describes U.S. laws as prohibiting discriminatory practices based on "race, color, religion, sex, national origin, disability, *or* age."[22] It would be logical, then, for organizations concerned with securing identity-based rights to respond to these categories and focus their resources on one identity feature or another.

Working within this framework also enables organizations to deepen their expertise over time with respect to the legal doctrine, the social science, and the networks of scholars, professionals, and community organizations, all of which tend to vary by identity category.[23] Groups focused on race discrimination, for example, tend to have deep knowledge of voting rights and public education data and the related, complex statutory and constitutional doctrine. Groups focused on LGBT issues tend to know the social science data that may best influence judges hearing sexual orientation discrimination cases, as well as the complex, variable ways that courts have responded to sexual-orientation-based distinctions over time. And organizations focused on women's rights know the ins and outs of the extensive body of statutory and constitutional sex discrimination law. If a group were to organize itself for the purpose of pursuing intersectional claims, it would need to amass this expertise in multiple areas, which is, from a time and resources investment standpoint, less efficient than focusing more specifically on the challenges presented by one group.

The relatively low success rate of intersectional claims presumably also reinforces the prevailing orientation toward unitary identity. While few courts have rejected these claims outright, there has been almost no success in having courts embrace either the full nuance or complexity of identity.[24] These losses are unlikely to be causal factors shaping the landscape, given that the real numbers are so small, but they have no doubt provided some reinforcement for the status quo.

Finally, cognitive preferences or biases may also be responsible for the single-identity focus of law reform organizations (as well as the single-identity focus of antidiscrimination law). As many scholars have observed, human cognitive functioning relies on the simplification of categories to facilitate decision-making in complex situations (Hamilton Krieger 1995: 1161; Wax 1999: 1129; Travis 2002: 481). The very project of demanding recognition of complexity seems to cut directly against this apparently ingrained preference for simple, clear categories. The tendency of individual rights groups to orient themselves toward a single identity may be understood thus either as reflecting this deep-rooted element of human cognition or as capitalizing, instrumentally, on an approach that courts and others are most likely to follow.

Cross-identity *amicus* briefs: a site for studying intersectionality in practice

Despite their identity-driven boundaries, law reform organizations interact across identity with some regularity, including, as noted above, by filing *amicus* briefs in each other's cases. This section introduces the general strategic and practical considerations that influence *amicus* brief participation and the rules and norms that render *amicus* briefs fertile sites for analyzing the ways that law reform groups navigate between their own and other identity categories.

Most basically, law reform organizations' decisions about *amicus* participation come either when a group is solicited to file (or join) an *amicus* brief or when a group handling litigation decides to seek *amicus* briefs from colleague organizations to bolster its claims.[25] Necessarily, then, organizations must face resource allocation questions in deciding whether they have staff available to oversee the group's *amicus* participation or to solicit participation from "outsider" groups. In some cases, participation can require substantial resources, especially if a group decides to draft its own brief[26] or to expend significant time soliciting and assisting with another group's brief. In others, fewer resources may be required. A group might merely be asked to sign on to a brief drafted by another organization[27] or a law reform organization handling a case might simply include an "outsider" group in a broad solicitation effort.

But although resource allocation questions may be significant, the expressive functions served by *amicus* briefs are equally, if not more, important in shaping organizations' decisions to participate – and, in turn, contributing to the briefs' value as a site for examining cross-identity collaboration. Specifically, a leading function of *amicus* briefs is to communicate an organization's position, not only to the court but also to constituents and the broader public.[28]

By virtue of their participation, *amici* signal that the identity group members whose rights are at issue in the case before the court are not alone in their quest for justice. They also create for themselves a platform for entering the public debate about an issue they see as relevant to their own organizational mission. For example, a women's rights organization's decision to file a brief in support of a case involving sexual orientation discrimination against a lesbian might be intended to highlight a shift away from an earlier time during which many women's rights organizations disassociated themselves from lesbians. In a related way, *amicus* participation might signal the women's rights group's sense of itself as a civil rights movement leader that should support other civil rights groups' efforts, including those not directly related to the women's rights mission. Yet again, the women's rights organization might sense that a victory in the lesbian rights case will provide either direct or indirect support for the organization's own agenda. The next section will distill these varying interests in greater detail; for purposes here, the important point is that *amicus* briefs provide a unique site for identity groups to situate themselves in relation to others.

This means, of course, that evaluations of costs as well as benefits will shape a law reform group's decision to participate as *amicus* in a cross-identity case. While it is difficult to predict in the abstract what might spark opposition to any particular filing, group members might object that the filing group is squandering its resources on issues outside its mission or, more seriously, harming itself by associating itself in some way with the "other" identity group. More generally, organizations might be concerned that over-participating in cases outside of their core mission might dilute the value of their participation in cases seen as most important to their work.

Social movement and coalition theorists reinforce the likely influence of these considerations that are associated with the expressive functions of *amicus* briefs. As the social movement literature indicates, a group's view of itself in relation to other social movement organizations and the political process will influence the group's actions (Della Porta and Diani 1998; McAdam *et al.* 1996; Morris and McClurg Mueller 1992).[29] Coalition theorists remind us, too, that the social movement's status and the prevailing perceptions of political and legal opportunity structures will also affect decision-making.[30]

Yet some might argue that the outcome orientation of the adversarial litigation process distorts the "true" nuanced views of groups about the relationships among identity categories and renders *amicus* briefs suspect as a site for study. Concerns might be raised, too, about whether the litigation superstructure, with its restrictive format for presenting claims and its formal dispute resolution process, might skew the analysis. My view, however, is that the obvious structural constraints of litigation serve as an asset by reminding us that organizations' views can never be isolated fully from the context in which they are expressed. This reminder, in turn, reinforces the point that context influences the conceptualization of identity, whether in an *amicus* brief filed to serve instrumental aims or in political organizing, social networking, academic deliberation, or even a hostile work environment.

In other words, identity categories – and their intersections – are always contingent.

Moreover, the rules and norms of litigation, and, in particular, *amicus* participation, are also assets to the project here, in that they provide unique access to the views of identity-based groups. Most practically, filing rules require *amicus* organizations to include a statement of interest that describes the group's concern with the case before the court. These statements explicitly elaborate how *amicus* organizations see the relationship between their constituent identity and the identity category in the case before the court. Of course, a given statement is unlikely to express all aspects of an organization's views. Yet it must say enough about the connection between the two identity groups to persuade the court to accept the brief for filing.[31]

Further, *amici* are at a slight remove from the rules and norms that constrain the parties before the court. Advocates for the parties (i.e., the plaintiff(s) and defendant(s) in a particular case) must concentrate only on legal issues immediately relevant to their clients. *Amici*, on the other hand, are freer to offer wide-ranging legal analyses and to mesh their legal theories with social science analysis, personal narratives to dramatize the issue at hand, and any other perspective so long as it is arguably relevant to the case before the court. A group concerned with race- or ethnicity-based discrimination, for example, would be free to use its *amicus* brief to show the race-related implications of a case concerned primarily with sex discrimination (*Nguyen v. INS* 2001).

Thus, even given the inevitable influence of instrumental concerns that shape participation in both litigation and social movements, identity groups have broad expressive leeway for achieving their strategic aims through *amicus* briefs. Their choices can, consequently, reveal a great deal about the role of identity categories both individually and in interaction with one another.

Excavating theories of identity from practice

With an understanding of the single-identity law reform organizations and the multiple influences on the organizations' *amicus* participation, we can now examine in greater detail whether and how *amicus* briefs engage with the complex conceptualization of identity that intersectionality theorists have highlighted. In this section, I analyze several interests that appear to shape law reform organizations' understanding of cross-identity relationships, recognizing that each interest's influence is also mediated by the array of dynamics just discussed. I do this based on a study of *amicus* briefs filed during the past two decades by the major identity-based law reform groups in cases involving identity-related claims.[32] The analysis is driven, as well, by my own intuitions developed during two decades of involvement with law reform organizations.[33]

While I identify four "interests" that shape cross-identity relationships, the categorization is not intended to announce a strict separation. Indeed, the interests articulated below often overlap. Still, pulling them apart supplies a heuristic for tracing the distinct ways in which advocates conceptualize and portray the interdependence among identity categories.

The four interests are:

1 the legitimation interest, which influences social movement leaders to lend their authority or legitimacy to support the claims of a more marginalized identity group;
2 the civil-rights-friendly environment interest, which prompts *amici* to support the development of civil-rights-protective doctrines where those doctrines are not seen as closely implicating their constituents' interests;
3 the mutual interests in effective antidiscrimination law, which leads *amici* to address a procedural or substantive antidiscrimination law issue in a case involving a "different" identity group because the issue will directly affect discrimination cases brought by the *amici* organization's constituents; and
4 the overlapping identities interest, which captures participation by *amicus* organizations that see their constituents' identity category and legal status as bound up and overlapping in important ways with the particular identity group before the court.

The discussion that follows will elaborate the conceptualization of identity and cross-identity relationships embodied in each of these interests. The first two interests, which are closely related to each other, suggest that the identity categories at issue overlap minimally, if at all. The second two more strongly embrace the interdependence among identity categories, albeit in rather different ways. The entire set can be read, then, as describing an ascending integration of identity categories across conventional boundaries.

The legitimation interest

Law reform organizations typically solicit legitimation-oriented briefs when they determine that another identity-based organization can add value to a case by lending its reputation and its "authority" on a particular issue. Typically, the solicited group will enjoy better established civil rights protections and/or some special connection to an important issue in the case before the court.[34] By participating as *amicus*, the solicited group can, arguably at least, make the plaintiff organization's claim seem less marginal, both to the court and to external audiences, than it might otherwise appear. In addition, in contexts where advocates seek to have established precedent related to one identity group applied to another, support for that move from the already-protected group may provide some reassurance and reinforcement to the court.

This approach reveals several important aspects of cross-identity relationships in law reform. First and most basically, it shows that the status hierarchy among identity groups is a strong factor in cross-identity practice, with some identity groups having far more value than others. It is difficult to imagine, for example, that advocates handling a racial equality case would solicit an *amicus* brief from, say, a gay rights organization, because legal protections for race, while still contested, are far more established than they are for sexual orientation.[35] Consequently, there is little that a gay rights group could add, either by way of reputation or authoritative interpretation of gay-rights-related cases, that could bring significant benefit to a racial equality case.

Conversely, gay rights organizations often go to great lengths to solicit *amicus* briefs from racial equality organizations on the theory that these groups can lend their legitimacy to efforts by lesbians and gay men to establish similar protections. In a case challenging the denial of marriage rights to lesbian and gay couples in New York (Hernandez 2006: 338), for example, the gay rights organizations handling the case made extensive efforts to obtain an *amicus* brief from LDF, which, as noted earlier, is the largest national law reform organization to focus on race and is most closely associated with advocacy for African Americans. LDF agreed, and filed a brief that played exactly the authoritative and legitimacy-reinforcing role just described. The organization explained that *Loving* v. *Virginia* (1967: 1), the United States Supreme Court's major precedent that invalidated racially discriminatory marriage laws, should also be applied to invalidate discrimination against same-sex couples in marriage law (Brief of NAACP Legal Defense and Education Fund 2006: iii, 3; Brief of NAACP Legal Defense and Education Fund 2007).

Note that for this legitimacy-enhancing function to work to greatest effect, the *amicus* organization must play the role of identity group "outsider" rather than "intersector." The precise value of having an organization like LDF support a gay rights claim is that the organization is presumably sharing its reputation out of commitment to principle rather than out of self-interest. If the organization is perceived as a direct beneficiary of the rights being sought, its authoritative status is diminished. To the extent LDF were to frame its interest in the case in terms of an intersectional concern for its gay African American constituents, thereby heeding the theory's insights about the complexity of identity, it would lose some of the reputational capital it brought to the case.

Indeed, in its brief, LDF stated that its interests extend to "the constitutional and civil rights of all Americans" but in summarizing its argument made clear that it also saw racial and sexual-orientation-based identities as distinct (Brief of NAACP Legal Defense and Education Fund 2006: iii, 3). At the same time that it stressed the relevance of *Loving* v. *Virginia* to marriage rights for same-sex couples, the brief noted the many differences between "the historical experience in this country of African Americans, on the one hand, and gay men and lesbians, on the other" (ibid: 3).[36]

Civil-rights-friendly environment interest

The interest in a civil-rights-friendly environment reflects the view, held by many law reform groups, that civil rights are interdependent and protections will not be truly secure for anyone unless they are secure for all. *Amici* may thus be motivated to expend resources on participation as *amicus* in a case, even though their constituents' rights will not be directly implicated by the court's decision. Simply put, by expressing cross-group solidarity through the filing of an *amicus* brief, advocates are, in effect, supporting an environment in which all civil rights protections stand a greater chance of flourishing.

This interest can be understood, in part, as the flipside of the legitimation interest because it helps explain why an "outsider" group with little to gain directly from a case might nonetheless dedicate its resources to filing a legitimacy-enhancing *amicus* brief. The LDF marriage brief, for example, highlighted the organization's "interest in the fair application of the Due Process and Equal Protection Clauses of the New York Constitution, which provide important protections to African Americans and to all New Yorkers …" (ibid: 1–2). In terms of the discussion here, LDF can be characterized as taking the view that African Americans will be better off to the extent the state's constitutional law is interpreted to support rather than limit civil rights, even if race-related rights are not the subject of the newly developed doctrine.

This interest in engendering a civil-rights-friendly environment is not limited to an *amicus* group's consequentialist desire to gain attenuated benefits from positive litigation outcomes. Another motivator may be a law reform organization's expectation that participation as *amicus* will enhance the group's status in the eyes of its constituents as well as the broader community of individuals and organizations concerned with civil rights. Yet another prompt for *amicus* participation might be entirely non-instrumental, resting instead on the normative, good faith view that supporting another identity group's effort to achieve civil rights is the right thing to do, without regard to benefits that might inure to the participating organization. Parsed further, this interest could be said to rest on groups' respective perceptions that there is a civil rights "community" and that membership in that community ought to include expressions of support for other community members' cases.[37]

Because an interest in expressive effects outside of litigation prompts much of this type of *amicus* participation by "outsider" organizations, it can have the additional effect of strengthening and supporting civil rights coalitions.[38] For example, in a prominent women's rights case concerning a military school's refusal to admit women (Virginia 1996: 515), the Mexican American Legal Defense and Education Fund was among a large group of civil rights organizations to sign an *amicus* brief elaborating the standard of review that should be applied to sex discrimination by government bodies (Brief of National Women's Law Center *et al.* 1995). MALDEF's statement of interest indicated only that the organization has often been involved in challenges to unequal rules and policies in education cases (ibid: 30). The brief did not otherwise mention Mexican Americans or Latinos at all, suggesting that it was not aimed to further readers' understanding of Latinas as a social group whose members reside at the intersection between the missions of MALDEF and the women's rights organizations that were backing the litigation.[39] How, then, to explain MALDEF's participation? Although the organization has some overlapping interest in eliminating discrimination in education, an interest that will be discussed momentarily, its participation can also likely be explained by the organization's interest in expressing its membership in a broader civil rights community. And, for the women's rights organizations, MALDEF's sign-on enabled a related sort of expression, providing a platform for showing that a diverse coalition supported their position.[40]

As with the legitimacy-enhancing brief, the civil-rights-friendly, coalition-focused brief derives its value from *amicus* organizations' retaining the separateness of their identities rather than destabilizing intergroup boundaries. These solidarity-oriented briefs, while enthusiastically committed to their arguments, ordinarily leave in place background assumptions regarding the separateness of identity categories or work to reinforce them rather than to minimize the differences between the *amici* and the identity group seeking the court's protection. This, again, has the effect of rendering *amici* as providing "outside" support, at least to the degree they are seen as not concerning themselves with constituents identical to those before the court.[41]

The mutual interests in effective antidiscrimination law

The third prompt for cross-identity practice derives from the *amici* groups' recognition that they share, with the identity group before the court, a direct interest in ensuring effective rules and doctrine for the enforcement of antidiscrimination measures. These briefs, which account for the largest number of filings, recognize that the *amicus* group members' fates, even if not their identities, are bound up with the identity group before the court.

Unlike in *amicus* briefs prompted by the two interests just discussed, the *amici* motivated by this interest are not trying to present themselves as complete outsiders; indeed, their point is that the groups' fates are interdependent. Yet their briefs also do not seek to destabilize identity boundaries in the way that intersectionality theory demands.

Instead, "mutual interests in effective antidiscrimination law" briefs tend to focus not on the relationship across identity categories at all, but rather on the shared interest of all groups in a particular interpretation of antidiscrimination law or procedure. Their point, in other words, is to demonstrate that the court's decision will affect protections for a diverse set of people. The rhetorical impulse is thus to show the court a slippery slope that will likely reach dangerously beyond the category of people before the court. Although *amici* often do this by concentrating on the broad reach of the antidiscrimination issue at bar, they also sometimes use their briefs to show how their own constituents (as distinct from the parties before the court) may be rendered especially vulnerable by a negative ruling in the case.

In a recent sex discrimination case before the U.S. Supreme Court, for example, several racial and ethnic equality advocacy organizations joined together to file an *amicus* brief (Brief of the Lawyers' Committee for Civil Rights Under Law 2006). At issue was not the law of sex discrimination *per se* but rather the law prohibiting unlawful retaliation against employees who file discrimination claims. The Court's decision in the case was sure to affect race discrimination claimants directly in addition to affecting the sex discrimination plaintiff whose case was to be decided. The racial and ethnic groups' *amicus* brief focused only on the retaliation law; no mention was made of how the interactions of race and sex could affect retaliation against a targeted employee (ibid). A similar group of organizations filed an *amicus* brief in a case alleging a violation of the Americans with Disabilities Act, again not for the purpose of addressing the connection between race, ethnicity, and disability discrimination but instead to address the challenge to the federal government's authority to enact antidiscrimination measures (Tennessee 2004: 509).[42]

Other *amicus* briefs influenced by this interest come closer to addressing specific identity categories, but, similarly, their concern is with showing how the set of problems faced by one identity group plays out in related ways for other identity groups, rather than with challenging the perceived boundaries among categories. Consider, for example, *Saint Francis College v. al-Khazraji*, which addressed a race discrimination law's coverage of Arab Americans (Saint Francis College 1987: 604).[43] A companion case raised a similar question about discrimination against Jews (Shaare Tefila Congregation 1987: 615). The case might have presented an opportunity for *amici* to challenge the governing single-identity paradigm by exposing the complexity of the "race" category. Yet the brief filed by the Puerto Rican and Mexican Legal Defense and Education Funds focused instead on the ways in which a negative decision in the case could destabilize legal protections that reached their own constituents as well. Because the antidiscrimination statute at issue in the case was so important as a "means of redress to Hispanics victimized by discrimination," the organizations wrote in their statement of interest, a decision that Arab Americans and Jews were not protected by the statute might cast doubt on the law's availability "as a means of combating discrimination against Hispanic Americans" (Brief of Mexican American Legal Defense and Education Fund 1987). The point, in other words, was not that the category "Hispanic" had any overlapping relationship with the category "Arab" or "Jew" but rather that a narrow interpretation of the governing law would cause harm extending beyond the identity groups before the court.

Similarly, in a recent sex discrimination case concerning different immigration sponsorship rules for U.S. citizen mothers and fathers (Nguyen 2001: 53), the Asian American Legal Defense and Education Fund filed an *amicus* brief aimed at bringing the interests of Asian Americans into the case. Like the PRLDEF/MALDEF brief in *Saint Francis College*, however, the brief's interest was not in the overlap of identity categories. Instead, as the AALDEF brief explained, the organization was interested in the case because "the legal and factual problems presented [regarding foreign-born children's immigration status]... affect large numbers of Asian children." (Brief of Asian American Legal Defense and Education Fund 2001: 1).

In *Romer* v. *Evans* (Romer 1996: 620), which addressed a state constitutional amendment that barred antidiscrimination protections uniquely for gay people, the cross-identity briefs likewise concentrated on shared problems without addressing the connections among identities. One, which included NAACP LDF, MALDEF, and the Women's Legal Defense Fund, focused on shoring up the broad principle, already established in the contexts of race and sex, that laws enacted for the purpose of thwarting political participation by a group of people are impermissible. The brief acknowledged that the discrimination against gay people by the measure at issue bore "an unsettling resemblance" to attacks on Jews and African Americans (Brief of NAACP Legal Defense and Education Fund 1996: 15), thus positioning the identities as related in their experience of the harms at issue, but also distinct. A separate *amicus* brief filed by AALDEF, PRLDEF, and other politically oriented civil rights organizations similarly stressed the measure's infringement of political rights and drew connections to cases invalidating race-based political participation limits, focusing, again, on the commonality of the injury, not the commonality among the identities at issue (Brief of Asian American Legal Defense and Education Fund 1996).[44]

Although these briefs may serve legitimation or civil-rights-friendly environment interests in the ways just discussed, they do not tend to foreground questions of identity at all, much less reify differences among identity groups in service of their arguments. Yet they also do not seek to destabilize inter-identity boundaries as intersectionality theory does. Instead, because the *amici* in this category have a mutual interest in effective antidiscrimination laws, their briefs focus on cross-group vulnerabilities and largely sidestep questions of how the different identities interrelate.

The overlapping identities interest

The final interest that shapes the filing of cross-identity *amicus* briefs comes somewhat closer to intersectionality theory, in that the *amici* are concerned directly with the integration of particular identity categories. According to briefs motivated by this interest, the close relationship between two different identity categories requires protections be granted to the "other" group as a means of ensuring meaningful protection for the *amicus* group's own constituents. Unlike the interdependent "mutual interest in effective antidiscrimination law" brief, however, the slippery slope presented here is particular to the identity groups involved. This type of brief asks the court to recognize the interrelationship of the *amicus* group and its unprotected counterpart. Put metaphorically, if civil rights law is seen as an umbrella protecting some but not others, this type of advocacy seeks to broaden the umbrella's reach to another group in the interest of keeping the umbrella functional for themselves.

Intersectionality theory suggests that the preferred strategy for defining unprotected outsiders into the protection of antidiscrimination law would be to challenge the boundaries of identity categories that leave some outside and others in. Briefs motivated by an interest in overlapping identities, however, do not focus on challenging the perceived boundaries between identity groups so much as on advocating a reading of settled antidiscrimination law to reach discriminatory *acts* that had previously been seen as outside the law's scope. Put another way, *these briefs challenge the conceptualization of discrimination rather than the conceptualization of the identity categories.* They do so by first distilling core principles underlying existing law and then showing how those principles would be intolerably infringed and weakened if they are not applied to punish the challenged discriminatory act.

Consider, for example, a brief filed on behalf of women's rights organizations in a suit brought by lesbian and gay couples seeking marriage rights. The brief first describes the *amicus* organizations in terms of their commitment to eradicating *actions* that embody sex and gender stereotypes rather than by the *identity* of their constituents. It then pursues this act-oriented framing in its legal argument. Rather than addressing the relationship between the identity categories of "woman" and "lesbian," the brief spotlights the principles undergirding existing prohibitions against governmental perpetuation of gender stereotypes.

> By excluding same-sex couples from the institution of marriage, the state gives legal support to the belief that a marriage and a family are not proper if they allow a man to act "like a wife" or "like a mother" or permit a woman to act "like a husband" or "like a father." That message undermines the ability of all Californians to achieve their full

potential, both within marriage and outside, without regard for gender stereotypes.

(Application to File *Amici Curiae* Brief in Support of
Respondents and Proposed *Amici Curiae* Brief of
Amici Concerned with Women's Rights 2007)

In some respects, this approach resembles the legitimacy-enhancing and solidarity roles discussed earlier in connection with LDF's marriage brief (NAACP Legal Defense and Education Fund 2006) in that women's rights organizations, relative to gay rights organizations, enjoy greater status and stronger legal protections and are seen as authorities on sex discrimination doctrine. By focusing on the overlap in the identity categories, however, we see the different treatment of identity here. While legitimacy and solidarity-oriented briefs derive much of their authority through the status of their signers as outsiders to the immediate concerns of the litigation, this type of brief's power lies, in part, in the *amicus* group's admission of self-interest. In this instance, the claim is that the established protections at issue must be construed to encompass a related identity group if they are to remain fully effective for the *amici*. The identity group is thus integrally related to the group in need of protection, even if that connection is not explored explicitly.[45] Although the relatively greater status of the women's rights groups as compared to the gay rights groups is undoubtedly useful for legitimacy and civil-rights solidarity purposes, those status concerns take a back seat to the focus on the shared vulnerability of women and lesbians to gender stereotyping.

Observations and next steps for theory and practice

As just shown, advocacy across identity categories takes a variety of (overlapping) forms. Yet, even in the most deliberately intersectional of the categories just described, the focus is not typically on engaging – or even acknowledging – the ways in which identities overlap, as is the mission of intersectionality theory. Instead, while the *amicus* organizations recognize the interdependence among identity categories to some degree, the focus is largely away from the specifics of identity and toward the shared interest, whether thickly or thinly conceived, in strong limits on would-be discriminators' discretion to draw identity-based distinctions.

Yet, despite this significant disjunction between intersectionality theory's exploration of complexity and identity-based advocates' embrace of conventional categories, the theory and practice have begun to converge in ways that may be interesting and productive for both. Broadly speaking, cross-identity practice may signal ways to move beyond the challenge that infinite complexity has posed for efforts to create a grand theory in this area. At the same time, intersectionality theories offer important challenges for identity-based advocates' relatively passive acceptance of the existing identity categories paradigm.

As noted at the chapter's outset, intersectionality theorists have themselves come to a frustration point with complexity-oriented analyses. Some have urged that efforts to create a "unified field theory" be abandoned (Cho 2002; Ehrenreich 2002: 266–71; Engle and Danielson 1995: xvii-xvx; Williams 2002: 493) in favor of theorizing intersections among "systems of subordination." Others have suggested that even these newer theories will not elide the difficulty of managing the often competing interests enmeshed in cross-group interactions (Chang & Culp 2002: 487; Cho 2002: 403; Williams 2002: 493).

The examination of cross-identity advocacy here reinforces the view that a grand theory of identity intersections may not be forthcoming, although it also suggests that grand theory may well help us unpack advocacy's starting premise: that identity – whether treated as simple or complex – is necessarily dynamic. Of course, this point is not entirely unknown to contemporary theorists, many of whom have recognized that the meaning and function of identity may shift in different contexts.

Yet a deep recognition of identity's dynamism spells trouble for theories that would support complex identity-based claims. Once an identity category's instability is conceded, it becomes more difficult to demand that the law be responsive to identity-based claims (Goldberg 2002: 629). Courts are accustomed to adjudicating rights based on clear categories. To determine whether a party before the court is entitled to a remedy, for example, a judge must first decide whether that party falls within a protected category. If the category lacks clear boundaries, this task becomes difficult, if not impossible, for a court to fulfill. This challenge arises, in part, because judicial legitimacy concerns lead most courts to avoid overt engagement with complex questions regarding definitions of social groups that arguably verge on the anthropological rather than the legal (Goldberg 2006: 1955). One might imagine the argument being made that, after all, if the theorists cannot hold identity steady, how can we expect courts to do so?

Yet, as identity-based advocacy highlights, identity categories function largely as pawns, sometimes there to be accepted or even capitalized upon and at other times to be relegated to secondary importance. One might argue that this fluid, instrumental treatment of identity categories is particular to practice, and especially litigation practice, which aims to create specific outcomes and will use strategically whatever is available, whether facts or law or some combination of the two, to achieve the desired aims. But, as suggested through the series of examples above, the shifting deployment of identity categories to enhance legitimacy, foster a civil-rights-friendly environment, achieve effective legal protections, or strengthen the reach of antidiscrimination principles cannot be so easily dismissed.

Identity can be pressed into service of these roles not only because its complexity subjects it to manipulation but also because the categories themselves cannot be meaningfully understood outside the context of their use. They have, as advocates have recognized, political, legal, and social valences, and even those valences are ever-shifting as they combine in new moments and new contexts. As Iris Marion Young has observed, social groups are "an expression of social relations; a social group exists only in relation to at least one other group" (Young 1990: 43). Identity categories likewise do not exist in a vacuum. To expect that any theory can provide a grand, acontextual, and noncontingent methodology for analyzing identity thus defies what we know about the variable ways in which identity matters in the world.

Identity theorists might also explore the move made in intersectional practice – especially in connection with the overlapping identities interest – away from problematization of identity categories and toward expanding the conceptualization of existing antidiscrimination principles to broaden restrictions on would-be discriminators. A move in this direction could nicely complement ongoing efforts to deconstruct the ways in which identity categories are used systemically to subordinate marginalized populations. To return to an earlier metaphor, a focus on broadening the umbrella's protected reach could fit nicely with work that seeks to understand how and why some identity groups wind up outside the umbrella altogether.

The challenge going forward is thus to develop theories that account for identity as both an internally and externally complex category. The current, varied practices of intersectionality that work with – and around – identity categories, together with the frustrations of identity theorists related to identity's infinite complexity make this an exciting moment for new theoretical work about identity itself.

Advocates can likewise benefit from the insights of intersectional theorists, who have observed, repeatedly, that to accept overly simplistic categories is to obscure lived experience. Current cross-identity practices, as outlined above, do little to contest the law's tendency toward oversimplification. This strategy is unsurprising in a context where litigation victories can be terribly important and where contesting identity categories may jeopardize efforts to obtain protection from identity-based harms. But, for many who experience vulnerability across multiple dimensions of identity, meaningful judicial recognition of intersectional harms could produce far more protective results.

As identity theory suggests, well-rounded protection can be achieved only by pressing courts to understand the analytic error in treating identity categories as independent of one another. By demonstrating, time after time, in brief after brief, that an individual does not exist as a person with a race in isolation from sex or sexual orientation, for example, advocates could go a long way toward pushing back against and perhaps even redirecting the judicial orientation toward simplification. Courts have little incentive to do this themselves; simpler identity claims are often easier to resolve (Goldberg 2002). But if advocates were even to avoid some of the unnecessary reification of identity boundaries – or, going further, to develop strategies for retaining legitimacy even while acknowledging intersectionality – the project of cross-identity litigation would be more profoundly transformative of the law and, likely, more protective of broader, more complex identities.

The apparent divergence between theory and practice thus may be cause for inspiration rather than dismay. By sketching and analyzing the ways that intersectionality is practiced, this chapter has aimed to expand the opportunities for advocates and scholars to ply that divergence in conversation with each other. With care, the divergence can continue to be a productive one, creating, in turn, far greater opportunities for expanding our understanding *and* realization of a society more genuinely protective and appreciative of its inevitable multidimensionality.

Acknowledgements

Thanks to Davina Cooper, Ariela Dubler, Elizabeth Emens, Robert Ferguson, Anna Gelpern, Emily Grabham, Olati Johnson, Gillian Metzger, Henry Monaghan, and Susan Sturm, for ongoing conversations about the ideas in this chapter and to Ethan Frechette, Benjamin Garry, and Michael Budabin McQuown for excellent research assistance.

Bibliography

American Civil Liberties Union, Immigrants' Rights Project. Online. Available HTTP: <http://www.aclu.org/immigrants/index.html> (accessed 21 October 2007).

American Civil Liberties Union Lesbian Gay Bisexual Transgender and AIDS Project, *About Us*. Online. Available HTTP: <http://www.aclu.org/getequal/aboutus.html> (accessed 21 October 2007).

Anderson, Ellen (2005) *Out of the Closet and Into the Courts: Legal Opportunity Structure and Gay Rights Litigation*, Ann Arbor: University of Michigan Press.

Areheart, Bradley Allan (2006) 'Intersectionality and Identity: Revisiting a Wrinkle in Title VII,' *George Mason University Civil Rights Law Journal*, 17: 199–235.

Asian American Legal Defense and Education Fund, *About AALDEF*. Online. Available HTTP: <http://www.aaldef.org/about.php> (accessed 21 October 2007).

Badgett, M.V. Lee *et al.* (2007) *Bias in the Workplace: Consistent Evidence of Sexual Orientation and Gender Identity Discrimination*. Online. Available HTTP: <http://www.law.ucla.edu/williamsinstitute/publications/Bias%20in%20the%20Workplace.pdf>.

Brief of the American Association on Mental Retardation, the American Orthopsychiatric Association, the ARC, the National Association of Protection and Advocacy Systems, the National Association for Rights Protection and Advocacy, and the American Network of Community Options and Resources in

Support of Respondents, Romer v. Evans (1996) 517 U.S. 620 (No. 94-1039), 1995 WL 17008437.

Brief of Amicus Curiae Asian American Legal Defense and Educational Fund, Inc. in Support of Petitioners, Nguyen v. INS (2001) 533 U.S. 53 (No. 99-2071), 2000 WL 1702027.

Brief for Amici Curiae Asian American Legal Defense and Educational Fund, Japanese American Citizens League, National Council of La Raza and Puerto Rican Legal Defense and Education Fund in Support of Respondents, Romer v. Evans (1996) 517 U.S. 620 (No. 94-1039), 1995 WL 17008434.

Brief of the Lawyers' Committee for Civil Rights Under Law, The Asian American Justice Center, The National Association for the Advancement of Colored People, and the Puerto Rican Legal Defense and Education Fund, Inc. as Amici Curiae in Support of Respondent, Burlington Northern and Santa Fe Ry. Co. v. White (2006) 126 S.Ct. 2405 (No. 05-259), 2006 WL 615159.

Brief of the Lawyers' Committee for Civil Rights Under Law, the National Asian Pacific American Legal Consortium, the National Association for the Advancement of Colored People, the Puerto Rican Legal Defense and Education Fund, People for the American Way Foundation, and the Anti-Defamation League as Amici Curiae in Support of Respondents, Tennessee v. Lane (2004) 541 U.S. 509 (No. 02-1667), 2003 WL 22733909.

Brief of Mexican American Legal Defense and Educational Fund and Puerto Rican Legal Defense and Education Fund as Amici Curiae in Support of Respondent, Saint Francis College v. Al-Khazraji (1987) 481 U.S. 604 (No. 85-2169) WL 880980.

Brief of NAACP Legal Defense and Education Fund, Inc. (LDF) (2006) *Brief for Amicus Curiae*. Hernandez v. Robles (2006) 821 N.Y.S. 2d 770. Online. Available HTTP: <http://data.lambdalegal.org/pdf/656.pdf>.

Brief of NAACP Legal Defense and Education Fund, Inc., *Brief for Amicus Curiae, In re Marriage Cases,* Case No. S147999 (Cal. S. Ct. Sept. 26, 2007 *but not docketed until Oct.* 4). Online. Available HTTP: <http://www.nclrights. org/site/DocServer/2007.09.26.Amicus.NAACP_Legal_Defense_Education_ Fund.B.pdf?docID=2081.

Brief for the NAACP Legal Defense and Educational Fund, Inc., the Mexican American Legal Defense and Educational Fund, and Women's Legal Defense Fund as Amici Curiae in Support of Respondents, Romer v. Evans (1996) 517 U.S. 620 (No. 94-1039), 1995 WL 17008435.

Brief of Amici Curiae National Women's Law Center *et al.* in Support of the Petitioner, United States v. Virginia (1995), 518 U.S. 515 (No. 94-1941), 1995 WL 703392.

Brown-Nagin, Tomiko (2005) 'Elites, Social Movements, and the Law: The Case of Affirmative Action,' *Columbia Law Review*, 105: 1436–528.

Buchanan, James M. (1965) 'An Economic Theory of Clubs', *Economica*, 32: 1.

Catholic League, *About Us*. Online. Available HTTP: <http://catholicleague.org/ about.php> (accessed 6 November 2007).

Chang, Robert S. and Culp, Jerome McCristal (2002) 'After Intersectionality,' *UMKC Law Review*, 71: 485–91.

Cho, Sumi (2002) 'Understanding White Women's Ambivalence Towards Affirmative Action: Theorizing Political Accountability in Coalitions,' *UMKC Law Review*, 71: 399–418.

Clark, Cindy, Sprenger, Ellen and VeneKlasen Lisa. (2006) *Where is the Money for Women's Rights?*. Online. Available HTTP: <www.awid.org/publications/where_is_money/web_book.pdf>.

Conaghan, Joanne (2008), 'Intersectionality and the Feminist Project in Law,' this volume.

Council on Foundations (2002) *Board Briefing: Duration of Funding*. Online. Available HTTP: <http://www.cof.org/files/Documents/Governing_Boards/bb4funding.pdf>.

Crenshaw, Kimberlé (1989) 'Demarginalizing the Intersection between Race and Sex: A Black Feminist Critique of Anti-Discrimination Doctrine, Feminist Theory and Anti-Racist Politics,' *University of Chicago Legal Forum*, 1989: 139–67.

Crenshaw, Kimberlé (1991) 'Mapping the Margins: Intersectionality, Identity Politics and Violence Against Women of Color,' *Stanford Law Review*, 43: 1241–99.

Crooms, Lisa A. (1997) 'Indivisible Rights and Intersectional Identities OR, 'What do Women's Human Rights Have To Do With Race Convention?,' *Howard Law Journal*, 40: 619–40.

Cunningham, E. Christi (1998) 'The Rise of Identity Politics I: The Myth of the Protected Class in Title VII Disparate Treatment Cases,' *Connecticut Law Review*, 30: 441–501.

Currah, Paisley (2006) 'Gender Pluralisms under the Transgender Umbrella,' in Paisley Currah, Richard M. Juang and Shannon Minter Price, eds, *Transgender Rights*, Minneapolis: University of Minnesota Press.

Davidson, Jon, *Lambda Legal's Analysis of H.B. 3685: Narrow Version of ENDA Provides Weaker Protection for Everyone*. Online. Available HTTP: <http://data.lambdalegal.org/pdf/enda_llanalysis_20071016.pdf> (accessed 5 November 2007).

Della Porta, Donatella and Diani, Mario (1998) *Social Movements: An Introduction*, Oxford: Blackwell.

Disability Rights Education and Defense Fund. Online. Available HTTP: <http://www.dredf.org/about.shtml> (accessed 21 October 2007).

Ehrenreich, Nancy (2002) 'Subordination and Symbiosis: Mechanisms of Mutual Support Between Subordinating Systems,' *UMKC Law Review*, 71: 251–324.

Engle, Karen and Danielson, Dan (1995) 'Identity Politics After Identity,' in Karen Engle and Dan Danielson, eds, *After Identity: A Reader in Law and Culture*, London: Routledge.

Frey, Andrew (2006) 'Amici Curiae: Friends of the Court or Nuisances?,' *Litigation*, 33(1).

Gamson, William A. (1961) 'An Experimental Test of a Theory of Coalition Formation,' *American Sociology Review*, 26: 565.

Gilmore, Grant (1977) *The Ages of American Law*, New Haven, CT: Yale University Press.

Goldberg, Suzanne B. (2002) 'On Making Anti-Essentialist and Social Constructionist Arguments in Court,' *Oregon Law Review*, 81: 629–61.

Goldberg, Suzanne B. (2006) 'Constitutional Tipping Points: Civil Rights, Social Change, and Fact-Based Adjudication,' *Columbia Law Review*, 106: 1955–2022.

Hamilton Krieger, Linda (1995) 'The Content of Our Categories: A Cognitive Bias Approach to Discrimination and Equal Employment Opportunity,' *Stanford Law Review*, 47: 1161–248.

Hayes, Christopher (2006) *The New Funding Heresies*. Online. Available HTTP: http://www.inthesetimes.com/article/2697/.

Hutchinson, Darren Lenard (2002) 'New Complexity Theories: From Theoretical Innovations to Doctrinal Reform,' *UMKC Law Review*, 71: 431–45.

Konrad, Rachel (2007) 'Diverse Groups File Legal Briefs Endorsing Same-Sex Marriage,' *The Mercury News*, San Jose: California.

Krislov, Samuel (1963) 'The Amicus Curiae Brief: From Friendship to Advocacy,' *Yale Law Journal*, 72: 694–721.

Lambda Legal Defense and Education Fund, *About Lambda Legal*. Online. Available HTTP: <http://www.lambdalegal.org/about-us/> (accessed 12 June 2008).

Lax, David A. and Sebenius, James K. (1991) 'Thinking Conditionally: Party Arithmetic, Process Opportunism, and Strategic Sequencing,' H. Peyton Young, ed., *Negotiation Analysis*, Ann Arbor: University of Michigan Press.

Leadership Conference on Civil Rights, *About LCCR*. Online. Available HTTP: <http://www.civilrights.org/about/lccr/> (accessed 21 October 2007).

Legal Momentum, *Mission and Vision Statement*. Online. Available HTTP: <http://legalmomentum.org/legalmomentum/aboutus/> (accessed 21 October 2007).

Levit, Nancy (2002) 'Theorizing the Connections Among Systems of Subordination,' *UMKC Law Review*,' 71: 227–49.

Lopez, Haney (2006) *White By Law: The Legal Construction of Race*, New York: N.Y.U. Press.

Lynch, Kelly J. (2004) 'Best Friends? Supreme Court Law Clerks on Effective Amicus Curiae Briefs,' *Journal of Law and Policy*, 20: 33–75.

McAdam, Doug, McCarthy, John and Zald, Mayer, eds. (1996) *Comparative Perspective on Social Movements; Political Opportunities, Mobilizing Structures, and Cultural Framings*, Cambridge: Cambridge University Press.

McCall, Leslie (2005) 'The Complexity of Intersectionality,' *Signs Journal of Women in Culture and Society*, 30(3): 1771–800.

Mexican American Legal Defense and Education Fund, *Mission Statement*. Online. Available HTTP: <http://www.maldef.org/about/mission.htm> (accessed 21 October 2007).

Morris, Aldon D. and McClurg Mueller, Carol, eds. (1992) *Frontiers in Social Movement Theory*, New Haven: Yale University Press.

Murray, Shaulagh (October 18, 2007), 'Quandary Over Gay Rights Bill: Is It Better to Protect Some or None?,' *Washington Post*, at A23.

NAACP Legal Defense and Education Fund, Inc., *Mission Statement*. Online. Available HTTP: <http://www.naacpldf.org/content.aspx?article=1133> (accessed 21 October 2007).

National Center for Lesbian Rights, *About NCLR*. Online. Available HTTP: <http://ncflr.convio.net/site/PageServer?pagename=about_overview> (accessed 21 October 2007).

National Legal Foundation. Online. Available HTTP: <http://nlf.net/> (accessed 6 November 2007).

Native American Rights Foundation. Online. Available HTTP: <http://www.narf.org> (accessed 3 November 2007).

Northwest Women's Law Center, *How We Make a Difference*. Online. Available HTTP: <http://www.nwwlc.org/difference/LGBTrights.htm> (accessed 18 June 2008).

Olson, Mancur (1965) *The Logic of Collective Action: Public Goods and the Theory of Groups* Cambridge: Harvard University Press (1971) (rev'd ed.).

Phelan, Shane (1994) *Getting Specific: Postmodern Lesbianism Politics*, Minneapolis: University of Minnesota Press.

Pierson, Paul (2000) 'Increasing Returns, Path Dependence, and the Study of Politics,' *American Political Science Review*, 94: 251.

Puerto Rican Legal Defense and Education Fund. Online. Available HTTP: <http://www.prldef.org (accessed 21 October 2007).

Putnam, Robert D. (2006) *Bowling Alone*, New York: Simon and Schuster.

Stone, Roger Alan (1992) 'The Mass Plaintiff: Public Interest Law, Direct mail Fundraising and the Donor/Client,' *Columbia Journal of Law & Social Problems*, 25: 197–241.

Sylvia Rivera Law Project, *Mission*. Online. Available HTTP: <http://srlp.org/index.php?sec=olA&page=about> (accessed 21 October 2007).

Tarrow, Sidney (1994) *Power in Movement: Social Movements, Collective Action and Politics*, Cambridge: Cambridge University Press.

The History of the ACLU Women's Rights Project. Online. Available HTTP: <http://www.aclu.org/FilesPDFs/wrp_history.pdf> (accessed 3 November 2007).

Thomas More Law Center, *About Us*. Online. Available HTTP: <http://www.thomasmore.org/qry/page.taf?id=23> (accessed 6 November 2007).

Transgender Legal Defense and Education Fund, *About Us*. Online. Available HTTP: <http://www.transgenderlegal.org/> (accessed 6 November 2007).

Travis, Michele A. (2002) 'Perceived Disabilities, Social Cognition, and "Innocent Mistakes,"' *Vanderbilt Law Review*, 55: 481–579.

U.S. Dept. of Labor (2005) *U.S. Bureau of Labor Statistics, Women in the Labor Force: A Databook*, Washington D.C. 10.S. Government Printing Office.

Wax, Amy L. (1999) 'Discrimination as Accident,' *Indiana Law Journal*, 74: 1129–231.

Wing, A.K. (2000) *Global Critical Race Feminism: An International Reader*, New York: New York University Press.

Williams, Joan C. (2002) 'Fretting in the Force Fields: Why the Distribution of Social Power Has Proved So Hard to Change,' *UMKC Law Review*, 71: 493–505.

Yoshikawa, Yoko (1998) 'The Heat is on Miss Saigon Coalition,' in David L. Eng & Alice Y. Hom, eds., *Q & A: Queer in Asian America*, Philadelphia: Temple University Press.

Young, Marion (1990) *Justice and the Politics of Difference*, Princeton: Princeton University Press.

Legislation

Table of cases

Notes

1 Some have called this post-intersectionality literature. (See Levit 2002: 227, but see Cho 2002: 399.)

2 Levit has further observed that "[a] deeper, epistemological problem of essentialism is its tendency to assume natural essences and to move away from explanations that comprehend the social construction of identity categories." (Levit 2002: 228) (citing Spelman 1988). In addition to the epistemological issues, Levit notes the power dynamic through which privileged identities may dominate at the expense of more subordinated groups. (Ibid: 227.)

3 As a result of these challenges, the intensive focus of some legal scholarship in the 1990s and early 2000s on elaborating comprehensive and complex identity theories, see *supra* note 1, has slowed considerably. While explorations of the law/identity relationship continue, they tend to be aimed not so much at developing a comprehensive theory of complexity as at understanding the legal and social location of specific aspects of identity (Lopez 2006), or advocating interpretation of antidiscrimination laws and doctrine to redress complex identity-based injuries (Areheart 2006: Crooms 1999: 620; Cunningham 1998: 441). Outside of legal scholarship, intersectionality remains a central, active analytic tool (McCall 2005: 1771).

4 Chang and Culp 2002: 485, arguing that the utility of intersectionality theory is limited because of the context-sensitive variations in the importance and interaction of various aspects of an individual's identity; Hutchinson 2002: 444:

> [T]he problem for coalition politics is not "What do we share?" but rather "What might we share as we develop our identities through the process of coalition?" Coalition cannot be simply the strategic alignment of diverse groups over a single issue, nor can coalition mean finding the real unity behind our apparently diverse struggles. Our politics must be informed by affinity rather than identity, not simply because we are not all alike, but because we each embody multiple, often conflicting, identities and locations.
>
> (quoting Phelan 1994: 140)

5 Cf. Gilmore 1977: 17, observing that academics and practitioners often differ in their analysis of legal problems.

6 Unlike the other groups mentioned here, Native Americans have a distinct legal status and unique sovereignty rights. Therefore, although law reform work on behalf of Native Americans includes some identity-based claims similar to those handled by other groups, much of the work involves rights claims that grow out of tribes' sovereign status (Native American Rights Foundation).

7 While "lesbian, gay, bisexual, transgender" sounds like a multiple rather than single identity category, most advocacy organizations working on LGBT issues conduct themselves as having a single-identity focus and maintain that discrimination based on sexual orientation and gender identity is closely, if not inextricably, related:

> Lambda Legal is a national organization committed to achieving full recognition of the civil rights of lesbians, gay men, bisexuals, transgender people and those with HIV through impact litigation, education and public policy work.
>
> (Lambda Legal November)

Davidson explaining decision to support version of Employment Non-Discrimination Act protecting gender identification as well as sexual orientation; Murray (2007: A23), reporting "more than 300 gay, lesbian, and transgender groups" opposed removing gender identity from Employment Non-Discrimination Act. In recent years, a new, smaller set of law reform organizations has been created to focus exclusively on transgender rights issues; see, for example, Transgender Legal Defense and Education Fund November:

> Transgender Legal Defense & Education Fund, Inc. is a national nonprofit civil rights organization committed to ending discrimination based upon gender identity and expression and to achieving equality for transgender people through public education, test-case litigation, direct legal services, community organizing and public policy efforts.

8 I focus in later discussion primarily on groups addressing race, ethnicity, sex, and sexual orientation because the identity categories they encompass have been among the leading concerns of intersectionality scholarship. Other identity-based advocacy groups that could profitably be considered include, for example, the Disability Rights Education and Defense Fund whose mission is "to advance the civil and human rights of people with disabilities" and groups working on behalf of immigrants (American Civil Liberties Union). Some groups that advocate on behalf of adherents to particular religions also conceive of

themselves as identity-based groups. (Catholic League, asserting mission of defending Catholics; Thomas More Law Center: "Our purpose is to be the sword and shield for people of faith …"; National Legal Foundation: "The NLF is a Christian public interest law firm.") A fuller discussion of the nature of identity and group formation is beyond this chapter's scope.

A multitude of other law reform organizations focus on civil liberties, poverty, gun control, drug use, the right to die, as well as on voting rights, access to courts, religious freedom, and related aspects of liberal democracy. On identity-related issues, however, these organizations might lend their support but they will rarely, if ever, take the lead.

9 Some smaller law reform organizations do not work against the background of a single-identity mission and, instead, hold themselves out as working deliberately and explicitly across categories. For example, the Northwest Women's Law Center's explicitly addresses the rights of lesbians *and* women more generally:

> The Law Center has been recognized as a regional leader in fighting for equality for all women. To further that work, we bring lawsuits and work to pass legislation that will put an end to discriminatory employment practices, criminal laws that target people based on their sexual orientation and family laws that fail to recognize and protect non-traditional families. (ibid)

This deliberately intersectional approach is not seen in larger, nationally focused organizations.

10 *Amicus curiae* briefs, also known as "friend of the court" briefs, can be submitted by people or entities who are not directly involved with the lawsuit at issue but who have some interest or expertise they would like the court to consider. Most often, *amici* must obtain the permission of the court and/or the parties to the case before the brief will be accepted for consideration.

Amicus briefs typically: 1) develop legal arguments not addressed by the parties to the lawsuit; 2) expand on (or limit) arguments the parties have made; 3) explore the practical or policy implications or historical context of a case; and/or 4) offer social science data relevant to the issue in the case and/or critique the data already presented to the court (Frey 2006: 65; Krislov 1963: 703). "The majority of [U.S. Supreme Court] clerks [surveyed] (56 percent) explained that *amicus* briefs were most helpful in cases involving highly technical and specialized areas of law, as well as complex statutory and regulatory cases" (Lynch 2004: 41).

11 For additional discussion of the complex nature of the "lesbian, gay, bisexual, and transgender" category, *see supra* note 7.

12 For detailed discussion of various intersectionality theories, see Conaghan, this volume.

13 As just noted, the analysis here is confined to U.S.-based organizations, which have a rich tradition of identity-based advocacy. Much room remains for a comparative approach, including both domestic and international law-focused non-governmental advocacy organizations, to enhance the project of mapping the relationship between identity-based theory and practice.

14 For further discussion of some of the leading organizations and their missions, see *infra* notes 15–24 and accompanying text.

15 See discussion above for additional discussion of the internal instability of these group categories.

16 See ACLU Lesbian Gay Bisexual Transgender and AIDS Project, "About Us," at http://www.aclu.org/getequal/aboutus.html (last visited Oct. 21, 2007) for the organization's mission statement. See American Civil Liberties Union, at http://

aclu.org/ (last visited 21 October 2007) for a list of the organization's programs and projects, which address an array of civil rights and civil liberties issues in addition to the types of individual rights matters discussed here.

17 See *infra* notes 32–37 and accompanying text.

18 James Buchanan's theory of clubs helps show how advocacy groups overcome collective action problems by gathering constituencies who will benefit from the groups' activities. If, on the one hand, a group acted on behalf of every identity sub-group conceivably falling within its umbrella, its mission might become so diffuse as to make the benefits essentially non-exclusive, stimulating collective action problems. If, on the other hand, a group acted on behalf *only* of a particular identity sub-group, the advocacy group might have difficulty mustering sufficient resources to be an effective agent of change (Buchanan 1965: 1; Olsen 1965).

19 Yoshikawa's article discusses a conflict initiated by Asian gay, lesbian, bisexual, and transgender organizations and social networks in 1991 regarding Lambda Legal's promotion of a controversial Asia-themed play, "Miss Saigon," for a fundraising event (Yoshikawa 1998: 41).

20 The U.S. Labor Department's statistics show that men earn more than women and whites earn more than people of color, with the exception of Asian workers, who earn more than whites. The point is true as well for sexual orientation- and gender identity-based distinctions, with heterosexual, non-transgender individuals typically out-earning their LGBT counterparts (Badgett *et al.* 2007: 5) (finding that gay men earn less than heterosexual men and noting several surveys showing transgender people typically experience disproportionately high unemployment and have disproportionately low incomes; the data on the relevance of lesbian identity to income is less conclusive). Many members of other identity groups are likewise vulnerable to economic marginalization or discrimination. (U.S. Dept. of Labor 2005).

21 Foundations can fill some of this gap, although grants sometimes come with restrictive conditions that limit an organization's discretion. Moreover, many foundations will not, as a matter of principle, undertake long-term funding, which means, for many organizations, that foundation funds are a less stable source than gifts from longstanding individual donors (Council on Foundations 2002; Clark *et al.* 2006: 39) (noting that changing funding priorities of large foundations has lead to a decline in funding for women's rights groups).

22 U.S. Equal Employment Opportunity Commission, "Discriminatory Practices," at http://www.eeoc.gov/abouteeo/overview_practices.html (last visited Oct. 21, 2007) (emphasis added); see also 42 U.S.C. § 2000e-5(k) (2000) (Title VII of Civil Rights Act of 1964); id. § 12205 (Americans with Disabilities Act of 1990); 29 U.S.C. § 621–34 (2000) (Age Discrimination in Employment Act of 1967). Of course, the law's distinctions between categories did not arise in a vacuum. Just as cultural factors and the existing legal framework may shape the advocacy organizations' single-identity approach, so too the advocacy groups may have shaped the law.

23 To a lesser but still significant degree, much of the identity-related social science that law reform groups rely on, including in their *amicus* briefs, focuses on single-identity traits. This phenomenon has spawned its own body of intersectionality literature (McCall 2005). Although a comprehensive effort to explain these parallel trends is beyond this chapter's scope, several points in the discussion below regarding why single-identity law reform organizations have thrived likely bear on the success of single-identity social science research as well.

24 See, for example, Levit, op. cit., p. 243 (criticizing judicial treatment of the "discrete and insular minorities" concern in footnote 4 of *United States* v. *Carolene Products*, 304 U.S. 144, 153 n.4 (1938), as "a check-off list" that has constricted courts' understanding of disadvantage). See also *Rabidue* v. *Osceola Refining Company*, 805 F.2d 611 (6th Cir. 1986) (treating sexual harassment claims as requiring conflict between interests of women and workers, notwithstanding women workers) (cited and discussed by Ehrenreich 2002: 260). See, for example, *Ingram* v. *West*, 70 F.Supp.2d 1033, 1036 (W.D.Mo. 1999) (recognizing a black, female, senior citizen as only belonging to multiple, separate protected classes); *Martin* v. *Healthcare Business Resources*, No. 00-3244, 2002 WL 467749, at *5 (E.D.Pa. 2002) (same); *Flint* v. *City of Philadelphia*, No. 98–5, 2000 WL 288114, *5 (E.D. Pa. 2000) (same). But see *Jefferies* v. *Harris County Community Action Ass'n*, 615 F.2d 1025, 1032 (5th Cir. 1980) (acknowledging that "discrimination against black females can exist even in the absence of discrimination against black men or white women."). See also Arehart (2006) (reviewing cases).

25 Although anyone may seek a court's permission to file an *amicus* brief in any case, law reform advocates frequently ask other identity-based legal groups, as well as social scientists, academics, and professional organizations, to file briefs in support of their claims, especially in appellate courts.

26 In some instances, the soliciting organization wants the potential *amicus* to write its own brief. But often, the soliciting organization will arrange for a law firm or other organization to draft the brief, which merely requires the solicited group to lend its organizational name, reviewing someone else's draft, and writing a statement of interest. But, in a world in which resources are scarce, the decision whether to either write or sign a brief nonetheless requires an organization to weigh the costs and benefits of participation (and, comparably, the organization planning the solicitation strategy must decide where to devote its energy).

27 In some instances, even when organizations have agreed to prepare an *amicus* brief, individuals who are not on the organization's legal staff but function instead in a "cooperating attorney" capacity might do the bulk of the drafting. Even these efforts, though, typically require substantial oversight by an organization staff member. In situations where an organization is signing on to another group's brief, the work required, including reviewing and commenting on the draft, can be relatively minimal.

28 Organizations regularly promote the filing of *amicus* briefs through their websites and press releases. For high-profile cases, the media sometimes reports on *amicus* brief filings as well:

> Hundreds of national civil rights groups, lawmakers, academics and cities submitted legal briefs to the California Supreme Court Wednesday in support of gay couples who are seeking to overturn state laws prohibiting same-sex marriage.
>
> (Konrad 2007)

29 Any discussion of a movement's views begs the question how those views are to be determined, given the diversity within any movement, just as there is within an identity group, as noted earlier. I will leave fuller exploration of that question to social movement theorists and simply observe that, when discussing a movement's views, I am addressing the dominant articulation of those views by dominant movement leaders. (Cf. Brown-Nagin 2005: 1443) (discussing the ways in which elite movement leaders shaped the social movement views

articulated in support of affirmative action in *Grutter* v. *Bollinger*, 539 U.S. 306 (2003) and *Gratz v. Bollinger*, 539 U.S. 244 (2003).)

30 Political (or legal) opportunity structure constitutes "consistent . . . dimensions of the political environment which either encourage or discourage people from using collective action." (Tarrow 1994: 18). For a discussion of legal opportunity structure in the context of litigation to secure rights for lesbians and gay men, see Anderson 2005: 114; Lax and Sebenius 1991: 153; Gamson 1961: 565).

31 As noted earlier, courts have discretion whether to accept *amicus* briefs that have been submitted for consideration. See *supra* note 10. The claims made in the statement of interest regarding the *amicus* group's connection to the case before the court are important to this determination.

32 While my study included all law reform groups' *amicus* briefs filed in the U.S. Supreme Court as well as selective lower court *amicus* briefs that might be characterized as cross-identity filings, this chapter does not present the entire study but rather draws from representative examples to illustrate the theory/ practice relationship that is this chapter's focus.

33 The most intense period of this involvement was during the 1990s, when I was a staff attorney with Lambda Legal Defense and Education Fund, where I oversaw the solicitation of *amicus* briefs in numerous cases and participated in evaluating and drafting *amicus* briefs in many others. This work brought me into contact with lawyers at many other identity-based law reform groups, including those discussed in this chapter. My involvement continues today through my role as Director of Columbia Law School's Sexuality and Gender Law Clinic.

34 To a degree, this practice of solicitation by reputation is common practice across all types of litigation, with *amicus* participation by the federal or state government, certain prominent officials, and particularly esteemed industry leaders or academics often considered valuable for their potential influence on the court hearing a case (Grutter 2003: 330).

35 While this phenomenon has not been documented formally, a survey of *amicus* briefs in race-related cases provides reinforcement for the proposition that LGBT organizations are not regularly solicited as *amici* in race-related cases.

36 Through this statement, LDF might also have intended to protect established race-based protections from being weakened by association with less secure gay rights claims or even to stake a position in the sometimes contentious public conversation about the relation between gay and African American identities. But, whatever the intent, the brief's articulation of the distinction between gay and African American people reinforces that the *amicus* support comes from an "outsider" group.

37 This begs further questions about the meaning and function of identity within this perceived civil rights community, including: 1) is the very idea of a civil rights community premised on providing a conceptual gathering place for separate identity groups that would not otherwise have great need to interact with each other?; 2) does this sense of community survive because it is in its members' self-interest to be perceived as making claims that extend beyond the distinct identity group they represent? Although fully engaging these questions is beyond the scope of this chapter, their presence illustrates how potentially valuable it is to analyze cross-group interactions not only for the insights they hold regarding social movement and coalition theory but also for their window onto the role of identity and cross-identity interactions.

38 Often this occurs when organizations sign onto briefs rather than write the briefs themselves. While this is relatively inexpensive to the signing group, which has only to review another organization's work, the participation is nonetheless

valuable to the soliciting organization, which is typically interested in the legitimacy-enhancing use of the organization's name and reputation rather than the attorney time expended on the project.

39 Unlike many of the other cases discussed in this chapter, *U.S.* v. *Virginia* was brought by the United States government rather than by a law reform organization. Still, the women's rights organizations played a significant role in gathering *amicus* briefs and telling the public story about the case (*History of the ACLU Women's Rights Project*: 4–5).

40 Of course, the power of coalitions in litigation should not be overstated. While legislators might be impressed with an advocacy group's broad array of supporters, courts do not face comparable institutional pressure to respond to constituents' preferences. They are, thus, less likely to be moved by sheer numbers than they are to be influenced by the participation of parties without a predictable self-interest in the case.

41 As a strategic matter, it would also often not be in the self-interest of *amicus* organizations to suggest that their constituents have vulnerabilities similar to the party before the court.

42 For an *amicus* brief that brought together a variety of law reform organizations, including identity-based groups, see brief of *Amici Curiae* the Lawyers' Committee for Civil Rights Under Law 2004; see also *Jones* v. *R.R. Donnelley & Sons Co.*, 541 U.S. 369 (2004) (in a civil rights claim under 42 U.S.C. § 1981 by an African American employee that implicated the statute's limitations period generally, a joint brief was filed by the Lawyers' Committee for Civil Rights Under Law, Mexican American Legal Defense and Education Fund, National Association for the Advancement of Colored People, National Asian Pacific American Legal Consortium, National Employment Lawyers Association, and the Puerto Rican Legal Defense and Education Fund in Support of Petitioners) (Jones 2004: 369); see also *National R.R. Passenger Corp.* v. *Morgan*, 536 U.S. 101 (2002) (in an employment discrimination case filed by an African American employee that implicated the statute of limitations for a federal antidiscrimination law, a joint *amicus* brief was filed by The Impact Fund, Disability Rights Education and Defense Fund, Public Advocates, Inc., The Western Center on Disability Rights, Protection and Advocacy, Inc., The Mexican American Legal Defense and Education Fund, Equal Rights Advocates, The Asian Pacific American Legal Center, the Legal Aid Foundation of Los Angeles, and The Michigan Civil Rights Division in support of the respondent; a separate joint brief was filed by The Lawyers' Committee For Civil Rights Under Law, The National Association For The Advancement Of Colored People, The Minority Business Enterprise Legal Defense And Education Fund, Inc., now Legal Defense And Education Fund, The National Women's Law Center, The National Partnership For Women And Families, The American Jewish Congress, AARP [an organization that addresses the needs of Americans age 50 and over], and The National Employment Lawyers Association also in support of the respondent) (National R.R. Passenger Corp. 2002: 101).

43 The U.S. Supreme Court ultimately found that coverage existed. Most other cases involving race and sex discrimination claims, and sex discrimination claims too, focus on the types of procedural and general doctrinal issues discussed above rather than on issues specifically related to identity.

44 Advocates for individuals with mental retardation also filed an *amicus* brief in *Romer*. They, too, did not focus on the overlap in identity categories. Instead, they stated their concern "about the shaping of this Court's equal protection doctrine for cases involving groups that have not been recognized as 'suspect,'

but where the challenged laws are the product of invidiously discriminatory motivation" (Brief of the American Association on Mental Retardation 1996: 1). In elaborating their argument, they continued to avoid an intersectional position, observing instead that "[i]t is our experience that combating patterns of bias has ... taken a different course for different groups" (ibid: 4).

45   This close connection of interests may be more easily developed when one aspect of identity is integrally connected to another. In this instance, lesbian identity is integrally connected to being a woman, at least to the extent the category "lesbian" is understood to encompass women who have an erotic attraction to other women. It may, but need not, follow that the legal vulnerability of lesbians might present a special risk to women whereas the legal vulnerability of another identity group, whether based on race, disability, or some other factor, is less likely to present that type of threat.

Chapter 6

Identifying disadvantage

Beyond intersectionality

Rosemary Hunter and Tracey De Simone

Introduction

This chapter deals with intersectionality as an analytical tool for understanding the nature and dynamics of subordination. Intersectionality analysis as developed within US critical race feminism incorporates two important claims: first, that the experience of Black women is not simply one of added oppressions (gender oppression plus racial oppression), but is specifically 'intersectional', that is, unique to women situated at the point of intersection of race and gender; and secondly, that shifting theory to the intersection, focusing on the position of marginalized rather than relatively privileged women, is likely to reveal forms of oppression hitherto invisible within mainstream feminist or anti-racist theorizing (Crenshaw 1991). In the words of Rebecca Johnson, 'The point of intersectional analysis is to see whether or not the experiences of those located at the intersections can provide insights crucial to the construction of better theories' (2005: 29).

These claims have inspired a considerable literature reporting accounts of and research into 'intersectional' experience. In terms of Leslie McCall's taxonomy of approaches to studying intersectionality, much of this literature has taken an 'intracategorical' approach (McCall 2005: 1780–82; reprinted in this volume). That is, it has focused on the experience of a single 'intersectional' group, such as women of colour, lesbians, working-class women or women with disability. In Australia, for example, this kind of approach has been taken by Indigenous women, who have trenchantly criticized white feminists for purporting to speak for them, and argued for the specificity of their experience (including the experience of being oppressed by white women), and hence their separate political position, as Indigenous women (e.g., O'Shane 1976; Behrendt 1993; Huggins 1994; Moreton-Robinson 2000). Australian multiculturalism also gave rise to the intersectional category of 'women from non-English speaking backgrounds' (NESB), a category which asserts both difference from the more privileged category of English-speaking women, and a commonality of experience among immigrant women for whom English is not their first language. There has been a considerable amount of research on, for example, the health and well-being of NESB women (e.g., Alcorso and Schofield 1991; Mason 1993; Easteal 1996), and on their position and experiences in the labour market (e.g., Alcorso 1991; Yeatman 1992; Alcorso and Harrison 1993; Junor 1994; Stephens and Bertone 1995; VandenHeuvel and Wooden 1996) and in the legal system (e.g., Keys Young 1994, Assafiri and Dimopoulos 1995, Domestic Violence and Incest Resource Centre 1996).

Intersectionality analysis has, however, been critiqued by those who argue that we all occupy a position at the intersection of multiple systems of privilege and/or subordination – that 'multidimensionality' is, in fact, a universal condition (e.g., Grillo 1995: 17; Hutchinson 2001: 312) – and by those who argue that there is no ontology of identity, what McCall has termed the 'anticategorical' approach (McCall 2005: 1776–8; see also Staunces 2003: 103; Milczarek-Desai 2005: 243–5). In either its modernist or postmodernist form, this critique tends to lead to the proposition that, rather than working from predetermined identity categories, it is necessary to examine the ways in which domination, subordination, and subjects themselves, are constructed in particular locations and contexts (e.g., Grillo 1995: 17; Hutchinson 2001: 312–13; Yuval-Davis 2006: 200).

This debate about whether subordination is best illuminated via an intersectional or a contextual analysis, whether it should be understood as an experience consistently related to identity or a variable product of particular institutional structures, is taken up here from the perspective of research into women's access to legal aid in Australia. It will be seen that while the research began with an intersectional analysis, its findings tended to support the argument for attention to context rather than identity.

Women and legal aid in Australia

Access to the legal system and to legal representation, to enable adequate pursuit of legal rights and the defence of legal proceedings, has been regarded as an important component of democratic citizenship. Legal aid systems in Western countries were established pursuant to this conception of citizenship, in order to ensure that people with legal needs were not denied access to the legal system or to an adequate defence by reason of limited resources. Nevertheless, legal aid has rarely been considered a 'core' welfare programme in the same way as health and housing (which undoubtedly address more widespread needs). While a comparatively generous legal aid scheme was established in England and Wales, legal aid provisions in other countries tended to be restricted in one way or another, for example being confined to the provision of limited, free legal services rather than funding for private representation, or subject to income thresholds set at quite low levels. As a general proposition, too, legal aid provisions in Western countries have declined since the 1970s, with the demise of welfare states and the rise of neo-liberalism, resulting in a revised conception of legal aid as a residual rather than universal programme, to be carefully targeted to those defined as the most needy (see, e.g., Moorhead and Pleasence 2003). The gendered, raced, and other consequences of these (re)distributional policy choices and changes have rarely been questioned (though see Addario 1998; Brewin 2004; New Zealand Law Commission 1999), although Australia represents something of an exception to this trend, with feminist activists and academics making considerable efforts to highlight the issue of gender difference in legal aid provision.

A study of women's access to legal aid was undertaken by the federal Office of Legal Aid and Family Services (OLAFS) in 1994, in response to feminist concerns that women were not receiving a fair share of the legal aid budget. The OLAFS report, *Gender Bias in Litigation Legal Aid*, found that in 1992/93,[1] women received only 37 per cent of net legal aid expenditure on representation services, and that while women made 39.5 per cent of legal aid applications, their success rate was lower then men's (OLAFS 1994: 8–9, 14, 24). The report made it clear that this gender bias was a product of indirect rather than direct discrimination against women (at 40). That is, legal aid policies and guidelines did not overtly distinguish between men's and women's applications. Rather, the adverse outcomes for women resulted from the differential treatment of legal aid applications relating to criminal law and family law matters. Women enjoyed an equal success rate with men in relation to criminal matters, and an equal or slightly higher success rate than men in relation to family law matters (at 19–21). But legal aid guidelines gave priority to criminal matters in which the defendant was potentially threatened with loss of liberty, criminal law applications outnumbered family law applications, criminal law applications had a higher approval rate than family law applications, and men made the majority of criminal law applications (over 80 per cent), while women made the majority of family law applications (over 70 per cent) (at 19–21, 34). Thus, in 1992/93, 72 per cent of all litigation legal aid grants were made in the area of criminal law, consuming 43 per cent of the total legal aid budget. By contrast, only 21 per cent of legal aid grants were made in the area of family law, consuming only 32 per cent of the legal aid budget (at 24).

The standard justifications for prioritizing criminal law in the expenditure of legal aid budgets are that criminal defendants face the overwhelming power and resources of the state, and therefore have the greatest need for legal representation; and the serious consequences of being found guilty of many criminal offences, i.e. deprivation of liberty. In Australia, these justifications were reinforced in a 1992 High Court decision, *Dietrich v R*,[2] which held that a fair trial for a person accused of a serious criminal offence includes a right to legal representation, and if the accused is unable to afford such representation, either it must be provided at public expense, or the trial should be stayed. By contrast, while the Family Court has repeatedly made statements about the iniquities and serious consequences of lack of legal aid funding for family law matters,[3] those statements have had no practical effect on legal aid grants policy.

The issue of women's inequitable access to legal aid was taken up by the Australian Law Reform Commission (ALRC) in its mid-1990s inquiry into women's equality before the law (ALRC 1994). The Commission drew a link between women's unequal status in society in general and their access to the legal system, and argued, among other things, that 'If legal aid was allocated solely on the basis of relative poverty, it could be expected that more women would receive it than men, given their inferior economic status' (1994: para 4.10). Other feminist arguments at the time also sought to counter the standard justifications for prioritizing criminal law in legal aid expenditure, pointing out (among other things) the potentially serious consequences for women of losing family law disputes, the significant inequality of resources often experienced by women in those disputes, and the problematic nature of policies which gave legal aid funding to the perpetrators of violent crimes but not to their victims (ALRC 1994: para 4.17; Mossman 1993: 47–50; see also Mossman 1994 and Mossman 1990). Two of the ALRC Commissioners, Reg Graycar and Jenny Morgan, published an article in which they deployed the rhetorically powerful metaphor of 'civil death' to describe women's inability to invoke the legal system to redress the harms they had suffered, and hence their lack of full enjoyment of citizenship (Graycar and Morgan 1995).

The ALRC recommended that the federal government (which at that stage contributed around half of national legal aid funding, with the states contributing the other half) should take a more directive role to ensure better use of legal aid funds and revised priorities to protect women's rights. In response, the then federal Labor government announced a National Women's Justice Strategy, which included the establishment of a national network of women's legal services, additional legal aid funding for civil and family law matters, and a commitment to refocus legal aid policies to redress gender bias (Commonwealth Attorney-General and Minister for Justice 1995). In mid-1996, however, the election of a new, Conservative federal government resulted in a reversal of legal aid policies. The government made cuts of $AU120 million[4] to federal legal aid funding over the four years 1997/98–2000/01, resulting in severe restrictions on legal aid for family law matters in particular. These included the introduction of capped funding in individual cases, a more stringent merit test, and new guidelines limiting the types of family law matters eligible for legal aid grants and mandating efforts to resolve disputes by mediation and other alternative means before grants would be made for court proceedings. While the federal legal aid budget has subsequently increased modestly, it still falls well short of the level of demand.

Needless to say, this has not been a climate conducive to addressing issues of gender bias in the distribution of legal aid funding. Gender monitoring undertaken by the Women's Legal Aid Unit of one of the state legal aid funding bodies, Legal Aid Queensland (LAQ), showed that in 2003/04, women made 37.5 per cent of legal aid applications in that state but received only 34.8 per cent of legal aid grants, and again had a lower success rate in their applications (69.9 per cent) than did men (77.6 per cent) (Women's Legal Aid 2005: 2, 7, 21). Similarly, the Women's Legal Aid report explained that it remains easier to obtain legal aid for criminal law because the majority of offences are not merit-tested (at 7), whereas all applications for family law are subject to both means and merit tests. Of all the legal aid grants made by LAQ in 2003/04, 64 per cent were in criminal law, compared to only 24 per cent in family law (at 21).

One notable difference between the 1994 OLAFS report and the 2005 Women's Legal Aid report, however, was that the latter included separate consideration of access to legal aid for Indigenous women, NESB women, women with disability, younger women, and women living in rural and regional areas. This demonstrated the permeation of the concept of intersectionality into feminist activist and policy circles. During the ten years that elapsed between the two reports, it had become much less acceptable to discuss 'women' as a unitary identity or policy category. At the same time, the particular 'intersectional' categories deployed in the Women's Legal Aid Report had become relatively entrenched in policy analysis as accepted sites of subordination. This policy context formed an important background to our research.

Women's disadvantage in access to legal aid: researching differences

Tracey De Simone, one of the authors of this chapter, is a former Coordinator of Women's Legal Aid. In the early 2000s she became concerned that the gender and intersectional monitoring undertaken by the unit was having little impact on organizational policies. While LAQ stated that its mission was to provide legal assistance to 'disadvantaged' Queenslanders, it seemed to have difficulty seeing any disadvantage to women flowing from policies that were, on their face, gender-neutral. These concerns were shared by Louise Whitaker, Coordinator of LAQ's Rural and Regional Access Strategies Unit. Tracey and Louise approached the other author of this chapter, Rosemary Hunter, a feminist legal academic who was then working at a Queensland university, to devise a research project which might help to demonstrate, and delineate the dimensions of, women's disadvantage in access to legal aid. After some discussion, we formulated a project which sought to go beyond the previous feminist analysis of legal aid provision, and which had the concept of intersectionality at its core.

Our basic premise was that in a climate of ongoing limitations on legal aid budgets, there was unlikely ever to be enough funding available to meet all demands or to address the issue of gender bias in the distribution of legal aid funds between criminal and family law *per se*. In this context, it was necessary to re-focus concerns about the gendered distribution of legal aid funds to the question of whether any particular groups of women were disadvantaged in access to legal aid for family and civil law matters. This question both accorded with Crenshaw's call to place 'those who currently are marginalized in the center' (1991: 212) and dovetailed with policies of targeting legal aid to those most in need. For the purposes of our research, this meant that rather than comparing the positions of 'men' and 'women' as singular categories, we focused solely on women (a controversial approach from the perspective of LAQ), and compared the positions of different groups of women. In McCall's taxonomy, our approach was 'intercategorical', focused on analyzing relationships of inequality between multiple social groups (McCall 2005: 1785–86).

Next, and for the purposes of comparison, we operationalized the notion of 'disadvantage' in access to legal aid by reference to three factors: whether any groups of women with legal needs disproportionately *failed to apply* for legal aid; whether any groups of women were disproportionately *refused* legal aid; and whether failures to apply for or refusals of legal aid had a particularly *adverse impact* on any groups of women, having regard to the alternative resources, support and strategies available to them to pursue legal proceedings. The methodology adopted to answer these questions was empirical, multi-faceted and triangulated, involving examination of LAQ application and refusal statistics over time, an in-depth, statistical analysis of a sample of 322 files over a two-year period in which women's applications for legal aid had been refused, and interviews with 152 of the women whose files were included in the refusal sample, 152 lawyers and community workers having contact with a range of social groups, 19 women representing themselves in court, and six LAQ grants officers. In order to keep the scope of the project within manageable bounds, we focused on legal aid applications in the areas of family law,[5] domestic violence and anti-discrimination. We also focused on applications to the main Brisbane office of LAQ, plus four regional offices that had historically high refusal rates for women's applications in those areas of law.

In order to collect empirical data that would enable us to compare the positions of different groups of women, we also found it necessary to engage in some *a priori* identification of groups of women who would be the subject of scrutiny. The groups we chose were Indigenous women, NESB women, women with disability, older women (aged 60+), younger women (aged 18–20), and women living in rural and regional areas. The reasons for choosing these groups were to some extent principled, but included a large element of pragmatism. In principle, women in these groups who met the legal aid means test (i.e., who had very low incomes) might be said to be 'doubly disadvantaged' in gaining access to the legal system. Not only did they live in poverty and face major financial barriers to accessing lawyers and the court system, but they also faced cultural, linguistic, informational, age-based, physical and geographical barriers to access, as well as misconceptions and sometimes prejudices on the part of key gatekeepers and decision makers in the system. Thus, we did not simply assume these women's disadvantage in accordance with accepted policy categories. But at the same time, there were other groups whom we did not include who might also be said to have faced multiple barriers in accessing the legal system, such as lesbians[6] and women with low levels of education. There may also have been different levels of disadvantage within some of the chosen groups, for example among very recently arrived African immigrant/refugee women as opposed to women in more established immigrant groups, or among women living in very remote, rural areas as opposed to those living closer to large, regional towns.

Pragmatically, however, we were compelled to choose groups that could be readily identified in LAQ statistics. The groups we chose could all be identified from questions on the legal aid application form, by virtue of the very fact that they constituted entrenched policy categories. Thus, the form included questions about Indigeneity, whether the applicant spoke a language other than English at home,[7] receipt of a disability pension, age, and postcode. By contrast, it did not ask questions about sexuality or education, so we had no way of statistically isolating sexual minorities and those with low educational levels. Receipt of a disability pension was a very under-inclusive proxy for actual disability, but this was the best we could do with the information available. We were also unable to distinguish between types of disability, in particular between physical disabilities, cognitive disabilities and mental illness. We could, theoretically, have distinguished between different immigrant groups because the form also asked about country of birth, but we were unable to gauge recentness of arrival because that information was not gathered, and in its absence, we had no principled basis for drawing distinctions. Pragmatically, again, if we had focused on particular countries or regions of origin, we would have been likely to end up with such small numbers in each group in our file sample that we would have been unable to make meaningful comparisons between them. This is a well-observed problem of combining statistical and intersectionality analysis (e.g., Merritt 2001: 732–5).

The 'rural and regional' category raised similar issues. LAQ had pre-existing lists of postcodes classified as 'rural' and 'regional'. We could have revised these categories, but this would have been time-consuming, and again we lacked a principled basis for doing so. The existing categories were also meaningful to LAQ in the context of its specialist Rural and Regional Access Strategies Unit. So once more, we took the line of least resistance. In gathering qualitative data through interviews with women refused legal aid, self-representing litigants, lawyers, community workers and grants officers, we could elicit more nuanced responses about groups of women perceived to experience disadvantage in access to legal aid, but the quantitative component of the research compelled us to utilize, and hence to some extent to reify, particular intersectional categories.

A further difficulty posed by our selection of particular 'target' groups of women to be the focus of our quantitative research was that 'characteristics' (Indigeneity, language background, disability, age) inevitably overlapped with geographical location. One way of dealing with this might have been to construct a whole series of groups for comparison (Indigenous rural, Indigenous regional, Indigenous metropolitan, NESB rural, NESB regional, etc.). Yet this would again have yielded such tiny numbers in most categories that statistical comparisons between them would have been meaningless. In practice, then, we made two kinds of comparisons: one between groups identified by characteristics (regardless of location), and the second between groups identified by location (regardless of characteristics). If both comparisons yielded statistically significant results, we would then look at the interaction between them, to see whether one had a stronger or more salient effect than the other. There was also the possibility of overlapping characteristics, that is, that any given individual might, for example, be both Indigenous and have a disability, or be NESB and older. In fact, only six women in the file sample had more than one targeted characteristic.[8] In this situation, we simply assigned each woman to a primary category of Indigenous or NESB, since these were defined so as to be mutually exclusive.

The violences thus inflicted on individual experience through the process of categorization for the purposes of statistical analysis might constitute an argument against attempting to combine intersectionality and quantitative research (or indeed against attempting to conduct quantitative research of any kind). Yet the outcomes of such research perhaps provide a better test of its value. The literature does include instances of statistical analyses using crude, problematical, intersectional categories nevertheless yielding important insights.[9] Merritt argues that given the need to select a finite range of categories for the purposes of statistical analysis, we should simply recognize that every analysis offers partial truths – necessarily limited but nonetheless contributing some new knowledge (2001: 744). Indeed, the same may be said of qualitative studies of intersectionality which, as noted earlier, also tend to focus on one or a confined range of intersectional categories to the exclusion of others (see Parashar 1993; McCall 2005; and also, e.g., Austin 1989; Collins 1991; Crenshaw 1991; Eaton 1994; Jacobs 2005).

But another potentially valuable function of quantitative analysis in this context is that it enables the claims of intersectionality analysis themselves to be tested. In our study of women's access to legal aid, an intersectionality analysis would hypothesize that Indigenous women, NESB women, women with disability, older and younger women, and women living in regional and rural areas would be differently situated, both as between each other, and in comparison to non-Indigenous, ESB women without disability aged 21–59, and women living in metropolitan areas. If these hypothesized differences failed to emerge, it would suggest that focusing on the position of marginalized women was not particularly illuminating, as it would be necessary to explain women's experiences in attempting to access legal aid by reference to other dynamics. The remainder of the chapter turns to this issue.

Research findings

The study certainly did not find an absence of differences or different levels of disadvantage in women's access to legal aid.[10] On the contrary, we found that 'the incidence of legal aid refusals is not randomly distributed across the applicant population', but rather, legal aid eligibility criteria, the application process, the decision-making process, and the way refusals were communicated had 'systematically adverse impacts on certain groups of women' (Hunter *et al.* 2006: 210). But these were not always the same groups of women. Nor, indeed, were they always the groups of women we had made the initial subjects of our investigation.

Different forms and sources of group disadvantage were identified by different elements of our data. Our interview data from lawyers and other service-providers did suggest that women in the target groups experienced particular disadvantages in the legal aid system. This was partly due to the fact that these groups were flagged by the interviewers as being of particular concern to the research, but even when specifically asked whether, in their experience, there were other groups of women who experienced disadvantages in accessing legal aid, apart from the ones identified, respondents generally reiterated the target groups (or sub-groups thereof): NESB women, rural women, women with mental health problems, older women and Indigenous women. The only other groups mentioned by a few respondents were women with low incomes or inaccessible assets who were ineligible for legal aid but could not afford legal representation, women in prison,[11] and lesbians. These responses tended to suggest that interviewees believed independently in the salience of the target groups in relation to barriers to accessing legal aid, perhaps because they too operated within the same policy context with its entrenched categories of disadvantage as did LAQ and the project itself.

At they same time, interviewees did have a tendency to disaggregate the target groups. Thus, rather than talking about 'NESB women' or 'women with disability' as a whole, they often identified disadvantages for sub-groups within those groups. This was particularly the case in relation to barriers which might render women in the target groups less likely than others to apply for legal aid in the first place. So, for instance, newly arrived immigrants, women with intellectual disability, and rural women were said to lack awareness of their legal rights (Hunter *et al.* 2006: 85–6). In relation to recent immigrants, a migrant resource centre support worker identified African women from Ethiopia and Sudan as new clients experiencing high levels of domestic violence but lacking suitable translated materials about their legal rights and remedies. According to this interviewee, Filipino women had encountered a similar situation in an earlier period.

Refugees and women from particular immigrant communities, Indigenous women from remote communities, rural women (in relation to domestic violence) and some older women were said to be reluctant to invoke the legal system to deal with their problems (at 86–7). In relation to older women, for example, one service provider observed:

> Women who are married to veterans … are often victims of domestic violence or mental health episodes. The veterans often have no control over their actions and the woman stays with him due to emotional issues. They're reluctant to seek help. Women who are victims of elder abuse are often not even known. Avoidance of any form of assistance or support is rife. Women 'hide' in the community and think they are the only one this is happening to.[12]
>
> (Hunter *et al.* 2006: 87)

Rural women in the Toowoomba and Southport regions, NESB women in the Southport region, Indigenous women and women with mental health problems were said to have limited access to lawyers, due variously to limited service availability, geographical distance, and lawyers' failure to use interpreters, failure to offer culturally appropriate services, and unwillingness to give the necessary time to take proper instructions (at 89–91). According to two interviewees, for example:

> Some solicitors won't be comfortable with communicating with an Indigenous woman or a woman from another race. They probably think she wouldn't know what's best for her.

> The needs of women with mental health issues are consistently unmet due to service providers' lack of understanding. Those women need extra assistance which is not always forthcoming. For example, it can take a lot longer for a lawyer to get instructions.
>
> (Hunter *et al.* 2006: 90)

In addition, NESB women, women with intellectual disability or mental health problems, older women and women living in particular regional areas were said to have limited access to support services that would refer them to Legal Aid (at 89, 91–9).

In sum, these interview responses, while apparently accepting the relevance of the target groups as categories of disadvantage, analyzed barriers to access to legal aid in terms that were both narrower and broader than the relevant intersectional categories. Only some sub-groups of the target groups were said to experience certain disadvantages (e.g., women with particular kinds of disability, women in specific immigrant groups, women living in particular areas or in particular family circumstances). But disadvantages and barriers to access also transcended (sub-)groups and were shared by women across the various identity categories. Some members of most of the target groups were disadvantaged in similar ways. The experiences of women in the target groups thus both diverged and converged. They were differentiated within each category, but they were also collectively differentiated from the experiences of women outside the target categories. These interview responses thus did not present a straightforward intersectional account of women's disadvantage in accessing legal aid.

The women refused legal aid whom we interviewed were even less likely to link their experiences with the legal aid system directly with any 'intersectional' identity. Rather, when asked whether there were any factors that made it difficult when they applied for legal aid, they identified a range of personal and structural barriers, such as (in declining order of emphasis) transport and mobility difficulties, difficulties with the legal aid application form, their emotional state, language difficulties, and difficulties with child care (at 110–11). In the words of one woman: 'forms, childcare and stress. Just being there' (at 110). Nevertheless, these barriers were often indirectly related to identity categories. Difficulties with transport and mobility and childcare were particularly mentioned by rural and regional women (at 111); difficulties with the application form were particularly mentioned by Indigenous women (at 112); language difficulties were particularly mentioned by NESB women (at 114); although these difficulties were also experienced by some women in other groups. In relation to emotional well-being, however, some of the sources of stress related directly or indirectly to identity (chronic mental health conditions, lack of child care, poverty), but others related to the particular need for legal assistance (the impact of domestic violence, separation, or discrimination in the workplace on the woman's mental state) (at 115–16). As in the case of the lawyers and service providers, then, the difficulties identified by the women interviewed appeared to subtend rather than being straightforwardly aligned with particular target groups.

The qualitative components of the research – which were, necessarily, our only sources of information about barriers to and experiences of applying for legal aid – thus gestured towards the existence of some other dynamic, apart from intersectional experience, creating disadvantages in women's access to legal aid. This was brought into clear focus by our quantitative analysis of refusal files. There turned out to be relatively few statistical differences between women in the target groups and women who did not share any of the targeted characteristics in relation to refusals of legal aid and subsequent actions, and once more, such differences as did emerge were rarely confined to a single target group. For example, older women, NESB women, rural women and metropolitan women were most likely to be refused legal aid on the basis of the means test (i.e. their income and/or assets) (at 135); and NESB women, women with disability and older women tended to be more accepting of the institutional decision to refuse aid, and hence less likely to appeal against the decision (at 183–4), although women in other target groups were also deterred from appealing for a variety of reasons, resulting in an overall appeal rate of only 15 per cent (at 178).

Moving away from identity categories, the statistical analysis demonstrated a clear inequity between women living in the Brisbane metropolitan area and those living in the regional areas studied, which was related to the way legal aid budgets were distributed within LAQ. The annual grants budgets for LAQ regional offices were fixed by reference to historical relativities, regardless of changes in population or levels of demand in different regional areas over time. As a result, the approval rates for women in all areas of law in all of the regional offices examined were lower than the approval rates in the central office in Brisbane (at 79). The organizational budget distribution model thus systematically disadvantaged women living in non-metropolitan areas.

Inconsistencies and inequities also emerged between regional offices. Local decision-making cultures thrived in each of the offices, with little centralized oversight beyond the measurement of performance against a handful of key performance indicators (KPIs). Some of those local cultures proved to be hostile to women. For example, compared to the size of the local population, the Cairns office of LAQ (north-east Queensland) gave low levels of advice and received a low number of applications from women in relation to domestic violence, and it had the highest refusal rate for women in domestic violence applications. NESB and Indigenous women were particularly disadvantaged in this respect, with Indigenous women refused legal aid for domestic violence matters at a higher rate than Indigenous men (against a background of endemic violence against women in Indigenous communities). But more generally, the Cairns office refused legal aid to women in all target groups at higher than average rates (at 83). Similarly, the Southport office of LAQ (south-east Queensland) did not appear to be woman-friendly. Out of all the offices studied, it had the highest refusal rates for women for family and anti-discrimination law matters, and it also had high rates of refusal for NESB women and women with disability in domestic violence matters (at 84). Thus, geographical location was a particular disadvantaging factor for women living in these areas by virtue of the shortcomings of the local Legal Aid office.

Refusals of legal aid for all women were, however, most prominently associated with the type of matter raised in the application. Existing eligibility tests and guidelines had systematically adverse impacts on particular kinds of applications, regardless of the identity characteristics of the applicant. So, for example, in family law, women making applications to secure their children's residence and regulate the other party's contact regime following separation routinely fell outside the guidelines specifying that aid would only be granted where there was a 'substantial dispute' between the parties (at 139). Often, in these situations, there had been a history of violence in the relationship and/or disrupted and disruptive contact, and the woman was seeking a court order so as to provide more stable and predictable arrangements for herself and the children. However, the other party might deny that there was any problem or any need for court orders, and so the dispute would be classified as not 'substantial' and aid would be refused (see also Rendell *et al.* 2002: 70). Similarly, women seeking court orders for no contact between the children and their father, due to fears of violence, child abuse or abduction, were caught by the guideline that required legal aid applicants to provide independent evidence of good reasons for denial of contact (Hunter *et al.* 2006: 140). Given the insidious nature of domestic violence, such evidence would not always be available. This evidential hurdle was compounded by the fact that the requirement for independent evidence was not specified on the legal aid application form, and was in any event interpreted differently by different grants officers (at 141). Consequently, there was a substantial number of refusals of aid due to failure to provide independent evidence.

Women responding to (and seeking to resist) court applications for contact brought by the other party found themselves entangled in a particular element of the legal aid merit test which required that the benefit of granting aid or the detriment to the applicant if aid was not granted must justify the legal costs involved 'having regard to other demands for legal aid on the office'. In these cases, grants officers tended to reason that the court would inevitably grant some form of contact to the father, and the benefit to the mother of achieving her preferred contact regime as opposed to what the father wanted was too slight to justify a grant of aid (at 144–5).

Our follow-up interviews found that negative outcomes occurred in the majority of family law cases in which aid was refused (at 200). That is, either an unsatisfactory status quo was maintained, the situation became worse, or court orders were made to the woman's detriment. For example one Indigenous woman with a white ex-husband:

> initially had residence of her children but lost it after she self-represented in court. The other party was also self-represented, but had more financial resources and previous experience in army prosecutions. She now saw her children every 2–8 weeks and paid significant child maintenance.
>
> (Hunter *et al.* 2006: 203)

And an NESB woman 'had a contact order in place but felt vulnerable being alone and given the past history of domestic violence. She was seeking more certainty in contact times but was unable to achieve that outcome' (at 204).

This was the area of law in which women most needed a lawyer in order to achieve a positive outcome, but in the absence of legal aid, a lawyer was usually unaffordable, and women either tried to represent themselves, calling on whatever other limited forms of support and assistance they could muster, or were simply unable to pursue court orders (at 193–4, 202–4). Some women did manage to raise the money to brief a private lawyer, but while they might then have achieved a more satisfactory outcome to their court proceedings, they also found themselves impoverished or saddled with long-term debt as a result (at 203).

In domestic violence cases, women responding to protection order applications found themselves particularly disadvantaged by legal aid eligibility rules. The legal aid merit test and priorities for domestic violence cases understandably favoured applicants for protection orders. However the trend had emerged of abusive men applying for protection orders for themselves, as a form of retaliation or continued abuse against their (ex-)partners, relying on some kind of defensive violence on the woman's part as a basis for the order. Sometimes these were cross-applications to a woman's primary application, and sometimes they were applications in circumstances where the woman already had an order in her favour. In these cases, the distinction between target and perpetrator of violence did not map onto the positions of applicant for and respondent to a protection order. Rather, the perpetrator was the applicant and the target the respondent. Nevertheless, women in this position were routinely denied legal aid by virtue of their role as respondent, regardless of the fact that an order against them would perpetuate abuse and diminish their safety, by portraying them as equally violent and rendering their own order less meaningful and effective (at 147–8). On the other hand, women refused aid for domestic violence matters were most likely to achieve a positive outcome to their case in any event (at 200). It appeared that in the absence of legal representation, other court support services such as police and domestic violence workers were available to fill the gap, suggesting that there could be greater coordination between Legal Aid and court support programmes, and more effective targeting of legal aid, in this area.

Anti-discrimination cases formed only a very small proportion of legal aid applications, resulting in a total of only nine anti-discrimination files in our refusal sample. While it is difficult to generalize from this small number, the files were rich in detail, and follow-up interviews with the applicants elicited stories of lengthy struggles for justice. Because grants officers had relatively limited experience with anti-discrimination applications, it appeared that several of the files had been assessed – and refused aid – using the wrong criteria (at 150). In addition, because anti-discrimination applicants were most likely to have been or still be in employment, they were most likely to fail the means test (at 134–5). The means test operated on a sliding scale depending upon the applicant's income and assets, whether they were single or living with a partner, and their number of dependents. At the lowest threshold (and assuming they also passed the merit test), applicants were entitled to legal representation free of charge. Above that, they were assessed to pay a contribution towards the cost of representation, up to a second threshold, beyond which they were not eligible for legal aid. Within the contribution band, the applicant would only receive aid if the amount of contribution assessed was lower than the level of the grant available. Proceedings were divided into stages, with fixed, lump-sum grants payable to the recipient's legal representative at stages prior to the final trial of the matter (at which point a fixed, daily rate was paid). In anti-discrimination proceedings, the first two stages, involving preparing and lodging an anti-discrimination complaint, and representing the client at a conciliation conference, attracted quite low grants, whereas if the matter did not settle at that stage, the final proceedings could be lengthy and expensive. Nevertheless, some of the applicants were refused aid because the level of contribution they were assessed to pay exceeded the amount of a first or second stage grant. They were not encouraged or advised to re-apply if their matter did not settle and needed to proceed to trial (at 159–60).

All of the anti-discrimination applicants refused legal aid experienced a negative outcome to their case – they either withdrew their complaint or agreed to a settlement they considered unsatisfactory (at 204), in some cases after pursuing the matter for a considerable period at enormous personal and/or financial cost:

> One entered conciliation without a lawyer, but the respondent was represented by a lawyer whom she found to be rude and intimidating. She then borrowed $10,000 and hired her own lawyer. Negotiations dragged on for two and a half years, by which time her health was suffering. She finally accepted a settlement offer in the interests of her health. The settlement was much higher than the respondent's initial offer, but had cost her $12,000 in legal fees.

> [A] woman who represented herself did so because she was a single mother, was not currently working, and would have had to sell her house in order to pay the legal fees. She faced solicitors on the other side who bullied her and tried to wear her down with attrition tactics. The case dragged on for three years, and after this time, her health was clearly suffering. Eventually she was offered a settlement to which she agreed because she was unable to continue any longer. She had wanted to achieve a change of policy and culture in the organization for the benefit of future women employees, but was unable to do so.

> (Hunter *et al.* 2006: 204–5)

Finally, the statistical analysis revealed some overriding patterns among the refusal files that affected all or the majority of the women concerned, regardless of characteristics, geographical location, or type of matter. Two-thirds of the women refused legal aid had filled out the legal aid application form themselves, without assistance from a professional adviser (at 106). If someone applies for legal aid through a lawyer who is one of LAQ's 'preferred suppliers', the lawyer completes a short version of the form, fills out a checklist certifying the applicant's eligibility under the various tests and guidelines, and submits it electronically to LAQ, where it will be lightly scrutinized by a grants officer before aid is (usually) granted. Applicants may also seek assistance to complete the application form from a community legal centre or from an LAQ advice solicitor or counter staff, although such assistance appeared to be relatively infrequently available in practice (at 108). Grants officers readily agreed that people who completed the application form without assistance were likely to have a lower success rate, because they either failed to complete the form appropriately, or failed to provide additional information required (such as bank statements or tax returns, proof of receipt of welfare benefits, or other supporting documentation) (at 109–0).

Technically, if a grants officer received an incomplete application, they could ask the applicant to provide the further information, and then make their decision once the application was complete. But at the same time, one of the KPIs to which grants officers were subject was a time standard of five days to decide legal aid applications. If the officer attempted to contact the applicant (and perhaps had some difficulty doing so) and then waited for the additional information to arrive, their performance against the five-day KPI would be compromised. So they had developed the practice of refusing the application (thereby making a decision within five days), but advising the applicant that they should provide further specified information and resubmit the application (at 153). Our statistical data indicated, however, that few women did provide the further information requested in this way (at 152), and our follow-up interviews indicated that this was generally because women did not understand the refusal letter (at 173). These letters were expressed in very formal, complex and forbidding language, difficult sometimes even for the researchers to comprehend. The women concerned simply grasped that their application had been rejected, and gave up on legal aid.

Another institutional factor resulting in what we could only describe as 'arbitrary, opaque and inconsistent decision making' over time (at 172) was LAQ's method of micro-budget management, colloquially known as 'the tap [being] turned on and off'. Performance against budget targets, overall and by individual office, was monitored on a monthly basis. If the overall budget or an individual office budget was tracking above target, a directive would be issued to tighten spending. Conversely, if the overall budget was tracking below target, a directive would be issued to spend more. Thus, in any given month, in any given office, depending on the latest directive, decisions on grant applications would be made that would not have been made on the same application last month, or would not be made in the same way next month. This had a particular effect in family law cases, as guidelines such as whether there was a 'substantial' dispute could be interpreted more widely or narrowly depending on whether the tap was turned on or off (at 168), but it also applied more widely to the application of the various elements of the merit test, and even to the supposedly objective operation of the means test.

This phenomenon bore a relationship to the other overriding statistical pattern in the refusal files, which was that 87 per cent of the women refused legal aid in the files we examined had a history of previous and/or subsequent dealings with LAQ, in seeking legal advice and/or applying for legal aid (at 126). Neither were these modest histories of encounters with the organization. These women had an average of 4.22 dealings with LAQ prior to the refused application we examined, and 2.2 dealings between the time of that application and the time we read the file, one to three years later (at 126). In 93 per cent of cases, these dealings concerned family law issues, and in 35 per cent they also concerned domestic violence issues (at 127). *All* of the NESB women had a history of dealings with LAQ concerning family law, and 92 per cent of them also had a history of dealings in relation to domestic violence (at 129).

This pattern can be explained by reference to a series of legal needs studies that have been undertaken in the UK in recent years (Genn 1999; Genn and Paterson 2001; Pleasence *et al.* 2004; Pleasence *et al.* 2006). These studies have involved large-scale population surveys asking about people's recent experience of non-criminal 'justiciable events' (that is, events that could have triggered civil legal action), and their actual response to those events. The studies have consistently found that some groups of people (who might broadly be categorized as 'socially excluded' (see, e.g., Pleasence *et al.* 2004: 9, 106)) tend to experience a complex web of related and concurrent legal problems, and that one frequently occurring problem 'cluster' consists of family law and domestic violence problems. Our research suggests that NESB women are especially vulnerable to this problem cluster, but it also suggests that this problem cluster may be more generally associated with further problems of lack of access to legal advice and assistance.

Interestingly, though, not all of the women's previous and subsequent encounters with LAQ had been unsuccessful. Indeed, their previous and subsequent applications for legal aid had been more often successful than unsuccessful (at 128). So they were not making repeated, fruitless applications, but rather applying now, or subsequently, because they had applied in the past and been successful, albeit in obtaining a limited grant of aid. This seems to illustrate how the phenomenon of the tap being turned on and off worked in individual cases. But, most importantly, the limited grants of aid obtained previously had obviously not solved these women's legal problems. So they appeared to have become stuck in a cycle of repeated returns, attempting to make headway, with legal aid sometimes provided and sometimes not, and problems sometimes abating and sometimes compounding, but never, quite, going away.

It was also clear that LAQ was neither aware of nor concerned about this pattern of engagement. When people sought advice from LAQ or applied for legal aid, their history was checked only to the extent that it was 'relevant', which for most grants officers was confined to previous files dealing with the same type of matter (at 130). Only one of the grants officers interviewed considered family law and domestic violence issues to be relevant to each other (at 130). And when an applicant's history was checked, it was with an eye to factors such as how long the matter had been going, the cost so far, whether the same dispute had been raised previously, when the most recent orders had been made, and recidivism, with the aim of weeding out unmeritorious applications (at 130). There was no notion that repeated advice-seeking and applications might indicate that the applicant was experiencing some kind of major problem, or that the legal aid system might be failing these applicants. At the time of the research, there was a proposal to establish a new civil law scheme to assist vulnerable clients, identified as those experiencing multiple problems associated with domestic violence. But the proposed assistance was to consist only of advice, 'minor assistance' (help with filling out forms, writing letters, etc), and referrals to other support services (at 131). Such assistance would be unlikely to resolve the client's legal problems or prevent them from escalating.

In summary, then, our qualitative and quantitative research data combined to suggest that thinking in terms of intersectional categories was not the most useful way of analysing women's disadvantage in access to legal aid. While there did appear to be some relationship between disadvantage and identity, the overwhelming dynamic creating disadvantage in access to legal aid was institutional: legal aid eligibility tests and guidelines, the way that grants were structured, and LAQ's policies and practices – its application procedures, KPIs, decision making cultures, budget management processes, and failures of communication. Even treatment that might appear from the perspective of individual applicants to be arbitrary had a structural basis (the tap turned on and off). Asking a question more detailed than one of simple gender difference in access to legal aid certainly resulted in a more complex answer, but it was not the kind of complexity we expected. LAQ's failures of recognition had less to do with identity categories than with its inability to see around corners of its own construction.[13]

Conclusion

In Leslie McCall's 'intercategorical' study of wage inequalities, having 'arrived at the complex outcome that no single dimension of overall inequality can adequately describe the full structure of multiple, intersecting, and conflicting dimensions of inequality', she concluded that different contexts reveal different configurations of inequality, and it is the nature and extent of such differences and inequalities that need to be explored (2005: 1791). Our own intercategorical research ultimately arrived at the same point. Disadvantage in access to legal aid did not result from, nor could it be mapped onto, pre-determined identity categories, but rather was constructed within the particular institutional context of the legal aid system. That context sometimes brought particular elements of identity to the fore, but most often created its own categories of exclusion: those who lacked access to a lawyer to make a legal aid application; those whose financial position and/or legal problems did not fit legal aid guidelines and eligibility tests (as interpreted) but who nevertheless needed some form of legal intervention and could not afford to pay for their own representation; and those whose cluster of domestic violence and family law problems could not be solved by a limited grant of legal aid. These were the women who were 'most disadvantaged' in – and *by* – the legal aid system, and who conversely had the greatest need for legal assistance. Their experience in applying for legal aid was crucially shaped by institutional policies and practices. In order to overcome their disadvantage, therefore, it would be necessary not to redistribute resources so as to empower any particular group/s of women, but directly to confront and change those policies and practices of exclusion.[14]

Our research adds to the literature which suggests that paying attention to context, institutional dynamics and local practices is a more fruitful starting point for analysing processes of subordination than an intersectional approach which explores experience in categorical terms. It is arguable that this kind of conclusion is likely to result from any intercategorical study. Intersectionality analysis has yielded many valuable insights by looking at intersectional identities one at a time. But once we begin to look at several categories alongside each other, to aggregate and compare experiences between categories, localized similarities and internal differences will inevitably emerge. This is emphatically *not* to say that all oppressions are essentially the same – very clearly they are not. But it is to say that the question of whether experiences are shared or not, and the particular sources and dynamics of exclusion and subordination, need to be explored in a range of institutional contexts. This represents a substantial field of investigation beyond intersectionality.

Acknowledgements

The research on which this chapter is based was funded by an Australian Research Council Linkage grant, with Legal Aid Queensland as the Industry Partner. We would like to thank the ARC and the LAQ Board for their financial support, our collaborator Louise Whitaker, our researchers Jane Bathgate and Alicia Svensson, all those who agreed to be interviewed and to have their files read for the project, and the two reviewers who provided challenging comments on an earlier draft of the chapter. The views expressed in the chapter are those of the authors alone.

Bibliography

Addario, L. and National Association of Women and the Law (1998) *Getting a Foot in the Door: Women, Civil Legal Aid and Access to Justice*, Ottawa: Status of Women Canada.

Alcorso, C. (1991) *Non-English Speaking Background Immigrant Women in the Workforce*, Wollongong: Centre for Multicultural Studies.

Alcorso, C. and Harrison, G. (1993) *Blue Collar and Beyond: The Experiences of Non-English Speaking Background Women in the Australian Labour Force*, Canberra: AGPS.

Alcorso, C. and Schofield, T. (1991) *The National Non-English Speaking Background Women's Health Strategy*, Canberra: AGPS.

Assafiri, H. and Dimopoulos, M. (1995) 'The legal system's treatment of NESB women victims of male violence', *Criminology Australia*, 6: 20–2.

Austin, R. (1989) 'Sapphire bound!', *Wisconsin Law Review*, 1989: 539–78.

Australian Law Reform Commission (1994) *Report No 69, Part I – Equality Before the Law: Justice for Women*, Sydney: Australian Law Reform Commission.

Behrendt, L. (1993) 'Aboriginal women and the white lies of the feminist movement: implications for Aboriginal women in rights discourse', *Australian Feminist Law Journal*, 1: 27–44.

Brewin, A. (2004) *Legal Aid Denied: Women and the Cuts to Legal Services in BC*, Vancouver Canadian Centre for Policy Alternatives.

Collins, P.H. (1991) *Black Feminist Thought: Knowledge, Consciousness and the Politics of Empowerment*, New York: Routledge.

Commonwealth Attorney-General and Minister for Justice (1995) *The Justice Statement*, Canberra: AGPS.

Crenshaw, K.W. (1991) 'A Black feminist critique of antidiscrimination law and politics', in D. Kairys (ed.) *The Politics of Law: A Progressive Critique*, New York: Pantheon.

Domestic Violence and Incest Resource Centre (1996) *Not the Same: Conference Proceedings and a Strategy on Domestic Violence and Sexual Assault for Non-English Speaking Background Women*, Melbourne: Domestic Violence and Incest Resource Centre.

Easteal, P. (1996) *Shattered Dreams: Marital Violence Against Overseas-born Women in Australia*, Canberra: AGPS.

Eaton, M. (1994) 'Abuse by any other name: feminism, difference, and intralesbian violence', in M.A. Fineman and R. Mykitiuk (eds) *The Public Nature of Private Violence: The Discovery of Domestic Abuse*, New York: Routledge.

Genn, H. (1999) *Paths to Justice: What People Do and Think About Going to Law*, Oxford: Hart Publishing.

Genn, H. and Paterson, A. (2001) *Paths to Justice Scotland: What People in Scotland Think and Do About Going to Law*, Oxford: Hart Publishing.

Graycar, R. and Morgan, J. (1995) 'Disabling citizenship: civil death for women in the 1990s', *Adelaide Law Review*, 17: 49–76.

Grillo, T. (1995) 'Anti-essentialism and intersectionality: tools to dismantle the master's house', *Berkeley Women's Law Journal*, 10: 16–30.

Halley, J. (2006) *Split Decisions: How and Why to Take a Break from Feminism*, Princeton, NJ: Princeton University Press.

Hernandez, T.K. (2006) 'A critical race feminism empirical research project: sexual harassment and the internal complaints black box', *UC Davis Law Review*, 39: 1235–304.

Huggins, J. (1994) 'A contemporary view of Aboriginal women's relationship to the white women's movement', in N. Grieve and A. Burns (eds) *Australian Women: Contemporary Feminist Thought*, Melbourne: Oxford University Press.

Hunter, R., De Simone, T. and Whitaker, L., with Bathgate, J. and Svensson, A. (2006) *Women and Legal Aid: Identifying Disadvantage – Final Report*, Brisbane: Griffith University and Legal Aid Queensland. Online. Available HTTP: <http://www.griffith.edu.au/centre/slrc>.

Hutchinson, D.L. (2001) 'Identity crisis: "intersectionality", "multidimensionality", and the development of an adequate theory of subordination', *Michigan Journal of Race and Law*, 6: 285–317.

Jacobs, B. (2005) 'Gender discrimination under the Indian Act: Bill C-31 and First Nations women', in G. MacDonald, R.L. Osborne and C.C. Smith (eds) *Feminism, Law, Inclusion: Intersectionality in Action*, Toronto: Sumach Press.

Johnson, R. (2005) 'Gender, race, class and sexual orientation: theorizing the intersections', in G. MacDonald, R.L. Osborne and C.C. Smith (eds) *Feminism, Law, Inclusion: Intersectionality in Action*, Toronto: Sumach Press.

Junor, A. (1994) *Beyond Pool Stirring: Non English Speaking Background Women and Labour Market Programs*, Sydney: Association of Non English Speaking Background Women of Australia.

Keys Young (1994) *Quarter Way to Equal: A Report on Barriers to Access to Legal Services for Migrant Women*, Sydney: Women's Legal Resources Centre.

Mason, C. (1993) *Mental Health Issues for Women from Non-English Speaking Backgrounds*, Canberra: Commonwealth-State Council on Non-English Speaking Background Women's Issues.

McCall, L. (2005) 'The complexity of intersectionality', *Signs: Journal of Women in Culture*, 30: 1771–800.

Merritt, D.J. (2001) 'Constructing identity in law and social science', *Journal of Contemporary Legal Issues*, 11: 731–45.

Milczarek-Desai, S. (2005) '(Re)locating other/third world women: an alternative approach to *Santa Clara Pueblo v. Martinez*'s construction of gender, culture and identity', *UCLA Women's Law Journal*, 13: 235–91.

Moorhead, R. and Pleasence, P. (2003) 'Access to justice after universalism: introduction', *Journal of Law and Society*, 30: 1–10.

Moreton-Robinson, A. (2000) *Talkin' Up to the White Woman: Indigenous Women and Feminism*, Brisbane: University of Queensland Press.

Mossman, M.J. (1990) '"Shoulder to shoulder": gender and access to justice', *Windsor Yearbook of Access to Justice*, 10: 351–63.

Mossman, M.J.(1993) 'Gender equality and legal aid services: a research agenda for institutional change', *Sydney Law Review*, 15: 30–58.

Mossman, M.J. (1994) 'Gender equality, family law and access to justice', *International Journal of Law and the Family*, 8: 357–73.

New Zealand Law Commission (1999) *Women's Access to Legal Services*, Wellington: Law Commission.

Office of Legal Aid and Family Services (1994) *Gender Bias in Litigation Legal Aid*, Canberra: Commonwealth Attorney-General's Department.

O'Shane, P. (1976) 'Is there any relevance in the women's movement for Aboriginal women?', *Refractory Girl*, 12: 31–4.

Parashar, A. (1993) 'Essentialism or pluralism: the future of legal feminism', *Canadian Journal of Women and the Law*, 6: 328–48.

Pleasence, P., Buck, A., Balmer, N., O'Grady, A., Genn, H. and Smith, M. (2004) *Causes of Action: Civil Law and Social Justice*, Norwich: TSO.

Pleasence, P., with Balmer, N. and Buck, A. (2006) *Causes of Action: Civil Law and Social Justice,* 2nd edn, Norwich: TSO.

Rendell, K., Rathus, Z. and Lynch, A. for the Abuse Free Contact Group (2002) *An Unacceptable Risk: A Report on Child Contact Arrangements Where There is Violence in the Family*, Brisbane: Women's Legal Service.

Staunces, D. (2003) 'Where have all the subjects gone? Bringing together the concepts of intersectionality and subjectification', *NORA: Nordic Journal of Women's Studies*, 11: 101–10.

Stephens, J. and Bertone, S. (1995) *Manufacturing Uncertainty: Non-English-Speaking Background Women and Training*, Canberra: AGPS.

VandenHeuvel, A. and Wooden, M. (1996) *Non-English-Speaking-Background Immigrant Women and Part-Time Work*, Canberra: AGPS.

Women's Legal Aid (2005) *Gender Equity Report 2005: A Profile of Women and Legal Aid Queensland*, Brisbane: Legal Aid Queensland.

Yeatman, A. (1992) *NESB Migrant Women and Award Restructuring: A Case Study of the Clothing Industry*, Canberra: AGPS.

Yuval-Davis, N. (2006) 'Intersectionality and feminist politics', *European Journal of Women's Studies*, 13: 193–209.

Table of cases

Notes

1 The Australian financial year runs from 1 July to 30 June, hence annual figures reported as, e.g., 1992/93 refer to the financial year 1 July 1992–30 June 1993.

2 (1992) 177 CLR 292.

3 E.g., *McOwan and McOwan* (1994) FLC 92-451; *T* v. *S* (2001) 28 Fam LR 342; *In the Marriage of S* (1997) 22 Fam LR 112. In *Re JTT; ex parte Victoria Legal Aid* [1998] HCA 44, the High Court held that the Family Court had no power to order the provision of legal aid to any party in family law proceedings.

4 Roughly equivalent to £48 million.

5 The area covered by this term is known as 'private' family law in the UK. In practice, it meant disputes over residence and contact arrangements for children following their parents' separation, as legal aid was not available for divorce proceedings and was only available for property proceedings in extremely limited circumstances.

6 Barriers for lesbians include ignorance and homophobia on the part of police and court staff in the context of domestic violence, the fact that family law jurisprudence may be less well developed or possibly adverse to their claims, and general difficulties with finding empathetic legal representatives.

7 In fact, while we assumed that this question would be used to identify applicants of non-English-speaking background, this turned out not to be the case. After the project commenced and we requested historical application and refusal statistics from LAQ, we discovered that responses to this particular question on the application form were not entered into LAQ's database. Rather, LAQ identified 'non-English-speaking background' by reference to the question about country of birth, combined with its own categorization of 'English-speaking' and 'non-English-speaking' countries. This, of course, was a far from reliable indicator, for example in the case of people born in South Africa, or who were not members of the ethnic majority in their country of birth, such as Maori in New Zealand.

8 This very low number may be attributable to the fact that we were dealing with a population of women who had both applied for, and been refused, legal aid. This population was dominated by women not falling into one of the target groups, so that we had to over-sample from the target groups in order to obtain sufficient numbers of files in each category to enable meaningful statistical comparisons. Women with more than one targeted characteristic may not have applied for legal aid in the first place, for the reasons suggested later in the text. If they did apply, it appears that their applications were likely to be successful.

9 For example Hernandez (2006). Hernandez studied the use of internal complaint procedures for sexual harassment by 'White Women' and 'Women of Color'. Although she acknowledged that 'Women of Color' are not a homogeneous group, the small number of her survey respondents made it necessary for non-white women to be statistically analysed as a single category. Despite these various theoretical and methodological problems, the study showed that 'Women of Color' were significantly less likely than 'White Women' to use internal complaint procedures. This, in turn, had serious repercussions, given anti-discrimination case law requiring employees to invoke internal procedures before filing complaints with external bodies or bringing court proceedings. This doctrine was thus shown to have a systematically adverse impact on the ability of 'Women of Color' to obtain remedies for sexual harassment.

10 For the full report of the study, see Hunter *et al.* (2006).

11 We did, in fact, early on explore the possibility of including women in prison in our research, but the numbers of such women applying for and being refused legal aid in Queensland in the areas of law on which we were focusing were so tiny that we decided not to to attempt to investigate this group.

12 Note that interviewees were guaranteed confidentiality so individual sources of quotations cannot be identified. Interview transcription was also done in summary form rather than verbatim, so that 'quotations' represent the key points made by interviewees rather than their precise words.

13 This phrase is adapted from Halley (2006: 321), although she uses it in a different context to talk about the limitations of US legal feminism.

14 Our report to LAQ recommended a number of changes to existing practices and policies in relation to community education and outreach, the legal aid application process, eligibility criteria and their application, the refusal and review process, and client service (see Hunter *et al.* 2006: Ch. 10). LAQ is currently in the process of addressing these recommendations, for example letters and factsheets have been rewritten in plain English, and revision of the legal aid application form is under way.

Chapter 7

Intersectionality

Traumatic impressions

Emily Grabham

Introduction

Introduced as a method of integrating anti-essentialist perspectives into feminist perspectives on law, intersectionality has now achieved a wide degree of currency within legal and policy discourses on equality. In this chapter I interrogate intersectionality for its effects as a technique of governance. I draw on Wendy Brown's analysis of rights claims in *States of Injury* to argue that intersectionality cannot challenge law's disciplinary constructions of identity and that it in fact functions as an 'anatomy of detail' which supports law's propensity to classify. Moving away from the regulatory effects of intersectionality within law, I aim to reframe my understanding of the liberal subject's experience of inequalities through the cultural functions of trauma (Cvetkovich, 2003), and the role of impressions in connecting questions of justice with emotional and physical encounters (Ahmed, 2004). Viewing discrimination claims as expressions/impressions of trauma may, paradoxically, give us new ways of viewing complex inequalities, shifting the focus of intersectionality away from disciplinary identity categories and towards the cultural circulation of emotions.

Intersectionality

Intersectional analysis grew from critiques in the 1980s and 1990s which fundamentally challenged the arrangement of feminist theory and praxis around white women's experiences and priorities (see for example, Harris, 1990; Williams, 1991). Like many other academic methods of analysis, intersectionality responds to political work that was, and is, taking place within activist spheres, as people engaged in activism around race, gender, disability and poverty attempt to address, and strategise around, complex forms of inequality. An early example was the work of the Combahee River Collective, which used a sophisticated form of systems theory to integrate into black feminist scholarship an understanding of class, gender and sexuality (see Cooper, 2004: 44). More recent examples of activist projects which explicitly foreground anti-essentialist approaches include the Safra Project in the United Kingdom, which provides advice and support for lesbians, trans women and bisexual women who identify either culturally or religiously as Muslim and the Sylvia Rivera Law Project (SRLP), based in New York, which campaigns around trans issues.[1]

Intersectionality is not, therefore, reducible to an academic, or even legal framework, but describes a much broader field of practice and analysis engaged in critiquing hierarchical and categorical concepts of oppression (see, for example, MacDonald *et al.* 2005). Importantly, critical race, LatCrit and feminist scholars have also used it to interrogate academic environments. Angela Harris has written about working to maintain an analysis of heteronormativity within the field of critical race studies (Harris, 1999), whilst Francisco Valdes has argued for an analytics of queer interconnectivity to work with and through intersections of sex and race within sexual minority scholarship (Valdes, 1995). This work reminds scholars of the practical applications of intersectionality theory within the academy.

In the legal arena, the work of Kimberlé Crenshaw, specifically her 1989 piece 'Demarginalizing the Intersection of Race and Sex: A Black Feminist Critique of Antidiscrimination Doctrine, Feminist Theory and Antiracist Politics', has been instrumental in turning a critical gaze onto the categorising function of equality and anti-discrimination laws and policies (Crenshaw, 1989). As Crenshaw argued in that article, maintaining a focus on the 'archetypal' female or Black legal claimant leads to the wholesale exclusion of people who exist at the intersections of these subject positions: Black women. Following Crenshaw, many legal scholars and activists have used an analytics of intersectionality to deconstruct essentialist identity positions in favour of focusing on the 'intersections' – the spaces where subjects are more than their categorisations as women or Black. The motivation for such a move within feminist and queer legal scholarship is to challenge the grounding of legal and political claims in 'unified' notions of identity and to trace the complex forms of inequalities that get lost in traditional categorical analysis (see, for example, Duclos, 1993; Hutchinson, 1997). In this way, intersectionality provides a vitally important vehicle for anti-essentialist work in the field of feminist legal theory and practice.

Nevertheless, there have been problems with the development and application of intersectionality analysis. According to Davina Cooper, one significant issue is how to conceive the intersection (Cooper, 2004: 48). What does the intersection look like and what are its effects? Intersectionality implies a model through which it would be possible to exercise more power in one aspect of one's identity than in another. It might be possible to say that an individual is privileged by her ethnicity and subordinated by her gender, for example. But this would require a polarised analysis that would view the individual either at the midpoint of different social positions, or as see-sawing between them (ibid). Social location is lived in much more complex ways than this, but the metaphor of the intersection appears too static to respond to such complexities.

For her part, Joanne Conaghan argues in this collection that intersectionality has reached the limits of its potential for the feminist project in law (Conaghan, this volume). In her opinion, intersectionality does not have a sufficiently nuanced vision of the complexities of inequality, and this is partly because it prioritises a focus on the individual and on identity formation, and does not adequately address social processes and relations (ibid). She argues that earlier work in socialist/materialist feminism was more successful in this regard. As she puts it:

> ... intersectionality is rather limited in its theory-producing power. In particular, while it acts as an aid to the excavation of inequality experiences at a local level, it tells us little about the wider context in which such experiences are produced, mediated and expressed
>
> (ibid: 28).

Applying this mode of analysis leaves scholars with very few strategies for countering 'law's repressive, inegalitarian effects', leading many to reference intersectionality merely as an 'exhortation' to pay attention to the complexities of identity (ibid). Furthermore, as Conaghan points out, intersectionality has an investment in the representative function in law. It implies that requiring the law to represent complex inequalities more effectively is in itself a politically powerful strategy (ibid).

Whilst there are clearly many different ways in which the term can be used, I refer to intersectionality as an approach within law which aims (1) to challenge or destabilise traditional legal categories of identity and their necessary separation in law, and (2) to take account of varied and complex types of inequalities and the ways in which they are experienced by subjects who do not 'fit into' those categories. There have been many analyses, and applications of, intersectionality outside the legal arena and I will not be addressing these in this chapter (see, for example, Yuval-Davis, 2006). There is a perception that intersectionality has become less relevant in fields outside of law: that it was useful for a period but has given way to less instrumentalist modes of analysis. It is also possible to argue that intersectionality only becomes relevant if you are not already addressing the complex nature of inequalities. For example, Dean Spade points out that work by the Sylvia Rivera Law Project on trans people and prisons brings together analysis of, and activist responses to, the prison-industrial complex, gender discrimination and poverty, but SRLP activists have not felt the need to name this work as specifically intersectional.[2] All of these points have aided my thinking in this area.

In this chapter, I use a case study from my time in practice as a discrimination lawyer to think through some of the questions around intersectionality and rights claims arising from Wendy Brown's influential critique in her 1995 book *States of Injury* (Brown, 1995). Briefly put, Brown argues that identity claims, and particularly legal rights claims, are based on an investment in powerlessness and injury which holds very little scope for political action. Tracing the effects of such investments, she argues instead for a politics based on "I want this for us" rather than "I am". One of the aims of this chapter is to use Brown's analysis of identity politics to address some of the problems with the ways in which intersectionality analysis has been mobilised within feminist legal theory and practice.

The next section sets out my case study. In the third section, I will discuss Brown's analysis of identity politics in more detail and use it to raise some questions about intersectionality. In particular, following Brown's analysis, I am sceptical about the possibility of using intersectional arguments within law to 'represent' complex identities and contest complex inequalities. Within the disciplinary system of law, focusing on the 'intersections' between categories merely leads to the production of 'more' categories, thereby supporting the law's propensity to classify. Whilst not coming to any conclusion on the question of engaging with law in this area, I move instead to a reconsideration of Brown's concepts of 'pain' and 'injury'. I argue that by investigating 'trauma' as the mundane experience of subjects under liberalism, it is possible to develop a picture of intersectionality which does not rely on governmentally produced identity categories. Part of this re-framing of intersectionality requires moving away from an idea of rights claims as being necessarily institutional projects. Some examples of discrimination law litigation can be viewed in extra-institutional terms, as instances of subjects making an impression on the law: bringing to the law their experiences of the powerful, distributive functions of emotions. By focusing on impressions in this way, it is, arguably, possible to uncover forms of inequality that are organised out of more disciplinary accounts of intersectionality.

Case study: M.

After qualifying as a solicitor in 2002, I worked for a short time as a legal advisor for the London-based organisation Lesbian and Gay Employment Rights (otherwise known as LAGER) in 2003. LAGER was set up in the 1970s as a collective, the aim of which was to advise and represent lesbians and gay men on employment-related disputes, including discrimination.[3] For most of the time that I was working for LAGER, UK legislation addressing sexual orientation discrimination in the workplace had not yet come into force. Although much of our work was related not to discrimination but to wages claims or unfair dismissal, nevertheless we tried to find legal routes around the lack of discrimination legislation, and this often involved making human rights arguments or trying to establish other forms of new legal points on behalf of our clients. We were assisted in this by a number of barristers who were willing to provide tribunal representation and expert advice for free.

I began at LAGER with a background in corporate law, having trained in employment litigation from the employer's perspective. However, prior to training as a solicitor I had studied feminist legal theory, and intersectionality in particular, for my LLM degree in Canada. When I began work at LAGER, I wanted to find ways, wherever possible, of putting into practice the feminist anti-essentialist work I had come across in Canada. This took many forms: it related to the ways that we conducted ourselves as 'lawyers', but it also related to the arguments we used on behalf of clients and the way we constructed cases. When M. contacted LAGER, she was also aware of the theoretical work on intersectionality, and we agreed that we would try to construct her claim as an intersectional claim.

M. is a trans woman and out lesbian, of middle-class white British background, who came to LAGER having experienced discrimination[4] at work spanning sexism, transphobia and homophobia. The discrimination consisted of overtly transphobic comments by colleagues, belittling references to M. (a senior manager) being a 'girl', and a consistent and unexplained failure, over a period of years, to promote M. despite qualifications and performance that colleagues in other organisations had recognised as being excellent. In one situation, a colleague referred to 'uncovering' M.'s trans status by saying to her: 'It's your big hands and feet that give you away'. M. later said:

> I remember what I thought about that comment was that it was so gross, it offended so many things in one easy go … And I was thinking – what to say? So I said: 'I'm always interested in that kind of comment … because, you know, I have a twin sister and our hands and feet are the same size.
>
> (interview with M., 2004: 5)

Understandably, M. herself could not identify one sole 'discriminatory ground' that accounted for the way she had been treated overall. During our first face-to-face interview, she told me that she was acutely aware of the way that her colleagues were reacting to her status as a woman, a lesbian and a trans person, and she did not think one could be separated from the other. We submitted M.'s claim to the tribunal on the basis of all three 'non-privileged' grounds: sex, gender reassignment (as UK discrimination law refers to trans status), and sexual orientation. The sex and gender reassignment parts of the claim were covered by the Sex Discrimination Act 1975 (SDA). At that time, the Employment Equality (Sexual Orientation) Regulations had not yet come into force. This meant that there was no legislation addressing sexual orientation discrimination in the workplace. Our argument was that following the Human Rights Act, the definition of 'sex' in the SDA should be interpreted to cover sexual orientation so as to give effect to M.'s European Convention rights to private and family life, freedom of expression and non-discrimination.[5] In their judgment of June 2003 in the joined cases of *Pearce* and *MacDonald*, the House of Lords struck down that argument.[6] As a result of that decision, we had to remove the sexual orientation aspect of M.'s claim.

As the case continued, we faced the exchange of 'further and better particulars'. Requests for further and better particulars are questions that one side can send to the other to clarify the legal and factual arguments. The request we received from the respondent's solicitor, which the tribunal had endorsed, included a question along the following lines: 'Please specify the ground of discrimination on which the applicant states each of the alleged acts took place'. Having consulted the barrister in this case, we responded to the request by stating that each of the alleged acts took place on 'one or more of the following grounds: sex, sexual orientation, and/or gender reassignment'. We did this for two main reasons, both of which were connected with the question's implicit reliance on a legal chronology of events. First, we wanted to prove a 'continuing act' of discrimination to be sure that the discrimination fitted within the three-month time limit for bringing a claim. And second, we did not want to assist the categorising function of the law by defining each act as a manifestation of only one type of discrimination.

Due to LAGER's closure, my involvement in this case ended shortly after the exchange of further and better particulars, and I later heard that the case had been settled. It would therefore be very difficult to discuss whether an intersectional approach was developed at a further stage. But in a previous article, I have tried to theorise how the intersectional discrimination in this case could never be captured through legal procedures, as well as categories, available to lawyers at the time (Grabham, 2006). I wanted to think about how discrimination law, with its emphasis on making claims 'in time' (i.e. three months after the act of discrimination, under UK law) and on establishing 'continuing acts' of discrimination, effectively embeds a separate grounds approach through imposing restrictive chronologies on forms of discrimination which, in practice, shift over time and which do not merely consist of easily discernable 'acts'.

My focus here, by contrast, is on thinking through in more depth what the political implications were of advising M. on her 'intersectional' rights claim. This case study in particular raises a number of questions about engaging with law to obtain redress for discrimination and in order to challenge inequalities. First, there is an assumption that turning to the law in this situation was a potentially beneficial strategy for M. And second, by attempting to bring an intersectional claim, I was also, as Joanne Conaghan has pointed out, invested in law's representative function (Conaghan, this volume). I wanted to bring M.'s complex identity and experiences to the law as an 'intersectional' claim, but I was not sure what I wanted the law to do with them beyond that. And in trying to work on these questions in more depth, I have found Wendy Brown's work on 'wounded attachments' useful and challenging.

Trauma, ressentiment and intersectionality

Wendy Brown argues in *States of Injury* that the politics of identity in contemporary liberal society is based on an investment in powerlessness and injury that undercuts its apparently emancipatory goals (Brown, 1995; see also Brown, 1993). Her project is not to critique rights claims as such, but rather to explore what it is about the way that identities are constructed that leads to self-subversive effects when those identities are politically articulated (Brown, 1995: 55). Brown refers to marginalised groups' rejection of humanist inclusion in favour of a view of exclusion as alterity and an understanding of the role of the margins in the construction of the centre (ibid: 53). Following Foucault, she then situates her analysis of identity within an understanding of how disciplinary power works on subject formation (ibid: 65). She traces how surveillance, classification and minute regulation normalise as social categories those positions that we might otherwise describe as social behaviours embedded in complex historical and political circumstances: the 'crack mother', for example (ibid: 58). With these 'subjectivising conditions of identity formation' (ibid: 55) in mind, Brown asks what does politicised identity want (ibid: 62)? And what 'logics of pain' exist that operate to contain the emancipatory objectives of marginalised groups (ibid)?

At this point, Brown brings in the concept of 'ressentiment', partly understood through the writings of Nietzsche. Ressentiment is 'the moralising revenge of the weak' or '"the triumph of the weak as weak"' (ibid: 66–7). It is the result of the tensions that come about when liberalism promises both equality and universal individual freedom (ibid: 67). All liberal subjects are situated within a realm that promises them equality – promises them the conditions in which they can realise their dreams, and presumes that they have the capacities to do so, but which is actually underpinned by a variety of social inequalities that prevent them from achieving this. Brown (following Nietzsche) presents two possible responses to this invidious state of affairs: subjects can either turn the suffering on themselves or they can externalise it (ibid).

According to Brown, politicised identity is what ensues when subjects turn the suffering outwards, because identity itself is always a reaction to something outside of oneself (ibid: 69). Identity constituted through ressentiment encounters three things that it finds attractive: recognition, revenge, and a place to locate the suffering. In this way, identity becomes reliant on the subjection that it supposedly challenges. The problem with such an approach is that ressentiment holds no promise for the future and no space for political action beyond constantly re-iterated pain (ibid: 70). Whilst Nietzsche counsels forgetting as a means of escaping the trap of ressentiment, Brown finds this to be too harsh a response to pain that has itself arisen through socially-sanctioned forms of forgetting. Instead, she argues for a 'slight shift' in the articulation of political claims based on identity, away from 'I am' and towards instead 'I want this for us': a shift from 'being' to 'wanting' (ibid: 75).

Applying Brown's analysis to the case study, it is possible to consider discrimination law in terms of its investment in 'wounded attachments'. This could arguably consist of two moves: the turn to law, first, and then, within law, the turn to rights expressed through categories of identity. Both moves are intrinsic to disciplinary societies with their basis in liberalism, and both moves are, arguably, deeply connected with political paralysis within oppositional movements. As Brown states:

> Politicised identity, premised on exclusion and fuelled by the humiliation and suffering imposed by its historically structured impotence in the context of a discourse of sovereign individuals, is as likely to seek generalised political paralysis. ... as it is to seek its own or collective liberation through empowerment. Indeed, it is more likely to punish or reproach... than to find venues of self-affirming action.
>
> (Brown, 1995: 71)

Within this logic, we externalised M.'s pain onto the institutional system of the law, a politically paralysed system embedded in disciplinary identities. And the only difference between our apparently subversive intersectional claim and one that relied merely on a single category of discrimination was that we were trying to draw links between the various normalised categories of identity that discrimination law requires. As a result, it is evident that deploying intersectional arguments in M.'s case could not challenge the law's basis in disciplinary constructions of identity.

Following on from this, it is worth using Brown's critique to investigate the political purchase of intersectionality analysis more generally within law. Brown's work and intersectionality analysis both contest the turn to legal rights in pursuance of counter-hegemonic political goals. Both approaches also deconstruct, although in different ways, the identity positions – or categories – that are supposed to ground political claims. Theorists deploying intersectional analysis take an approach that looks to the inadequacy of these positions for capturing experiential complexities and the interlocking function of oppressions, whilst Brown takes a broadly Foucauldian approach that focuses on how these identities are naturalised as social positions through regulatory and disciplinary techniques.

Nevertheless, Brown's analysis of late-modern identity politics prompts a number of questions about the deployment of intersectionality within law, which build on the critiques that I have mentioned above. Intersectionality relies on the very same categories – the same distilled social positions – that it looks to displace, and this means that there is a foundational assumption that the categories are distinct. As Davina Cooper puts it, this 'ontological fallacy' assumes that 'the axes have an existence apart from the ways in which they combine' (Cooper, 2004: 48). She states:

> Models that emerge as rough approximations, developed by humans in an effort to try to understand the social, become reified as phenomena with an independent and prior existence. Discrete axes of gender, class, race and age do not exist independently on some distant plane prior to their convergence in the form of distinct social permutations. Rather, identifying axes of class, gender, race and age occur in the course of making sense of social life.
>
> (ibid)

Cooper goes on to argue that models relying on groups, rather than axes, lead to a similar ontological problem which assumes that different groups exist prior to inequalities and which does not view group classifications as the effects of power (ibid: 49–50). She proposes an analytics based instead on visualising social inequality in terms of 'organising principles' – focusing on how gender, race, disability and age are the effects of technologies of power instead of axes of inequality or the conditions by which some people are subordinated by other people (ibid: 51). Such an analysis would presume the already intersecting nature of inequalities (ibid), and I will return to this later.

In the meantime, within a disciplinary society based on liberal norms, attempts at 'making sense of social life' through an abstract formulation of the liberal subject reduce identity positions to depoliticised 'interests' (see Brown, 1995: 56). As Brown puts it: '(t)he abstractness of the "we" is precisely what insists upon, reiterates, and even enforces the depoliticised nature of the "I"' (ibid: 57).[7] In other words, fighting to obtain individualised rights for abstract liberal subjects cannot be politically empowering or transformative. This might provide a clue to why mobilisations of intersectionality analysis within feminist legal studies, and within my own experience of practice, appear unsatisfactory. On the one hand, intersectionality analysis is presented as a challenge to abstract and depoliticised theories of identity formation: it has been deployed in expressly concrete and politicised ways – to uncover the marginalising effects of discrimination laws on Black women. In this way, intersectional analysis could challenge the normalisation – as social categories – of behaviours and positions that are themselves enmeshed in complex configurations of power. It could assist in bringing into view what

Brown terms 'politicised identity formation' by articulating political demands based on recognising the contingent effects of power and ultimately resisting the abstract articulation of political demands as mere 'interests'.

On the other hand, many forms of intersectional analysis, and especially the way that I applied intersectionality to law in M.'s case, do not interrogate social positions as effects of power. Articulations of intersectionality that focus on combinations or syntheses of legal categories, as well as on the intersections, are very often based on the same depoliticised categories which Brown speaks of in her account. This is evident within the sentencing decisions which Toni Williams writes about in her chapter in this collection (Williams, this volume). Williams examines legislative reforms in Canada which have attempted to reduce the over-incarceration of Aboriginal people with the use of intersectional analysis at the sentencing stage, and she shows that these reforms have increased the level of incarceration of Aboriginal women. She concludes that the sentencing process receives feminist knowledge – analyses of intersectional inequalities leading to Aboriginal women's contact with the criminal justice system – in ways that have 'failed to ameliorate the substantive inequality that Aboriginal women encounter' (ibid: 20). There is no reason to suppose that intersectional arguments on behalf of claimants in discrimination cases will be received any differently. Indeed, if we take on board Brown's critique, then intersectionality in discrimination law relies on a combination of 'wounded attachments' – identities that have been constituted through turning pain outwards onto the law. In this way, intersectionality does not challenge law's own role in supporting a politics of ressentiment, and the effects of such a failure, as Williams points out, have a considerable material effect on the lives of subordinated subjects depending on the area of the law to which they are applied.

Viewing intersectional analysis in the context of the genealogy of identity claims in liberal society gives us more of an understanding why it has not had the radical effects in discrimination law that we might have wished for. If single-ground rights claims are based on disciplinary identities, then intersectional rights claims (and many forms of legal intersectional analysis) are no less bound to these categories. Using more categories in legal analysis, or focusing on the intersections between legal categories, does not of itself challenge the regulatory function of liberal identity. Indeed, the precision required for intersectional perspectives can be seen to approximate the 'anatomy of detail' that goes into the production of subjects for surveillance and regulation. Drawing on Foucault, Brown argues that a wide range of social identities are produced through discourses of the state and consumer capitalism that rely on such an 'anatomy of detail' (Brown, 1995: 58). She gives as an example the state's construction of the welfare subject across categories of disability, motherhood, age and race (ibid). She furthermore argues that these categories 'cross-cut juridical identities' (ibid). In this way, the disciplinary construction of social positions as identities can be seen to rely on methods of identification which operate outside, or across, legal categories of sex, race, gender, disability, age and sexual orientation. The construction of the welfare subject is already, in some senses, intersectional, and it is no less disciplinary for that.

In M.'s case, we tried to bring in an intersectional analysis by resisting the allocation of acts to particular grounds of discrimination, thus keeping in view many grounds at once. This strategy mirrors the practice in some legal jurisdictions of allowing intersectional claims by expressly or implicitly providing for more than one ground to be argued, and it also runs into the same problems. Allowing 'many grounds', or arguing 'gender reassignment' alongside 'sex' and 'sexual orientation' is arguably merely another way of extending the classificatory function within the disciplinary production of identities. Brown gives the example of a local anti-discrimination ordinance in Santa Cruz, which prohibits discrimination on the basis of 'sexual orientation, transsexuality, age, height, weight, personal appearance, physical characteristics, race, colour, creed, religion, national origin, ancestry, disability, marital status, sex, or gender' (Brown, 1995: 65). She argues that this ordinance normalises positions that potentially subvert the law, and that it is an example of how contemporary politicised identity 'potentially accelerates' the surveillance and classification functions of disciplinary power (ibid).

I would argue that a similar acceleration happens when, for example, the South African Bill of Rights contains an equality provision (section 9(3)) that prohibits discrimination on 'one or more of the following grounds' from a wide-ranging list.[8] This approach presents intersectionality as merely a new 'form' of discrimination, akin to defining it as yet another identity, instead of allowing it to question the constitution of the identity subject positions. A similar approach could be found in the Canadian Supreme Court shortly after the 2000 decision in *Law* v. *Canada*, which brought in a new test for equality under section 15 of the Canadian Charter of Rights and Freedoms (Grabham, 2002). The court's approach after this case was, in certain circumstances, to treat intersectional discrimination as 'analogous' to the grounds that were already set out in section 15 (ibid: 650–51). Where it has been recognised, therefore, intersectional discrimination has often been expressed as a 'new' ground: yet another form of legally intelligible identity.

Wounded attachments/everyday trauma

Not only does intersectionality analysis in law fail to challenge categories, therefore, it actually deepens and extends the law's impetus towards the regulatory production of identities. Intersectionality, on these terms, helps to produce the legal 'truth' of inequalities through classification (cf. Dean, 1999). It produces a field of vision in which the anatomy of the legal subject, and the field of the inequalities she/he faces, appear to be totally amenable to surveillance. The implied motivation for pursuing such a 'freedom project' is that by focusing on the intersections between pre-existing regulated identities, the legal subject will be able to utilise the law to further their own emancipation. In a peculiarly legal paradox, intersectionality implies escape, but also, as we have already seen, relies on the law's capacity to represent the subject.

With this in mind, I would like to think about whether we can gain fresh perspectives on the role of intersectionality in legal discourse by revisiting the 'suffering' or 'ressentiment' at the heart of the turn to rights. Despite her arguments about the disciplinary production of identities in rights discourse, Brown still retains an account of subjectivity and the lived experience of power relations in late-modern society that implies a degree of agency on the part of legal/liberal subjects. By tracing the contours of the 'pain' or 'trauma' that results from subjects' positions within power relations, it might be possible to get back to what Davina Cooper would theorise as the already intersecting nature of inequalities (Cooper, 2004), but this time specifically through an account of how subjects experience enmeshed inequalities on the mundane, everyday level.

One way of approaching this task is to take on board the reasons for victimhood and the 'politics of recrimination' in Brown's account (Brown, 1995: 53) and look for examples where political subjects have formed alternative responses that do not end with ressentiment. Brown speaks of the two alternatives available to the liberal subject when caught in the tension between the mirage of freedom and self-determination and the (often) disempowering effects of social forces. These two alternatives are turning the blame inwards, as we have seen, and finding an external site (ibid: 67). The external site for blame becomes the basis for ressentiment. Yet these need not be the only options.

At this point, Ann Cvetkovich's work on trauma becomes useful. Cvetkovich emphasises the importance of public action and anger in living with, and responding to, trauma (Cvetkovich, 2003). Her avowedly feminist project acknowledges the impact of large-scale events such as wars, genocide and the holocaust, but focuses heavily on how trauma 'digs itself in at the level of the everyday', including for people who have survived forms of sexual trauma such as incest (ibid: 20). Cvetkovich uses an approach that itself challenges many of the usual feminist narratives: 'I found what I was looking for in lesbian subcultures that cut through narratives of innocent victims and therapeutic healing to present something that was raw, confrontational, and even sexy' (Cvetkovich, 2003: 4).

Cvetkovich presents a sex-positive approach to trauma, which focuses on the experiences of women, queers, butches, femmes and Aids activists. One example Cvetkovich gives is the feminist punk band Tribe 8's performance at the 1994 Michigan Women's Music Festival, which was preceded by their self-description in the programme as a 'blade-brandishing, gang-castrating, dildo-swingin', bullshit-detecting, aurally pornographic, Neanderthal-pervert band of patriarchy-smashing snatchlickers' (ibid: 83). Some protestors argued that Tribe 8's music would trigger flashbacks in survivors of incest and sexual violence because their performance contained light whipping and one scene in which lead singer Lynn Breedlove cut off a strap-dildo with a knife (ibid: 84). Yet as Cvetkovich points out, some band members also self-identified on stage as sexual abuse survivors and they explained how they used their music to express how they reacted to their experiences (ibid: 85). As Cvetkovich points out, '(t)heir performance blurs the distinctions between pro-sex practices, sexual violence, and incest survivorhood in order to reveal that their intimate connections may be productive rather than a cause for alarm' (ibid: 86).

Cvetkovich breaks from theorists who attempt to universalise trauma in attempting, for example, to find and set out the core symptoms for post-traumatic stress disorder, and she rejects the relegation of sexual trauma to the private sphere, insisting instead on an approach that recognises the impact on public spheres of intimacy and affect (ibid: 32). She acknowledges work on the 'trauma culture' of the United States, and its signalling of a political sphere in which the archetypal citizen is an injured victim. In particular, she takes on board Brown's work on ressentiment (ibid: 15). Nevertheless, in Cvetkovich's view, counterpublic spaces are already providing the opportunity for people to articulate trauma in a way that is confrontational and explicitly political, and which does not look to the state or to legal redress for a 'quick fix' (ibid: 16).

Brown and Cvetkovich's accounts overlap in the way they situate what they variously term 'suffering' or 'trauma' in relation to conditions of inequality in late modernity. For Brown, the pain of the liberal subject is always situated within power, and it is intimately connected with the subject's failure to achieve what it is expected to achieve: 'the failure to make itself in the context of a discourse in which its self-making is assumed' (Brown, 1995: 67). As Brown points out, Nietzsche calls this failure 'suffering', and Brown also herself refers to it as 'hurt' and 'pain'. This archetypal suffering, in Brown's account, is so unbearable that it requires action of some sort, whether conscious or unconscious. For her part, as we have seen, Cvetkovich makes clear that she does not want to confine her understanding of 'trauma' to the experiences of large-scale events, but wants to develop an account of the mundanity of trauma: its embeddedness in everyday life. This, I would argue, coincides with Brown's understanding of failure as a state of being intimately connected with one's position within power relations.

More than that, I think that where Brown and Cvetkovich's accounts resonate with each other is through the way that they focus on the lived experience of power configurations. Cvetkovich states that she wants to 'think about trauma as part of the affective language that describes life under capitalism' (Cvetkovich, 2003: 19). Referring to the connection between the term 'trauma' and the development of theories of 'railway shock' in the nineteenth century, she argues that '(t)rauma and modernity thus can be understood as mutually constitutive categories; trauma is one of the affective experiences, or to use Raymond Williams's phrase, "structures of feeling," that characterises the lived experience of capitalism' (ibid: 17). For Brown and Cvetkovich, then, capitalism and/or liberalism (and I understand these terms do not map directly onto each other) variously provide the structural overlay for subjects' experiences and result in mundane affective economies for the relatively disempowered which can be described through the language of 'ressentiment' or 'trauma'.

Where they differ, however, is in the way they view the consequences of these affective economies. In Cvetkovich's account, subjects who experience trauma can turn the pain outwards, to an external site, yet this does not result in the 'culturally dispersed paralysis and suffering' (Brown, 1995: 55) that Brown equates with ressentiment. Cvetkovich states that the cases she finds interesting 'offer the unpredictable forms of politics that emerge when trauma is kept unrelentingly in view rather than contained within an institutional project', and she continues: 'My investigation of trauma thus becomes an inquiry into how affective experience that falls outside of institutionalised or stable forms of identity or politics can form the basis for public culture' (Cvetkovich, 2003: 16–17). This arguably represents a third potential option available to Brown's liberal subject: the expression of trauma and anger, in this example through cultural media such as music and performance, instead of institutionally-based ressentiment, on the one hand, or turning the pain inwards, on the other. Where ressentiment aims to overcome the hurt, find a 'culprit' and displace the hurt through assigning it to an external site (Brown, 1995: 68), Cvetkovich's examples of trauma combine responses to the hurt of anger and aggression with counter-cultural sexual practices or politicised music, comedy or writing.

Traumatic impressions

By suggesting such an analysis, I do not wish to naturalise these emotions by implying that there is something 'authentic' about trauma, or something more 'healthy' about it than ressentiment. Instead, what is helpful about Cvetkovich's analysis is that from a similar motivation to understand the lived experiences of power relations as Brown, she examines extra-institutional, rather than rights-based, expressions of 'pain'. Using both Brown's and Cvetkovich's perspectives gives us a broader understanding of the subjectivities of inequalities. Nevertheless, within these accounts there remains a need to focus on the physicality of power relations: the ways in which emotional experiences of living through capitalism or neo-liberalism are so intensely embodied on an individual level, and it is at this point that Sara Ahmed's work on impressions becomes useful.

Ahmed mobilises the concept of impressions within an overall project of investigating the 'cultural politics of emotion' (Ahmed, 2004). In effect, impressions describe how emotions are socially and historically mediated, and how they reside outside the individual subject. Impressions are shaped by contact with objects and also by historical and cultural memories (ibid: 7). Ahmed uses the example of a child who sees a bear and runs away in fright. The bear is not inherently dangerous or fearsome. Instead of merely being a useful instinctive reaction to a dangerous animal, this child's fright is shaped by cultural stories about the fearsome bear, and the fright takes effect as a physical impression of the risks of coming into contact with the bear (ibid). The fear does not reside in the bear, nor in the child, but in the contact between bear and child and in the cultural stories that circulate about the bear. As Ahmed puts it: '(i)t is not simply that the subject feels hate, or feels fear, and nor is it the case that the object is simply hateful or is fearsome: the emotions of hate and fear are shaped by the "contact zone" in which others impress upon us, as well as leave their impressions' (ibid: 194).

These impressions are intensely embodied phenomena which draw on histories of meaning that we may find very difficult to reframe in any one instance. They might attach or 'stick' to some objects and pass over others (ibid: 8). Ahmed is careful to avoid replicating both a model of emotion as interiority – emotions being the expression of internal feelings, and the theory of emotions as a sociological form – Durkheim's view of emotions operating from the outside in as a form of binding for the social body (ibid: 9). Instead, she suggests that 'emotions create the very effect of the surfaces and boundaries that allow us to distinguish an inside and an outside in the first place' (ibid: 10).

Surfaces and boundaries can be physical, delineating the limits of the body. In this sense, the inside and the outside can be an expression of the limits of corporeality: where the flesh ends. Impressions have their effect here through intensifications of feeling: awareness of the body, and the limits of the body, through physical sensations such as pain (Ahmed gives the example of stubbing one's toe) (ibid: 24). Here, the boundary that determines 'inside' as something separate from 'outside' is the skin, and the skin has the dual role of containing the flesh but also being a surface upon which others, and objects, can impress on us (ibid: 25). And the reason why it is important to trace the effects of impressions is because they carry the force of histories of oppression into the ways that we relate to each other physically and emotionally. Ahmed states:

> Through emotions, the past persists on the surface of bodies. Emotions show us how histories stay alive, even when they are not consciously remembered; how histories of colonialism, slavery, and violence shape lives and worlds in the present.
>
> (Ahmed, 2004: 202)

Impressions, as combinations of sensations and emotions, shape the movements of our bodies towards and away from objects and each other in ways that replay racism, colonialism and rigid gender norms. In M.'s case, the comment about M.'s 'big hands and feet' drew on histories of fear and disgust around trans bodies, and on an investment in the concept of 'appropriate' sex characteristics. The effects of these histories on the physical and emotional encounters that M. had with her colleagues recall Ahmed's account of one of Audre Lorde's childhood experiences. Sitting on a subway train, Audre gradually realises that the reason why a white woman (flaring her nostrils) is pulling her coat closer to her and not letting it stray across the seat towards her is not because there must be some form of roach on the seat, but instead because she does not want her clothing to come into contact with a black child (ibid: 53). Ahmed shows how the movements in this encounter – the flicking away of the coat, the flared nostrils – redefine social and bodily integrity (ibid). The white woman's body is aligned through the emotion of 'hate' with the community, threatened with contamination from the black body (ibid). As Ahmed indicates, rather than seeing emotion as a psychological disposition, it is useful to see it as an organising factor (Ahmed, 2001). Hate, for example, gets stuck to some bodies: aligned with them, through force. Hate can be distributed (ibid: 346); it functions as an affective economy (ibid: 348).

Ahmed's work on impressions opens up a new avenue for thinking about trauma and about intersectionality. Mundane, everyday trauma, of the type that Cvetkovich theorises, is enmeshed in the impressions that we make on each other, which combine inequalities and the histories of inequalities with emotions, physical encounters, and intensifications of feeling. Physical encounters, movements towards and away from other people in acts of affection, violence or aversion are determined by, and determine, one's position in relation to power relations. The liberal subject might respond to such trauma through 'ressentiment': engaging with a politics of injury through rights claims, intersectional or not, or she might engage in counter-cultural modes of performance or communication. Either way, if emotions function as affective economies, then paying attention to the impressions that subjects make on one another can allow for a political reading of encounters that goes beyond the individual subject and beyond the law's construction of individuals through disciplinary identities. With this in mind, describing M.'s experience in legal terms as 'intersectional' invokes her identity as a trans woman and a lesbian but it says nothing about the productive force of the encounter between her and her colleague in aligning her body, through hate and fear, as a threat. Focusing on impressions – the physical and affective encounters between subjects and the histories on which these encounters draw – acknowledges the instrumental and distributive function of emotions: as Ahmed puts it, the way that emotions get stuck to bodies.

Concluding remarks

The application of anti-essentialist approaches to legal theory and practice has resulted in the widespread adoption of intersectionality analysis in law and policy. Intersectionality has been an important contribution to feminist legal theory, in particular, leading to much work that interrogates the silences, invisibilities and oppressive effects of law on racialised subjects in particular. Yet the more disciplining aspects of intersectionality discourse have been overlooked. Intersectionality is now arguably the product of the regime in which it operates and which it was conceived to contest. It supports law's classifying impulse to the extent that focusing on the 'intersections' has merely resulted in the disciplinary production of more identities. And in many ways it is an archetypal governmental discourse, presuming, as it does, an all-seeing optics of detail in which the vissicitudes of experience and identity can be set out and examined.

With these problems in mind, it might be a surprising move to focus instead on the 'trauma' and 'pain' experienced by subjects under liberalism. However, by investigating trauma as a mundane state of being, produced across physical and emotional encounters, it is possible to approach the complexity of inequalities without prioritising governmentally produced identity categories and without thereby contributing to the production of 'new' categories. Instead of locating intersectionality within the legal subject herself, through a trans lesbian who cannot bring a claim expressing her identity in a meaningful way for example, it is possible to focus instead on how different histories of oppression converge through and across the way that people interact.

I am not necessarily interested in what this 'means' for the conduct of legal cases. But it is worth noting that there are other ways of viewing law other than as an institutional project, especially if trauma is re-thought. Where I would depart from Cvetkovich's account is her positioning of legal redress as a 'quick fix' (Cvetkovich, 2003: 16). Drawing on Ahmed's work, but this time in a slightly different way, I would argue that subjects make an impression on the law when they make rights arguments, and these impressions circulate within law as traces of the hurt and trauma that they have experienced. Discrimination claims, in these terms, are not a politically empowering strategy, but neither are they a 'quick fix'. They result from mundane, painful experiences of inequality and subjects' attempts to make sense of these experiences through narrative and other forms of 'public' engagement. They may not be expressly counter-cultural, but they do give rise to a 'public culture' (Cvetkovich, 2003: 17) which goes beyond immediate engagement with the law, and they can be viewed as analogous to the expressions of trauma that Cvetkovich cites. Impressing on the law can be viewed, in terms of its effects, in a similar framework to writing a novel about sexual abuse, for example (*Bastard Out of Carolina* by Dorothy Allison; see Cvetkovich, 2003: 94–110). It is not simply a matter of declaring/constructing your identity in order to obtain legal redress: it is a lower-level process that relies on touch, emotions and perceptions, and which leaves traces of subjects' anger and trauma within the law itself (Johnson, 2007). It is also possibly more of a forward-looking, 'I want this for us' (as Brown would put it) form of action than traditional, institutional, conceptions of rights might allow. Viewing discrimination claims as expressions/impressions of trauma may, paradoxically, give us new ways of viewing complex inequalities, shifting the focus of intersectionality away from disciplinary identity categories and toward the cultural circulation of emotions.

Acknowledgements

Many thanks to Davina Cooper, Didi Herman, Jane Krishnadas and Anastasia Vakulenko for comments on earlier drafts of this piece. An earlier version of this chapter was presented at 'Critical Legal Theory? Postgraduate Projects in the Making', Altonaer Stiftung für philosophische Grundlagenforschung, Hamburg, 21–23 June 2007. Thank you to the participants there for useful comments and discussion.

Bibliography

Ahmed, Sara (2001) 'The Organisation of Hate' *Law and Critique* 12: 345–65.

Ahmed, Sara (2004) *The Cultural Politics of Emotion* Edinburgh University Press, Edinburgh, UK.

Brown, Wendy (1993) 'Wounded Attachments' *Political Theory* 21: 390–410.

Brown, Wendy (1995) *States of Injury: Power and Freedom in Late Modernity* Princeton University Press, Princeton, New Jersey.

Cooper, Davina (2004) *Challenging Diversity: Rethinking Equality and the Value of Difference* Cambridge University Press, Cambridge, UK.

Crenshaw, Kimberlé (1989) 'Demarginalizing the Intersection of Race and Sex: A Black Feminist Critique of Antidiscrimination Doctrine, Feminist Theory and Antiracist Politics' *The University of Chicago Legal Forum* 139–67.

Cvetkovich, Ann (2003) *An Archive of Feelings: Trauma, Sexuality and Lesbian Public Cultures* Duke University Press, Durham NC.

Dean, Mitchell (1999) *Governmentality: Power and Rule in Modern Society* Sage, Thousand Oaks CA.

Duclos, Nitya (1993) 'Disappearing Women: Racial Minority Women in Human Rights Cases' *Canadian Journal of Women and the Law* 6: 25–51.

Grabham, Emily (2002) 'Law v Canada: New Directions for Equality under the Canadian Charter?' *Oxford Journal of Legal Studies* 22: 641–61.

Grabham, Emily (2006) 'Taxonomies of Inequality: Lawyers, Maps and the Challenge of Hybridity' *Social and Legal Studies* 15: 5–23.

Harris, Angela (1990) 'Race and Essentialism in Feminist Legal Theory' *Stanford Law Review* 42: 581–616.

Harris, Angela (1999) 'Building Theory, Building Community' *Social and Legal Studies* 8(3): 313–25.

Hutchinson, Darren Lenard (1997) 'Out Yet Unseen: A Racial Critique of Gay and Lesbian Legal Theory and Political Discourse' *Connecticut Law Review* 29: 561–645.

Johnson, Toni (2007) 'Sexuality and Asylum: Narrativising Discourses of Resistance Through the "Imaginary Domain"', draft PhD thesis, University of Kent.

MacDonald, Gayle, Rachel L. Osborne and Charles C. Smith (eds) (2005) *Feminism, Law, Inclusion: Intersectionality in Action* Toronto: Sumach Press.

Valdes, Francisco (1995) 'Sex and Race in Queer Legal Culture: Ruminations on Identities and Inter-Connectivities' *Southern California Review of Law and Women's Studies* 5: 25–71.

Williams, Patricia (1991) *The Alchemy of Race and Rights* Harvard University Press, Cambridge UK.

Yuval-Davis, Nira (2006) 'Intersectionality and Feminist Politics' *European Journal of Women's Studies* 13(3): 193–210.

Table of cases

Interviews

Telephone interviews with M., 24 August 2004.

Notes

1 For the Safra Project, see www.safraproject.org/ and for the Sylvia Rivera Law Project, see www.srlp.org/.
2 Conversation with Dean Spade, 25 May 2007.
3 LAGER did later change its policies to include bisexual people, but never explicitly included trans people. This was an issue that divided LAGER management committee members and employees.
4 I do not find the term 'discrimination' particularly helpful, but I cannot find a better term to describe what happened in this context. In addition, 'discrimination' was the legal term that we used throughout the case.
5 Article 8: right to private and family life. Article 10: freedom of expression, and Article 14: right to non-discrimination.
6 *MacDonald v AG for Scotland, Pearce v Governing Body of Mayfield School* (2003) UKHL 34.
7 See also page 56, where she states that '(t)he abstract nature of liberal political membership and the ideologically naturalized character of liberal individualism together work against politicized identity formation'.
8 Section 9(3): 'The state may not unfairly discriminate directly or indirectly against anyone on one or more grounds, including race, gender, sex, pregnancy, marital status, ethnic or social origin, colour, sexual orientation, age, disability, religion, conscience, belief, culture, language and birth.

Part III
Power relations and the state

Chapter 8

Transitional intersections

Gender, sect, and class in Northern Ireland

Eilish Rooney

Introduction

The 'war on terror' has revived international interest in the conflict in Northern Ireland (Campbell and Connolly 2003).[1] In the aftermath of 9/11 Prime Minister Blair quickly claimed that the British government's expertise in handling 'terrorism' in Northern Ireland would be made available to the Bush administration (ibid). Discussions of the London bombing (7 July 2005) frequently included comparisons with Irish Republican Army (IRA) bombing campaigns in Britain, with contributions invited from 'experts' on the basis of their experience of 'terrorism' and the Northern Irish conflict. This conflict which was often characterized in the latter part of the twentieth century as a nineteenth century anachronism in the modern world (Deane 1999), at the start of the twenty-first century is considered by some as a 'model' of how democratic states might manage 'terrorist' threat. A key element in the management of the Northern Ireland conflict discourse is a state-sponsored community relations narrative that centres on dysfunctional sectarian opposition primarily between working class Catholic and Protestant men (Rooney 2006a). Women rarely feature whilst the gendered and social class dimensions of these 'identities' are also invisible and largely unexamined in mainstream academic research. In this essay intersectionality is discussed as a beneficial form of analysis for bringing women and social class into view and for enabling us to see how women's invisibility in conflict discourses operates to the disadvantage of the most marginalized Catholic and Protestant women in this context. Intersectional analysis further helps to illuminate critical questions of recognition and redistribution in post-conflict transitions such as that in Northern Ireland.

At a time when the narrative emerging in relation to the transition in Iraq is one of violent sectarian opposition between Sunni and Shia Muslims and Kurds (women are again invisible), this chapter contends that intersectional analysis can help deepen understanding of such complex situations. It contributes to a growing body of critical reflection in the transitional justice literature on the Northern Irish conflict (Campbell and Ní Aoláin 2002–03).

One leading study to critique the claim that Northern Ireland provides a model of how democratic states can successfully manage 'terrorist threat' does so through an analysis of the British state's decision to militarize the management of civil disturbance in Northern Ireland at a key early stage (Campbell and Connolly 2003). The role of women, which is decisive in the curfew event central to this analysis, is mentioned only in passing whilst the authors conduct a forensic analysis of military action.[2] The Catholic Falls district, where the curfew was imposed, was one of the most impoverished parts of Northern Ireland at the time. Almost forty years later, it remains one of the most deprived areas (Noble *et al.* 2005). Arguably the area posed a greater security threat to the state after the curfew than before. The argument in this chapter is that bringing women's agency into view and tackling poverty experienced by people living in areas such as this is crucial to building a more secure future for everyone in Northern Ireland. This is not solely a problem of Catholic disadvantage. Recent statistics reveal that the poorest Protestant areas are experiencing deepening levels of poverty in the aftermath of the peace process (CAJ 2006a). These statistics indicate that there is a reduction in religious and political inequalities amongst the poorest people in Northern Ireland not because things are improving for the Catholic poor but because the poorest Protestants are closing the gap. There is a levelling downwards. Deepening levels of Protestant poverty allied to alienation from political accommodation may yet pose a threat within a state whose status is now subject to the vicissitudes of the ballot box.[3]

On a common-sense level, women may reasonably be assumed to be a peripheral concern of states dealing with 'terrorist threat' given the dominance of men and masculinity invested in the construct and concrete experience of both 'threat' and 'security'. However, in the aftermath of the invasion of Iraq and in the 'transitional' phase of setting up democratic institutions there, Northern Ireland has become a destination for high-level political and civic delegations of Iraqi women.[4] They come to learn how women in a violent conflict, 'divided' by religion and politics, have managed to overcome division and unite in common cause. In these visits the Iraqi delegates meet with women's groups from working-class Catholic and Protestant districts. These women's groups have also been the subject of an influential feminist literature that highlights how women in different violent conflicts manage to overcome division and build alliances in what appear to be the most unlikely circumstances.[5] The women's groups visited by the Iraqi delegations organize in neighbourhoods where social need indices place them amongst some of the most deprived areas in western Europe (Hamilton and Fisher 2002). The groups themselves limp along on insecure funding, dependent upon state and state-related agency support that generally stipulates a 'community relations' (i.e. Catholic–Protestant) dimension to their work (Rooney 2002). The appalling degree of poverty experienced by women in these neighbourhoods is neither an issue of public debate nor is it on the equality agenda in Northern Ireland. The focus of this agenda is the persistent unemployment differentials between Catholic and Protestant men.[6] In the West Belfast constituency, the location of the curfew area that was referenced earlier, almost half of the electoral wards have child poverty levels of over 80 per cent (Rooney 2004). The impact of these and other inequalities upon the poorest women has never been comprehensively studied. Yet women in poverty are the most likely to bear the burdens of rearing children alone, to be in the low-paid and unofficial labour market, to have lower disposable income and, when married, to have a smaller share of and less control over family incomes (Daly 1989). Almost two-thirds of the income support claimants in Northern Ireland are women (Moore *et al.* 2002). Furthermore, there is a correlation between inequality and poverty and areas that have 'suffered the most and been most involved in the conflict' (Hillyard *et al.* 2005). The areas that posed the highest security threat to the state during the conflict are those with the deepest levels of deprivation. The social and generational impacts of political and religious inequalities fuelled the conflict. This is recognized in the equality strand of the Good Friday Agreement (Agreement) where the first two dimensions of inequality named are those of religious belief and political opinion.[7] However, on the matter of women's poverty in Northern Ireland there is a resounding silence not alone in public debate but also in the literature.[8] Women are simply not on the equality radar. Where they do come into view they do so in the women's groups visited by the Iraqi delegations, and in some feminist literature, as remarkably able to overcome discredited sectarian politics.

The virtual invisibility of women in Northern Ireland's conflict discourse is reflected in the equality agenda where the notable focus is on resilient unemployment differentials between Catholic and Protestant men. Women, and the impacts of these differentials on their lives, are unexamined even though the data is readily available.[9] Intersectional analysis foregrounds this neglect and calls attention specifically to women's inequalities in these circumstances. This chapter discusses intersectionality as a missing and beneficial form of analysis for the investigation of how women figure in conflict discourse and what impact this has on the most marginalized women's lives. Whilst policy discourse uses fixed categories for referencing statistical data and revealing patterns of political and religious inequalities, in places such as Northern Ireland, the deconstructive, theoretical dimension of this chapter calls for critical caution in relation to these same categories. Social categories and 'identities' are products of particular historical circumstances. They change and are changeable. This analysis provides pragmatic and theoretical lessons helping to illuminate the role of law and policy in such situations. The wider horizon of this essay is the possible application of the analytical tools of intersectionality to other conflicted and transitional contexts where 'identity' narratives emerge and appear to float free of the political economy of gender in state or regime reform or reconstitution. This wider theoretical horizon is glimpsed throughout the chapter, but my anchor is the here and now and the current challenges of Northern Ireland's transition.

There are three parts to the chapter. The first section 'Women in view' explores the invisibility of women and gender in the Northern Irish conflict narrative. The role of women in conflict narratives is a precarious one. For the most part they are an invisible presence. On occasion the female figure is hailed into prominence and functions in a symbolic way that neither disturbs the pervasive masculinity of the discourse nor questions women's stereotypical depiction in the narrative. I argue that this precarious role is also vital. It sustains a narrative fiction that conflicts are gender-free. Following from this, the second section 'Theory in place' probes the benefits of intersectionality theory as a way to interrogate primary binary ways of thinking about and analysing sectarian oppositions in Northern Ireland. In this instance, as is generally the case when conflicts are described as 'sectarian', sect references the historical role of religion in state formation whereby one religiously defined political and/or ethnic group can exercise power over the other. The complex legacy of this exercise of power in Northern Ireland is evident in the reported indices of deprivation that continue to show deep rooted political and religious inequalities (CAJ 2006a, Noble *et al.* 2005). This chapter calls for an analytic approach that begins the work of integrating regimes of state formation with gender and class inequalities in order to comprehend the challenges facing law and policy in transition. This preliminary work is undertaken with the aid of postcolonial theory in the third section 'Gender in a state'. The implications of this analysis are examined for feminist theory and politics premised, as Bottomley (2004) argues from the perspective of feminist jurisprudence, on the unitary if categorically unstable category 'woman'. Intersectionality exposes the 'illusory sameness' suggested by the very terms (such as Catholic and Protestant) used to describe dimensions of inequality and discrimination in Northern Ireland.

The chapter develops Joan Scott's (2001) insight that 'identities don't pre-exist their strategic political invocations'. 'Strategic political invocations' of Catholic and Protestant (and 'woman' for that matter) in the Northern Irish context illustrate and affirm her point. Furthermore, intersectionality functions here as a conceptual framework or heuristic device for asking questions otherwise not asked, for seeing women otherwise hidden from view (or seen only within a certain frame) and for describing the kinds of things to consider especially in the transitional process in Northern Ireland when sect, and the relationship with the state that it denotes, is being institutionalized in post-agreement mechanisms of governance (Rooney 2000a).[10] Just as critical race feminists in the US devised intersectionality as a tool to elucidate how gender is hidden within discourse on 'race', it can be applied to similar effect in relation to sect in Northern Ireland. The chapter ends with 'Transitional conclusions' where what has gone before is drawn together in the context of seeing the 'liberal democratic state' of Northern Ireland as a 'moment' of

European modernity. Postcolonial state–citizen relations in Northern Ireland are living evidence of the state's founding faultlines of gender, sect and class under pressure. In other words Northern Ireland is a most apposite site for the deployment of intersectionality.

Initially, it may seem an unlikely location within which to apply this complex theoretical paradigm.[11] Intersectionality with its triad of 'race/class/gender' originally designed in a US context, poses fundamental challenges in the Northern Irish transitional process. Billed as the latest 'fast travelling theory' (Knapp 2003), the theoretical paradigm of intersectionality, that promises so much by way of an escape from the cul-de-sac of disconnected, deconstructing differences, appears to be heading for a roundabout in the metropolis of feminist theory in the US.[12] Or so it seems – from a distance. The 'distance' that Northern Ireland is from any site of theory production is all important. First, it is a society in transition from over thirty years of violent political conflict involving sect and politics in state formation (in this context the intersectional triad becomes gender/sect/class). Whilst the conflict has not been about religion *per se*, in that it has not been a dispute concerning doctrinal or theological matters, it cannot be understood without recognition of the historical interplay of sect and politics in political power relations between Britain and Ireland (Brewer and Higgins 1998). Intersectionality theory in this situation is useful because it brings women to the fore and gender and class into play in comprehending intersecting dimensions of inequality and discrimination as constitutive of state–citizen relations. Second, the virtual invisibility of women in Northern Irish conflict discourse is reflected in the equality agenda where, as already noted, the focus is on the resilient unemployment differentials between Catholic and Protestant men. Women, and the impacts of these differentials on their lives, remain unexamined (Rooney 2006b). The move of intersectionality foregrounds this erasure and, in this analysis, calls attention to women's socio-economic circumstances. Finally, the poorest people have suffered the most in the conflict. Whilst women's groups from poor neighbourhoods are showcased to international delegations and in the feminist literature for admiration, women in the most disadvantaged neighbourhoods bear the heaviest burdens. Intersectionality further focuses the spotlight on these women and supports the argument that addressing the corrosive social impacts of women's poverty may provide a strategic approach for building durable stability in a state established on the basis of sect and the political affiliation it denotes.[13] The application of intersectionality in the post-Agreement transitional context has the pragmatic aim of introducing women's equality into the frame. An integral theoretical aim is to show how including women and developing gender sensitive analyses destabilizes the hegemonic masculinity of the discourse. The masculinity of the discourse is exposed by making women visible. This helps to deepen understanding of contemporary conflicts and related historical processes of state or regime formation in modernity and the central role of integrated regimes of inequality in all of this.

Women in view

The tasks of addressing women's inequalities in a sectarian society in 'transition' from armed conflict are complex and vital. The first thing is to notice the invisibility of women and gender in explanations of the conflict itself, then to see how this invisibility is reflected in the equality agenda. The focus of the equality debate in Northern Ireland is the persistent sectarian unemployment differentials between Catholic and Protestant men. The impact of these upon the poorest women has never been examined and is never an issue for debate. As noted above, these women are more likely to be lone parents, to have lower disposable income and less control over family incomes; they fill the ranks of the low-paid and unofficial labour market (Daly 1989). They are the poorest group of people in any category referenced in the legislation. Intersectional aspects of recognition and redistribution in feminist critical race theory are useful for the analysis of gender inequalities in this context. Of first importance are the forms of concealment that constitute and govern public discourse and their implications for feminist thinking particularly in relation to political agency and coalition building across intersections of gender, sect and class. Being invisible in the discourse, or being assumed to be included though not mentioned, is one form of concealment. Mentioning 'women' in the literature whilst failing to bring the concept of gender into play is another, as is the focus upon gender as a neutral category which bypasses women.[14] In the Northern Ireland context there is the additional political gesture of avoiding allusions to women in the context of sectarianism. This works to conceal women, obviate gender and ignore the many inegalitarian consequences of sectarianism including its social divisiveness. This avoidance is significantly breached on occasions when women are hailed in particular ways into the narrative. Then the erstwhile concealed female presence often carries powerful rhetorical authority in contemporary conflicts.[15]

If you want to learn about women in the Northern Irish conflict, you would do well to steer clear of the mainstream academic analyses and key texts. In the vast literature generated by this conflict, women are either invisible or assumed to be included (McGarry and O'Leary 1995).[16] Occasionally, women are mentioned in passing in an author's effort to include them in an index. Indeed, the odd reference only serves to underscore their absence. This absence may initially seem simply a matter of common sense – men dominate in the politics, in the war and in the negotiations, so the discourse simply reflects the 'reality' of sex segregation. But this uncritiqued 'common-sense' reality is a disappearing act of 'legitimizing discourses' whereby women's invisibility goes unnoticed and unremarked (Lauret 2000).[17] Along with it, also unnoticed, goes any critique of the hegemonic masculinity of the discourse.[18] The 'disappearance' of women in the literature of the Northern Irish conflict is a discursive mechanism whereby women's subordination is 'routinely accepted' (Thomson 2006). Women are not 'there' in the discourse; neither are they 'there' in the power play where things happen. Effectively, they are kept apart from the conflict in the literature and are simply not visible in any way that reflects their presence in the population or understands their positioning in the gender regime and their role in conflict and transition. The masculinity of key actors is also unnoticed and taken for granted.[19] In the study of the Falls Road curfew, referenced at the start of this chapter, the masculinity of key actors is unremarked and taken for granted (Campbell and Connolly 2003). Local women from outside the curfew area marched with prams and children through armed military barriers to deliver food. They dramatically brought the curfew to an end. In the article they 'walk' onto the page and then disappear whilst the authors compare army and police arrests. All of those arrested were men. Presumably, given the time when this occurred, all those conducting the arrests were men. The article provides a valuable critique of the militarization of civil disturbance in Northern Ireland at an early decisive stage. Its focus on state intervention means that social class, gender, masculinity and women's agency in this important event are unexamined. The invisibility of women in Northern Ireland's mainstream academic conflict discourse means that the dynamic of what went on in the private sphere of the home and its political outworking in the public sphere is also closed to critical scrutiny.

Women are not treated as actors in the conflict narrative but as bystanders to the main event – a man's war. There are basically three observable approaches: women are invisible, or mentioned in passing, or referenced only in particular ways. The comprehensive University of Ulster's CAIN website is typical. Here the category 'women' is treated as a theme along with 'education' and 'attitudes'.[20] The investigation of how gender regimes inform and even constitute what is visible or what appears to be there for analysis in conflicts seems like a detour away from the politics of a given event or period, into a diversion on 'women in conflict'. Sometimes this work compounds the problem it seeks to remedy. The sole focus on women and avoidance of masculinity (and often of women's agency in conflict) reinforces the separation of women within the mainstream literature.[21] This separation is deepened when the only women who come to prominence in the Northern Ireland conflict appear to be uncomplicated by sectarian and class tensions and discriminations.[22] The men who dominate the narrative, on the other hand, appear to definitively embody disdained sectarian tensions as they threaten state stability. The avoidance of any critique of masculinity in this context also allows these gendered roles to escape critical scrutiny.

The preoccupation of most writers on this conflict has been in the more marketable arena of 'power politics', with the personalities, political parties and armed groups involved. In other words, it has focused on those who, when it comes to negotiations, do the negotiating. Other preoccupations in the literature are around matters to be negotiated: arms, prisoners, policing, victims, criminal justice, and, less so, human rights and equality; added to these are the challenges of the transitional period (Campbell *et al.* 2003). The urgency of addressing matters related to conflict, and of influencing policy and politics, as well as the legitimate aim of catching an academic market in the wake of a new 'war on terrorism', all seem to mitigate against the theoretical tasks of gender analyses of the Northern Irish conflict. It is with these theoretical tasks in mind that this chapter undertakes an analysis of gender and women's equality in transition.

The invisibility of women and the absence of gender awareness in the established literature on the Northern Ireland conflict are core to understanding how women get left out of account in the context of the transition. The precarious role of women in conflict narratives discursively maintains the invisibility of gender regimes operating within transitions. This precarious role is vital in sustaining the narrative fiction that conflicts are gender-free. Indeed, the massive literature and mainstream analysis of the Northern Irish conflict is gender-free. Women's invisibility in conflict narratives conceals how gender regimes frame what is in view. The masculinity of key actors is also invisible. Yet, gender as a key organizing principle of conflicts, one that structures the discursive 'frame for understanding', to use Butler's (2002) phrase, is nowhere examined in relation to Northern Ireland.[23]

Theory in place

The search to see and understand how women figure in societies fissured by conflicts around 'identity' led me to intersectional theory and efforts to analyse the interrelations of gender, sect and class. More specifically, intersectionality helps to reference how race and/or sect, class and gender work as integrated regimes of inequality within historical processes and, as such, has several benefits for thinking about the role of law and policy in conflict and transition. First, the introduction of gender deconstructs the primary, binary way of thinking about equality in terms of sectarian oppositions between men. It brings women into the frame. To some extent this mirrors the US experience, where race becomes the intersectional move qualifying the dominance of gender oppositions in 'race-free' feminist theory. At the same time, intersectionality qualifies the dominance of race oppositions in 'gender-free' race theory. Intersectional theory further qualifies gender/sect categories with the introduction of social class. It is used in this chapter to bring into view issues of poverty.

The thesis under construction is that gender regimes play a key role in conflicts, disadvantaging women in particular ways and the poorest women more than others. First and foremost, women are rendered invisible in conflict narratives and then left out of account in the implementation of beneficial equality provisions (Rooney 2004). Social identities, constituted through contested processes of state or regime formation, are not separable from gender and social class inequalities. Discursive gender regimes structure these conflict discourses in ways that 'preclude certain kinds of questions' and construct certain kinds of narrative (Butler 2002). Influential in these preliminary efforts to bring gender, sect and class into view and into play in understanding the Northern Ireland conflict are a range of feminist theorists who explore hegemonic silences within different discourses and their real world impacts on women's lives.[24] A useful tool in this exploration is feminist discourse analysis applied to how women are sometimes hailed into view in conflict narratives. This may be decisive at key moments when the presence of 'women' in the narrative confers legitimacy and authority particularly to violent action taken by states on behalf of women but from which women are normatively excluded.[25] The presence of 'women' can powerfully confer legitimacy and authority in contemporary war rhetoric.[26] Women are hailed into view but also kept apart, noticeable by their erstwhile absence from the mainstream account. The 'women' of these discourses are not the key actors, nor do they direct the action.[27] They are there to be noticed, admired, and protected. In these situations their presence rhetorically advances the political perspective dominant in the narrative. The apparent powerlessness of women in this narrative is at times strategically deployed in the management of the conflict to strong effect. To appear to be on the side of 'women' and to have women onside is occasionally an unassailable strategic position in the management of the discourse of modern conflicts.[28] This is the case for state as well as non-state actors. This challenges the common sense assumption, noted earlier, that women are a peripheral concern of states dealing with 'terrorist threat'. The sometimes decisive role of women in conflicts may be a powerful ideological and discursive resource. The 'woman' depicted, constituted and claimed by (and occasionally laying claim to) this discourse is a discursive construction with material and rhetorical effects. It is a construction of gender 'difference' at times deployed for quite specific political ends.[29]

The recognition of how gender difference operates in these contexts goes some way to bringing women into view. However, as Crenshaw (2004) comments, the knowledge that gender difference exists is only part of the theoretical work needed to understand what is going on: 'The struggle over which differences matter and which do not is neither an abstract nor an insignificant debate among women. Indeed, these conflicts are about more than difference as such; they raise critical issues of power' (ibid: 411). The conflicts referred to by Crenshaw are feminist disputes over theory and practice in relation to race in the US. Of particular interest, in relation to a society in transition from violent political conflict, is how gender regimes operate in a sectarian society that is 'politically divided' over the status of the state itself. The challenge eventually is to apply the theory-under-construction to the problem of the absence of the most marginalized women from the equality debate in Northern Ireland. As noted above, women's invisibility in the equality agenda and literature is reflective of women's precarious role within the conflict discourse. Moreover, introducing women into an apparently gender-free agenda reveals how gender is decisive. This chapter argues that these discourses are constituted by an absence of women. The work of asking questions otherwise not considered involves deconstructing dominant frameworks of understanding. The theory being discussed prepares the way for this approach. Throughout, I bear in mind the challenge from feminist jurisprudence that the critical testing ground of theory is not simply internal coherence but 'an ability to deliver' (Conaghan 2000: 364–5). Further research and debate on women's equality in Northern Ireland's transition is needed to inform the implementation of the equality legislation. Progress on the policy front that advances the intersectional equality provisions in the new legislation could deliver positive impacts for the most marginalized women in Northern Ireland.

My theoretical approach to gender is 'intersectional' although I do not confine the search for insight to any single discipline area. I draw upon Knapp's (2003) useful discussion and definition of gender within the frame of feminist sociology as a central, intersectional axis of dominance and inequality that structures contemporary society. Also pivotal are Conaghan's (2000) insights from feminist jurisprudence into how gender is both 'ignored and enshrined' in legal theory and discourse that has specific real world impacts that disadvantage women in general. Conaghan's point that the significance of gender is not 'practically diminished by its relative invisibility' leads her to argue for the creation of 'new knowledges which have the capacity both to liberate women … and subvert the hegemonic power of men' (ibid: 360–4). This 'new knowledge' is to be drawn from giving voice and authority to women and using women-centred approaches as a 'critical device'. The argument is altogether more complex than is allowed for in a brief reference, but what is useful and problematic is the assertion that giving voice to women will elucidate the problems of gender, class and sectarian inequality in a place such as Northern Ireland. Women's accounts will generally reflect their political location and relationship to the state (it may work better in relation to legal discourse that, as well as being blind to gender, appears to make no distinction between women). Giving 'voice to women' is important but it is not sufficient for the analysis that is required to understand what is going on. In the discourse of conflicts, such as that in Northern Ireland, selected women are sometimes reified (or 'enshrined' to use Conaghan's term) as victims, as peace-makers, as workers 'across the divide' – as specific kinds of discursively rendered symbolic presences that advance particular political understandings as well as perspectives on what it is to be a woman in this situation.

Simply mentioning women in the academic literature or even focusing on women where they are to be found in a conflict – as victims or less often as prisoners or activists and so on – may reveal little about the gender regime of conflicts. Indeed, the focus upon women in conflicts, whilst ignoring intersectional dimensions (see S.75 Northern Ireland Act 1998) or adopting a 'taken-for-granted' attitude towards gender as synonymous with 'all women', may compound the problem. It is not that everything is 'gender' nor that 'gender is everywhere'; 'it is simply the case that nothing is ontologically protected from [gender] that nothing is necessarily or naturally or ontologically not [gender]' – which may be very like saying that gender is everywhere, but it is not.[30] In this regard, the academic task is to develop ways to answer the question posed by Scott (2003: 378): 'how, in what specific contexts, among which specific communities of people and by what textual and social processes has meaning been acquired?' This chapter goes further and raises the questions: 'what are the material effects of these processes for women in conflicts?' and pragmatically 'what can law and policy do to offset these adverse effects in transitions?'

Post-structural deconstruction of power as diffused through society rather than located solely in the state (Parpart 1993: 440) is also useful and problematic when addressing questions about the state in a situation of conflict such as is the case for the British state in Northern Ireland. The mobilization of state power when the existence of the state itself is under attack is intensified through the state's ability to 'control knowledge and meaning, not only through writing, but also through disciplinary and professional institutions, and in social relations' (ibid). The management of conflict discourse is of fundamental importance. The British state's paradigmatic community-relations approach to the management of the Northern Irish conflict has resulted in a welter of 'community relations' research and attitude surveys that remove from the frame intersectional religious and political inequalities; moreover, they reframe the state's responsibilities with regard to these.[31] This discourse helps to generate the terms within which sectarianism in Northern Ireland is understood as dysfunctional attitudes belonging to Catholics and Protestants, or as a pathological problem that the 'two communities' share equally.[32] Structural inequalities disappear in a discourse that appears to provide recognition of 'difference' whilst collapsing this difference into a matter of problematic attitudes without redistributive policy implications.[33] The approach is similar to multicultural discourse around racism in Britain and elsewhere. Potential sources of conflict are handled by the state through an identity discourse that appears to accommodate (and construct) difference whilst doing nothing to materially change the circumstances that give rise to racism and its discriminatory consequences. This is carried through in the state-managed narrative of the Northern Irish conflict in a range of discourses which include formal social policy, community relations and equality as well as jurisprudence and state rhetoric on the use of force (Ní Aoláin 2000).[34]

Despite their invisibility in these discourses, women and gender play key roles in all of this, locally and internationally, as well as in historical processes that predate violent conflict. Much is at stake in the introduction of women and intersectional gender analysis into the frame.

Gender in a state

Understanding how gender and women have figured in 'historical processes that, through discourse position subjects and produce their experiences', to use Scott's (1992) analysis again, is virtually unexamined in British–Irish state-building colonial relations. The 'transitional moment' arguably opens a critical space to redress this in the postcolonial theoretical literature that is currently emerging in Ireland.[35] For instance, in a study of the term 'terrorist' in a formative moment of its deployment in British–Irish relations, Mac Suibhne and Martin (2005) examine the operations of gender in state mobilizations of fear and its role in state formation.[36] With regard to modern-day state derogations from human rights conventions in 'emergencies' (such as the 'war on terror'), gender plays a role in serving to legitimize derogations, as well as legitimizing discourses of state violence as reactive and designed for protection rather than aggression. The valorized but subordinate role of women (not powerful enough to be responsible for threat and most in need of protection) has been discursively deployed to justify war as a form of protection even of 'enemy women'.[37] The emergence of postcolonial theory in Ireland contributes critical understanding of gendered forms of nation-state–citizenship formation. This analysis has contemporary relevance for women's citizenship and reproductive rights in the Republic of Ireland.[38] Whilst the transitional justice literature augers caution on the transformative potential of the 'transitional moment', this (lengthening) moment in Ireland, North and South, opens critical space for transformative reflections on times past and their relevance for the present.[39]

Insights from feminist postcolonial theory, located within cultural studies in the US, are useful here as well. This theory places gender within the frame of colonial state-building strategies of 'divide and rule'. Valuable for reflections on the Northern Irish context is the over time sedimentation of intersectional inequality this entails (Shohatt 2002). Shohatt contributes to the 'identity' as 'difference' debate and argues that the 'question of differences [is] not about some essentialist ideas about differences ... but about positioning *vis-à-vis* the histories of power, especially since the advent of colonialism' (ibid: 75). The enforced confrontation of dependent cultures and peoples with dominant discourses (even apparently progressive ones around 'equality' and 'human rights') is a rich source of critical reflection on 'master narratives' and their real world impacts (Afshar 1996). As already noted, women in Northern Ireland occupy an unstable and precarious position in these discourses. Northern Ireland is 'not an irredeemable authoritarian state but a leading western democracy' (Campbell *et al.* 2003). Unlike other modern liberal democratic states, however, Northern Ireland has had to come to terms 'with institutional failure of a degree to which, on the state's definition, should have been impossible' (ibid). It has never achieved the collective amnesia regarding its coercive origins that pertains elsewhere (for instance in most European states) or that was asserted during the conflict by the political elite in the Republic of Ireland.[40] Ireland's national narrative continues to unravel and be remade and contested in ways that leave open both claims about its historical origins and questions of what it means to be a citizen in either jurisdiction on the island. At a time when nationalist (mainly Catholic) and unionist (mainly Protestant) identifications are institutionalized in the arrangements for power-sharing in Northern Ireland, the material and cultural weight of institutionalized sectarianism and its impact upon the poorest people can be undermined through the implementation of equality and policy commitments in the Agreement.[41] The tense political problems involved in institutional reform, and the consequences for power sharing and citizenship, suggest some of the complex issues involved in claims about women's equality in transitioning societies. The equality and human rights legislation deriving from the Agreement, and the commissions set up with oversight functions, arguably provide institutional mechanisms for tackling these problems and building a more just and stable society.

In order to enable us to get closer to seeing how to quantify and do something about women's inequalities, however complex the context, Conaghan (2000) calls for a 'focus on the concrete material details of women's lived existence' (ibid: 369). When this is applied to women's lives in Northern Ireland, it is productively problematic. Conaghan's concerns are with academic feminism and the women's movement. She suggests that a focus on material details is one way to avoid the 'trap' of essentialism as well as the academic trick of privileging theory that has lost hold of feminist politics. She proposes the focus on material details as a way to recuperate feminism from what she identifies as an affliction affecting academics, 'on the one hand, embracing intellectual trends which direct them away from the political concerns of the women's movement; on the other hand, unwilling to empty feminism of its traditional political content' (op. cit. supranote 14: 355). This 'affliction' has emerged in very different and instructive ways in Northern Ireland where the 'traditional political content' of feminist politics has emerged from and had to contend with the sectarianism of a state in conflict. In some areas this has led to a marriage of convenience between government sponsored 'community relations' funding and women's groups in the 'women's sector' (Rooney 2002).[42] Not surprisingly, one outcome is that organizations in the women's sector have developed strategies to secure funding by developing networks that represent Catholic and Protestant working-class women's groups. These alliances have mutually beneficial results in the most unpropitious circumstances. That the women's sector is sometimes showcased to international delegations as being 'above' sectarian politics is essentially a political trade-off about which many women are fully cognizant (Rooney 2002). The sector is subject to the vicissitudes of political developments and relies on treating 'women' as though they are a group uncomplicated by sectarian inequalities, class tensions and discriminations. The urge for women's unity in the wider Western feminist political project of 'global sisterhood', for instance, finds remarkable fulfilment in the 'woman' from Northern Ireland who occasionally comes to prominence.[43] This figure, like the female figure critiqued in race-free feminist theory, is without colour and without class, or her religion, race, sect or class does not appear to matter (Newman 1999).[44] She seems to affirm a dream of uniting women in their 'own interests' despite political and religious inequalities (Cockburn 1998).[45] In Northern Ireland this figure poses no threat to the state and makes no redistributive equality demands. Indeed, her prominence is arguably premised on this conservative function.[46] The integral roles of sectarian state formation and citizenship, of masculinity and social class are erased in the same manoeuvre. The silences about gender, sect and class are paid for by the poorest women whose circumstances are rendered invisible to the equality agenda.[47]

The legitimate strategic aim to advance women's interests in the women's sector, in Northern Ireland, has often led to a pragmatic approach that 'enshrines' or invents a unity of women otherwise 'divided' by intersections of gender, sect, and class.[48] The extent to which political and religious inequalities matter in Northern Ireland is not addressed. The unified 'woman' in the women's sector is an outcome of 'strategic essentialism' that provides marginal benefits for local groups.[49] This is not to say that the sector can be expected to take the lead in the debate required to tackle women's poverty. The local work of women's education, training and personal development is important for the women concerned and undoubtedly has impacts in local working class districts. A focus on sectarian discrimination in the sector could be divisive and detrimental to this fragile if exploitable 'unity'. As I say, there are costs for these discursive silences and they are unequally distributed.

In the context of Northern Ireland, the separation of women as apart from the conflict and the subsuming of gender into unitary notions of 'woman' serve to prohibit key considerations of women's equality from the debate required, especially in relation to tackling poverty. This separation derives from and reinforces how women are conditionally admitted to conflict narratives. The space reserved for women in mainstream discourse is one of innocence, victimhood or valorization – they are interdependent (Rooney, 2000b). The separation of this configured woman as apart from the conflict supports the contention that gender is a powerful principle in discursive constructions of modern conflicts.[50] Gender figures in militarized, masculinized, mobilizations of men, often in the defence of what is characterized as feminine – the home ('homeland') and the family ('nation') (Yuval-Davis 1997).[51] The configuration of woman as essentially peaceful is also a powerful narrative trope in the discourse and, as has been demonstrated, in state-sponsored war rhetoric.

Transitional conclusions

Recognizing how women are configured in conflict discourses that have practical consequences for law and policy in transitions illustrates how intersectionality can deepen the understanding of conflicts by reframing the analysis in terms of intersecting dimensions of inequality and discrimination. In Northern Ireland these are constitutive of state–citizen relations. The linkage between structural causes of conflict and gender relations calls for an analytic approach that explores situated and integrated regimes of gender and class inequality in state formation. It suggests a practical and theoretical approach to excavating 'gender' which is otherwise hidden behind the highly visible, disdained, sectarian binaries of 'Catholic' and 'Protestant'. It questions the specific ways that gender may be rendered visible as well as occluded in contemporary conflicts. It further seeks to identify specific ways that gender and sect are integrated into economic class relations, what the consequences are, and how these may be made visible in order to be remedied. The application of such an analysis could prove beneficial to understanding conflicts more generally. It provides an interpretative framework for thinking through how intersections of gender, sect and class shape experience and agency in a given political moment (Hill-Collins 2004: 69–70).

Deployed in the context of a society in transition from armed conflict, the analytical tools provided by intersectionality theory enable us to see that struggles for political 'recognition' simultaneously may involve claims for 'redistribution' of economic resources. The key problem in this situation is that the former may be formally granted through power sharing but that economic 'redistribution' will be resisted or withheld. Current signs are that this is the case.[52] What is more, in Northern Ireland the social policy framework to target objective social need has been in place for over fifteen years.[53] However, the latest social need indicators show that the poorest areas are increasing in poverty and social exclusion (Rooney 2006b).

Sectarianism, or the structural working of sect in state formation, is not the same as race in the US. The construct and experience of 'race' cannot simply be replaced, as it were, with the construct 'sect'. Scott's (2001) insight into the site-specific construction of identities comes into play once more: 'identities don't pre-exist their strategic political invocations'. The academic task carried forward in this essay is to investigate the material and social implications of these strategic political invocations in a range of discursive sites. Intersectionality theory functions as a conceptual framework or heuristic device for asking questions and describing the kinds of things to consider in this undertaking and, as such, has application in a sectarianized society. As previously argued, this is especially so at a time when sect is institutionalized in post-Agreement mechanisms of governance (Rooney 2000a). At this stage it is crucial to recognize and redress past harms. What Hill-Collins (2004) has to say of race and state–citizen relations in the US is insightful and cautionary. She observes that this relationship created 'immutable group identities' (ibid: 67). Integral to making race matter, she avers, is the related 'state distribution of social rewards to group membership [that] fosters a situation of group competition for scarce resources, [in the US] policing the boundaries of group membership becomes more important' (ibid: 69). Democratic participation in Northern Ireland is based upon and derives from the political affiliation and historical experience that sect broadly denotes. Whilst political and religious inequalities, and relationship with the state, are most evident in the marginalized Catholic and Protestant working-class urban and rural areas, this is where 'competition for scarce resources' is at a premium. This is where deprivation has to be tackled on the basis of objective social need. Women are invisible in the competition for 'scarce resources' but addressing women's poverty in deprived neighbourhoods may be a strategic way of defusing the competition and making life better for everyone.

Finally, the liberal democratic state of Northern Ireland might be seen as a 'moment' of European modernity. It is a place where unresolved, postcolonial state–citizen relations and contemporary indices of social deprivation are living evidence of state founding faultlines of gender, sect and class under pressure. This essay argues that in this context gender is constitutive of sect and class. The faultline metaphor is useful when applied to the intersectional triad in Northern Ireland. 'Catholic' and 'Protestant' identities are contingent, more complex than the labels allow and they are changing, sometimes it seems with a slowness associated with geological faultline formation. Elsewhere, nation-state founding faultlines upon which stable democratic polities are based are less visible. Arguably, from an Irish and European feminist perspective, intersectionality and critical race theory have been about exposing subordinations of nation-state formation in modernity. Nationalist and race politics (and arguably that of other so-called 'identities') are not merely an effect of modern state formation, but, as Wimmer (2002) argues, 'modernity itself rests on a basis of ethnic and nationalist principles'.[54] When the work of intersectional analysis is undertaken in Northern Ireland, the observation made by Knapp (2003) from a German perspective is pertinent. She reflects that the intersectional triad of race, class and gender – originating in the US context – has on its 'transatlantic route to Old Europe [become a] radical historical reminder of the dark sides of modernity' (ibid). She calls for critical attention to be paid to the 'uncanny and tense historical synchronicity' between the promise of universal rights and the invention of 'difference and inequality along the lines of gender/class/race' in the legitimizing politico-scientific discourses of modernity. Whilst this is a challenge for another day, it suggests the critical and figurative reach of the theoretical paradigm of intersectionality.

For now in Northern Ireland/ the North of Ireland the progressive challenge of the transitional moment is one where law and social policy may be used to implement a longer term social transformation that empties gender, sect and class of discriminatory weight and significance. It is a transition to a hoped-for future in which intersectional explanations of such categories are unnecessary and without contemporary political significance. That may be a utopian transition I am imagining. So be it. Socialist and feminist imaginings have been fuelled by utopian as well as dystopian imaginings albeit that 'topias', as well as transitions, need to be treated with critical caution.

Acknowledgements

The initial research for this chapter was undertaken with support from the Transitional Justice Institute, University of Ulster and developed as a Visiting Scholar on the Feminist Legal Theory Programme, Emory University Law School, 2006. I am grateful to the editors for valuable critical comments.

Bibliography

Afshar, H. (1996) *Women and Politics in the Third World*, London: Routledge.

Alison, M. H. (2003) '"We are fighting for the women's liberation also": A Comparative Study of Female Combatants in the Nationalist Conflicts in Sri Lanka and Northern Ireland', unpublished thesis, Queen's University Belfast.

Aretxaga, B. (1997) *Shattering Silence: Women, Nationalism, and Political Subjectivity in Northern Ireland*, Princeton, NJ: Princeton University Press.

Bottomley, A. (2004) 'Shock to Thought: An Encounter (of a Third Kind) with Legal Feminism', *Feminist Legal Studies*, 12: 29–65.

Brewer, J. and Higgins, G. (1998) *Anti-Catholicism in Northern Ireland, 1600–1998: The Mote and the Beam*, London and New York: Palgrave McMillan.

Butler, J. (2002) 'Explanation and Exoneration, or What We Can Hear', *Social Text* 72, 20: 177–88.

CAJ (Committee on the Administration of Justice) (2006a) *Equality in Northern Ireland: The Rhetoric and the Reality*, Belfast: Shanways.

CAJ (Committee on the Administration of Justice) (2006b) *Briefing on Religious and Political Inequalities in Northern Ireland*, Belfast: CAJ.

CAJ (Committee on the Administration of Justice) (2006c) *'Lifetime Opportunities': Government's Anti-Poverty and Social Inclusion Strategy for Northern Ireland: Briefing Note*, Belfast: CAJ.

Campbell, C. and Connolly, I. (2003) 'A Model for the "War on Terrorism?" Military Intervention in Northern Ireland and the Falls Curfew', *Journal of Law and Society*, 30: 341–75.

Campbell, C. and Ní Aoláin, F. (2002–03) 'Local Meets Global: Transitional Justice in Northern Ireland', *Fordham International Journal*, 26: 871–92.

Campbell, C., Ní Aoláin, F. and Harvey, C. (2003) 'The Frontiers of Legal Analysis: Reframing the Transition in Northern Ireland', *Modern Law Review*, 66/3: 317–45.

Carroll, C. and King, P. (eds) (2003) *Ireland and Postcolonial Theory*, Cork: Cork University Press.

Chang, R. S. and Culp, J. M. Jr. (2002) 'Symposium: Theorizing the Connections Among Systems of Subordination Responses and Commentary', *University of Missouri Kansas City Law Review* 71.

Cockburn, C. (1998) *The Space Between Us: Negotiating Gender and National Identities in Conflict*, London and New York: Zed Books.

Conaghan, J. (2000) 'Reassessing the Feminist Theoretical Project in Law', *Journal of Law and Society*, 27/3: 351–85.

Connell, R. W. (1995) *Masculinities*, Cambridge: Polity.

Crenshaw, K. (2004) 'Mapping the Margins: Intersectionality, Identity Politics, and Violence Against Women of Color', *Stanford Law Review*, 1241 (1991); reprinted in L. Richardson, V. Taylor and N. Whittier (eds) *Feminist Frontiers* (1983; 6th edn), Boston: McGraw-Hill.

Crilly, A., Gordon, H. and Rooney, E. (2002) 'Women in the North of Ireland: 1969–2000', in A. Bourke *et al.* (eds) *The Field Day Anthology of Irish Writing: Volume V: Irish Women's Writing and Traditions*, Cork: Cork University Press in association with Field Day.

Daly, M. (1989) *Women and Poverty*, Dublin: Attic Press.

Deane, S. (1991) 'Wherever Green is Read', *Revising the Rising*, Derry: Field Day.

Dodds, A. (2003) 'Review: *Nationalist Exclusion and Ethnic Conflict: Shadows of Modernity*, A. Wimmer, Cambridge: Cambridge University Press, 2002', *Contemporary Political Theory*, 2/2: 251.

Droichead an Dóchais (2005) *'Too Much Hurt': The Long Term Impact of a Conflict-Related Traumatic Incident in an Urban Area*, Belfast: Droichead an Dóchais. Online. Available HTTP: http://www.thebridgeofhope.org/index_files/articles/too%20much%20hurt%20final.pdf (accessed 28 February 2007).

Ehrenreich, N. (2002) 'Subordination and Symbiosis: Mechanisms of Mutual Support Between Subordinating Systems', *University of Missouri Kansas City Law Review* 71: 251–324.

Fearon, K. and McWilliams, M. (2000) 'Swimming Against the Mainstream: The Northern Ireland Women's Coalition', in C. Roulston and C. Davies (eds) *Gender, Democracy and Inclusion in Northern Ireland*, Basingstoke: Palgrave.

Hamilton, D. and Fisher, C. (eds) (2002) *Mapping West Belfast: A Statistical Overview of Socio-economic Disadvantage*, Belfast: West Belfast Economic Forum.

Hanafin, P. (2003) 'Valorising the Virtual Citizen: The Sacrificial Grounds of Postcolonial Citizenship in Ireland', *Law, Social Justice & Global Development Journal* Available HTTP: http://www2.warwick.ac.uk/fac/soc/law/elj/lgd/2003_1/hanafin/hanafin.rtf (accessed 25 February 2007).

Hill, M. (2003) *Women in Ireland: A Century of Change*, Belfast: The Blackstaff Press.

Hill-Collins, P. (2004) 'Some Group Matters: Intersectionality, Situated Standpoints, and Black Feminist Thought', *Fighting Words: Black Women and the Search for Justice*, Minnesota: University of Minnesota Press, 1998; reprinted in L.

Richardson, V. Taylor and N. Whittier (eds) *Feminist Frontiers* (1983; 6th edn), Boston: McGraw-Hill.

Hillyard, P., Rolston, B., and Tomlinson, M. (2005) *Poverty and Conflict in Ireland: An International Perspective*, Dublin: Combat Poverty Agency.

Honig, B. (1992) 'Towards an Agonistic Feminism: Hannah Arendt and the Politics of Identity', in J. Butler and J. Scott (eds) *Feminists Theorize the Political*, New York and London: Routledge.

Knapp, G.-A. 'Race, Class, Gender: Reclaiming Baggage in Fast-travelling theories ...', Keynote paper presented at European Intertexts Conference on Women's Writing in English as Part of a European Fabric, Hungary, June 2004 (on file with author).

Lauret, M. (2000) '"Race" and the Difference it Makes', *Women: A Cultural Review*, 11/1–2: 156–60.

Lorentzen, L. A. and Turpin, J. (eds) (1998) *The Women and War Reader*, New York and London: New York University Press.

Mac Suibhne, B. and Martin, A. (2005) 'Fenians in the Frame: Photographing Irish Political Prisoners, 1865–68', *Field Day Review*, 1: 101–19.

McCall, L. (2005) 'The Complexity of Intersectionality', *Signs*, 30/3: 1771–1800.

McCormack, I. and McCormack, V. (1995) 'More Bangs For Your Buck: Once For Jobs and Once For Justice', *Irish Reporter*, 17: 9–10.

McCrudden, C. (2003) 'Taking the Equality Agenda Forward', *Economic Bulletin*, 10/2: 5–11.

McGarry, J. and O'Leary, B. (1995) *Explaining Northern Ireland*, Oxford and Cambridge, MA.: Blackwell.

McKitterick, D., Kelters, S., Feeney, B., and Thornton, C. (1999) *Lost Lives: The Stories of the Men, Women and Children who died as a result of the Northern Ireland Troubles*, Edinburgh: Mainstream Publishing.

McMinn, J. (2000) 'The Changers and The Changed: An Analysis of Women's Community Education Groups in the North and South of Ireland', unpublished thesis, University College Dublin.

Miller, R. (2004) 'Social Mobility in Northern Ireland', in B. Osborne and I. Shuttleworth (eds) *Fair Employment in Northern Ireland: A Generation On*, Belfast: The Blackstaff Press and the Equality Commission for Northern Ireland.

Moore, R. (1993) 'Proper Wives, Orange Maidens or Disloyal Subjects: Situating the Equality Concerns of Protestant Women in Northern Ireland', unpublished thesis, University College Dublin.

Moore, T., *et al.* (2002) *Gender Equality in Northern Ireland*, Northern Ireland Assembly Research Paper 28/02, April; Northern Ireland Office Research and Library Services.

Newman, L. M. (1999) *White Women's Rights: The Racial Origins of Feminism in the United States*, New York and Oxford: Oxford University Press.

Ní Aoláin, F. (2000) *The Politics of Force: Conflict Management and State Violence in Northern Ireland*, Belfast: The Blackstaff Press.

Ní Dhonnchadha, M. and Dorgan, T. (eds) (1991) *Revising the Rising*, Derry: Field Day.

Noble, M., *et al.* (2005) *Measures of Deprivation in Northern Ireland*, Belfast: Northern Ireland Statistical Research Agency.

OFM/DFM (2004) *Indicators of Social Need for Northern Ireland*, Belfast: Northern Ireland Office. Online. Available HTTP: http://www.ofmdfmni.gov.uk/hbai.pdf (accessed 27 November 2006).

OFM/DFM, Gender Equality Unit (2005) *Gender Matters, 2005–2015*, Belfast: Northern Ireland Office. Online. Available HTTP: http://www.ofmdfmni.gov.uk/gendermatters.pdf (accessed 26 November 2006).

OFM/DFM, Equality Directorate Research Branch (2007) *Labour Force Religion Survey*, Belfast: Northern Ireland Office. Online. Available HTTP: http://www.northernireland.gov.uk/news/news-ofmdfm/news-ofmdfm-june-2007/news-ofmdfm-200607–labour-force-survey.htm (accessed 23 January 2008).

Osborne, B. and Shuttleworth, I. (eds) (2004) *Fair Employment in Northern Ireland: A Generation On*, Belfast: The Blackstaff Press and the Equality Commission for Northern Ireland.

Parpart, J. L. (1993) 'A Post-Modern Feminist Critique of Women and Development Theory', *Development and Change*, 24/3: 439–64.

Rawi, M. (2004) 'Rule of the Rapists', *The Guardian*, 12 February.

Rooney, E. (1995) 'Women in Political Conflict', *Race & Class*, 37/1: 51–7.

Rooney, E. (1999) 'Book Note: "Taking it Personally: Women & War", in L A Lorentzen and J Turpin (eds) *The Women & War Reader* New York and London, NY University Press', *Journal of Peace Research*, Vol. 3/5: 607–17.

Rooney, E. (2000a) 'Women in Northern Irish Politics: Difference Matters', in C. Roulston and C. Davies (eds) *Gender, Democracy and Inclusion in Northern Ireland*, Basingstoke: Palgrave.

Rooney, E. (2000b) 'Learning to Remember and Remembering to Forget: *Beloved* from Belfast', in L. Pearce (ed) *Devolving Identities: Feminist Readings in Home and Belonging*, Aldershot: Ashgate.

Rooney, E. (2002) 'Community Development in Times of Trouble: Reflections on the "Community Women's Sector" in the North of Ireland', *Community Development Journal: An International Forum: Ireland, Corporatism & Community Development: Special Issue*, 37/1: 33–46.

Rooney, E. (2003) 'Beyond Sex and Gender? A Belfast Response to Wendy Brown', *Feminist Theory*, 4/3: 371–5.

Rooney, E. (2004) 'Counting Women's Equality in West Belfast and Finding Failings in the Northern Ireland Equality Commission', *Women's Studies Review*, 9: 151–9.

Rooney, E. (2006a) 'Reflections on Northern Irish Women: Gendered Narratives of Absence and Silence', *Irish Feminist Review*, 2: 20–35.

Rooney, E. (2006b) 'Women's Equality in Northern Ireland's Transition: Intersectionality in Theory and Place', *Feminist Legal Studies*, 14/3: 353–75.

Roulston, C. and Davies, C. (eds) (2000) *Gender, Democracy and Inclusion in Northern Ireland*, Basingstoke: Palgrave.

Scott, J. W. (1992) '"Experience"', in J. Butler and J. Scott (eds) *Feminists Theorize the Political*, New York and London: Routledge.

Scott, J. W. (2001) 'Fantasy Echo: History and the Construction of Identity', *Critical Inquiry*, Winter, 127/2. Online. Available at HTTP: http://www.uchicago.edu/research/jnl-crit-inq/issues/v27/v27n2.scott.html (accessed 27 November 2006).

Scott, J. W. (2003) 'Deconstructing Equality-Versus-Difference: or, The Uses of Poststructrualist Theory for Feminism', in E. R. McCann and S. Kim (eds)

Feminist Theory Reader: Local and Global Perspectives, New York and London: Routledge.

Shohatt, E. (2002) 'Area Studies, Gender Studies and the Cartographies of Knowledge', *Social Text*, 20/3: 67–78.

Shohatt, E. (n.d.) 'Reflections by an Arab Jew', *Bint Jbeill*. Online. Available at HTTP: http://www.bintjbeil.com/E/occupation/arab_jew.html (accessed 25 February 2007).

Thomson, Michael (2006) 'Masculinity, Reproductivity and Law'. Online. Available at HTTP: www.ccels.cf.ac.uk/literature/publications/2005/thomsonpaper.pdf (accessed 27 November 2006).

Ware, V. (2000) 'References', *Feminist Review*, 66: 157–60.

Wimmer, A. (2002) *Nationalist Exclusion and Ethnic Conflict: Shadows of Modernity*, Cambridge: Cambridge University Press.

Yuval-Davis, N. (1997) *Gender and Nation*, London: Sage Publications.

Zalman, A. (2003) 'Out of the Rubble: Competing Perspectives on the Lives of Afghan Women', *The Women's Review of Books: A Feminist Guide to Good Reading*, April. Online. Available at HTTP: http://www.wellesley.edu/womensreview/archive/2003/04/highlt.html (accessed 27 November 2006).

Notes

1 Northern Ireland is a contested designation; many who oppose or question the union with Great Britain refer to the 'North of Ireland'.

2 The authors focus upon arrests and the criminal proceedings that followed to demonstrate that military action had an adverse impact in terms of brutality and effectiveness.

3 In the Good Friday/Belfast Agreement the British and Irish governments agreed that the territorial integrity of each sovereign state would be subject to the democratic mandate of citizens voting in Northern Ireland (Campbell *et al.* 2003). A majority voting for a unitary Irish state would thereby alter the territory of the United Kingdom and the Republic of Ireland.

4 For instance the Iraqi women's visit to Belfast in April 2005 was organized by the Iraqi Women's National Commission (details supplied by Ann Hope).

5 For examples see Roulston and Davies (2000); Cockburn (1998).

6 Some progress has been made. However, Catholic men remain twice as likely to be unemployed as Protestant men (OFM/DFM 2004).

7 The equality strand is given effect in the Northern Ireland Act 1998, S75 of which requires public authorities in carrying out their duties in Northern Ireland to: pay due regard to the need to promote equality of opportunity between persons of different religious belief, political opinion, racial group, age, marital status, or sexual orientation; between men and women generally; between persons with a disability and those without; and between persons with dependants and persons without.

8 A recent landmark review of fair employment legislation in NI contains no chapter on women (Osborne and Shuttleworth 2004). There is in this publication not even a page-numbered reference for 'women' in the index. Chapter 3, 'Social mobility in Northern Ireland', explores patterns of social mobility by religion and gender (Miller 2004: 49–64). In this, 'gender' is equivalent to 'neutral' sex difference.

9 OFM/DFM's latest Labour Force Religion Survey (2007) shows that women in Northern Ireland are at the bottom in terms of labour force equality and that Catholic women are 50 per cent more likely to be unemployed than Protestant women.

10 The NI Assembly functions through 'weighted majorities' based upon unionist (mainly Protestant) and nationalist (mainly Catholic) political representation.

11 The frequently noted 'complexity' of intersectionality is examined in McCall (2005). See also Chapter 2 in this volume.

12 For the emergence of 'post-intersectionality' see Chang and McCristal Culp (2002); also Ehrenreich (2002); however, McCall (2005) argues that intersectionality points up the limitations of 'gender' as a single analytical category and is the 'most important theoretical contribution that women's studies ... has made so far' (1771).

13 Research to support this strategic approach comes from a study of conflict related trauma experienced by second-generation young people where respondents stressed the positive importance and influence of women's parenting (Droichead an Dóchais 2005: 10).

14 This treats gender as having evenly balanced outcomes for women and men and is the approach adopted by OFM/DFM (2005), in its consultation document on gender in Northern Ireland.

15 For instance see citations below to how the protection of Afghan women was cited by the US administration as reason for the invasion of Afghanistan.

16 There is no reference to either women or gender in this standard text.

17 Lauret (2000) uses the term 'legitimizing discourses' to reference political appropriations of 'black identity' as positive acts of self-assertion.

18 Hegemony here is meant in the Gramscian sense referring to the maintenance of and consent to class inequalities in democratic society (Connell 1995: 77, cited in Thomson, 2006: 4).

19 Over 95 per cent of conflict-related deaths in the North were of men, and working-class areas paid the highest human costs (McKitterick et al. 1999; Hillyard et al. 2005).

20 CAIN (Conflict Archive on the Internet) http://cain.ulst.ac.uk/

21 For a survey of feminist work in Northern Ireland, see Rooney (1995), Crilly et al. (2002); for an all-Ireland survey, see Hill (2003); notable feminist studies include Aretxaga (1997) (Republicans), Cockburn (1998) (cross-community), and two unpublished dissertations, Moore (1993) (Protestant women), Alison (2003) (Republican women combatants).

22 For instance, the women of the Northern Ireland Women's Coalition (NIWC) were depicted as above sectarian division (Rooney 2003).

23 Butler's (2002) article examines what was able to be 'heard' and what was silenced and excluded from the post 9/11 public discourse in the explanatory framework that emerged.

24 They include Conaghan (2000) (law); Knapp (2003) (sociology); Parpart (1993) (development); and others. Each is engaged in specific scholarly terrain on the work of excavating hidden structures of power and oppression.

25 For instance, in addition to the de facto activation of the self-defence provisions of the UN Charter, the US administration cited the defence and protection of Afghan women as justification for overthrowing the Taliban regime in October 2001.

26 Five weeks after the invasion of Afghanistan, First Lady Laura Bush claimed, 'The fight against terrorism is also a fight for the rights and dignity of women' (Rawi 2004).

27 Some women in Afghanistan attempted to influence political action prior to the war. The Revolutionary Association of Women of Afghanistan (Rawa) gave footage of the execution of its leader, Zarmeens, to the BBC and CNN, only to be told that it was too shocking to broadcast. After September 11, 2001 the footage was aired repeatedly. Rawa's photographs documenting Taliban abuses of women were used without the organization's permission. The photos were reproduced as flyers and dropped by US warplanes as they flew over Afghanistan (Rawi 2004).

28 Unassailable until a feminist and human rights literature emerges to challenge the rhetoric, as has happened in the US and from Afghanistan in the wake of the war (Zalman 2003).

29 See for instance Rooney (2002) for a discussion of the high-profile 1998 Vital Voices women's conference on democracy attended by Hillary Clinton in Belfast where, in the context of building consensus for the Agreement, the contentious issue of local democracy was not on the agenda.

30 This citation adapts Honig's (1992) analysis of Arendt on the everywhereness of 'politics' (225).

31 This literature is vast. For a sample, visit: ARK Northern Ireland Social & Political Archive at http://www.ark.ac.uk/; Conflict Archive on the Internet (CAIN) at http://cain.ulst.ac.uk/othelem/organ/docs/crcpubs.htm; Northern Ireland Community Relations Council publications at http://www.community-relations.org.uk/services/publications/.

32 Shohatt's (n.d.) pertinent reflection on the characterization of the Middle East conflict as one of neat 'national and ethnic divisions', leads her to assert that, 'War ... is the friend of binarisms, leaving little place for complex identities'.

33 The pervasiveness of this approach and its discursive and discriminatory impacts cannot be examined here. Suffice to cite McCrudden's (2003) warning that 'if inequality is not tackled, sectarianism will not be tackled. Community relations activity that is not based on a notion of tackling inequality is community relations built on sand' (6).

34 On the disjunction between state rhetoric in the management of conflict discourse and 'actual practices of conflict management' through, for instance, the uses of force and legal processes, see Ní Aoláin (2000: 16).

35 The integration of postcolonial theory into the field of Irish studies is a relatively recent development (Carroll and King, 2003).

36 The authors argue that the period studied (1865–8) is an 'allegorical staging of one of the founding mythologies of the modern state. The condemnation of violence legitimates state violence and new modes of power, but presents this institutionalized violence as reactive and as designed to ensure the protection of citizens' (116).

37 See earlier citation with regard to the protection of Afghan women.

38 See Hanafin's (2003) reading of women's citizenship as one based upon self-sacrifice in the postcolonial Republic of Ireland.

39 See Campbell and Ní Aoláin, (2002–03: 876).

40 Deane's (1991) essay, cited earlier, was published with a range of academic views on the 1916 Irish rising to mark its 75th anniversary in 1991. The editors, and others, had originally hoped to organize a conference in Dublin on this founding event in modern Irish history. Official support was not forthcoming, and given that 'general discussion had been curiously muted, not to say inhibited', the writers settled for a publication, in the belief 'that, as a reaction, amnesia – private or communal – is both unhealthy and dangerous' (Ni Dhonnchadha and Dorgan 1991: ix). Hanafin (2003) also notes the amnesia in Irish society around

the state's foundation in violence (p.8). However, he also reports a strategic, post-conflict revival in elite claims to this historical inheritance.

41 The British government committed to, 'progressively eliminating the differential in unemployment rates between the two communities by targeting objective need' (Agreement: 24).

42 The 350 to 400 women's groups comprise the 'women's sector' and have attracted international feminist attention and admiration (Roulston and Davies 2000; Cockburn 1998; McMinn 2000). This is seen as a form of civic feminism overlapping with but distinguished from Republican feminism in that no formal position is taken on the constitutional question of state formation and citizenship in Northern Ireland (Aretxaga 1997; Rooney 2000a).

43 The Global Sisterhood Network is at: http://home.vicnet.net.au/~globalsn/. See Bottomley (2004) for analysis of the theoretical and practical problems posed by the unitary 'figure of woman' that emerges for stout defence in feminist jurisprudence.

44 Newman (1999) is critical of race-free feminist theory. Her study of US feminists provides evidence of 'feminist racism' and suggests that 'whiteness' lay at the heart of the feminist project. A political movement that demanded rights for women in general was capable of eliding smoothly into a women's rights agenda that explicitly privileged one racialized group of women at the expense of another (Ware 2000).

45 Cockburn (1998) recognizes this issue in her study of the Women's Support Network, which represents women's centres in Catholic and Protestant working-class districts of Belfast. For an analysis of the women's sector and government-sponsored community relations funding, see Rooney (2002).

46 For instance, the 'women's sector' is treated as non-political in a community relations discourse where 'politics' is construed as a disdained sectarian category (Rooney 2002). As noted above, the NIWC was represented as being beyond disdained sectarian division whilst the party itself envisioned a society freed from such divisions (Fearon and McWilliams 2000). It adopted a 'no position' position on the status of the Northern Ireland state.

47 There is no comprehensive study of women's poverty available in Northern Ireland; for a local analysis of women's poverty in the poorest constituency of West Belfast see Rooney (2004); for a critique of the failure of the Northern Ireland Equality Commission to include all of the S.75 grounds in its submission to the Committee for the Elimination of Discrimination Against Women, see Rooney (2006).

48 Efforts have been made to engage with feminist theorists but there is no local debate (Rooney 2003).

49 For a discussion of 'strategic essentialism', see Conaghan (2000: 368–9).

50 For a range of feminist perspectives on this, see Lorentzen and Turpin (1998); a review of this text is in Rooney (1999).

51 Cockburn (1998) discusses Yuval-Davis (1997) on how constructions of nationhood involve specific notions of both 'manhood' and 'womanhood' within which women are subordinate. Cockburn also suggests that 'if you see home as a "golden cage" you might suspect that homeland too has its contradictions'.

52 Recently reported indices of deprivation, that comparatively ranks electoral wards, indicate that the situation is worsening. Between 2001 and 2005, 12 of the 17 West Belfast wards, referred to earlier, increased their rank of deprivation. A leading human rights non-governmental organization, the CAJ, finds that 'Northern Ireland is one of the most unequal societies in the developed world, and the inequality is increasing' (CAJ, 2006b: 6).

53 This policy was intended to target those people objectively shown to be in greatest need. Originally it had no funding stream and was ineffective (McCormack and McCormack 1995). It has recently been replaced by a new anti-poverty strategy entitled, 'Lifetime Opportunities' available at: http://www.ofmdfmni.gov.uk/antipovertyandsocialinclusion.pdf. For an important critique of this policy see CAJ (2006c). Research remains outstanding on women's poverty.

54 See review in Dodds (2003: 251).

Chapter 9

Minority politics in Korea
Disability, interraciality, and gender

Eunjung Kim

Introduction

In the 1990s, South Korea has witnessed the growing visibility of resistance movements and pluralized activisms by minorities (*sosuja*) addressing multiple forms of social injustice. Occurring alongside larger existing movements of laborers, women, and disabled people, minority movements employ human rights discourse as a tool for raising awareness of severe marginalization. The National Human Rights Commission of the Republic of Korea, under the Nobel Peace Prize laureate, President Kim Dae Jung's leadership, was created in 2001 in an increased effort to enhance human rights in general. In 2006, the Commission released the National Action Plan for the Promotion and Protection of Human Rights (NAP). The NAP classifies "vulnerable social groups and minorities" according to eleven categories:

1   Disabled persons [Temporary workers with no benefits];
2   Irregular workers;
3   Migrant workers–refugees;
4   Women;
5   Children, juveniles;
6   Aged persons;
7   Disease sufferers [People with certain diseases or who have a history of stigmatizing disease];
8   Soldiers and riot/auxiliary police;
9   Persons living in social welfare facilities;
10   Sexual minorities;
11   North Korean displaced persons.[1]

The Commission states that the NAP "serves as a master plan for a country's human rights policies, represents a comprehensive national plan on human rights policies designed to improve legal and institutional mechanisms and practices relating to human rights" for the upcoming five years (National Human Rights Commission 2006: 9).

Each category includes people marginally positioned by unique historical circumstances which make them vulnerable in Korean society to violations of their human rights. For example, the number of temporary workers and laborers with no benefits increased after the economic crisis in 1997 when the International Monetary Fund's restructuring program under globalized neoliberalism embraced a greater labor market flexibility that caused massive lay-offs and job insecurity without providing other means of social security. The category "disease sufferers" not only includes people currently having a stigmatizing disease such as AIDS but also includes people with a history of having a disease like Hansen's Disease (leprosy), extending stigma beyond the presence of disease.[2] "Sexual minorities" include transsexual people and people who have same-sex relations.[3] The "soldiers and riot/auxiliary police" category addresses human rights violations within the armed forces including frequent violence against and the unexplained death of soldiers in the armed forces and requires full disclosure of this information to family members and the public.

Nevertheless, these classifications do not seem to consider sufficiently the intersectional effects of marginal categories. For example, while efforts have been made by the NAP to address overlapping populations such as disabled women and immigrant women, both mentioned under the general category of "women", disabled women and their experience are not registered under the category of "disabled persons." "Persons living in welfare facilities" includes people in private institutions, including nursing homes, and residential institutions in which 82 percent of people are disabled and elderly (NAP). This category reflects ongoing problems raised by disability activists about inhumane conditions, violence, and fraudulent use of funds in large-scale private residential facilities. Furthermore, the separate categories do not adequately capture those dynamics of disability, job security, and immigration affected by patriarchal social structures and gender discrimination. In many cases, the creation of a minority category gives no indication about how to determine who belongs primarily to the category.

This chapter examines the conflictual sites of different minority groups in South Korea and the effects on intersectional subjectivities provisionally formed in between identity categories. The emergence of disabled women in between disability rights movements and women's movements is one strong example of an intersectional identity position. Disabled women's new identity challenges previous activisms' prioritized identities such as gender *or* disability. However, the legal framework to safeguard disabled women from sexual violence considers disability identity as qualification for eligibility but defines disability as the complete lack of capability. In order to interrogate the categorical constructions, I trace the historical interconnection of stigma between interraciality and disability. The contemporary politics of the international marriage business between Korean disabled men and Vietnamese women illustrates conflicts and exploitation as well as intersections of minority groups in Korea. I argue for a theory of multiple consciousness about systems of oppressions – a theory that imagines new subject positions erased by dominant identities and that examines both the privileged and marginalized positions produced by classification of bodies.

Disabled women or female disabled persons

The exploration of a space in between categories and the need for a new identity that grasps liminal experiences offer useful insights for articulating the difficult processes of disabled women's subject-making in South Korea. For example, when the disabled women's movement emerged, two different words were used by activists to name themselves because no category existed previously to label their new position. One is a combination in one word of women and disabled people, *yŏsŏng-changae-in* (women-disability-person), which means "female disabled persons"; the other word uses disability in its adjectival form to modify women, *changae-yŏsŏng* (disability-women), which means "disabled women". These neologisms demonstrate both the difficulty of escaping established categories and the interstitial politics of disabled women. The debate over the two terms was never settled, and both words are currently used by the media interchangeably without invoking a sense of political incorrectness. Nevertheless, various organizations in the disabled women's movement apply the two usages differently depending on whether they wish to give political emphasis to the female identity of disabled women or accent women as a subcategory of disabled people.[4] While it is evident that disabled women's positions are formed by the categories of "disability" and "female gender," the question remains which category represents the more determining identity. In terms of social classifications, which identity names the common denominator and which identity becomes the qualifying adjective?[5] Is there an essential disability experience not determined by gendered norms? Is there a female experience that is not enforced by the "ability/disability system" of a society (Garland-Thomson 2002)? These are questions about classification that touch upon both minority identity politics and the intersection of subject positions.

Ella Shohat envisions intersectionality as crossings between class, racial, national, sexual, and gender-based struggles, describing them as "axes of stratification" (1998: 1).[6] In my speculation, linear axes may cross from time to time, creating multiple intersections between separate trajectories of oppressions. Separate constructions of individual forms of oppression, even if they intersect at numerous points for people who belong to multiple categories, do not negate the existence of the nonintersecting essence of each trajectory unmediated by other identities. On the contrary, people with single identity markers of gender or race are not free from the influence of other privileged identities that are disguised as "nonidentities" (McRuer 2003). Thus, the identities of these people should be understood in relation to nonidentity and its effect on identity category making. Intersectionality, when based on linear axes, can leave essentialism unchallenged because, in that framework, each oppression is assumed to have an essence that does not intersect with that of other identities.[7]

Because many people consider disabled people an internally undifferentiated group, recognizing the gender of disabled people raises concerns about dividing and weakening the power of the disability rights movement in general. For example, Disabled People International recently included the statement "disabled women are not a group separate from disabled people" in a discussion paper on the integration of women's issues at a UN convention (Arnade and Häfner 2005). The question of whether "disabled women" is a defining category has not been fully accepted by the disability community in general. The problem is that the two groups, women and disabled people, are frequently set against each other in cultural and political representations – a conflict that further silences disabled women. Consider that the remarks "disabled men are feminine" or "pregnant women are disabled people" are perceived as discriminatory because of stigmas attached to femininity or disability constructed prior to the alienation of disabled men or pregnant women. Rosemarie Garland-Thomson (2002) addresses this tension between femininity and disability. The language of deficiency and abnormality, according to her, is used to devalue women who are already seen as inferior to men. As a result, women have been associated historically with disability in Western culture. Such an interpretive move efficiently invokes one oppressive system to deprecate people marked by another system of representation (Garland-Thomson 2002: 8). This representational process has obscured the experience of disabled women because when femaleness registers as disability, hierarchies based on ability and disability status among women are trivialized. Furthermore, when anti-stigma movements try to emphasize women's competency as the basis of equality by saying "women are not disabled" or "disabled men are not feminine," the stigma attached to femininity or disability remains intact or is strengthened because the hierarchy between femininity and masculinity remains unquestioned. Caught in between, disabled women find it difficult to combat their devaluation in these mutual negations. When one minority group tries to seek equality by breaking away from the stigma produced by association with another group, the claim of equality can further naturalize the other minority group's alienation.

Although the remarkable emergence of the disabled women's movement indicates a new challenge to both mainstream Korean society and the disabled people's movement, the legislative grouping of disabled women does not always provide an effective position for forwarding critiques of social hierarchies. The attention to disabled women can also be bound by essentialist thinking about which aspects of oppression are based on identity either as women or as disabled persons. Research projects addressing the experience and oppression of disabled women were conducted as a result of the emergence of the disabled women's movement in the late 1990s and its entrance into the international arena after the Fourth Beijing World Conference on Women in 1995. Researchers employed the strategy of identifying the reality of disabled women based on mathematical formulations by using the terms "double oppression" or "triple oppression" (Oh and Kim 2000).[8] Disabled women are understood in this framework as a group produced by combining two existing social groups (or three, including lower class). Disabled women experience discrimination as disabled people in the area of education, employment, and accessibility of the built environment; and discrimination as women in the area of reproduction, sexual violence, marriage, and domestic roles (Oh and Kim 2000). Oh and Kim largely define disability discrimination within the public sphere but formulate gender discrimination within the domestic sphere. However, the binary of public versus private proves to be problematic in theorizing disabled women's everyday experiences. When public transport is made physically accessible, resolving disability discrimination, disabled women still experience frequent harassment by men and women when they use public transport. Disabled women are hired in irregular, low wage, and traditionally feminized positions, such as phone operators, more than disabled men. Such complicated workings of sexism and ableism often blur the public/private binary.

Sexual violence has been identified as the most urgent matter that has to be addressed for disabled women. Disability rights activists supported creating special consideration for victims with a disability in the Special Act on Sexual Violence of 1994 (Sŏngp'okryŏk T'ŭkbyŏlbŏp). As a result, a provision was included in 1994 regulating a harsher sentence for raping disabled women. However, because the provision only included "physical disability" as a victim's identity for the law to be applied, cases against women with cognitive or mental disabilities were often dismissed. Later in 1997, disability activists were successful in their efforts to amend the law in order to include the rape cases of women with cognitive disabilities; the 1997 amendment includes "mental disability" in order to address nonphysical disabilities. Provision 8 of the Special Act on Sexual Violence on disabled people reads: "a person who has sexual intercourse with a woman or assaults a person using the status of incapability of defense caused by physical or mental disability should be convicted on the basis of the Criminal Code 297 (rape) or 298 (forceful assault)." In other words, the law defines sexual intercourse (kanŭm) as rape when it occurs not by using physical force but by taking advantage of a disabled victim's vulnerability.

The provision poses two problems: the definition of disability as incapability of defense and the definition of rape as the use of force. Korean criminal law and its interpretation determine rape by the degree of force used against the victim, not by lack of consent. Violated persons often have to prove the presence of force by reporting defensive wounds on their bodies. If the violated person has a disability (or is considered to have one under provision 8), inability to defend oneself because of disability has to be proven for the code to be applied. Therefore, if a woman does not have the physical ability to defend herself against force, she cannot presumably exercise her right to consent to sexual relations. This means disabled women, if they are proven incapable of defending themselves physically or mentally, cannot consent to sex under the special legislation without it being rape. Naming any sexual relations of women with different physical and cognitive capabilities as rape denies disabled women's sexual desires and sexual agency. Alternatively, if a woman does not have a disability, the ability to defend is assumed automatically; to establish rape, she must show with her body signs of the violence that overpowered her resistance. Consequently, the burden of proof weighs on disabled women to demonstrate the preexistence of total defenselessness caused by disability. The legislative system forces sexual violence victims either to be identified as disabled, which equates complete incapability of defense with disability, or to be identified as nondisabled and have physical wounds to prove that they tried to defend themselves.

The preemptive indistinctness between rape and sexual intercourse encourages legal action to dismiss rape cases by casting in doubt the existence of the victim's disability. Thus, despite concerned professionals' initial reaction that the legislation could be overprotective and violate disabled women's freedom to have sexual relations, the legislation does not function as a protective tool. On April 20, 2005, Pusan (Busan) Kodŭng Pŏbwŏn (Higher Court) exonerated the defendant Kim, because even though the victim had a cognitive disability according to professionals, the court found that she was not disabled. During the trial period, the victim had to go through intellectual ability tests to prove her disability, and the tests determined that she had in fact the ability to defend herself, thus negating her disability status. The Sexual Violence Counseling Center for Disabled Women released a statement rejecting the court's decision, arguing that Kim's acquittal proved that the human rights of disabled women are not protected in Korea, because the identification of disability is dependent upon the power of the court and appointed professionals to define women as either disabled or nondisabled, no matter how the women identify themselves (Changae Yŏsŏng Sŏngp'okryŏk Sangdamso 2005)[9].

The example of sexual violence shows the inadequacy of identity based on legislation for ensuring human rights. Here disability identity functions merely as a screening condition for the legislation to be applied. The special legislation fails to address the vulnerabilities of disabled women that are created by society. Rather, due to the assumed lack of physical and cognitive ability to defend oneself, the legislation situates vulnerability within disabled women's bodies. Although disabled women's new subject positions articulate their unique identity and experiences, legislation that relies on the false separation between disabled and nondisabled persons assumes disability as well as gender identification as stable, measurable, and absolute. Thus, this legislation and its narrow interpretation fails to address rape as an action conditioned by the social tolerance of gendered violence and not by a victim's particular characteristics. In this scheme, disabled women are characterized as completely powerless victims and nondisabled women are thought able to defend themselves against rape if they do not consent. Both presumptions derive from a misogynous attitude that denies the existence of rape and places the blame on women's "innocence" or "promiscuity". It is important to think about how to eschew essentialist distinctions between disabled and nondisabled women and men and how to arrive at noncoercive and more flexible conceptions of disability and gender identity that do not deny either individual agency or the spectrum of different abilities and genders.

Interracial bodies, disability, and nationality

To understand how a minority subject is interpolated by the state and subjected to control or protection, it is crucial to engage in a genealogical exploration of the political relationship among many identities. Disability, femininity, sexuality, and race – particularly in post-war South Korea – demarcate the interlocking construction of problematized bodies managed together with nationality. Intersectionality here represents the organically interdependent construction of categories that need one another, rather than depending on the image of multiple, separate axes. My goal in this section is to provide a brief examination of such interdependent categories. In 1954, South Korea's Ministry of Health and Social Affairs started issuing annual statistical reports on populations that were considered to need the state's protection and surveillance. The first report included "leprosy patients, mixed-blood children, widows, drug addicts, patients with infectious diseases, and prostitutes" (Ministry of Health and Social Affairs 1954). A year later the categories of people with disabilities ("physically handicapped") and disabled veterans ("disabled soldiers") joined the catalog (1955). Whereas disability, interraciality, prostitution, and diseases were juxtaposed for the purpose of public health surveillance in the 1955 report, the first nationwide census of "handicapped" children conducted in 1961 by the Korean Child Welfare Committee classified interraciality and diseases under the category of "handicaps" (1962).[10] The children of mixed races were listed alongside children with various physical and sensory impairments, classified according to physical, mental, and social handicaps: "children with limb handicaps; audio-visual; mental; speech impediments; miscellaneous deformities; social handicaps (children of mixed racial parentage)" (ibid: 86). Although there was a distinction made among physical, mental, and social conditions, disability in general was not understood as solely an individual body's functional difference but rather as connected to the presence of external prejudice and stigma related to differentness.

Nonetheless, the stigma of interraciality was specifically constructed through its association with female gender and the lack of authentic Koreanness. The survey defined interracial children as "those children born of Korean *mothers* and foreigners," which excludes Chinese and Japanese (Korea Child Welfare Committee 1962: 91; emphasis added). By eliminating other East Asian ethnicities, the screening focused on the visibility of non-East Asian characteristics.[11] The survey was therefore designed specifically to count only children of Korean women and American military service men who had been born outside of marriage. The children were further classified into "white", "black", and "others" according to identifiable skin color, immediately reducing interracial children's race to that of the fathers and denying the heritage of Korean mothers. The survey also noted that interracial children who were born through legitimate marriages should be excluded from the definition of "handicap".

After World War II and the Korean War, being labeled as interracial (*t'uigi* in the derogatory Korean vernacular term) referred to children born to Korean prostitutes and American soldiers. Women who worked in the U.S. camp town (*kijich'on*) were often called pejoratively "*yanggongju*" (Yankee princess or Western princess), with the connotation of being "vulgar, low, dirty, and socially shameful," but also called "patriots" who contributed to Korean economy and US–South Korean security alliance by servicing American soldiers (Kim, H. 1997:180). In postwar Korea, the term, *yanggongju* has expanded to include "GI Brides", or Korean women in interracial marriages with soldiers (ibid:178).

Until the end of the twentieth century, the popular term for interracial people was *honhyŏla*, meaning "*children* with mixed blood" (not people or adults), implying figuratively that all interracial people have been infantilized, alienated, and marginalized in Korea and literally that most of them were presumably exiled from Korea before they grew up (National Human Rights Commission 2003: 6–7). The Korean Nationality Act defined nationality based on patrilineal heritage, granting nationality to people born to Korean fathers until the 1997 amendment. The focus on patrilineal heritage is more than just a sexist policy; it reflects how gender and reproduction were viewed in modern Korea. According to its hegemonic ideology, Korean nationality was made of one ethnicity (*minjok*),[12] and when a Korean woman gave birth after having a relationship with a foreign man without legally marrying him, that woman's body was considered to be violated or contaminated. To protect the symbolic and biological status of nationality from contamination, interracial people could not achieve Korean citizenship while growing up in Korea during the 1960s and 1970s.[12] Consequently, the newly emergent population of interracial people after the war – later called "Amerasians" – was stigmatized because the mothers supposedly prostituted themselves to Western foreigners.

The article by Anne Davidson in the 1961 survey report explains the reason why only certain interracial children were considered disabled. "Most of the mixed racial children in Korea," she writes, "are illegitimate because their mothers are casual or regular prostitutes of foreign servicemen" (Davidson 1962: 73). According to Davidson, the prostitutes' status depends on American men and socially acceptable marriage:

> If a western marriage is registered, the Korean community accepts it, but if the eastern custom is followed in a mixed marriage, the western country may not recognize it legally. When there is a marriage by Korean custom, as long as her "husband" remains in Korea, she is a respectable member of society, but when her "husband" leaves and returns to his own country, leaving her behind, everyone feels that he is a deserter. She is then thrust back into the community as an outcast and joins the group of cast-off wives, and other rejected people. Her chances of rehabilitation become very small.
>
> (Davidson 1962: 71)

The stigma of interracial children does not originate from their bodily characteristics but from their family arrangement and the lack of social sanction, the absence of a patriarch, and their mothers' prostitution, which causes disease and "feeble-mindedness" (Davidson 1962: 74). Davidson links prostitution, disability, and interracial reproduction directly. Davidson's description also suggests a hierarchy between Western and Korean culture. Of sole importance is the recognition of marriage by the husband's family, even if the wife's family has accepted the marriage.

Based on patrilineal ideology, governmental policies considered interracial people who were fathered by Americans to be Americans, thus construing them as national others. Therefore, a major policy of the government was to send interracial children "back" to the U.S. by migration or adoption. In the 1960s, those children were placed in segregated special schools and began to learn English as part of their curriculum in primary school in order to prepare for emigration (National Human Rights Commission 2003: 31–32). By 1968, 7,164 interracial children were adopted by U.S. citizens (Ministry of Health and Social Welfare 1968). In 1974, the category of "mixed blood" had disappeared from the annual statistical reports on public health and also from the disability category without a clear explanation. I speculate that the removal of the category does not necessarily reflect an actual decline in the number of interracial people. When forcing them to migrate was the primary goal, tracking their existence and integrating them into Korean society may have become insignificant. The comprehensive report on the lives of interracial people by the National Human Rights Commission states that the social integration of interracial people almost disappeared as an issue after 1982 from the media (2003).[13]

The removal of the interracial category from public health reports also reflects the transition of public health policy toward more medically configured disability and disease management divorced from the role of social stigma. Interracial people's lives in Korea were marked by rejection, exclusion, institutionalization, lack of education and employment, and poverty – all of which characterize life with disability in many aspects, including that of interracial people with physical and cognitive disabilities. This history of the construction of interraciality during the U.S. military occupation and afterwards, provides evidence that stigmatizing the body requires an association with the already devalued characteristics of other identities. The flexibility of disability as a category, one including interraciality in Korean history, cements a radical solidarity between the seemingly separate categories of disability and race. Furthermore, this solidarity allows us to recognize the positions of interracial people with disabilities as well as interracial sex workers who do not distance themselves from the stigma of prostitution.

However, in the discourse of contemporary minority activism, the human rights of interracial people often fails to mention the connection to other stigmatized groups, such as prostituted mothers and disabled people. Rather, human rights discourse often breaks away from other associated, stigmatized identities and attempts to valorize itself through qualifications of belonging to the dominant society, such as citizenship. In 2004, in order to generate awareness of interracial people's human rights, the National Human Rights Commission started broadcasting a television announcement. The announcement shows a series of still headshots of six people, one woman and five men, taken by the photographer Yi Jae Gap. Accompanied by inspirational music, the camera slowly zooms in on each photo to capture in-depth the gaze of the person. Each individual has an expressionless face looking back at the camera. These images compel viewers to meet the gaze of the person in the photo and to confront the long-avoided reality of interracial people's alienation. Following the photo of one person, the image of a Korean Resident Registration Card is given with the name of the birthplace in Korea. The ID card demonstrates the fact that these people are not foreigners but Koreans. Accompanying the photos, a man narrates the following: "My name is Bae Gi Cheol. I am Korean. Only because of different skin color, people say that I am different from them". The slow narration with pauses in between words demonstrates effectively that he speaks Korean as his mother tongue. At the end of the announcement, an official female voice addresses the audience with corresponding subtitles, "If you accept difference, you will see the world without discrimination".

Arguably, this television campaign is an attempt by the government to change the public understanding of "Koreanness" as not limited to Korean ethnicity. Meanwhile, it frames Koreanness as the ground of equality and human rights in specific ways, for example, speaking Korean, having a Korean name and official documentation, and being born in Korea. In fact, the announcement does not address interracial people's nationality based on their Korean heritage. The announcement presents an interesting contrast to the media frenzy about the American football player, Hines Ward, accepted as Korean in 2006. Because his mother is a Korean who was married to American G.I. and later emigrated to the U.S., he was claimed as one of "us" and awarded honorary Korean nationality. In the television announcement, however, the possibility that the interracial subjects may have one Korean parent is not included as evidence of their Koreanness. The audience is not informed that they are descendants of foreigners or interracial people with Korean heritage. This absence is an attempt to dissociate the widely held stigma that interracial people are "tainted" children of prostitutes. Moreover, this formulaic remaking of interracial people as Koreans ignores the human rights of many illegal immigrant laborers, while appealing to a liberal sentiment about diversity and who belongs to the nation. The employment of Korean nationality as the basis of social acceptance poses a significant problem because the act of claiming human rights reinforces other privileges of nationality. If the contemporary anti-stigma minority movement does not recognize its organic connection to other related stigmatized groups, it will end up reinforcing and justifying the oppression of other groups. The danger in claiming minoritized others as one of "us" is that it ignores connections between minoritized people and creates further minority factionalism.

The limitations of human rights grounded on nationality and citizenship, exemplified in the national human rights promotion for interracial people, become more evident if we take into account the impact of the international marriage trade on Korean minority men. The international marriage business in Vietnam targeting Korean men with intellectual or physical disabilities has become more visible since 2002 as a major consumer market. More and more billboards and banners about international marriage have appeared nationwide with the phrase "Marry a Vietnamese Virgin." In smaller font, most of the billboards say "For older, disabled people, first-time or second-time marriage."[14] Given that culturally and legally sanctioned marriage is heterosexual in present-day Korea, "people" here means "men" because the word "virgin" (ch'ŏnyŏ) largely designates females (Kim and Chivers 2005). The number of agencies that promote Vietnamese brides for "second-rate" Korean men, including disabled, rural, older, or divorced men, has increased, and with them, new advertisements with new phrases appear in many regions throughout the country. Some billboards include the disturbing phrase, "they never run away" in order to appease potential customers' fears about images of immigrant brides from China who "defraud" their Korean husbands and run away.[15] Other signs state that no payment is due until the marriage actually occurs. These statements reflect the view that these women are commodities (Kim and Chivers 2005).

More detailed advertising flyers distributed in the streets and subway stations in Seoul describe Vietnamese women as best suited for marriage with marginalized Korean men because these women admire Korean culture and men as affluent and caring. Such perceptions seemingly develop because of popular Korean television shows and films consumed in Vietnam. The flyers describe Vietnamese women as submissive, subservient, sacrificial, chaste, smart, possessing "beautiful faces, bodies, and similar ethnic origin to Koreans," and willing to "serve the parents-in-law and never divorce due to their traditional beliefs." The disparity between the economic situations and cultural enterprise of Vietnam and Korea allows for an intercultural hierarchy that supposedly compensates for disabled men's marginal status in South Korea.[16] The promotion emphasizes the invisibility of interracial characteristics of the second generation because Vietnamese presumably look similar to Koreans.

The association between disability and the bride business evolved before the international marriage trade between Korean men and foreign brides became popular. On the second of August 1990, *Kungmin Ilbo* (*Citizens Daily*) sensationally described Korean women in the marriage business as victims of trafficking. The article claimed that five Korean women were sent to marry "mentally retarded" men in Japan by a bride business agency ("Japan–Korea" 1990). This description sets up the disability of a husband as a horrifying condition that the Korean women are forced to accept. In the past, Korea was one of the countries from which women migrated to get jobs overseas or for a better life through marriage. The increasing rate of international marriage between foreign women and Korean men reflects Korea's transition from an export country that sends women away, to an import country that brings in foreign women. Countries sending brides to Korea now include China, Vietnam, the Philippines, Mongolia, Thailand, and Cambodia (Kang 2005).[17]

The commercial penchant for treating women as commodities, in addition to the racism displayed in the advertisements, invokes concerns about immigrant women's human rights. In fact, the overwhelming number of advertisements about tourism to Vietnam sponsored by the bride business has disturbed many people, including Vietnamese university students in Korea. Human rights activists have started demanding legislation that bans the commercial advertisement of women (Cho 2007). The media, concerned about human rights violations in these marriages, often portray one side as the victim while ignoring the other side's marginality. The media tell horror stories about domestic abuses against immigrant women. These abuses include mental and physical disabilities resulting from the marriages but also note that the women are abused by concealment of their husband's disability status prior to the marriage (Im 2004; C. H. Kim 2007). The media also portray disabled men as victims of women who run away from marriages after they have achieved legal status in Korea (Chŏng 2000; C. Yu 2006). Sensational depictions of each party's victimizations reflect the marginal status of disabled men and immigrant women in marriage arrangements.

Men's privilege, based on gender and nationality, and women's able-bodiedness form the ground on which both groups exploit each other.

The international marriage business illustrates the politics involved when multiple groups, marginalized on the basis of class, age, disability status, gender, and nationality, seek normalized lives. The mutual exploitation between groups can be tracked in marriage, caring labor, sexuality, reproduction, and cultural norms – all of which undergird the fantasy of the sanctioned heterosexual family. The discourse of one group's exploitation, i.e. Korean disabled men or nondisabled immigrant women as abused and defrauded by the other party, encourages the public to uphold the image of extreme vulnerability and pity for minority life. Inevitably, without understanding the system of marriage, which includes increased global migration, limited employment, and poverty, injustice can be easily blamed on another party.

How might we understand the alienation in marriage arrangements sought as a solution to marginalization? It is important to consider individuals' everyday life situations by giving attention to multiple systems of oppression. For example, the marriage transaction involves the devaluation of disability and unmarried life, the language and cultural differences of the spouses, legal naturalization of immigrants, and public attitudes about domestic violence. All of these factors help to construct the vulnerability of marginalized lives that exist under complicated circumstances leading individuals to choose the purchased marriage as an option, but rarely a viable one. The solution to isolation and limited social interactions, resources, and employment cannot be easily provided by women from "lesser" cultures.

If an identity-based approach to human rights does not examine the "constitutive historicity" of categories and the erasure of differences, the liberation of one group will not necessarily bring about democratic changes in the social structure (Butler 1993). While the demands of Korean disabled men and their families for marriage as a solution to personal care, reproduction, and sexual fulfillment created a new international marriage market, disabled women did not invite social attention on similar terms. Rather, the disabled women's movement stresses the dangers that disabled women face in marriage; disabled women confront in their marriages unique problems of violence, economic dependence, and reproductive risk often not addressed by nondisabled women's movements (T'a-Ri 38–43). Heavily gendered aspects of marriage, reproduction, and family life create an overly conflicted space for disabled women simply to demand access. Furthermore, when immigrant brides have a disability, they are considered undesirable or sent back to their home countries (Kim, 2003; Hu, 2003). If we are to decouple the identities used by oppressive formations, whether disability-maleness-heterosexuality or femaleness-heteronationality-ablebodiedness, it is important to pay attention to the perspectives of the erased groups lost in between minority groups because they represent the multiple structures involved – in this case, the perspectives of Korean and Vietnamese disabled women toward the cultural imperialism and discrimination that they experience in the marriage market and family life.

Concluding remarks: intersectionality and interminority consciousness

As feminism faces the challenge of incorporating race, sexuality, class, disability, age, and nationality, a new feminist subject position is needed. This position aims at eradicating multiple forms of subordination and generating a transnational democratic citizenship. Presumed impermeability between separate identity categories represses the voices of multiply identified people and standardizes intragroup differences. It also produces distance and tension between different groups on the margins (Crenshaw 1997a). For this reason, communication is often more complicated between two oppressed groups than between the dominant group and an oppressed group. Multiple identities for women of color based on their gender, race, ethnicity, disability, sexuality, class, nationality, and other differences are possible; however, these identities often lie in contradiction, for the act of claiming one identity requires the reservation of one and distance from another. Trina Grillo addresses this conflict by warning against the very use of multiple identities. "We speak with multiple voices," she states, "only because we have categories that describe these voices as separate from one another" (1995: 17). Moreover, many discussions of intersectionality recognize that political identities are grounded in categories enforced by the dominant culture. Donna Haraway speaks to this point:

> Gender, race, or class consciousness is an achievement forced on us by the terrible historical experience of the contradictory social realities of patriarchy, colonialism, and capitalism....Which identities are available to ground such a potent political myth called 'us,' and what could motivate enlistment in this collectivity?
>
> (Haraway 1991: 155)

Although acts of reappropriating dominant cultural denominations as self-claimed identities may empower certain groups, people who are not called upon as primary subjects in identity politics do not automatically benefit from such empowerment. Silenced by external oppressions, internal hierarchy, and a sense of loyalty to an oppressed community, marginal people with multiple markers struggle against the fragmentation of their experiences by uneasy identity politics connected to dominant cultures and political activism alike. As the construction of South Korean minority categories shows, modern forms of subjugation often arrange gender, disability, race, class, nationality, and sexuality as interdependent coordinates of marginalization.

In *Looking White People in the Eye* (1998), Sherene Razack addresses the importance of examining the analytical tools of racism, sexism, and subcategories of women. She argues:

> Analytical tools that consist of looking at how systems of oppression interlock, differ in emphasis from those that stress intersectionality. Interlocking systems need one another, and in tracing the complex ways in which they help to secure one another, we learn how women are produced into positions that exist symbiotically but hierarchically.
>
> (Razack 1998: 13)[18]

Understanding symbiotic relationships in the construction of marginality demands attention to the fact that the body cannot be divided into countable marginalized identities when one marginalization is enabled by another identity. The imposition of stigma upon a certain unfamiliar body relies on existing stigmas, building an association between the established stigmas of one group and those of the unfamiliar group. For example, newly emergent interracial populations in Korea were immediately associated with the stigma of prostitution, and simultaneously, the livelihood of mothers accused of prostitution were affected by the birth of interracial children. Reasserting the humanity of stigmatized groups by applying other identity qualifications, such as nationality, masculinity, or sanctioned family, presents a challenge to multiply identified minorities striving toward shared equality. Disability studies has criticized political theories including feminism and anti-racism for distancing themselves from disability and not recognizing their naturalization of disability stigma. Mitchell and Snyder, for example, argue that:

> Race, feminist, and queer studies have all participated to one degree or another in a philosophical lineage that seeks to distance those social categories from more "real" biological incapacities.
>
> (1997:6, cited in Snyder and Mitchell 2006:17)

Moreover, they propose that claims to equality often rely on the exclusion of disability:

> Thus, in order to counteract charges of deviance historically assigned to blackness, femininity, or homosexuality, these political discourses have tended to reify disability as "true" insufficiency, thereby extricating their own populations from equations of inferiority.
>
> (Snyder and Mitchell 2006:17)

In parallel, the disability rights movement and disability studies also need to develop multiple consciousness about transnational contexts beyond Western cultures, including a recognition that gender, race, sexuality, age, class, nationality and other differences constitute hierarchies within the broad category of disability.

The 2005 amendment of the National Human Rights Commission Act (2001), which currently serves as a foundation for Korean anti-discrimination law unrelated to group-membership, offers a different starting point from the eleven categories of minorities discussed at the opening of my argument. It defines the violation of the constitutional right to equality as

> discrimination without reasonable grounds [in the areas of] employment, resource distribution, education, and sexual harassment [based on] gender, religion, disability, age, social status, birthplace, country of origin, ethnicity of origin, appearance or physical condition, marriage status, pregnancy or reproduction, family type or family situation, race, skin color, ideology or political opinion, criminal record, sexual preference, educational career, or the history of having a disease.
> (Ministry of Government Legislation, Article 2–4)

This extensive list encompasses significant social and cultural designations that maintain hierarchy, privilege, and stigma in South Korea, without resorting to exclusivity of conditions to constitute minority membership. Although it does not engage the intersectional effects of the listed conditions, it neither relies on proof of minority membership for people to be protected under anti-discrimination legislation nor assumes that a person has monolithic marker of marginalization. Multiple consciousness about systems of oppressions, achieved by reconsidering parallel and interdependent categories, is imperative to fight the forces that create inequality among people.

Acknowledgments

My work on this chapter is deeply indebted to a number of scholars whose ideas are incorporated here. I express my gratitude to Tobin Siebers whose feedback was vital to improving this chapter. I also thank Kyeonghee Choi, Sally Chivers, Mark Sherry, Michael Gill, Michelle Jarman, David Mitchell, Katrin Schultheiss, and Sharon Snyder who encouraged me to work on this issue and provided an enormous amount of help and discussion along the way. I am also indebted to many activists involved in the disabled women's movement in Korea. I also thank the editors of the volume and the anonymous reviewers who provided great help.

Bibliography

Amerasian Act. (1982) U.S. Public Law 97–359.

Arnade, S. and Häfner, S. (2005) "Towards Visibility of Women with Disabilities in the UN Convention." Disabled Peoples' International (ed), a paper presented at Comprehensive and Integral International Convention on the Protection of the Rights and Dignity of Persons with Disabilities in Berlin, July 2005. Online. Available HTTP: <http://v1.dpi.org/lang-en/resources/details.php?page=278> (accessed 26 September 2006).

Butler, J. (1993) *Bodies that Matter: On the Discursive Limit of "Sex,"* New York: Routledge.

Changaeyŏsŏng Sŏngp'okryŏk Sangdamso [Sexual Violence Counseling Center for Disabled Women] (2005) "Official Announcement on Busan Court's Ruling Acquittal in the Case of the Woman with Cognitive Disability." Online. Available. HTTP: <http://www.was.or.kr> (accessed 5 January 2006).

Cho, H. (2007) "Vietnamese Virgin Billboards will Disappear." *Han'gyŏre Sinmun* [Han'gyŏre Newspaper], 30 January.

Chŏng, H. (2000) "Marriage Scam of Mongolian Women." *Munhwa Ilbo*, 27 March.

Coleman, L.M. (2006) "Stigma: An Enigma Demystified," in L. Davis (ed.) *Disability Studies Reader*, 2nd edn, New York: Routledge.

Collins, P.H. (2000) *Black Feminist Thought: Knowledge, Consciousness and the Politics of Empowerment*, 2nd edn., New York: Routledge.

Crenshaw, K. (1997a) "Intersectionality and Identity Politics: Learning from Violence against Women of Color," in Wendy K. Kolmar and Frances Bartkowski (eds) *Feminist Theory*, 2nd edn, [2003], Boston: McGraw-Hill College.

Crenshaw, K. (1997b) "Beyond Racism and Misogyny: Black Feminism and 2 Live Crew," in Diana Tietjens Meyers (ed.) *Feminist Social Thought: A Reader*, New York: Routledge.

Davidson, A. (1962). "The Mixed Racial Child," in Korean Child Welfare Committee (ed.) *Handicapped Children's Survey Report*, Seoul: Korean Child Welfare Committee.

Fine, M. and Asch, A. (eds) (1988) *Women with Disabilities: Essays in Psychology, Culture and Politics*, Philadelphia, PA: Temple University Press.

Garland-Thomson, R. (2002) "Integrating Disability, Transforming Feminist Theory," *NWSA*, 14(3):1–32.

Goffman, E. (1963) *Stigma: Notes on the Management of Spoiled Identity*, New York: Touchstone.

Grillo, T. (1995) "Anti-Essentialism and Intersectionality: Tools to Dismantle the Master's House," *Berkeley Women's Law Journal*, 10: 17–30.

Haraway, D. (1991) "A Cyborg Manifesto: Science, Technology, and Socialist-Feminism in the Late Twentieth Century," *Simians, Cyborgs and Women: The Reinvention of Nature*, New York: Routledge.

Hull, G., Scott, P.B., and Smith, B. (eds) (1982) *All the Women Are White, All the Blacks Are Men, but Some of Us Are Brave : Black Women's Studies*, Old Westbury: Feminist Press.

Im, Y. (2004) "Immigrant Women, Vulnerable to Trafficking and Violence." *Yŏsŏng Sinmun* [*Women's Newspaper*], 10 December.

Kang, C. (2005) "One out of Four Rural Bachelors Marry Foreign Women." *Kyŏnghang Sinmun* [*Tendency Newspaper*], 28 June.

Kim, C.H. (2007) "Does Paying Money Make Beating Okay?: International Marriage, Bruised by Verbal, Physical, and Sexual Violence." *Kungmin Ilbo* [*Citizens Daily*], 2 February.

Kim, E. and Chivers, S. (2005) "Trafficking Care: Race and Gender in In-Home Care Program," paper presented at Hidden Cost, Invisible Contribution Symposium at Trent University in Peterborough, Canada, 8–10 June.

Kim, H.S. (1997) "Yanggongju as an Allegory of the Nation: Images of Working-Class Women in Popular and Radical Texts," in E.H. Kim and C. Choi (eds) *Dangerous Women: Gender and Korean Nationalism*, New York: Routledge.

Kim, S. (2003) "Marriage Scam, Nat'asha and I," *Han'gyŏre 21* 450, 13 March. Online. Available HTTP: <http://www.hani.co.kr/section-021003000/2003/03/021003000200303130450014.html> (accessed 20 Mar 2006).

Korean Child Welfare Committee ([1961] 1962) *Handicapped Children's Survey Report*, Seoul: Korean Child Welfare Committee.

Kungmin Ilbo [Citizens Daily] (1990) "Japan–Korea Match Making Scam. Five Korean Virgins were Sent to Marry Japanese Disabled Person", 2 August.

Lloyd, M. (2005) *Beyond Identity Politics: Feminism, Power and Politics*, London: Sage.

McRuer, R. (2003) "As Good As It Gets: Queer Theory and Critical Disability," *GLQ: A Journal of Lesbian and Gay Studies,* 9(1–2): 79–105.

Ministry of Government Legislation (2001) *National Human Rights Commission Act.* Online. Available. HTTP: < http://www.klaw.go.kr>, accessed 23 May 2006.

Ministry of Health and Social Affairs (1954–1999) *Pogŏn Sahoi T'onggye Yŏnbo [Annual Statistics on Public Health and Social Affairs]*, Seoul: Ministry of Health and Social Affairs.

National Human Rights Commission (2003) *Kijich'on Honhyŏlin In'gwŏn Siltae Chosa [Army Base Mixed Blood People Human Rights Reality Survey]*. Online. Available HTTP: <http://www.humanrights.go.kr/> (accessed 2 April 2005).

National Human Rights Commission (2004) "Public Announcement." Video file. Online. Available. HTTP: <http://www.humanrights.go.kr/> (accessed 23 May 2005).

National Human Rights Commission (2006) "Kukga In'gwŏn Chŏnch'aek Kibon Kyehoik Kwŏngoan" [National Action Plan for the Promotion and Protection of Human Rights (NAP)]. Online. Available. HTTP: <http://www.humanrights.go.kr/> (accessed 27 November 2006).

O, T'aejin (2005) "Imported Brides," *Chosun Ilbo*, 27 June.

Oh, H.G. and Kim, C.A. (2000) *Yŏsŏng Changaeingwa Ijungchabyŏl [Women with Disabilities and Double Discrimination]*, Seoul: Hakchisa.

Onishi, N. (2007) "Betrothed at First Sight: A Korean–Vietnamese Courtship," *The New York Times*, 22 February.

Pak, H. (1996) "Scam Marriage of Korean Chinese is a Problem," *Seoul Sinmun [Seoul Newspaper]*, 4 March.

Razack, S.H. (1998) *Looking White People in the Eye: Gender, Race and Culture in Courtrooms and Classrooms*, Toronto: University of Toronto Press.

Shohat, E. (ed.) (1998) "Introduction," *Talking Visions: Multicultural Feminism in a Transnational Age*, New York: New Museum of Contemporary Art.

Snyder, S.L. and Mitchell, D.T. (2006) *Cultural Locations of Disability*, Chicago, IL: University of Chicago Press.

T'a-Ri (2003) "'Yŏjŏnhi Nae Sarmŭn Kodan Hada': Changaeyŏsŏng-gwa Kyŏlhon" ["My Life is Still Tiring": Disabled Women and Marriage], *Konggam [Empathy]*, 6: 38–43.

Yang, H. (1997) "Remembering the Korean Military Comfort Women: Nationalism, Sexuality, and Silencing" in E.H. Kim and C. Choi (eds) *Dangerous Women: Gender and Korean Nationalism*. New York: Routledge.

Yu, C. (2006) "Old Bachelors with Disability Cried Twice," *Kangwŏn Ilbo* [*Kangwŏn Daily*], 9 January. Online. Available. HTTP:<http://www.kwnews.co.kr/sub/search/default.asp?p=%C0%E5%BE%D6%C0%CE%B3%EB%C3%D1%B0%A2> (accessed 12 Feb 2007).

Yu, H. (2003) "Marriage or Dangerous Shopping," *Han'gyŏre 21* 450. 13 March./20 March. Online. Available. HTTP: < http://www.hani.co.kr/section-021003000/2003/03/021003000200303130450023.html> (accessed 20 March 2006).

Notes

1 The terms are translated into English by the Commission in the English version of the report.

2 Building upon Erving Goffman's description of stigma as equivalent to "undesired differentness" (1963:5), Lerita M. Coleman defines stigmatization as what "occurs only when the social control component is imposed, or when the undesired differentness leads to some restriction in physical and social mobility and access to opportunities that allow an individual to develop his or her potential" (2006: 149). This essay adopts Coleman's definition of stigma and extends it to incorporate moral and hygienic judgments constructed around undesired differentness. In particular, the essay focuses on the classification of persons simultaneously as a byproduct and precondition of stigmatization. The use of attributes of one group as a tool of inscribing stigma on another group creates further tensions among stigmatized groups in both stigmatizing and destigmatizing processes.

3 The Criminal Act defines rape as an act of a man against a woman and does not include sexual violence between same sex individuals. Moreover, the Military Criminal Act defines same-sex relations as "sodomy." The NAP addresses the legal discrimination against sexual minorities as well as the public's resistance to their gathering together and exchanging information. The NAP emphasizes sexual minorities' rights to existence, safety, employment, and freedom from prejudice and discrimination, as well as their right to national health insurance coverage for sex-reassignment surgeries.

4 Changaeyŏsŏng Konggam (Women with Disabilities Empathy) is one of the few organizations including the term "disabled women" in their Korean name. I was one of the advocates of the term "disabled women," arguing that "women" and "people" are redundant, as in "female disabled people," for designating personhood and that gender should not be treated as an additive feature. My argument was that disability should be treated as a changeable trait by social standards as well as gender. Now I am open to both terms because I do not think that one identity should be prioritized over the other.

5 I focus on identity as a social classification rather than an individual psychological and cultural identification, although the two are interrelated. Legal and political categories of minority groups and identifiability are a more important point of inquiry in this essay. Whether or not a disabled woman chooses to identify as a disabled person or a woman primarily is also influenced by social interactions and the political system.

6 Feminist legal theorist, Kimberlé Crenshaw suggests the notion of political intersectionality, along with structural and representational intersectionality (1997b), seeking to explain the systems of privilege and the problem of monolithic identity politics on which anti-discrimination legislation is based in the U.S.

7 Trina Grillo explains the relationship between essentialism and identity: "Essentialism is the notion that there is a single woman's, or Black person's, or any other group's experience that can be described independently from other aspects of the person – that there is an essence to that experience" (Grillo 1995: 20). Kimberlé Crenshaw distinguishes intersectionality from anti-essentialism (1997a).

8 Similarly, Western scholars such as Michelle Fine and Adrienne Asch use of the term "double oppression," albeit in a scare quote, in their classic book *Women with Disabilities* (1988). Accordingly, they highlight the core of disabled women's experience as rolelessness, which makes disabled women a kind of "social nomad."

9 After this chapter was written, the case was reconsidered in the Supreme Court of Korea and the court revoked the previous ruling in July 2007. The Supreme Court states that the definition of disability has to be understood broadly considering not only the degree of disability but also social relationships, power dynamics and contexts. This ruling addresses some of the problems raised in this chapter, although the problem of the term "defenselessness" as a basis of protection remains.

10 The survey was conducted by trained local agents from all precincts, who visited each household and recorded the number of children and the characteristics of their bodily conditions in order to identify the welfare needs of "handicapped" children nationwide. The survey was funded by various North American organizations, including the U.S. Army, Pearl Buck, and Christian missionaries in Korea. This explains the survey's particular focus on interracial children and the U.S. adoption policy.

11 Although racialization and discrimination existed against Japanese and Chinese immigrants, there was a significant number of unmarked interethnic descendants in Korea.

12 *Minjok* refers to people who belong to a common ethnic group, such that all Koreans are assumed to constitute one homogenous Self. Invocation of this national self affirms a unified identity, based on an unchangeable essence that is transmitted through blood and homogeneous culture (Yang, H. 1997:128).

13 There was some exceptional application of the territorial principle (*jus soli*) for abandoned babies, whose father's nationality could not be identified and who were born in Korea. The government has allowed Amerasian children to be registered under the mother's name since 1980 without any information about the father (National Human Rights Commission 2003: 20). An amendment was made in 1997 to give nationality to people if either one of their parents is Korean.

14 In 1982, the U.S. legislated the Amerasian Act, which provided full and automatic citizenship for certain Amerasians migrating to the U.S. It states: "in order to qualify for benefits under this law, an alien must have been born in Cambodia, Korea, Laos, Thailand, or Vietnam after December 31, 1950, and before October 22, 1982, and have been fathered by a U.S. citizen" (U.S. Public Law 97–359). Migration provided only a partial "solution" to the marginalization of interracial people in Korea. Given that the U.S. army had been stationed in Korea since 1945, the window of birth years between 1951 and 1982 was not

inclusive enough for many people born before 1951. When the legislation was enacted, many interracial adults in their thirties found it hardly viable to enter the U.S. through adoption (National Human Rights Commission 2003).

15 On February 22, 2007, *The New York Times* reported this phenomenon under the title, "Betrothed at First Sight: A Korean–Vietnamese Courtship" (Onishi). The article explains the reasons for the increase in Korean–Vietnamese marriages with two factors, rising social status of women and sex-screening technology, i.e. female fetus abortion that causes a surplus of unmarried men.

16 Among many newspaper articles reporting marriage fraud cases for Korean–Chinese brides, *Seoul Sinmun* (*Seoul Newspaper*) reported the danger of an increasing number of scammed marriages by brides who used marriage as a way to migrate to South Korea, took money from the husband's family, and ran away (Pak 1996).

17 International or interracial marriage has not been a very popular phenomenon but has been traditionally considered taboo. Commercialized interracial and international marriage practices have emerged in Korean public culture since the 1980s. In the late 1980s, rural areas were being depopulated at a high rate. The difficulty that men in agricultural areas had in getting married emerged as a social issue. Urban women were depicted in the media as not wanting to marry rural men, to work in agriculture, or to accept traditional extended family living with parents-in-law. Unmarried males were considered more problematic than unattached females. In 1990, regional offices and agricultural associations began to promote international marriage between Korean men and Korean-Chinese women, even though the illegitimate trafficking in foreign brides already existed (O 2005).

18 In 2005, 27.4 percent of men in the agricultural and fishing industries married foreign women (Kang 2005).

19 Patricia Hill Collins also carefully distinguishes her theoretical concept, the "matrix of domination," from intersectionality (2000: 18). In 1978, the Combahee River Collective used the term "interlocking systems of oppressions" to describe the importance of collective political solidarity. See the group's essay in the edited volume by Hull *et al.* (1982).

Chapter 10

Migrant women destabilizing borders

Citizenship debates in Ireland

Siobhán Mullally

Introduction

In June 2004, a referendum on citizenship was held in Ireland. The referendum and subsequent constitutional amendment led to restrictions being imposed on the constitutionally protected right to citizenship by birth. The citizenship referendum followed a period of heated debate on the meaning of citizenship and the terms on which migrant families would be allowed to remain in Ireland. This chapter examines the challenge posed by the migrant female subject to Ireland's citizenship laws and the potential of intersectionality analysis to respond to that challenge and support strategic political engagement with questions of migration and citizenship.

Intersecting, as Conaghan notes elsewhere in this volume, can denote passing or crossing. Intersectionality analysis would seem particularly apt, therefore, to examine the experiences of migrant women who cross borders, and who, in doing so, expose themselves to the risk of status related inequalities and exclusions. At a time when sovereignty is shrinking, the state acts upon vulnerable categories of migrants (often asylum seekers) to reestablish and affirm its power to control borders. Lubhéid notes in the Irish context:

> While childbearing by asylum seeker women is represented as a threat to the sovereignty of the nation-state, in fact, their presence has allowed the State to refashion the national imaginary, reinvent itself, and implement new strategies of sexualized, racialized governance.
>
> (Lubhéid 2004: 344)

Although reproduction and sexuality were at the centre of the citizenship debates, the constructions of gender and sexuality that underpinned debates on the need for reform were often ignored by anti-racist and migrant rights campaigners. This chapter, drawing on feminist intersectionality analysis, explores the moral panic that both sensationalized – through their 'hyper visibility' – and silenced migrant women coming to Ireland. Migrant women, particularly Black women from the South, were represented as dangerously fertile foreign bodies, threatening the boundedness of the nation-state. Positioned as 'undeserving poor' or 'citizen tourists', exploiting the logic of free market citizenship, the embodied migrant woman evaded and undermined the state's immigration controls, threatening the integrity of the nation-state. Familiar gender tropes were deployed by the state, as migrant women were 'fixed' into pre-defined categories of threat to the national interest. At the same time, the state highlighted the instability linked with migrant women's bodies, the potential to reproduce, and the inability of the state to limit or constrain this potential.

Intersectionality analysis is deployed here in this chapter as a tool to highlight the ways in which migrant women were positioned, reduced, and essentialized, in the citizenship debates in Ireland. In this context, intersectionality analysis assists us in highlighting the gendered, racialized configurations of migrant women that were often overlooked in critiques of the citizenship debates. Also becoming visible through such analysis, are the privileges and inequalities that go with citizenship status, inequalities that are linked with inherited statuses, and that push and pull women through difficult journeys (Schachar 2003). Through such journeys, migrant women, crossing borders, are potentially at the intersections of many overlapping axes of discrimination. Neither the categories of gender or 'race' adequately capture the obstacles, the multiple forms of exclusion experienced, however. The question for us, here, is how far intersectionality analysis can take us. In particular, can it support strategic political and legal engagement so as to bring about improvements in the lives of migrant women?

The *jus soli* principle and citizenship debates in Ireland

The debate on birthright citizenship placed migrant women's roles in reproduction at the centre of legal and political debate in Ireland. Migrant women's bodies, their sexuality and reproductive roles became the subject of heightened scrutiny, with newspapers reporting daily on the numbers of migrant women availing of maternity services in Irish hospitals. Of course, the intersection of gender, national identity and reproduction is not new to Ireland. Women's reproductive rights in Ireland have long been a contested terrain. Defining Ireland in exclusively 'pro-life' terms served as a distinguishing mark of Irish identity. The family, sexuality and reproductive rights fell within the boundaries of the private, the sphere of domestic jurisdiction and served to underpin the nation-state's claim to a distinct cultural identity. This assertion of national identity provided a commonality and sense of solidarity in a nascent nation-state, scarred by the trauma of partition and civil war. It also, as with much of identity politics, elided differences within, silencing, in particular, women who did not fit with the mythical female figures that personified the Irish nation-woman.[1] In the citizenship debates in Ireland, women were defined yet again by their reproductive roles and, yet again, the assertion of reproductive autonomy was rejected as a threat to the nation's ethno-cultural identity. These debates reveal both the gendered and racialized underpinnings of such nationalistic identity claims. The exclusivity of the family unit that is provided with constitutional protection was also revealed. Migrant families, denied the protection of the state, were not considered to be 'indispensable to the welfare of the Nation or the State' (see: article 41, Irish Constitution).

In 1998, following peace negotiations and the conclusion of the Good Friday Agreement in Northern Ireland, a new article 2 was inserted into the Irish Constitution,[2] giving constitutional recognition to the right to citizenship by birth.[3] This affirmation of birthright citizenship coincided with a constitutional amendment recognizing the 'diversity of identities and traditions on the island of Ireland.'[4] The coincidence of increasing immigration in Ireland with the Good Friday Agreement and constitutional change, has been described by the Irish Supreme Court as an 'accident of history.'[5] It is an 'accident' that provided the Irish government with an opportunity to develop an open and inclusive concept of citizenship. That opportunity, at least for the moment, however, appears to have been passed by.

This search for defining attributes of the nation is not unique to Ireland. As Iris Young points out, nationalist ideologies have always tended to define their groups in either/or terms (Young 2000: 252). The nation is conceptualized as strictly bounded between insiders and outsiders, as nationalists struggle to define attributes of national identity or character that all members share. The representation of Ireland as mother and the nation as a family were established signifiers of community and common lineage (Quinn 1997; Boland 1989). The largely middle-class Gaelic League, founded in 1893 to promote Irish literature and culture, idealized mother and home as 'the repository of spiritual, moral and affective values' (Quinn 1997: 41). Women were constructed as the bearers and cultural reproducers of the future nation. For the Gaelic League, the domestic sphere was the site of a nationalist pedagogy, a pedagogy that conflated women's roles with motherhood and quiet domesticity (Butler 1901).

Against this background, assertions of reproductive or sexual autonomy have been perceived as threatening, destabilizing forces. The autonomy and agency of migrant women, often pregnant, crossing Ireland's borders, deciding when and where to give birth, destabilized the certainties and limits of border control. Migrant women coming to Ireland and bearing children posed a threat to the racial homogeneity of the nation, revealing the exclusivity of Irish understandings of 'the nation', 'the family' and 'the citizenry' (Lentin 2003). While Irish nationalism celebrated women's roles as mothers, migrant women's reproductive roles were not to be celebrated. Mother Ireland was to remain 'white' Mother Ireland.

The 1937 Constitution of Ireland, Bunreacht na hÉireann, had left open the question of how citizenship was to be allocated, providing only that citizenship status would be determined in accordance with law.[6] It was presumed that the *jus soli* principle of citizenship by birth would continue to apply as part of the inherited body of common law. In 1956, the Irish Nationality and Citizenship Act was passed, providing for citizenship by birth or descent. The primary concern within the legislature was to ensure that all those born in the island of Ireland would be entitled to citizenship. Citizenship laws could transcend the partition of the island into North and South. The still nascent project of nation-building required an open and inclusive concept of citizenship. Emigration and depopulation were threats to the project of nation-building and so the *jus sanguinis* principle, allowing for citizenship by descent, was also provided for. This inclusive concept of citizenship was not all-embracing, however. From the beginning, we see the association of 'otherness' with danger. Speaking on the passage of the Irish Nationality and Citizenship Act in 1956, Deputy Esmonde noted that while the entitlement to citizenship by birth was desirable, 'in one sense', such an entitlement also carried with it a 'certain amount of danger'. There were, he noted, 'a great number of people [in the world] who would be undesirable to us in Ireland'.[7] Esmonde's comments reflect an assumed commonality within the Irish nation and a denial of the humanity of the stranger. This assumption and denial was to continue to surface in debates on immigration and citizenship in Ireland.

The case of *Osheku* v *Ireland*[8] was one of the earliest cases to deal with the right to family life in the context of immigration decisions. Gannon J, speaking for the High Court, concluded that the fundamental rights protected by the constitution were not absolute. In an oft-quoted statement, he defended a quintessentially state-centred view on the limits and scope of fundamental rights. There were, he said, 'fundamental rights of the State itself as well as fundamental rights of the individual citizens, and the protection of the former may involve restrictions in circumstances of necessity on the latter'.[9] In a statement that reflects the exclusionary impulse behind the nation-state, he noted that the 1935 Aliens Act reflected the philosophy of the nation-state: 'Its unspoken major premise is that aliens have, in general, no right to be on the national territory'.[10] As we shall see, it is this exclusionary impulse that has guided, or misguided, legislative and judicial responses to the claims made by migrant families in Ireland.

The position of children born in Ireland to third country national parents was the subject of greatest debate in the 1990 decision of the Supreme Court, *Fajujonu* v *Minister for Justice*.[11] The *Fajujonu* case involved a husband and wife, of Nigerian and Moroccan nationality respectively. The couple were living in Ireland, without documentation. When the matter finally came before the Supreme Court, Mr and Mrs Fajujonu had been resident in the state for more than eight years. The third-named plaintiff, their eldest daughter,

Miriam Fajujonu, was born in Ireland and a citizen by birth. The Fajujonus had two further Irish citizen children. Finlay CJ, speaking for the majority of the Supreme Court, concluded that a citizen child had a constitutional right to the 'company, care and parentage of their parents within a family unit'. Subject to the 'exigencies of the common good', this was a right, he held, which could be exercised within the state. Particular emphasis was placed on the Fajujonus' residence for 'an appreciable time' within the state. Walsh J, concurring with the majority judgment, placed greater emphasis on the rights of the family as a constitutionally protected unit and the need to protect the integrity of the family. The children, he said, were of tender age, requiring the society of their parents. In the particular circumstances of this case, to move to expel the parents would be inconsistent with the constitutionally protected rights of the family.[12]

The findings of the Supreme Court and, in particular, the judgment of Walsh J, reflect the cardinal value of citizenship for a child: 'the ability to enjoy the company, care and parentage of their parents within a family unit within the State'. In the *Fajujonu* case, the family had withstood the test of time, resident in Ireland for almost eight years prior to the Supreme Court judgment. In the Court's judgment, immigration is not represented as a threat to the state or the process of nation-building. The representation of migration in the courts was to change significantly over the next decade, however.

Following on from the *Fajujonu* judgment, applications for residence from undocumented migrant parents were routinely granted. However over the next decade, the migration context in Ireland was to change dramatically. The number of migrant parents claiming residency on the basis of Irish citizen children increased from approximately 1,500 in 1999 to over 6,000 in 2001. At the beginning of 2003, more than 11,500 applications for residence from undocumented migrant parents were pending with the ministry. As the numbers of families claiming residence rights increased, political pressure to deny these claims grew. Bowing to this pressure, the Minister for Justice, Equality and Law Reform began to refuse or stay applications in late 2002, leading finally to the Supreme Court judgment in the *L.* and *O.* cases in January 2003.[13] By this time, the right to citizenship by birth had been enshrined as a constitutional right, following the Belfast Agreement and the Nineteenth Amendment to the Constitution Act, 1998.[14]

The *L.* and *O.* cases involved two families of Czech Roma and Nigerian origin, each with Irish citizen children. Deportation proceedings were commenced against *L.* and *O.* following the failure of their asylum applications. Seeking a judicial review of the deportation orders, *L.* and *O.* both asserted a right to exercise a choice of residence on behalf of their citizen children, and on behalf of their children claimed the right to the company, care and parentage of their parents within the state. The majority of the Supreme Court distinguished the *Fajujonu* case on the basis of the length of time the parents had lived within the state and the changing context of immigration in Ireland since then. Using the terms of Finlay CJ's judgment in *Fajujonu,* the majority of the Supreme Court concluded that neither family had been within the state for 'an appreciable time', such as to give rise to a right to residence. Keane CJ distinguished the nature of citizenship claims enjoyed by children and adults. While an adult citizen had an automatic right to reside in the state, he said, the position of minors was 'significantly different'.[15] The right to reside within the state could not vest in a minor until she or he was capable of exercising such a right. And, while the parents could assert a choice of residence on behalf of their citizen children, any claims made by the parents were subject to the exigencies of the common good. The requirements of the common good were defined by the Court solely with reference to the State's interest in controlling immigration and in maintaining the 'integrity of the asylum system'.

The *L.* and *O.* cases also raised questions concerning the constitutional commitment to protecting the 'inalienable and imprescriptible' rights of the family. Article 41 of the constitution assigns the family an exceptionally important status and role in the 'welfare of the Nation and the State'. The rights of the family are described in the constitutional text as being 'antecedent and superior' to all positive law, including, this would suggest, to immigration and asylum law. Ireland's commitment to the protection of the family unit has frequently been invoked as a marker of Ireland's distinct national identity.[16] In *McGee* v *Attorney General,* Walsh J noted that the family, as the 'natural primary and fundamental unit group of society', had rights that the state could not control.[17] In the *L.* and *O.* cases, however, the court concluded the state's right to control immigration, and to safeguard the integrity of the asylum and immigration systems took priority over any claims asserted by undocumented migrant family units. Only certain kinds of families, it would seem, are deserving of the constitutional protection afforded by the very entrenched provisions on family life.

The findings of the Supreme Court in the *L.* and *O.* cases stand in marked contrast to the court's deference to the family unit in previous cases. Just one year earlier, in the *N.W.H.B* case, Keane CJ held that the family, because it derives from the 'natural order', was endowed with an authority that the constitution itself recognized as being superior even to the authority of the state. He went on to argue that the constitution outlawed any attempt by the state to usurp 'the exclusive and privileged role of the family in the social order.'[18] In the same case, Murphy J noted that the express terms of the constitution relegated the state to a subordinate and subsidiary role.[19] The circumstances that could justify intervention by the state in the family unit, he said, must be exceptional indeed. Such exceptions have been found to arise where the best interests of the child required intervention. In the *L.* and *O.* cases, however, this line of reasoning was turned on its head, with the

State's interest in immigration control invoked to challenge the exercise of parental authority and to undermine the child's best interests.

The role of law, understood as referring to positive legal texts, differs markedly in these cases. Contrast the subordinate and subsidiary role given to the state in the *N.W.H.B.* case with the following statement on migration from Denham J in the *L.* and *O.* cases:[20]

> Over thousands of years waves of people have come ashore on the island of Ireland. However, the island found by those early migrants was very different from the Ireland of today. The differences included those of the landscape, society and governance. [...] Today Ireland is not covered by great oak forests. Raths have been replaced by housing estates and apartment blocks. The Brehon law has been displaced by modern Irish law. The principles and law governing Irish society today come from the people and are to be found in the Constitution of Ireland, 1937, and the legislation of the Oireachtas. It is to that Constitution and law we must look to determine the issues of our times. The days when migrating people would sail long boats up an Irish river, pull the boat up the shingle, and set up home in Ireland, without recourse to a central government, are long gone. *Today people who migrate to Ireland may arrive by many means but they must comply with the Constitution and the law.* (emphasis added)

The role of the state and the law in racializing the Irish 'people' here referred to, is central. Migrant women, at the intersections of the state's racializing processes, threaten to destabilize both the gendered and racialized identities constructed by the State. In response to this threat, we see the 'Constitution and the law' invoked to position migrant women as strangers, as other. Drawing on intersectionality analysis, to engage in a re-reading of the legal texts, allows for the possibility of a fuller representation of the experiences of migrant women in Ireland, who through their roles as mothers, were central figures in these cases. It plays an important role in highlighting the subjective experiences of gendered racialized subjects, who are not deemed to be deserving of the protection of the Constitution and the law. It does not, however, give us the resources to propose legal and political reforms or to challenge the normative underpinnings of border controls.

Removing the right to citizenship by birth: migrant women challenging borders

Despite the Supreme Court judgment in the *L.* and *O.* cases and change in practice, migrant women continued to travel to Ireland and to give birth to their children within the state. Predictions that the judgment would stem the flow of inward migration to the state failed to materialize. The government decided, therefore, to take further action and in April 2004, announced its intention to hold a referendum on a proposed constitutional amendment, to impose restrictions on the right to citizenship by birth where a child was born within the state to non-Irish nationals.[21] In the months preceding the citizenship referendum, the Minister for Justice Equality and Law Reform, Michael McDowell, repeatedly emphasized the crisis posed to the State's maternity services by migrant women arriving in Ireland:

> Our maternity services come under pressure because they have to deal at short notice with women who may have communication difficulties, about whom no previous history of the pregnancy or of the mother's health is known ... Hospitals cannot predict the demand on resources from month to month.
>
> (McDowell 2004: 1)

The migrant woman, because of her possible childbearing role, posed a threat to the state's overriding concern with immigration control. Predictability in immigration numbers could not be guaranteed. In presenting the proposed amendment, the government was anxious to portray its move as a compassionate one, designed to minimize the risks faced by migrant women taking 'hazardous journeys' to come to Ireland at late stages of their pregnancy. To reduce such risks, it was necessary, they said, to remove the incentive that induced women to take such journeys in the first place. This meant removing the right to citizenship by birth (ibid.).

Discussion of migrant women's childbearing and reproductive roles allowed for a circulation of racist imagery, in a way that was unsanctioned. Media headlines included: 'Racial Time Bomb Set to Explode as Crisis Deepens' (*Irish Independent*, 27 January 2002); 'State Alert as Pregnant Asylum Seekers aim for Ireland' (*Irish Examiner*, 4 December 2001) and 'Non-nationals Fuel Pregnancy Crisis' (*Irish Examiner*, 21 February 2001). In 2002, an elected councillor (member of local government) publicly commented that 'refugees and asylum seekers are breeding like rabbits here' (*Irish Times*, 16 April 2002). This reiteration of racialized imagery, through reproduction and sexuality, contributed to a climate of inequality and fear. The National Consultative Committee on Racism and Interculturalism reported that pregnant Black women and Black women with children were becoming targets of verbal and physical abuse (*Irish Times*, 14 March 2002). The National Women's Council of Ireland, representing more than 300,000 women, responded to the government's proposal by calling for a no vote in the referendum. The government, they said, was blaming migrant women and children for the state's repeated failure to properly resource the Irish maternity and health services. What was needed, they argued, was 'a fair and comprehensive immigration policy that is compassionate, anti-racist and recognizes the rights and needs of women' (National Women's

Council of Ireland 2004: 1). The Irish Human Rights Commission (IHRC), in presenting its observations on the proposed referendum, pointed out that much of the evidence offered in support of the proposed amendment was anecdotal in nature and inconclusive (IHRC: 2004). Specifically, the commission concluded that the data offered was insufficient to allow anyone to draw inferences as to the motives of non-national parents giving birth in Ireland to the extent argued by the government. Such particularities were erased as all migrant women were presented as a threat to the state's interest in immigration control or as victims of unscrupulous traffickers. The commission also pointed out that the proposed changes were discriminatory, as they imposed restrictions on one category of citizens with 'no substantial historical or familial connection to Ireland', while not addressing the citizenship entitlements of other equivalent groups, including those who obtained citizenship by descent without having to establish any substantial connection with the state (ibid. para.5).

Despite these concerns, however, the electorate voted, by a majority of almost four to one, in favour of the proposal. The Nationality and Citizenship (Amdt) Act, 2004, subsequently enacted, provides that children may acquire citizenship by birth only if their parents have been lawfully resident in the state for three years or more. Nira Yuval-Davis's commentary on 'eugenicist' and 'Malthusian' arguments in nation-building can assist in probing these developments further (Yuval-Davis 2000: 24–9). Malthusians fear overpopulation and stretched resources, as evidenced in the stress on maternity services, and 'thin end of the wedge' arguments about citizenship tourism. Additionally, by introducing the three-year residence requirement, bad genes were to be kept provisionally out of the gene pool. The state's bio-political function is to keep alive the valuable members of its population, here defined by access to citizenship and protections of family unity. 'The "we" of the Irish State thus staves off the threat to its resources [...] by re-legislating them away from access' (Garner 2007: 446).

The position of migrant families with citizen children born prior to the commencement of the 2004 Act was finally addressed in January 2005, when the government announced the introduction of a new set of procedures to assess residency applications (Dept. of Justice, Equality and Law Reform: 2005). Although the move to end the uncertainty surrounding the legal status of many immigrant families has been welcomed, the process has attracted criticism. Again a reluctance to protect the right to family life of migrant families is evident. Applicants for residence were required to sign a declaration on family reunification, accepting that permission to remain in the state does not give rise to any 'legitimate expectation' that family members living abroad would be given permission to reside in Ireland.[22] The declaration raises, yet again, the question of whether and how the right to family life of migrant families is valued. Announcing the introduction of the new proposals, the Minister for Justice, Equality and Law Reform, Michael

McDowell, stated that residence would only be granted to those parents who could show that they have 'not been involved in criminal activity' and are 'willing to commit themselves to becoming economically viable'(Dept. of Justice Equality and Law Reform: 2004). As yet it is unclear how a criminal record that arose in an applicant's country of origin will be considered or whether this reference will be limited to non-political crimes. The requirement of 'economic viability' raises questions as to whether a parent that is unable to be economically self-sufficient will be denied residence.

This latter requirement echoes the distinctions made by the European Court of Justice in the *Chen* case, a case that arose prior to the citizenship referendum in Ireland, and added a further legal twist to the domestic debates.[23] Man Lavette Chen, a Chinese national and mother of a Chinese national child, went to Northern Ireland to give birth to her second child, Catherine. Catherine acquired Irish citizenship by virtue of being born on the island of Ireland. Chen and her daughter, Catherine, subsequently moved to Cardiff in the UK, and applied for a long-term residence permit. Their application was refused. On appeal, the Immigration Appeals Authority referred the case to the ECJ for a ruling as to whether Community law conferred a right of residence in the UK to Catherine and her mother. The Advocate General Tizzano, issuing his opinion on 18 May, 2004, concluded that a young child who is a national of a member state has a right to reside in another member state so long as he or she has sickness insurance and sufficient resources so as not to become 'an unreasonable burden' on the public finances of the host member state.[24] In addition, he concluded that to deny Chen's right to residence in the UK would render her daughter's right of residence totally ineffective. The Advocate General's opinion was upheld by the ECJ in its ruling on 19 October 2004. The court dismissed the UK's contention that Chen should be denied residence because she had improperly exploited Community law in deciding to give birth in Northern Ireland so as to secure Irish and consequently EU citizenship for her daughter. The UK, the Court concluded, was attempting to impose additional conditions on the acquisition of rights arising from the grant of nationality by another member state.[25] Chen had acted within the boundaries of the law and should not be subject to further limiting requirements.

The court's judgment reflects one of the fundamental inequalities in Community law. Catherine and her mother, if not independently wealthy, could not have availed of the freedoms of Community law under either Article 18 EC or Directive 90/364. Catherine's status as a citizen of the union could not ensure the cardinal value of citizenship, the right to reside in the country of which one is a national. That right was subject to having sufficient independent resources so as not to become 'an unreasonable burden' on the host state. Despite these limits, however, the *Chen* judgment does go some way towards recognizing the networks of relationships into which a child is born and his or her dependency on those relationships for the effective vindication of Community rights. The role of the mother as carer is recognized as being essential to the effective vindication of the child's right to nationality and residence. This relational understanding of the EU citizen recognizes, albeit with many limitations, a citizen child's right to family life and a relational understanding of the subject of rights. In contrast, the Irish Supreme Court, in the *L.* and *O.* cases, was willing to effectively deny the children's right to residence within the state by deporting their carers and subjecting the children to *de facto* deportation. The child's right to residence, as an Irish citizen, was qualitatively different and would not be vindicated by the state until the child was capable of exercising such a right on his or her own behalf.[26] This limited understanding of the child as a bearer of rights allowed the state to justify its failure to vindicate the citizen child's right to residence. Despite the well-entrenched family life and fundamental rights provisions in the Irish Constitution, Community law, with its relatively underdeveloped rights jurisprudence, ultimately granted the citizen child greater protection than did Irish constitutional law.

Migrant women did not fall easily within the protections provided by 'mother' Ireland. Asking the gender and immigration status questions, noting and giving voice to those specific axes of exclusion and discrimination, brings to the fore the racializing function that citizenship and residence laws can serve, and their specific impact on women engaged in a process of reproduction. Despite the constitutional recognition of the 'diversity of identities and traditions on the island of Ireland' (article 3), the more open and inclusive conception of citizenship that came with the *jus soli* principle is lost. Migrant women, unless satisfying minimal residency requirements, could not reproduce the Irish nation.

Family values and reproductive rights in ireland: gendered borders and gendered identities

Women's assertion of reproductive autonomy in Ireland has required the crossing of many borders, both the territorial borders of the state and the jurisdictional borders between international and domestic law. In May 1971, almost one hundred women boarded a train in Dublin. They travelled to Belfast, where they purchased large quantities of contraceptives. They returned to Dublin by train, marching illegally through the customs barriers at Connolly Station waving banners, posters and condom balloons. The 'Condom train', as it subsequently became known, transgressed many boundaries. In crossing Ireland's disputed border with Northern Ireland and openly flouting the legislative ban on importing contraceptives, the women's movement challenged the borders set by the conservative Catholic consensus in the Republic of Ireland. They exposed the inequalities between women, North and South, and the closure of Irish society to difference in matters of sexual and reproductive health. They also exposed the hypocrisy of a state that laid territorial claims to Northern Ireland but refused to accommodate religious diversity in matters concerning sexuality and reproduction (Jackson 1993; Connolly 2002).

Women seeking to terminate their pregnancies have been forced to leave the state and have travelled, usually to the UK, to access safe abortion services. Women have also sought to transgress the borders of domestic law, appealing to international and European human rights standards, pointing to the gender-differentiated nature of Irish citizenship and seeking support for their claim to reproductive autonomy in treaties such as the 1979 UN Convention on the Elimination of All Forms of Discrimination Against Women, the 1966 International Covenant on Civil and Political Rights and the European Convention on Human Rights. In the past, women had left the state to access contraceptives. Today, more than 5,000 women travel to the UK each year to access safe abortion services.

In 2002, while yet another referendum on abortion was taking place, the rights of the 'unborn' were being tested again in Ireland's Supreme Court.[27] *Baby O. and Another* v. *Minister for Justice Equality and Law Reform* involved a Nigerian woman who was seven months pregnant and subject to a deportation order from the state, following a failed application for asylum. The woman challenged the validity of the deportation order, arguing that the state's duty to defend and vindicate Baby O.'s right to life prevented the state from deporting her to Nigeria, where infant mortality rates were substantially higher and the standard of living substantially lower. The Attorney General, acting on behalf of the Minister for Justice, Equality and Law Reform, appealed to the common good, to the need to defend and vindicate the territorial integrity of the state, and to the minister's right to deport failed asylum seekers.[28] The Supreme Court agreed with the submissions of the Attorney General. The threat posed by higher infant mortality rates could not invoke the protection of Article 40.3.3°.[29] The state's duty to defend and vindicate the right to life of the unborn did not extend to ensuring the health and well-being of Baby O., or even to ensuring a safe delivery. Article 40.3.3° could not be relied on to invoke unenumerated social and economic rights, which the court held, were not implicit within the constitutionally protected right to life.[30] The court upheld the deportation order and also refused a final application to stay the order pending a petition to the European Court of Human Rights. The 'common good' required a speedy deportation of the mother and foetus. Again, the narrative of nation was to prove exclusionary. The self-styled 'pro-life' movement, preoccupied with another referendum on abortion, had little to say in support of Baby O. or her mother.

The Treaty on a Constitution for Europe, concluded under the Irish Presidency of the EU, is supplemented by a protocol, providing that the constitutional prohibition on abortion in Ireland would not be affected by the adoption of a Constitution for Europe.[31] Again we see the limits of the

European integration project and the willingness of states to accommodation difference through limits imposed on women's reproductive health (Mullally 2006). Against the background of this political wrangling, more than 5,000 women will continue to travel to the UK each year to terminate their pregnancies. For unemployed women or women earning low wages, this freedom to travel remains illusory (ICCL 2005). For asylum-seeking women, the freedom to travel does not exist. Travel documents, however, have been provided on an ad-hoc basis for asylum-seeking women wishing to travel to the UK to avail themselves of abortion services, raising questions as to the legality of the legislative restriction imposed on travel for such women and conversely, of the legality of the State's ad-hoc response (*Irish Independent*, 15 October 2001). The Irish Human Rights Commission in its submission to the CEDAW Committee on Ireland's *Combined Fourth and Fifth Reports* under the UN Convention on the Elimination of All Forms of Discrimination Against Women notes that the number of women from immigrant communities seeking the services of crisis pregnancy agencies has risen significantly and that an increasing number of reports of back street abortions amongst immigrant communities are under investigation by the police force (IHRC 2005). The failure to safeguard the reproductive rights of specific groups of women, such as asylum-seeking women, was highlighted by the CEDAW Committee in its Concluding Observations on Ireland's second and third periodic reports (CEDAW 1999: para.185).[32] The UN Human Rights Committee highlighted Ireland's obligation, under article 7 of the ICCPR and General Comment no. 28, to ensure access to safe abortions for women who have become pregnant as a result of rape (UN Human Rights Committee 2000: para.18).[33] For asylum-seeking women, such access is not ensured, given the travel restrictions imposed while waiting for determination of asylum claims. This raises questions as to whether women are being compelled to continue with pregnancies, whether 'forced pregnancies' are occurring, contrary to the state's human rights treaty obligations.

In responding to a changing migration context, Ireland has failed to 'turn the gaze back', to reflect upon its own history of seeking refuge and economic prosperity on distant shores. For Irish women, 'turning the gaze back' reveals the many reasons why women migrate and cross borders. For many Irish women in the nineteenth and twentieth centuries, migration represented economic opportunity, but also a route through which reproductive autonomy and sexual desire could be pursued. As a result, migrant Irish women were frequently identified as a threat to communally oriented Irish modernity (Gray 2004b). Though migration concealed differences in sexual practices and identities, anxiety about reproductive and sexual autonomy amongst the diaspora remained. Assertions of individualism and autonomy in matters of reproduction and sexuality, whether at home or amongst the diaspora, threatened the unity of a nascent nation-state and the process of nation-building – a process that sought to identify distinct markers of

Irish identity, amongst these, 'pro-life' and 'pro-family' traditions rooted in Roman Catholicism. Appeals to the sanctity of family life and to 'pro-life' traditions, have served to limit women's human rights claims in Ireland since the foundation of the state. The priority accorded to such appeals have led to repeated attempts to restrict women's freedom to travel and to a notion of citizenship that is deeply gendered. While such attempts have often focused on restricting women's freedom to exit the state, legal responses to migrant women's assertion of reproductive autonomy have sought to restrict entry to the state. Common to both sets of legal responses is the curtailing of women's reproductive autonomy.

Concluding remarks

Migrant women coming to Ireland have turned debates on reproductive rights on their head, exposing the hypocrisy of a state that purports to defend and vindicate the right to life of the unborn and to protect the family. Migrant women's assertion of reproductive autonomy, in choosing to give birth within the state and secure citizenship status for their children, has been met with a rapid unfolding of legal restrictions, designed to remove incentives for women who may wish to come to Ireland. In the citizenship debates in Ireland, the familiar gender tropes – of women as wives, mothers, victims or demonized 'others' – were evident yet again. Migrant women were victims of unscrupulous smugglers, forced into taking 'hazardous journeys' or were 'demonized others', responsible for the crisis in the state's maternity services, the dilution of cultural identity and violation of the state's borders. In the *Chen* case, Chen stood accused of abusing immigration law and policy, despite the fact that she acted clearly within the boundaries of the law. In later reports on the case, it emerged that Man Lavette Chen and her spouse were seeking to avoid the constraints of China's one-child policy. The complexity of the migrant female subject, the push and pull factors that might have induced her to migrate, however, were largely ignored.

The voices of migrant women were rarely heard in the citizenship debates as legal interventions were designed and pursued solely from the perspective of the state's interest in immigration control. Women's agency or reproductive autonomy was not foregrounded in these debates as it is not foregrounded in abortion debates and debates on reproductive health in Ireland. The legal and political responses to immigration in Ireland, at times disciplinary and at times punitive, have not sought to empower women's human rights but rather to restrict women's mobility and agency. Such responses are not, of course, unique to Ireland. Drawing on intersectionality analysis to explore these debates reveals the many facets of the strategies of exclusion and distancing that shaped the citizenship reforms in Ireland.

In the citizenship debates, we see both the vilification and increasing control of migrant women's bodies. A limited form of national sovereignty is reasserted, underpinned by a racism that functioned through reference to reproduction. Reproduction was understood as 'gendered, classed, racialized labour that can be carried out for the state – or against the State' (Luibhéid 2003: 85). Migrant women's assertion of reproductive autonomy threatened to destabilize the racial homogeneity of the nation-state. In response to this 'threat', Ireland introduced citizenship laws that sought, yet again, to restrict women's autonomy, mobility and agency.

Intersectionality analysis, as an analytical tool to explore the citizenship debates in Ireland, brings to the fore the intersections of gender, class, 'race', and immigration status in political and legal discourse. Intersectionality analysis takes us beyond the limits of identity politics, recognizing differences within groups, further refining our understanding of group based disadvantage. This potential can be seen in an expanded analysis of the citizenship debates in Ireland. Though critics of the rush to reform citizenship laws expressed concern at the potential for moral panic on questions of 'race', there was at the time little attention paid to the positioning of migrant women as foreign fertile bodies, and the impact of such positioning on women's lives.

The test for feminist theory, as Joanne Conaghan has noted elsewhere, is 'its ability to deliver' (Conaghan 2000). In recounting this narrative of Ireland's recent citizenship reforms, I am suggesting the need for further fragmentation, for further dissection of the categories of gender and race, to take account specifically of the phenomenon of migration and immigration status. Immigration status then becomes visible as yet another site of discrimination and inequality. Proposals for reform, strategic engagements with law and policy making processes can draw on the intersectional analyses to expand the scope of reform initiatives. Immigration status has frequently been ignored in analyses of discrimination and subordination. Iris Young's earlier work exemplifies such analyses, adopting a 'nationally insular approach' to the significance of citizenship (Bosniak 2006: 144n23). In her more recent work, however, Young includes discussion of immigration status in her examination of the structures of subordination in liberal democratic societies (Young 2002). The increasing recognition of inequalities linked with immigration status can be found in other writings. As Bosniak notes, the category of immigration status is appearing with more frequency in various 'catalogues of subordination axes' (Bosniak 2006: 11). It is not enough, however, to simply add immigration status to the list of categories of social exclusion, or to 'laundry lists' of prohibited grounds of discrimination. The question that remains is whether intersectionality analysis can take us beyond this additive solution, the 'add and stir' proposals so criticized by earlier feminist responses to 'women and law' initiatives. As Conaghan notes, the potential of intersectionality analysis to critique identity politics is limited. Identity categories remain at its core, albeit further delimited. The push to feminist praxis, the impulse for reform underpinning Kimberlé Crenshaw's early invocations of intersectionality, are lost in this project of 'limitless possibilities and limited potential' (Conaghan, this volume). Intersectionality analysis, while useful, does not provide us with the methodological resources necessary to challenge the global distributive effects of extant systems of inherited citizenship statuses. Neither does it give us the normative resources necessary for an emancipatory feminist politics, a politics that challenges the enduring structural inequalities experienced by migrants and assists in bringing about systematic changes in the gendered regimes that regulate migration.

Missing from the moral panic on citizenship reforms was any considered analysis of the significance of citizenship, and the legitimacy or otherwise of established pathways to citizenship. While intersectional analysis provides a useful starting point from which to better understand the mechanisms of exclusion that operate through citizenship laws, it does not give us the tools necessary to build a feminist praxis on citizenship. Citizenship status, like property, brings with it considerable privileges and rights, which may be ascribed through birth or blood. The global inequalities that are linked with citizenship status require much greater interrogation, as do the structures and processes that perpetuate the distancing and dehumanizing of immigrant others. If feminist praxis is to move beyond explaining or describing, albeit in more complex and nuanced ways, mechanisms of exclusion and discrimination, greater attention needs to be paid to the distributive consequences of citizenship status. The implications of such consequences for feminist engagement are only recently being addressed in Ireland, in the aftermath of a bruising referendum. For such engagement, more than the tools of intersectionality analysis will be required. The normative basis for citizenship status, its role and value, its potential both to include and exclude, need much further probing and excavation.

Acknowledgements

I am grateful to the editors for their many helpful comments and suggestions on earlier drafts. This chapter forms part of an Irish Research Council for Humanities and Social Sciences research project on *Gender, Diversity and Multiculturalism in Contemporary Ireland*.

Bibliography.

Bhabha, J. (2003) 'The citizenship deficit: on being a citizen child', unpublished paper, copy on file with the author.

Boland, E. (1989) *A Kind of Scar,* Dublin: Attic Press.

Bosniak, L. (2006) *The Citizen and the Alien: Dilemmas of Contemporary Membership*, Princeton, NJ: Princeton University Press.

Butler, M. (1901) *Irish Women and the Home Language*, Gaelic League Pamphlets No.6, Dublin: Gaelic League.

Committee on the Elimination of Discrimination against Women (1999), *Concluding Observations: Ireland,* U.N. Doc. A/54/38 (1 July 1999).

Conaghan, J. (2000) 'Reassessing the feminist theoretical project in law', *Journal of Law and Society* 27: 351–85.

Connolly, L. (2002) *The Irish Women's Movement: From Revolution to Devolution,* London: Palgrave.

Constitution Review Group (1995) *Report of the Constitution Review Group,* Dublin: Government of Ireland Publications.

Cullen, P. (2002) 'What's to befall these Irish children?' *Irish Times,* 9 April.

Department of Justice, Equality and Law Reform (2004) 'Minister announces revised arrangements for processing claims for permission to remain from parents of Irish born children' (14 December), available online at: http://www.justice.ie.

Department of Justice, Equality and Law Reform (2005) 'Minister announces details of revised arrangements for residency' (14 January), available online at http://www.justice.ie.

Fletcher, R. (2001) 'Post-colonial fragments: representations of abortion in Irish law and politics', *Journal of Law and Society,* 28: 568–89.

Garner, S. (2007) 'Babies, bodies and entitlement; gendered aspects of access to citizenship in the Republic of Ireland', *Parliamentary Affairs,* 60: 437–51.

Gray, B. (2004a) *Women and the Irish Diaspora,* London and New York: Routledge.

Gray, B. (2004b) 'Remembering a "multicultural" future through a history of emigration: Towards a feminist politics of solidarity across difference', *Women's Studies International Forum,* 27: 413–29.

Harvey, C. and Livingstone, S. (1999) 'Human rights and the Northern Ireland Peace Process', *European Human Rights Law Review,* 2: 162–77.

Harvey, C.J. (2000) 'Governing after the rights revolution', *Journal of Law and Society,* 27: 61–97.

Harvey, C.J. (2001) *Human Rights, Equality and Democratic Renewal in Northern Ireland,* Oxford: Hart.

Haughey, N. (2002) 'Pregnant Blacks facing citizenship jibes – Report', *Irish Times,* 14 March.

Hesketh, T. (1990) *The Second Partitioning of Ireland: the Abortion Referendum of 1983,* Dun Laoghaire: Brandsma Books.

Hickey, D. (2001) 'State alert as pregnant asylum seekers aim for Ireland', *Irish Examiner,* 4 December.

ICCL (Irish Council for Civil Liberties (Women's Committee)) (2002) *The Need for Abortion Law Reform in Ireland: The Case against the Twenty-fifth Amendment of the Constitution Bill, 2001,* Dublin: Irish Council for Civil Liberties.

IHRC (Irish Human Rights Commission) (2004) *Observations on the Proposed Referendum on Citizenship,* Dublin: Irish Human Rights Commission.

IHRC (Irish Human Rights Commission) (2005) *Submission to the UN Committee on the Elimination of All Forms of Discrimination Against Women,* Dublin: Irish Human Rights Commission.

Jackson, N. (1993) 'Family law: fertility and parenthood', in A. Connolly (ed.) *Gender and the Law in Ireland,* Dublin: Oak Tree Press.

Keane, S. (2002) 'Councillor says asylum seekers are "breeding like rabbits"' *Irish Times,* 16 April.

Kingston, J. and Whelan, A. with Bacik, I. (1997) *Abortion and the Law,* Dublin: Roundhall Sweet and Maxwell.

Lentin, R. (2003) '(En)gendering Ireland's migratory space', paper presented at Migrant Women: Transforming Ireland Conference, Dublin.

Luibhéid, E. (2003) 'Globalisation and sexuality: redrawing racial and national boundaries through discourses of childbearing', paper presented at Migrant Women: Transforming Ireland Conference, Dublin, March 20–21.

Luibhéid, E. (2004) 'Childbearing against the state? Asylum seeker women in the Irish Republic', *Women's Studies International Forum,* 27: 335–49.

McDowell, M. (2004) 'Proposed citizenship referendum', *Sunday Independent,* 14 March.

Mullally, S. (2005a) 'Debating reproductive rights in Ireland', *Human Rights Quarterly,* 27: 78–104.

Mullally, S. (2005b) 'Citizenship and family life in Ireland: asking the question "who belongs?"', *Legal Studies,* 25: 578–600 .

Mullally, S. (2006) *Gender, Culture and Human Rights: Reclaiming Universalism,* Oxford: Hart.

National Women's Council of Ireland (2004) Press Release, 8 June.

O'Reilly, E. (1992) *Masterminds of the Right,* Dublin: Attic Press.

Pearce, P. (1903) *An Claidheamh Soluis,* editorials, 11 April and 28 November.

Phelan, D.R. (1992) 'Right to life of the unborn v promotion of trade in services: the European Court of Justice and the normative shaping of the European Union', *Modern Law Review* 55: 670–89.

Quinlan, F. (2001) 'Non-nationals fuel pregnancy crisis', *Irish Examiner,* 21 February.

Quinn, A. (1997) 'Cathleen Ni Houlihan writes back: Maud Gonne and Irish National Theatre', in A. Bradley and M. Valiulis (eds) *Gender and Sexuality in Modern Ireland*, Amherst, MA: University of Massachusetts Press.

Riegel, R. and Niland, G. (2002) 'Racial time bomb set to explode as crisis deepens', *Irish Independent*, 27 January.

Schachar, A. (2003) 'Children of a lesser state: sustaining global inequality through citizenship laws', in S. Macedo and I.M. Young (eds) *NOMOS: Child, Family, and the State*, New York: New York University Press.

Sheehan, A. (2001) 'Asylum seekers allowed to travel for abortions', *Irish Independent*, 15 October.

Smyth, A. (ed.) (1990) *The Abortion Papers: Ireland,* Dublin: Attic Press.

Toomey, D. (ed.) (1997) *Yeats and Women,* Basingstoke: Macmillan.

UN Human Rights Committee (2000) *Concluding Observations of the Human Rights Committee: Ireland,* UN Doc. CCPR/CO/69/IRL (20 July).

Walter, B. (2001) *Outsiders Inside: Whiteness, Place and Irish Women,* London: Routledge.

Young, I.M. (2000) *Inclusion and Democracy,* Oxford: Oxford University Press.

Young, I.M. (2002) 'Status inequality and social groups', *Issues in Legal Scholarship,* Berkeley Electronic Press, Article 9. Available online at: http://www.bepress.com/ils/iss2/art9.

Yuval-Davis, N. (2000) *Gender and Nation,* London: Routledge.

Table of cases

Notes

1 'Cathleen Ni Houlihán' is one of W.B. Yeats's most popular poems. It is now accepted that it was in fact co-written by his patron, Lady Gregory.
2 See: Agreement between the Government of the United Kingdom of Great Britain and Northern Ireland and the Government of Ireland (British–Irish Agreement) and the Agreement reached in Multi-Party negotiations (Belfast Agreement), concluded 10 April 1998, reproduced in: (1998) 37 ILM 751. See generally: Harvey, C. and Livingstone, S. (1999), Harvey, C.J. (2001), Harvey, C. (2000).
3 See: Nineteenth Amendment to the Constitution Act, 1998. The full text of article 2 of the Constitution of Ireland (as amended) reads:

> Article 2.
> It is the entitlement and birthright of every person born in the island of Ireland, which includes its islands and seas, to be part of the Irish Nation. That is also the entitlement of all persons otherwise qualified in accordance with law to be citizens of Ireland. Furthermore, the Irish nation cherishes its special affinity with people of Irish ancestry living abroad who share its cultural identity and heritage.

4 See Article 3 of the Irish Constitution, inserted following the enactment of the Nineteenth Amendment to the Constitution Act, 1998.
5 See *Lobe and Osayande* v. *Minister for Justice, Equality and Law Reform*, [2003] IESC 3 (23 January 2003) per Fennelly J, para. 451.
6 Article 9 of the Constitution.
7 Deputy Dr Esmonde, *Dáil Debates*, vol 154, 29 February 1956, Irish Nationality and Citizenship Bill, 1955 – Second Stage paras. 1014–1015.
8 [1986] IR 733.
9 Ibid. p. 746.
10 Ibid. p. 745.
11 *Fajujonu* v. *Minister for Justice* [1990] 2 IR 151; [1990] ILRM 234.

12 In a statement that is likely to have relevance to many families facing deportation proceedings in the future, Walsh J went on to point out that deportation proceedings could not be taken against a family that included citizen children, simply because of poverty, particularly where that situation of poverty was induced by the absence of a work permit.
13 Above n. 5.
14 See above n. 2 and n. 3.
15 Above n. 5 per Keane C J para. 34.
16 See *Norris* v. *Ireland* Judgment of 26 October, 1988. 13 EHRR 186.
17 [1974] IR 284, at p. 310.
18 *North Western Health Board* v. *HW and CW* [2001] 3 I.R. 622.
19 Ibid. p. 732.
20 Supra n. 5, per Denham J. para. 1   .
21 The Twenty-seventh Amendment of the Constitution Bill 2004 proposed that a new section be added to Article 9 of the Constitution to read as follows:

> 9.2.1 Notwithstanding any other provision of this Constitution, a person born in the island of Ireland, which includes its islands and its seas, who does not have, at the time of his or her birth, at least one parent who is an Irish citizen or entitled to be an Irish citizen is not entitled to Irish citizenship or nationality, unless otherwise provided for by law.

22 See: Department of Justice, Equality and Law Reform, Application Form IBC/05.
23 Case C-200/02 *Chen* v. *Secretary of State for the Home Department*, 19 October 2004.
24 See Article 1(1) of Directive 90/364.
25 Above n. 23, para. 39.
26 Above n. 15 per Keane CJ.
27 *Baby O.* v. *Minister for Justice, Equality and Law Reform*, [2002] 2 I.R. 169.
28 Ibid. p.173.
29 Ibid. per Keane CJ, p. 182.
30 Ibid. p. 182.
31 See: Treaty establishing a Constitution for Europe, Protocol on Article 40.3.3 of the Constitution of Ireland, O.J. C 310/377 (2004).
32 Concluding Observations of the Committee on the Elimination of Discrimination Against Women: Ireland. 01/07/99. UN Doc. A/54/38, paras.161–201, para.185.
33 See also: CCPR/C/21/Rev.1/Add.10, CCPR General comment 28. 29/03/2000, para. 11.

Part IV

Alternative pathways

Chapter 11

Structural injustice and the politics of difference[1]

Iris Marion Young

Introduction

As a social movement tendency in the 1980s, the politics of difference has involved the claims of feminist, anti-racist, and gay liberation activists that the structural inequalities of gender, race, and sexuality were not well perceived or combated by the dominant paradigm of equality and inclusion. In this dominant paradigm, the promotion of justice and equality requires non-discrimination: the application of the same principles of evaluation and distribution to all persons regardless of their particular social positions or backgrounds. In this ideal, which many understood as the liberal paradigm, social justice meant ignoring gender, racial or sexual differences among people. Social movements asserting a politics of difference, and the theorists following them, argued that this difference-blind ideal was part of the problem. Identifying equality with equal treatment ignored deep material differences in social position, division of labor, socialized capacities, normalized standards and ways of living that continued to disadvantage members of historically excluded groups. Commitment to substantial equality thus required attending to, rather than ignoring, such differences.

In the context of ethnic politics and resurgent nationalism, another version of a politics of difference gained currency in the 1990s, which focused on differences of nationality, ethnicity and religion. It emphasized the value of cultural distinctness to individuals, as against a liberal individualism for which culture is accidental to the self or something taken on voluntarily. Most modern societies contain multiple cultural groups, some of which unjustly dominate the state or other important social institutions, thus inhibiting the ability of minority cultures to live fully meaningful lives in their own terms. Contrary to arguments for cultural neutrality which until recently have been the orthodox liberal stance, the politics of cultural difference argues that public accommodation to and support of cultural difference is compatible with and even required by just institutions.

I read my own major writing on the politics of difference as emphasizing the politics of positional difference. Both *Justice and the Politics of Difference*

(Young, 1990) and *Inclusion and Democracy* (Young, 2000a) critically assess the tendency of both public and private institutions in contemporary liberal democratic societies to reproduce sexual, racial and class inequality by applying standards and rules in the same way to all who plausibly come under its purview. Each book also contains, however, elements that relate more to the politics of cultural difference. *Justice and the Politics of Difference* refers to cultural claims of indigenous people and speaks approvingly of movements of structurally oppressed groups to resist stigma by constructing positive group affinities, which I understand more as a means to the achievement of structural equality, rather than an end in itself.

Justice and the Politics of Difference was published earlier than most of the work in recent political theory which I consider focuses on a politics of cultural difference. That body of work might be said to begin with Charles Taylor's essay, "Multiculturalism and the Politics of Recognition", and to receive its first book-length treatment in Will Kymlicka's *Multicultural Citizenship* (Kymlicka, 1995), which I will discuss later in this chapter.[2] Published after I began to see that different theoretical approaches to a politics of difference were solidifying, *Inclusion and Democracy* tries more self-consciously to distinguish a focus on structural inequality from a focus on injustice through cultural difference and conflict. While most of that book theorizes within the politics of positional difference, one chapter of *Inclusion and Democracy* articulates a relational concept of self-determination, to contrast with more rigid notions of sovereignty. Here I intend to contribute to discussions in the politics of cultural difference. One motivation for my writing this chapter is to sort out these distinctions more.

In this chapter[3] I first lay out and distinguish these two versions of a politics of difference, which I call the politics of positional difference (PPD) and the politics of cultural difference (PCD), respectively. Both versions challenge commitments to political equality that tend to identify equality with sameness and which believe that the best way to pursue social and political equality is to ignore group differences in public policy and in how individuals are treated. They both argue that where group difference is socially significant for issues of conflict, domination, or advantage, that equal respect may not imply treating everyone in the same way. Public and civic institutions may be either morally required or permitted to notice social group difference, and to treat members of different groups differently for the sake of promoting equality or freedom.

Despite these similarities, it is important to be clear on the differences between a politics of positional difference and a politics of cultural difference, for several reasons. In recent discussions of a politics of difference, I think that analysts sometimes merge the two models, or attribute features specific to one to the other as well. Such confusions can have the consequence that intended criticisms of one or the other are misdirected because critics misidentify them or import features of one into the other.

As I read it, Brian Barry's recent book, *Culture and Equality* (Barry, 2000) fails to distinguish any strands in the thick ball of theoretical writing that he winds together. As a result, he levels criticisms at some writers that may be more apt for others, and he sometimes merges positions in a way that confuses the debate more than clarifies it. Another motive for this paper, then, is to try to sort out some of this confusion perhaps made more apparent by work like Barry's.

Probably a more important reason to notice the difference between the two versions, from my point of view, concerns keeping in the foreground some issues of justice and ways of thinking about justice and difference that first motivated this line of theorizing a quarter century ago. In my observation, concerns and concepts more associated with the politics of cultural difference have tended to occupy political theorists in recent years, such as issues of autonomy for minority cultures or toleration of religious difference, than have concerns and concepts more associated with a politics of positional difference, such as the status meaning of occupational positions, and the normalization of attributes that count as qualifications for them. Failure properly to conceptualize the difference between these two models of a politics of difference may lead to obscuring certain specific forms of group based injustice, such as racism or the normalization of certain capacities, which cannot be reduced to issues of cultural difference. I think that much recent political theory concerned with group difference has indeed ignored such issues, which were central to the problematics that generated theorizing on the politics of difference in the 1980s.

Both versions of a politics of difference are important, and they sometimes overlap. The politics of positional difference is broader in the scope of the kinds of groups whose concerns it brings under inquiry, I will argue. Both models concern issues of justice. I will suggest, however, that the politics of positional difference concentrates on issues of structural inequality, while the main issues that arise in a politics of cultural difference concern freedom.

Politics of positional difference

This approach theorizes social groups as constituted through interactions that make categorical distinctions among people in hierarchies of status or privilege. The production and reproduction of "durable inequality", as Charles Tilly calls it, involves processes where people produce and maintain advantages for themselves and disadvantages for others, in terms of access to resources, power, autonomy, honor, or receiving service and deference by means of the application of rules and customs that assume such categorical distinctions (Tilly, 1998). As I think of it, major structural axes in modern societies include: the social division of labor; relative power to decide institutional actions, or to change the incentives faced by large numbers of people; the establishment and enforcement of hegemonic norms.[4] Among the structural social groups that raise issues of the politics of positional difference are groups structured by gender, class, so-called disability, race and racialization.

The politics of positional difference argues that public and private institutional policies and practices that interpret equality as requiring [a sameness approach] to group differences are not likely to undermine persistent structural group differences and often reinforce them. Even in the absence of formally discriminatory laws and rules, adherence to body aesthetics, struggles over power, and other dynamics of differentiation, will tend to reproduce given categorical inequalities unless institutions take explicit action to counteract such tendencies. Thus to remove unjust inequality it is necessary explicitly to recognize group difference and either compensate for disadvantage, revalue some attributes, positions or actions, or take special steps to meet needs and empower members of disadvantaged groups.

I will explicate three examples of structural inequality to which the politics of positional difference calls attention: the structural position of people with disabilities, institutional racism, and gender inequality.

Disability as structural inequality

Most writings on social justice either do not notice disability at all as raising issues of justice, or bring it up in order to assert that disability is an outlier category, which theories of justice may deal with after addressing more commonly experienced disadvantages which supposedly raise issues of justice in a more obvious way. John Rawls, for example, famously "puts aside" those disabilities "so severe as to prevent people from being cooperating members of society in the usual sense" (Rawls, 1993: 20) until the theory deals with the easier and more generally shared issues of justice. It is better to begin theorizing justice, he says, by assuming that 'everyone has physical needs and psychological capacities within the normal range' (ibid: 83).

Some philosophers recently have put this set of assumptions into question, and have begun to develop alternative analyses both of disability and justice (Kittay, 1999; Silvers, 1998). Considering the vast numbers of people who have impaired physical and mental capacities at some point in their lives, it is simply factually wrong to think of disability as a relatively uncommon condition not affecting how we should think about justice. I suggest that we can learn much about social justice generally as concerning issues of structural inequality, normalization, and stigmatization, if we decide to make disability *paradigmatic* of structural injustice, instead of considering it exceptional.

In his recent book attacking all versions of a politics of difference, Brian Barry devotes considerable space to defending a standard principle of merit in the allocation of positions. Merit involves equal opportunity in the following sense: it rejects a system that awards positions explicitly according to class, race, gender, family background, and so on. Under a merit principle, all who wish should have the opportunity to compete for positions of advantage, and those most qualified should win the competition. Positions of authority or expertise should be occupied by those persons who demonstrate excellence in particular skills and who best exhibit the demeanor expected of people in those positions. Everyone else is a loser in respect to those positions, and they suffer no injustice on that account.[5]

In this merit system, according to Barry, it is natural that people with disabilities will usually turn out to be losers.

> Surely it is to be expected in the nature of the case that, across the group (disabled) as a whole, its members will be less qualified than average, even if the amount of money spent on their education is the average, or more than the average.
>
> (Barry, 2000: 95)

Barry's is a common opinion. In our scheme of social cooperation, certain skills and abilities can and should be expected of average workers, and it is "in the nature of the case" that most people with disabilities do not meet these expectations. Thus they do not merit the jobs in which we expect these skills, and do not merit the income, autonomy, status, and other forms of privilege that come with those jobs. These people's deficiencies are not their fault, of course. So a decent society will support their needs and ensure them a dignified life, in spite of their inability to contribute significantly to social production.

One of the objectives of the disability rights movements has been to challenge this bit of liberal common sense. Most people who have not thought about the issues very much tend to regard being "disabled" as an attribute of persons: some people simply lack the functionings that enable normal people to live independently, compete in job markets, have a satisfying social life, and so on. Many in the disability rights movements, however, conceptualize the problem that people with disabilities face rather differently. The problem is not with the attributes that individual persons have or do not have. The problem, rather, is the *lack of fit* between the attributes of certain persons and structures, practices, norms, and aesthetic standards dominant in the society. The built environment is biased to support the capacities of people who can walk, climb, see, hear, within what are thought of as the "normal range" of functionings, and presents significant obstacles for people whose capacities are judged outside this range. Both interactive and technical ways of assessing the intelligence, skill and adaptability of people in schools and workplaces assume ways of evaluating aptitude and achievement that unfairly exclude or disadvantage many people with disabilities. The physical layout and equipment in workplaces and the organization of work process too often make it impossible for a person with an impaired functioning to use the skills they have.[6] Hegemonic standards of charm, beauty, grace, wit, or attentiveness position some people with disabilities as monstrous or abject.

These and other aspects of the division of labor and hegemonic norms constitute structural injustice for people with disabilities. Many people with disabilities unfairly suffer limitation to their opportunities for developing capacities, earning a living through satisfying work, having a rewarding social life, and living as autonomous adults. A liberalism [that ignores difference] can offer only very limited remedy for this injustice. It is no response to the person who moves in a wheel chair who tries to go to a courtroom accessible only by stairs that the state treats all citizens in the same way. The blind engineer derives little solace from an employer who assures him that they make the same computer equipment available to all employees. The opportunities of people with disabilities can be made equal only if others specifically notice their differences, cease regarding them as unwanted deviance from accepted norms and unacceptable costs to efficient operations, and take affirmative measures to accommodate the specific capacities of individuals so that they can function, as all of us should be able to, at their best and with dignity.

The 1990 Americans with Disabilities Act recognizes this in principle, inasmuch as it requires that employers, landlords and public services make "reasonable accommodation" to the specific needs of people with disabilities. It codifies a politics of positional difference. Unfortunately, the only enforcement power the ADA contains is permission to litigate infraction. Coupled with the cost-saving and fear-denying interests of most people who think of themselves as able-bodied, the ADA's limitations arguably conspire to reproduce these injustices to people with disabilities as a group.

I have begun with the example of injustice towards people with disabilities because, as I said earlier, I wish to suggest that it is paradigmatic of the general approach I am calling a politics of positional difference. It represents a clear case where difference-blind treatment or policy is more likely to perpetuate than correct injustice. The systematic disadvantage at which facially neutral standards put many people in this case, however, just as clearly does not derive from internal cultural attributes that constitute a group, "people with disabilities". It may be plausible to speak of a Deaf culture, to the extent that many Deaf people use a unique language and sometimes live together in Deaf communities. In a wider sense, however, there is no community or culture of people with disabilities. Instead, this category designates a structural group constituted from the outside by the deviation of its purported members from normalized institutional assumptions about the exhibition of skill, definition of tasks in a division of labor, ideals of beauty, built environment standards, comportments of sociability, and so on. The remedy for injustice to people with disabilities consists in challenging the norms and rules of the institutions that most condition the life options and the attainment of well being of these persons structurally positioned as deviant.

Issues of justice raised by many group-based conflicts and social differences, I suggest, follow this paradigm. They concern the way structural social processes position individuals with similar physical attributes, socialized capacities, body habits and life style, sexual orientations, family and neighborhood resources, and so on, in the social division of labor, relations of decision-making power, or hegemonic norms of achievement, beauty, respectability, and the like. The politics of positional difference focuses on these issues of inclusion and exclusion, and how they make available or limit the substantive opportunities for persons to develop capacities and achieve well being. I will now all too briefly discuss racism and gender inequality as further examples of such structural inequality.

Racial inequality

Clearly this chapter's purpose is not to give an account of the structural inequalities of institutional racism. In this context, I want to make only a few points about racial inequality and the politics of difference. Although I will focus on racialized processes of structural inequality in the United States, I think that racial inequality structures many societies in the world. As I understand it, racism consists in structural processes that normalize body aesthetics, determine that physical, dirty or servile work is most appropriate for members of certain groups, produce and reproduce segregation of members of these racialized groups, and render deviant the comportments and habits of these segregated persons in relation to dominant norms of respectability.

What distinguishes "race" from ethnicity or nation, conceptually? The former naturalizes or "epidermalizes" the attributes of difference.[7] Racism attaches significance to bodily characteristics – skin color, hair type, facial features, and constructs hierarchies of standard or ideal body types against which others appear inferior, stigmatized, deviant, or abject. In Western structures of anti-Black racism this hierarchy appears both as dichotomous and scalar. That is, racial categorization is organized around a Black/White dichotomy, and this dichotomy organizes a grading of types according to how "close" they are to Black (most inferior) or White (the superior).[8]

Processes of racialization stigmatize or devalue bodies, body types, or items closely attached to bodies, such as clothing; this stigmatization and stereotyping appear in public images and in the way some people react to some others. Racialization also involves understandings of the proper work of some and its hierarchical status in relation to others. The stigma of Blackness in America, for example, has its origins in the division of labor, namely slavery (see Loury, 2002). The slave does hard labor under domination, from which owners accumulate profits; or the slave does servile labor to attend the needs and elevate the status of the ruling group. While chattel slavery was abolished a century and a half ago, racialized positions in the social division of labor remain. The least desirable work, the work with the lowest pay, least autonomy, and lowest status, is the hard physical work, the dirty work, and the servant work. In the United States these are racialized forms of work, that is, work thought to belong to black and brown people primarily, and these increasingly are also foreigners. A similar process of racialization has occurred in Europe, which positions persons of Turkish, North African, South Asian, sub-Saharan African, and Middle Eastern origin as "Other", and tends to restrict them to lower status positions in the social division of labor.

Segregation is a third common structure of racial inequality. It is not uncommon for migrants to choose to live near one another in neighborhood enclaves. I refer to this process as "clustering", and the urban residential patterning it produces might be considered a manifestation of cultural differentiation. While residential segregation often overlaps with or builds on such clustering processes, segregation is a different and more malignant process. Even when not produced by legally enforced spatial exclusion, segregation is a process of exclusion from residential neighborhood opportunity that leaves the relatively worse residential possibilities for members of denigrated groups. The actions of local and national government, private developers and landlords, housing consumers, and others conspire – not necessarily by intention – to concentrate members of these denigrated groups. The result is that dominant groups derive privileges such as more space, more pleasant space, greater amenities, stable and often increasing property values, and so on.[9]

With segregation, the stigma of racialized bodies and denigrated labor marks space itself and the people who grow up and live in neighborhoods. People who live together in segregated neighborhoods, moreover, tend to develop group specific idioms, styles of comportment, interests, and artistic forms. These also are liable to be devalued and stigmatized by dominant norms. People who wish to appear respectable and professional, for example, had better shed the habits of walking, laughing, and talking in slang they have learned on the home block. If these are properly considered "cultural", they are better considered consequences of segregation and limitation of opportunity, rather than their causes. These structural relations of bodily affect, meanings and interests in the social division of labor, segregation, and normalization of dominant habitus operate to limit the opportunities of many to learn and use satisfying skills in socially recognized settings, to accumulate income or wealth, or to attain positions of power and prestige.

The main purpose of my all too brief account of racism here is to exhibit it as a set of structural relations in which processes of normalization have a large role. Being White is to occupy a social position, or set of social positions, that privileges some people according to at least the parameters I have outlined, and sets standards of respectability or achievement for the entire society. Being Black, or "of color", means being perceived as not fitting the standards, and often means being inhibited in one's ability to develop and exercise capacities. An anti-racist politics of difference argues that such liabilities to disadvantage cannot be overcome by race-blind principles of formal equality in employment, political party competition, and so on. Where racialized structural inequality influences so many institutions and potentially stigmatizes and impoverishes so many people, a society that aims to redress such injustice must *notice* the processes of racial differentiation before it can correct them. Even when overt discriminatory practices are illegal and widely condemned, racialized structures are produced and reproduced in some of the most everyday interactions in civil society and workplaces.

Projects to redress racial injustice must notice these everyday social processes as well. It is important that persons positioned similarly by racial structures be able to organize politically together to bring attention to these relations of privilege or disadvantage. While such organizing properly has some elements of the celebration of positive shared experience, or "identity politics", the primary purpose of such group based organizing is, or ought to be, to confront and undermine the structural processes that perpetuate the limitation of opportunities.[10] Anti-racist movements are and ought to be directed at government policy to intervene in the structures. Government is not the only agent for institutional change, however, and I will return to this point.

Gender inequality

At least as these appear in the literature of political theory, the politics of positional difference and the politics of cultural difference conceive women's issues differently. As I will discuss below, some proponents of a politics of cultural difference implicitly invoke gender justice under norms of equal treatment. As discussed by much of the literature, the political struggle consists in getting women recognized as the *same* as men in respect to having rights to autonomy. In the politics of positional difference, by contrast, feminist politics are a species of the politics of difference; that is, on this approach, in order to promote gender equality it is necessary to notice existing structural processes that differently position men and women. Let me explain.

In the last quarter century there have been many changes in gendered norms of behavior and comportment expected of men and women, with a great deal more freedom of choice in taste and self-presentation available to members of both sexes than in the past. Basic structures of gender comportment, assumptions that the normal body is implicitly male, the structures of heterosexual expectations, and the sexual division of labor nevertheless continue structurally to afford men more privilege and opportunity for access to resources, positions of power and authority, or the ability to pursue their own life plans.

People too often react to public evidence of female specific conditions with aversion, ridicule, or denial. Public institutions which claim to include women equally too often fail to accommodate to the needs of menstruating, pregnant, and breast-feeding women, for example. This sometimes discourages them from participation in these institutions. Sometimes the costs to women of being positioned as deviant in relation to normal bodies are small inconveniences, like remembering to carry tampons in anticipation that the women's room at work will not supply them. Sometimes, however, women suffer serious discomfort, threats to their health, harassment, job loss, or forego benefits by withdrawing in order to avoid these consequences. Including women as equals in schools, workplaces, and other institutions entails accommodating to our bodily specificity to the extent that we can both be women and excel in or enjoy the activities of those institutions.

These are stark examples of women's differences rendering us deviant in some settings. More broadly, much contemporary feminist theory argues that the social imagination of this [North American] culture projects onto women all the sense of vulnerability and chaotic desire attendant on being embodied and sexual beings. The norms of many public professional institutions, however, exclude or repress acknowledgement of bodily need and sexuality. The presence of women or womanliness in them, then, remains upsetting unless the women can present themselves like men.

The social differences produced by a gender division of labor constitute another axis of gender difference that renders women vulnerable to domination or exploitation or exclusion. Although there have been huge changes in attitudes about the capacities of men and women, and most formal barriers to women's pursuit of occupations and activities have been removed, in at least one respect change has been slow and minor. A structured social division of labor remains in which women do most of the unpaid care work in the family, and most people of both sexes assume that primary responsibility for care of children, other family members, and housecleaning falls primarily to women.

As Susan Okin theorized it more than fifteen years ago, this gender division of labor accounts in large measure for injustice to women, whether or not they themselves are wives or mothers. The socialization of girls continues to be oriented toward caring and helping. Occupational sex segregation continues to crowd women in a relatively few job categories, keeping women's wages low. Heterosexual couples sometimes find it rational to depend on a man's paycheck for their primary income. Thus women and their children are vulnerable to poverty in case they raise their children alone (Okin, 1989).

The structural positioning of women in the division of labor offers another instance of gender normalization. Most employers institutionalize an assumption that occupants of a good job – one that earns enough to support a family at a decent level of well-being and with a decent pension, vacation time, and job security – can devote himself or herself primarily to that job. Workers whose family responsibilities impinge on or conflict with employer expectations are deviants, and they are likely to be sanctioned for trying to combine real work and family responsibility.

Feminism construed as a politics of difference thus argues that real equality and freedom for women entail attending to embodied, socialized, and institutional sex and gender differences in order to ensure that women – as well as men who find themselves positioned like many women in the division of labor, comportment or taste – do not bear unfair costs of institutional assumptions about what women and men are or ought to be doing, who they feel comfortable working with or voting for, and so on. For women to have equal opportunities with men to attain positions of high status, power, or income, it is not enough that they prove their strength, leadership capacities or intelligence are as good as men's. This is relatively easy. It is more difficult to overcome the costs and disadvantages deriving from the application of supposedly difference-blind norms of productivity, respectability, or personal authority, that in fact carry structural biases against many women.

The project of this section has been to explain what I call the politics of positional difference, which I will now contrast with an approach many conceptualize as a politics of cultural difference. The problems of injustice to which the former responds arise from structural processes of the division of labor, social segregation and lack of fit between hegemonic norms and interpreted bodies. I have dwelt on injustice to people with disabilities, racial injustice and gender injustice in order to bring out social group difference not reducible to cultural difference, and in order to illustrate some diverse forms that these structural inequalities take. All concern, however, relations of privilege and disadvantage where some people's opportunities for the development and exercise of their capacities are limited and they are vulnerable to having the conditions of their lives and action determined by others without reciprocation. A politics of positional difference holds that equalizing these opportunities cannot rely on supposedly group-blind policies, because so many rules, norms and practices of so many institutions have group differentiating implications. Promoting justice requires some efforts that attend to such structural differences and attempt to change them, not only within law and public policy, but also in many other social and economic institutions and practices.

The politics of cultural difference

A politics of positional difference continues to have proponents among political theorists and those engaged in public discussion about the implications of group difference for values of freedom, equality, and justice. Indeed, I count myself as among them. What I am calling a politics of cultural difference has in recent years received more attention, both from political theorists, and in wider political debates.

I consider Will Kymlicka's book, *Multicultural Citizenship*, one of the earliest clear and thorough theoretical statements of this distinctive approach to a politics of difference. In that book Kymlicka explicitly distinguishes his approach to issues of group difference from one concerned with the situation of socially disadvantaged groups. "The marginalization of women, gays and lesbians, and the disabled," he says,

> cuts across ethnic and national lines – it is found in majority cultures and homogeneous nation-states as well as national minorities and ethnic groups – and it must be fought in all these places.
>
> (Kymlicka, 1995: 19)

Kymlicka does not elaborate this distinction between his approach to multiculturalism and that concerned with marginalized groups. It seems clear, however, that one basis of the distinction is that he thinks that groups defined by what he calls "societal culture" are different kinds of groups from the sort of group whose members face threats of marginalization or social disadvantage like that faced by women, sexual minorities, or people with disabilities. Let me fill that in with the account I have given above, that the latter are *structural* social groups, which is to say that what makes the group a group is that its members are similarly positioned on axes of privilege and disadvantage through structural social processes such as the organization of the division of labor or normalization.

The groups with which Kymlicka is concerned face distinctive issues, according to him, just because what defines them as groups is "societal culture". In his theory this term refers only to differences of nation and ethnicity. A "societal culture" is

> synonymous with 'a nation' or 'a people' – that is, an intergenerational community, more or less institutionally complete, occupying a given territory or homeland, sharing a distinct language and history. A state is multicultural if its members either belong to different nations (a multi-nation state), or have migrated from different nations (a polyethnic state), and if this fact is an important aspect of personal identity and political life.
>
> (ibid: 18)

The societal culture to which a person relates is an important aspect of his or her personal identity; his or her personal autonomy depends in part on being able to engage in specific cultural practices with others who identify with one another as in the same cultural group; on being able to speak the language one finds most comfortable in the conduct of everyday affairs; on having the space and time to celebrate group specific holidays and to display symbols important to the group. When the societal culture takes the form of nationality, this personal autonomy is tied to self-government autonomy for the group itself.

Kymlicka, along with most others who theorize the politics of cultural difference, thinks that most political societies today consist of at least two cultural groups, and often more than two. The question the politics of cultural difference poses is this: given that a political society consists of two or more societal cultures, what does justice require in the way of their mutual accommodation to one another's practices and forms of cultural expression, and to what extent can and should a liberal society give public recognition to these cultural diversities?

The politics of cultural difference assumes a situation of inequality common in contemporary polities in which members of multiple cultures dwell. It assumes that the state or polity is dominated by one of these cultural groups, which usually, but not always, constitutes a majority of the polity's members. The situation of political conflict the politics of cultural difference aims at is one where this dominant group can limit the ability of one or more of the cultural minorities to live out their forms of expression; or more benignly, the sheer ubiquity of the dominant culture threatens to swamp the minority culture to the extent that its survival as a culture may be endangered, even though the lives of the individual members of the group may be relatively comfortable in other ways. Under these circumstances of inequality of [or] unfreedom, members of embattled cultural groups frequently demand special rights and protections to enable their culture to flourish, and/or claim rights to a political society of their own, either within a federated relationship to that of the dominant culture(s), or by way of secession, within a state of their own.

The politics of cultural difference explicitly rejects political principles and practices which assume that a single polity must coincide with a single common culture. This implies rejecting as well the assumption held by many liberals that for the state and law to treat all citizens with equal respect entails that all be treated in the same way. Kymlicka distinguishes two kinds of cultural groups existing within today's multicultural politics: ethnic groups and national groups. Much of the response to his theory has focused on whether this distinction is viable, whether Kymlicka has made it correctly, and whether he has correctly identified the requirements of justice appropriate for each. Neither this distinction nor the debates it generates concern the major argument of this chapter.

Kymlicka's theory has received wide attention because within it he has identified and clarified many of the major issues of conflict and potential accommodation that arise in the contemporary politics of cultural difference, and most subsequent theories take these up and add to them. What does freedom of cultural expression require? Does it entail forms of public recognition of and accommodation to practices, symbols, and ways of doing things, and not just allowing group members private freedom to engage in minority practices and forms of expression? Where the rules of public regulation, employers, or others come into conflict with what members of cultural minorities consider culturally obligatory or necessary for the survival of their culture, does justice require exemption from those sorts of rules? Can cultural groups make a legitimate claim on the wider polity for resources necessary to memorialize their cultural past and the means to preserve its main elements for future generations? Do some cultural groups have legitimate claims to national autonomy, and if so, what does this imply for forms of self-government and relations with other groups? Does justice require that state and society take special measures to try to prevent members of cultural minorities from suffering a loss of opportunity or other disadvantage because they are committed to maintaining their cultural identity? Since cultural minorities often suffer political disadvantage in getting members elected to office and in voicing their interests and perspectives in representative bodies, does justice call for installing forms of group representation? Kymlicka considers the question of whether liberal polities ought to go so far as to tolerate practices that members of a culture regard as important but which a wider societal judgment finds violate standards of liberal accommodation and individual human rights. He argues that such practices should not be tolerated.

I have dwelt on Kymlicka's text because he, more explicitly than others, distinguishes the politics of cultural difference from what I call a politics of positional difference. With one important exception, moreover, the issues and arguments he advances in *Multicultural Citizenship* have set an agenda of theorizing that subsequent texts have debated and developed. To the issues Kymlicka treats, theorists of a politics of cultural difference have added another: the extent to which religious difference should be accommodated and affirmed in a multicultural liberal polity (Spinner-Halev, 2000). No doubt partly because issues of religious difference and perceived freedom of religious practice have become more prominent in political debates within European and North American societies, as well as in many other places, many theorists of politics and group difference have put religion alongside ethnicity and nationality as paramount forms of deep diversity.[11] The logic of religious difference and its implications for politics importantly diverges from ethnicity and nationality, at least because religious adherents often take doctrine and ceremony as not simply helping to define their identities, but also as obligatory for them. This raises the stakes in potential conflicts between majority commitments and the commitments of religious minorities.

Much recent theorizing about the politics of cultural difference takes issue with what writers charge is Kymlicka's overly homogeneous and overly bounded concept of societal culture. Joseph Carens, for example, argues that Kymlicka's concept of societal culture implicitly follows the logic of the concept of nation-state, even as the theory aims to challenge the singularity of one nation for each state (Carens, 2000). Ethnic and national groups, on his model, are each bounded by a singular understanding of themselves, in which place, language, history, and practice line up, and are differentiated from other groups. The motive for Kymlicka's theory is precisely to challenge the singularity of the self-conception of the nation-state; but his logic of group difference may follow a similar logic. Many others theorizing a politics of cultural difference raise problems with what they fear is an "essentialism" of cultural difference, where either participants or observers take a culture to be a coherent whole, relatively unchanging, and fully separate from other cultures. Against this, theorists such as Bhikhu Parekh and Seyla Benhabib offer a politics of cultural difference which puts dialogue among cultures at the center (Parekh, 2000; Benhabib, 2002). On the dialogic view, members of different cultural groups within a society often influence one another and engage in productive cultural exchange, and this interaction ought to be mobilized to resolve intercultural conflict.

Since both the theoretical approaches I have reviewed in this chapter are versions of a politics of difference, it should not be surprising that they share some features. I find two major similarities in the analyses and arguments of the politics of positional difference and the politics of cultural difference. Both worry about the domination some groups are able to exercise over public meaning in ways that limit freedom or curtail opportunity. Second, both challenge difference-blind public principle. They question the position that equal citizenship in a common polity entails a commitment to a common public interest, a single national culture, a single set of rules that applies to everyone in the same way. They both argue that commitment to justice sometimes requires noticing social or cultural differences and sometimes treating individuals and groups differently.

While they are logically distinct, each approach is important. The politics of cultural difference is important because it offers vision and principle to respond to dominative nationalist or other forms of absolutist impulses. We can live together in common political institutions and still maintain institutions by which we distinguish ourselves as peoples of cultures with distinct practices and traditions. Acting on such a vision can and should reduce ethnic, nationalist, and religious violence. The politics of positional difference is important because it highlights the depth and systematicity of inequality, and shows that inequality before the law is not sufficient to remedy this inequality. It calls attention to relations and processes of exploitation, marginalization, normalization that keep many people in subordinate positions.

My project in this chapter, then, is not to argue that political actors and theorists ought to accept one of these approaches and reject the other. I wish, rather, to argue that it is important to notice the difference between them, a difference sometimes missed in recent literatures. At the same time, I find that the two forms of argument are compatible in practice. Indeed, for some kinds of issues of group based politics and conflict, both forms of analysis are necessary. As I have indicated above, and will discuss again in the next section, for example, the oppression of minority cultures often merges into structural inequalities of racism insofar as it entails the limitation of opportunities for developing and exercising capacities.

Before turning to my worries about paying too much attention to a politics of cultural difference, let me conclude this section by addressing a question some readers may have. To what extent is this distinction in theoretical approaches the same as or similar to the distinction that Nancy Fraser has drawn between a politics of redistribution and politics of recognition? They are not in fact the same distinction at all. As I understand Fraser's categorization, both forms of a politics of difference I have articulated here fall under her category of a politics of recognition. Indeed, in her most recent statement of her theory, Fraser distinguishes what she calls a participatory parity approach – which roughly corresponds to what I call the politics of positional difference – and an identity politics approach – which roughly corresponds to what I am calling the politics of cultural difference (Fraser and Honneth, 2003). Insofar as there can be any comparison, that is, I think Fraser would categorize both approaches to the politics of difference I have described as different forms of a politics of recognition. Except for Charles Taylor, Fraser gives little attention to theorists I associate with the politics of cultural difference, and she favors the approach she calls participatory parity as a response to structural inequalities of gender, race, and sexuality.

I find this distinction between different forms of recognition politics useful. I continue to think, however, that it is too polarizing to construct economic relations, or redistribution, and culture, or recognition, as mutually exclusive categories. As I have tried to do in the first section of this chapter, it seems more useful to me to break out different aspects of the production of structural inequality such as normalization and the division of labor, each of which has both material effects on access to resources as well as the social meanings underlying status hierarchy.

Critical limits to the politics of cultural difference

The politics of cultural difference exhibits a different logic from the politics of positional difference. I have argued that each brings up important issues of justice relevant to contemporary politics and the two approaches are often compatible in a particular political context. To the extent that recent political theory and public discourse focus on the politics of cultural difference, however, debates about justice and difference become inappropriately narrowed. Some kinds of issues of justice retreat from view, and the discussion brings those that remain squarely under a liberal paradigm, which sometimes distorts their significance.

In this final section I will discuss three such worries with the ascendancy of issues of ethnic, national and religious difference in debates about justice and social group difference. The paradigm of the politics of cultural difference tends to underplay important issues of group difference such as those I have discussed in giving an account of the politics of positional difference. Here I will take one example: the paradigm of cultural difference obscures racism as a specific form of structural injustice. Second, I will discuss how the liberal framework under which the politics of cultural differences brings its issues focuses too much on the state in relation to individuals and groups, and does not see relations in civil society either as enacting injustice or as a source of remedy. Because many debates within the politics of cultural difference put their issues in terms of toleration, finally, I will argue that sometimes the politics of cultural difference itself expresses and reinforces a normalization that the politics of positional difference criticizes.

Tendency to obscure some issues of justice

As I discussed earlier, the politics of positional difference conceptualizes group difference primarily in structural terms. Social relations and processes put people in differing categorical social positions in relation to one another in ways that privilege those in one category in relation to another or others, both in the range of opportunities for self-development available to them, the resources they have or can access, the power they have over others or over the conditions of the lives of others, and the degree of status they have as indexed by others' willingness to treat them with deference or special respect. Class and gender are important structural axes in most societies. I have argued that physical and mental ability counts as another in our society that normalizes certain capacities. Race also names an important structural axis in most societies today.

The politics of cultural difference does not have a conceptual place for racial difference. To be sure, racialized social processes usually build on perceived differences in culture – language, religion, a sense of common lineage, specific cosmological beliefs, differing social practices, and so on. As I have discussed above, however, racialization and racism consist in a great deal more than that groups perceive themselves as distinct in relation to one another and refuse to recognize the culture of the others as equally legitimate to theirs. It even consists in more than that groups that perceive themselves as ethnically or culturally different have conflicts or are hostile to one another. Such ethnic or cultural difference becomes racial hierarchy when the groups interact in a social system where one group is able to extract benefits by its hierarchical relation to the other. This process involves constructing members of the subordinate groups as stereotyped and despised bodies; assigns them to menial, dirty or servile work, exclude them from high status positions, and tends to segregate the subordinate group from the dominant group.

The politics of cultural difference obscures the way that many group-based political claims and conflicts in contemporary multicultural societies involve both issues of cultural freedom *and* issues of structural inequality such as racism. Where there are problems of a lack of recognition of or accommodation to national, cultural, religious or linguistic groups in liberal democratic societies today (as well as others), these are often played out through dominant discourses that stereotype members of minority groups, find them technically inept or morally inferior, spatially segregate them and limit their opportunities to develop skills and compete for high status positions (Young, 2000a: 102–7)

Issues of justice for Latinos in the United States, for example, concern not only cultural accommodation and acceptance, but also exposure and criticism of institutional racism. Many believe that the two are deeply intertwined. Demands for and implementation of policies that mandate English only in public institutions such as courts and schools limit the freedom of some Latinos to express themselves freely, stigmatize them, and often limit their ability to develop marketable skills. The position of many Latinos is racialized, moreover, in that their brown skin and facial features categorize them as a group in the eyes of many Anglos, in spite of the fact that they or their parents hail from different parts of Latin America and experience differences of language and tradition among themselves. Within the dominant structures, "Hispanics" occupy particular positions in the social division of labor, and the benefits employers derive from this positioning are significant enough to limit the opportunities of members of this racialized group to move into other occupational positions (Young, 2000b).

Everywhere that indigenous people make claims to freedom of cultural expression and political self-determination, to take another example, they do so in the context of racialized structural inequality. Indians in North America, Aboriginals in Australia, indigenous people in Latin America, are all victims of historically racist policies of murder, removal, spatial concentration, theft of their land and resources, and limitation of their opportunities to make a living. Structures of racialized inequality runs deep in these societies and discrimination against, and stereotyping of, indigenous people persist.

Many conflicts over cultural toleration or accommodation in contemporary liberal democracies, in my observation, occur within a context of structural inequality between the dominant groups and cultural minorities. This is to say that what is at stake in many of these conflicts is not simply freedom of expression and association, but substantively equal opportunity for individuals from different groups to develop and exercise their capacities, and to have meaningful voice in the governance of the institutions whose roles and policies condition their lives. When the politics of cultural difference dominates political discourse on group difference, however, these issues are harder to raise and discuss. The weight of felt grievance about structural injustice then may load onto these cultural conflicts.

I have already alluded to the example of political conflict between Latinos and Anglos in the United States that may focus on cultural difference, but where structural inequality is also at stake. It seems to me that some group political conflict in multicultural European societies focuses on cultural difference in a context where structural inequality is a primary but understated issue. Many Muslim people dwelling in major European cities, for example, are victims of racial injustice. They are excluded from many opportunities for achieving status and income, they suffer stereotyping and objectification of their embodied presence, they lack recognized political voice, and they often live in segregated less desirable neighborhoods. The claims of such Muslims that they should have the freedom to wear headscarves or make their prayer calls in the public square in the European cities where they live should not be divorced from this context of broad and entrenched structural privilege of majorities, and social and economic disadvantage of minorities. The passion that often surrounds these debates may well be symptomatic of a failure to discuss seriously enough these issues of structural inequality.

State and civil society

The paradigm situation assumed by the politics of cultural difference is that of a society in which there is a plurality of ethnic, national, and/or religious groups, but in the current moment one or some of them tends to wield dominant power through the state. These dominant groups tend to bias state action and policy in ways that favor members of their groups – by declaring their language the official political language, for example, or making only those religious holidays celebrated by members of their group holidays recognized by the state. Cultural minorities resist this dominative power, and make claims on the state and on other members of their society to recognize their right to freedom of expression and practice, to exempt them from certain regulations on religious or cultural grounds, to recognize their language as one among several constituting the political community, to allow and support their children being educated in their language, to take special measures to assure representation of minority groups in political decision making, and many other claims for cultural recognition and freedom. Some minority groups claim to be distinct nations towards whom a right of self-determination should be recognized. There are many proposals and debates about what it can mean to accommodate such a right, not all of which involve creating a distinct sovereign state for the oppressed nationality, but most of which involve constitutional issues.

My purpose here is not to catalogue all the claims made under a politics of cultural difference nor to review the diverse positions people take in response to these claims. I have detailed this much in order to notice one thing: most of the issues that arise both in theoretical writing and public discussion about the politics of cultural difference concern state policy, regulation, or the organization of state institutions.

In this respect the politics of cultural difference usually comes within a liberal framework. One of the features of a liberal framework, as distinct from other possible frameworks in political theory, such as critical theory, republicanism or communitarianism, is that it presumes that political struggle is about state policy primarily. This liberal framework assumes a simple model of society as consisting of what is public – which coincides with what is under the administrative regulation of the state – and what is private, which is everything else. Under this liberal model, the main question is, what shall the state permit, support, or require, and what shall it discourage or forbid. Framing questions of the politics of difference largely in terms of what the state should or should not do in relation to individuals and groups, however, ignores civil society as an arena of action, institutional decision making, and political struggle. It tends to ignore ways that non-governmental institutions often exercise exploitation, domination and exclusion, as well as ways that private organizations and institutions can design remedies for these wrongs. The relations in which individuals and groups stand to one another within civil society, even apart from their relations to state policy, are very important both as causes of injustice and resources for remedying this injustice.[12]

The assumption that politics concerns primarily what the state allows, requires or forbids, moreover, can generate serious misunderstanding about positions taken by proponents of a politics of difference, particularly with the politics of positional difference. Brian Barry is a case in point. He quotes disapprovingly my claim in *Justice and the Politics of Difference* that "no social practices or activities should be excluded as improper subjects for public discussion, expression and collective choice," and then cites Robert Fullinwider's interpretation of this statement to the effect that I advocate political intervention and modification into "private choices" (Barry, 2000: 270).

The specter that Barry and Fullinwider fear is limitation of individual liberty backed by state sanction. Apparently they envision no object of public discussion and collective choice other than state policies and laws. Certainly these are important objects of public discussion and choice in a democracy. A political theory concerned with the production and reproduction of structural inequalities even when laws guarantee formally equal rights, however, must shine its light on other corners as well. Movements of African Americans, people with disabilities, feminists, gay men and lesbians, indigenous people, as well as many ethnic movements, realize that societal discrimination, processes of segregation and marginalization enacted through social networks and private institutions must be confronted in their non-state institutional sites. While law can provide a framework for equality, and some remedy for egregious violations of rights and respect, the state and law cannot and should not reach into every capillary of everyday life. A politics of positional difference thus recommends that churches, universities, production and marketing enterprises, clubs and associations all examine their policies, practices, and priorities to discover ways they contribute to unjust structures and recommends changing them when they do. Such a position is not tantamount to calling the culture Gestapo to police every joke or bathroom design. Numerous social changes brought about by these movements in the last thirty years have involved actions by many people that were voluntary, in the sense that the state neither required them nor sanctioned agents who did not perform them. Indeed, state policy as often follows behind action within civil society directed at undermining structural injustice as leads it.[13]

Seyla Benhabib distinguishes such a "dual track" approach to politics, which she associates with critical theory, and argues that liberal political theory typically ignores non-state dimensions of politics.

> In deliberative democracy, as distinguished from political liberalism, the *official* public sphere of representative institutions, which includes the legislature, executive and public bureaucracies, the judiciary and political parties, is not the only site of political contestation and or opinion and will formation. Deliberative democracy focuses on social movements, and on the civil, cultural, religious, artistic, and political associations of the *unofficial* public sphere, as well.
>
> (Benhabib, 2002: 21)

Barry, and others who consider issues of difference under a liberal paradigm, ignores this non-official public sphere of contestation and action, and thus "attempts to solve multicultural conflicts through a juridical calculus of liberal rights" (ibid). A conception of justice able to criticize relations of domination and limitation of opportunity suffered by gender, racialized, ethnic or religious groups must consider relations within private activities and civil society and their interaction with state institutions (ibid: 118–21).

Normalizing culture

I said that the logic of most theorizing in the politics of cultural difference, as well as the logic of many political debates about multiculturalism, assumes the point of view of a power or authority which deliberates about what practices, forms of expression, forms of civic and political association, and so on, should be allowed, encouraged, or required, and which discouraged or forbidden. Both theoretical and political debates in the politics of cultural difference, that is, often take the traditionally liberal form of debates about what should and what should not be tolerated.

Framing issues of difference in terms of toleration, however, often introduces a normalizing logic in debates about multiculturalism. The political questions debated often have this form: shall we tolerate this expression or practice that we find of questionable value or morality, for the sake of mutual accommodation and civic peace? Should we allow methods of processing animals for food which require that the animals be awake at the time of slaughter? I do not introduce this example to debate it, but rather as an example that this form is typical in multicultural debates. I think this form assumes the following. The primary participants in the debate are members of the "we", who argue among themselves for and against toleration. This "we" is the point of view of the dominant culture, which also assumes itself to have the power to influence the authorities who allow or forbid. While those holding the point of view debate among themselves whether toleration is the appropriate stance in this case, they all presume themselves to occupy a position as normal, which means not only in the statistical majority, but also holding values that lie within the range of acceptable and even good. Those whose practices the normalized "we" debates have little or no voice in the public deliberations. They are the object of the debates, but only weakly political subjects in it, if at all. The debate positions them as deviant in relation to the norm; as with all questions of toleration, the question is only, are these practices so deviant as to be beyond a line of permissibility? Those who find themselves positioned in this normalizing discourse often believe that the terms of the debate themselves are disrespectful, even before a resolution has been achieved. They also often believe that their being positioned as deviant makes them liable to other forms of denigration, exclusion, or disadvantage.

A funny inversion often happens to gender issues in this politics of cultural difference utilizing the normalizing logic implicit in many debates about toleration. I argued above that the politics of cultural difference obscures many issues concerning gender and justice that are matters of structural inequality. The politics of positional difference theorizes gender as a set of structural social positions. These structures operate in complex ways to render many women vulnerable to gender based domination and deprivation in most societies of the world, including Western liberal democracies.

You would never know it, however, to listen to gendered debates among contemporary theorists of the politics of cultural difference. Many of the political debates currently taking place about multiculturalism focus on beliefs and practices of cultural minorities, especially Muslims, about women. These debates are especially salient in Europe, though George W. Bush used these issues to great rhetorical effect to legitimate the U.S.-led invasion of Afghanistan which began in 2001 (Young, 2003). A great deal of the recent political theoretical literature taking the approach of a politics of cultural difference devotes considerable attention to the treatment of women by cultural minorities.

In many theoretical writings on multiculturalism, gender issues serve as the tests to the limits of toleration. Can we tolerate rules of a national minority that refuse to recognize the women who marry outside as group members? Can we allow Muslim women to accede to the pressure or expectation that they wear the hijab? Surely we cannot permit arranged marriages of teenage girls or female genital cutting under any circumstances.

My purpose in calling attention to the ubiquity of gender issues in contemporary political and theoretical debates on cultural difference is not to examine the arguments on various sides and take a position. I bring them up as instances of the normalizing discourse of toleration typical of the logic of the politics of cultural difference. The "we" in these questions occupies the position of the majority Western liberals. "We" can raise these questions about the extent to which the gender practices of the minority culture can be tolerated because among "us", women have the same freedom and autonomy as men. Our gender individualism is the norm against which the practices of many cultures come up deviant. Debates about gender in the politics of cultural difference thus serve the double function of positioning some cultural groups beyond the pale and encouraging a self-congratulatory arrogance on the part of the "we" who debate these issues. Given the extent to which, in even the most liberal of Western societies, vast numbers of women continue to be vulnerable to poverty, left to work one and a half times as many hours as men, and are victims of rape, battery, and sexual harassment, this discourse is ridiculous.

Conclusion

The purpose of this chapter has been to clarify differences in approaches to political and theoretical debates about whether and to what extent justice calls for paying attention to rather than ignoring social group differences. I have argued that the politics of cultural difference has more occupied political theorists in recent years than a politics of positional difference. This trend is lamentable, I have suggested, because it tends to narrow the groups of concern to ethnic, national, and religious groups, and to limit the issues of justice at stake to those concerned with freedom and autonomy more than equal opportunity to develop capacities and live a life of well being. Its reliance on a liberal paradigm, moreover, tends to limit politics to state policy and to reintroduce normalizing discourses into what began as denormalizing movements. My objective in making these distinctions and arguments has not been to reject the politics of cultural difference, but to encourage political theorists to recommit their attention to group differences generated from structures of power, the division of labor, and constructions of the normal and the deviant, as they continue also to reflect on conflicts over national, ethnic, or religious difference.

Bibliography

Barry, B. (2000) *Culture and Equality: An Egalitarian Critique of Multiculturalism*, Cambridge: Polity Press.

Benhabib, S. (2002) *The Claims of Culture: Equality and Diversity in the Global Era*, Princeton, NJ: Princeton University Press.

Carens, J. (2000) *Culture, Citizenship and Community: A Contextual Explication of Justice as Evenhandedness*, Oxford: Oxford University Press.

Chambers, C. (2002) 'All Must Have Prizes: The Liberal Case for Interference in Cultural Practices' in Paul Kelly (ed.) *Multiculturalism Revisited: 'Culture and Equality' and its Critics*, Cambridge: Polity Press, pp. 151–73.

Fanon, F. (1967) *Black Skins, White Masks*, New York: Grove Press.

Fraser, N. and A. Honneth (2003) *Redistribution or Recognition: A Philosophical Exchange*, London: Verso Press.

Gordon, L. (1995) *Bad Faith and Anti-Black Racism*, Amherst, MA: Humanity Books.

Gutmann, A. (2003) *Identity in Democracy*, Princeton, NJ: Princeton University Press.

Kelly, P. (2002) 'Defending Some Dodos: Liberty and/or Equality' in Paul Kelly (ed.) *Multiculturalism Revisited: 'Culture and Equality' and its Critics*, Cambridge: Polity Press, pp. 62–80.

Kittay, E.F. (1999) *Love's Labor: Essays on Women, Equality, and Dependency*, New York: Routledge.

Kymlicka, W. (1989) *Liberalism, Community and Culture*, Oxford: Oxford University Press.

Kymlicka, W. (1995) *Multicultural Citizenship: A Liberal Theory of Minority Rights*, Oxford: Oxford University Press.

Loury, G. (2002) *The Anatomy of Racial Inequality*, Cambridge, MA: Harvard University Press.

Okin, S. (1989) *Justice, Gender and the Family*, New York: Basic Books.

Parekh, B. (2000) *Rethinking Multiculturalism: Cultural Diversity and Political Theory*, Basingstoke: Palgrave Macmillan.

Rawls, J. (1971) *A Theory of Justice*, Cambridge, MA: Belknap.

Rawls, J. (1993) *Political Liberalism*, New York: Columbia University Press.

Schachar, A. (2001) *Multicultural Jurisdictions: Cultural Differences and Women's Rights*, Cambridge: Cambridge University Press.

Silvers, A. (1998) 'Formal Justice' in Anita Silvers, David Wasserman, Mary Mahowald (eds) *Disability, Difference, Discrimination: Perspectives on Justice in Bioethics and Public Policy*, Lanham, MD: Rowman and Littlefield, pp. 13–146.

Slaughter, T.F. (1983) 'Epidermalizing the World: A Basic Mode of Being Black' in Leonard Harris (ed.) *Philosophy Born of Struggle*, Dubuque, IA: Kendall Hunt Publishers, pp. 283–8.

Spinner-Halev, J. (2000) *Surviving Diversity: Religion and Democratic Citizenship*, Baltimore, MD: Johns Hopkins University Press.

Tilly, C. (1998) *Durable Inequality*, Berkeley, CA: University of California Press.

Young, I.M. (1990), *Justice and the Politics of Difference*, Princeton, NJ: Princeton University Press.

Young, I.M. (2000a) *Inclusion and Democracy*, Oxford: Oxford University Press.

Young, I.M. (2000b), 'Disabilities and the Definition of Work' in Leslie Pickering Francis and Anita Silvers (eds) *Americans with Disabilities: Exploring Implications of the Law for Individuals and Institutions*, New York: Routledge, pp. 169–73.

Young, I.M. (2000c) 'Structure, Difference, and Hispanic/Latino Claims of Justice' in Jorge Gracia and Pablo de Greiff (eds) *Hispanics/Latinos in the United States: Ethnicity, Race and Rights*, New York: Routledge, pp. 147–66.

Young, I.M. (2001) 'Equality of Whom? Social Groups and Judgments of Injustice' *Journal of Political Philosophy* 9: 1–18.

Young, I.M. (2003) 'The Logic of Masculinist Protection: Reflections on the Current Security State', *Signs: A Journal of Women in Culture and Society*, 29: 1–25.

Notes

1 This paper was originally intended to be delivered by the author at the workshop on Intersectionality, organised by the AHRC Research Centre for Law, Gender, and Sexuality, on 21 and 22 May 2005, at Keele University, UK. Unfortunately, Professor Young was unable to attend the workshop due to ill-health. Instead, she sent us this paper to be posted on the centre's website. This book's editors have lightly edited this paper for publication here, and are responsible for any changes of meaning.

2 Some of the ideas in *Multicultural Citizenship* appear in a less developed form in Kymlicka's *Liberalism, Community, and Culture* (Kymlicka, 1989).

3 Versions of this paper have been presented at the International Association of Feminist Philosophers, Gothenberg, Sweden, June 2004, and at a meeting of the Chicago area Conference for the Study of Political Thought at the University of Illinois at Chicago, November 2004. I have profited from discussions on those occasions. I am grateful to the following individuals for comments on earlier drafts: David Alexander, David Ingram, Anthony Laden, Patchen Markell, and David Owen.

4 I have elaborated a notion of structural group difference and structural inequality in several previous writings. See Young, 2000a pp. 92–102; Young, 2001.

5 I have argued that so-called merit standards often normalize attributes, comportments, or attainments associated with particular social groups, and thus often do not serve the impartial purpose they claim (Young, 1990: Chapter 7). Brian Barry aims to refute this critique in *Culture and Equality: An Egalitarian Critique of Multiculturalism* (Barry, 2000) at pp. 90–102. For a good reply to Barry on these points, from the point of view of a politics of positional difference, see Kelly, 2002 at pp. 62–80. See also Chambers, 2002 at pp. 151–73.

6 I have discussed this issue in another essay: see Young, 2000c.

7 I take the term "epidermalize" from Frantz Fanon, *Black Skins, White Masks* (Fanon, 1967), at pp. 110–112. See also Slaughter, 1983.

8 Lewis Gordon analyzes the logic of the dichotomy of anti-Black racism according to an existentialist logic of absolute subject and the Other (Gordon, 1995). I have brought a Foucaultian framework to articulate how racial dichotomy sets up norms that then organize bodies on a scale of better and worse; see Young, 1990, Chapter 5.

9 For a more thorough account of the distinction between segregation and clustering, and an account of the structural consequences of segregation, see Young, 2000a, Chapter 6.

10 I have made a longer argument to this effect in Chapter 3 of *Inclusion and Democracy* (Young, 2000a). See also Gutmann, 2003. Gutmann's analysis would

be even stronger if she theorized the social group as a product of structural processes of privilege rather than as a prejudicial ascription of denigrated status onto some people. Amy Gutmann well articulates a distinction between an "identity politics" which might take pride in ascriptive identity as such, on the one hand, and a group-based politics in which "the appropriate object of pride is not the ascriptive identity in itself but rather the identity's manifestation of dignified, self-respecting personhood, the personhood of someone who has overcome social obstacles because of an ascriptive identity," on the other (ibid: 136).

11 Texts that add a focus on religious difference, and separate it from but compare to issues of national and ethnic difference include Parekh, 2000; Shachar, 2001; Benhabib, 2002; and Gutmann, 2003.

12 In Chapter 5 of *Inclusion and Democracy* (Young, 2000a) I further discuss the virtues and limits of action in civil society for remedying injustice.

13 Brian Barry also blanches at the assertion I make in *Justice and the Politics of Difference* (Young, 1990) that remedy for normalizing social processes is "cultural revolution." In this phrase, which I borrowed from Julia Kristeva, "culture" refers to modes of comportment, gestures, speech styles and other modes of communication and how people understand these in the everyday lifeworld. "Revolution" may be a dramatic term. Eliminating ways that women, people with disabilities or poor people are sometimes denigrated, however, among other things requires changing some symbolic meanings and interactive habits or some people. In her reaction to the phrase, "cultural revolution," Amy Gutmann also manifests an assumption that state and law are the primary motors of social change to undermine injustice. Processes that now I would call "denormalization," must involve change to every interactive habit as well as institutional rule reform.

Chapter 12

Intersectional travel through everyday utopias

The difference sexual and economic dynamics make

Davina Cooper

Race, gender, and sexual orientation are not *things* like plants and fungi with separate and independent existences. They are concepts, used within systems of language and culture, to apportion and police regimes of power.

(Kwan 2002: 328–9)

Introduction

In all the discussion surrounding intersectionality, what has received limited attention are intersectionality's conceptual building blocks: axes, groups, identity, domination – the terms intersectionality scholarship relies upon. This is my focus here. Drawing on two case studies involving prefigurative social spaces, I want to revisit how we think about intersecting inequalities in a way that *recentres* inequality's relationship to wider structural processes. At the same time, I want to offer a perspective which is non-deterministic, which, in presenting a polycentric picture of inequality and structural processes, refuses to privilege particular formations of power or social fields *ab initio*. In other words, this is a perspective which recognises the dynamic, changing character of inequality, as it also recognises the many, varied structural tendencies – and I use *tendencies* to get away from thinking of structures as *things* – that shape (and are conditioned by) inequality.

To pursue this project, the chapter engages two main concepts: relations of inequality and social dynamics. Since the first is far more familiar – identifying the different forms institutionally organised collective inequality takes – as sexual orientation, socio-economic class, gender, race, and physical capacity,[1] amongst others – the conceptual focus in this chapter is on the second term, as well as the relationship between the two. I started using the term 'social dynamics' in *Challenging Diversity* (Cooper 2004) to identify a wide range of dynamic processes, from capitalism to community formation, and the intimate/impersonal. These processes, I suggested, combine and articulate features of social life in ways that drive both stability and change. They also offer, amongst other things, a way of thinking about inequality. While social dynamics do not, alone, explain *why* relations of inequality exist, they do identify significant aspects of *how* inequalities operate and *what* they consist of.

Yet, if organising principles, such as gender, race, sexuality and class, are shaped by specific social dynamics, how do we avoid returning to a model in which each socially generated register of inequality (gender, class, sexual orientation, race, physical capacity) gets hooked to a separate system of power (patriarchy, capitalism, heterosexuality, white supremacy, able-bodiedness)? How do we retain the primacy of connection while still being able to talk analytically about different registers, features or parts? This is a key challenge for my discussion of social dynamics and their relation to intersectional thinking, which I address conceptually and in relation to two very different sites: a women's bathhouse in Toronto, established in the late 1990s to encourage casual, 'raunchy' sex, and networks of multilateral trading that became popular in Britain in the 1990s, known as Local Exchange Trading Systems or Schemes (LETS).

Drawing on a secondary literature alongside interviews conducted from 2001–7 with participants and organisers, this discussion forms part of a larger, ongoing project on 'everyday utopias' – a term I use for sites and spaces which aspire to accomplish some routine aspect of social life in a more democratic, equal or freer fashion.[2] My first site, LETS, since inception in British Columbia, Canada in the 1980s, have worked to create empowering, economically fairer, more sociable forms of trading, as spatially defined communities cohere around buying and selling, usually small-scale and informal, goods and services (from homemade bread to gardening, decorating, dog-walking and lessons). Toronto Women's Bathhouse (TWB), by contrast, was established in 1998 as an occasional, open, party event held at men's bathhouses in the city. Combining the ethos of a men's bathhouse and a feminist social venue, TWB aimed to create a safe, adventurous sexual space in which women and trans participants could develop new sexual skills and experiment with no-ties sex.

I want to draw on these two sites to bring a fresh perspective to exploring relations of inequality, and the connections framed as intersectional. On the one hand, focusing on community spaces and networks that are small-scale, less complex, and oriented towards equality and justice, allows us to contemplate conditions of possibility for non-hierarchical forms of difference. At the same time, I want to explore what intersectionality can offer to thinking about prefigurative spaces. As a lens – or, more accurately, as a collective term for several lenses – does intersectionality bring the presence of inequality within everyday, equality-oriented utopias to the fore? And if it does, how should we understand this process – conceptually and empirically?

To pursue my analysis, I begin by setting out an understanding of social dynamics, focusing on the two dynamics at the heart of my discussion: the economic and the sexual. I then explore how a variable-scale analysis, linking relations of inequality to social dynamics, complicates those intersectionality approaches which frame inequality as an intra-societal process involving homologous structures (whether as axes, classes, or systems). The second half of the chapter advances this more conceptual discussion through two case studies. My aim there is two-fold: to explore the distinctive relationship between social dynamics and relations of inequality within alternative spaces, and then to complicate this understanding with an analysis grounded in thinking intersectionally.

Social dynamics

My initial use of social dynamics was to find a way around some of the problems I associated with dominant frameworks for thinking about inequality and intersectionality (Cooper 2004). In particular, I wanted to find an approach which treated inequality as something more than relations between groups, without going to the other extreme of a mono-centric, inflexible account of social structure. To explain how I ended up with the concept of social dynamics, I shall briefly map four alternative approaches which, between them, have tended to dominate feminist inequality and intersectionality discussion.[3]

The first account centres groups, defined by identification or social location. While groups may be framed in mono-dimensional or intersectional terms, key characteristics of a group-based approach are, first, that groups are explicitly or implicitly depicted as *severable* from the relations of power they encounter. And second, oppression or subordination tends to be portrayed as a negative property or burden which the group (temporarily) holds. The strength of this paradigm is that it treats 'minority' identity and experience as *more than* subordination. However, the cost is that the complex interconnections and inequalities generated by the social fabric – its processes, cycles, flows, procedures, norms and artefacts – get reduced to a model of conflicting group interests. Scholars vary in whether they adopt a weak or strong group-based account. The former suggests simply that categories, such as sex/gender, will endure (even as they get articulated over time in different ways); the strong version suggests that what group identities *mean* will also endure – giving groups a meaning, reality, and durability beyond current power formations.[4]

Intersectionality scholars divide in their relative willingness to give social categories ontological durability. What they converge more comfortably around is their shared concern that focusing on the multi-dimensional character of social subjects can lead to infinitely smaller, more finely categorised, and consequently less politically effective groupings.

Consequently, a second different perspective has tended to dominate intersectionality's lexicon. This draws on the language of axes or vectors to represent compound inequality as the place where axes meet. Evocative and engaging with its crossroads image, the drawback with this metaphor is two-fold. First, it depicts inequality as one straight line encountering another – in which each line represents a continuum of greater or lesser advantage.[5] Second, despite its figurative structuralism, this framework is subject-centred in that each configuration of criss-crossing axes tends to centre, and thus do little more than *define*, a particular individual or group experience – even as it recognises that the intersectional experience or compound identity accounted for may take an unexpected or contradictory form. Together, these drawbacks thwart intersectionality's capacity to illuminate the texture, systemic flows or practices that comprise the social landscape except as a confusion of diverse, infinitely interconnecting, vectors.

The second two sets of explanations offer a richer picture of the social landscape *qua* social formation – moving away, in the process, from intersectionality theory's heartland of identity characteristics or group-based power. The first, systems-based, approach sets up a hybrid structure or combination of interlocking systems as shaping, determining or governing social life (see Conaghan, this volume). The limits and weaknesses of this approach have been well-rehearsed – particularly its tendency to a reductionist functionalism unable to acknowledge (and even less illuminate) counter-hegemonic forms of agency, changing and contradictory social patterns, and new contenders for systemic status. However, what has received less attention within intersectionality writing is the contribution a more systemic or structuralist account offers – particularly its capacity to provide an analysis of complexly textured, interconnected social logics, such as capitalism, colonialism and kinship structures, which, while they *shape* relations of inequality, are not *reducible* to them.

The second of these last two approaches represents a step back from structural or systemic accounts. With its focus on how gendered, racialised, sexualised and other asymmetrical relational processes are accomplished in and through particular sites, this framework gives a more pluralistic, contingent and active account of how social life is shaped by inequality relations, one which recognises also the contradictory effects and reversals of these fractious power-oriented registers. Often read as 'gendering, racialising...' it covers a lot of ground. Hailing institutional structures through the terminology of inequality, it addresses how asymmetrical relations shape and occupy the terrain of state practice, while its lexicon flags the presence, within social and institutional life, of norms, values, structures, practices and beliefs historically associated with particular relations of hierarchy. Yet, 'gendering, racialising...' has two significant shortcomings from the perspective of my discussion here. First, its more poststructuralist understanding of social relations often leaves it unclear as to what, for instance, the gender of being 'gendered' refers to – is gender at heart about hierarchically ordered categories (even as it also secures and reproduces these categories) through institutional performances, or is its remit much wider embracing social features such as the public/private? Are such social features a *part* of gender or merely *articulated* to gender at particular historical moments? This raises a second concern. While it might prove insightful to talk about the gendered state, the series of articulations connecting gender to the state can become something of a 'black box'. So, explaining how governmental practices produce, sustain or impact upon gendered inequalities may be relatively straightforward; but how gender relations, values, epistemologies, and cultural practices connect to each other as well as to the state to structure *its* practice remains more opaque.

What analytical assistance can social dynamics offer? I want to suggest that by providing a partner term to relations of inequality, social dynamics necessarily narrow the latter's scope. Instead of gender having to do all the analytical work, what Kate Bedford describes as 'patterned links' – here, between gender and dynamics, such as the 'intimate/impersonal'[6] – help to flesh out how gender relations of inequality operate: how they can be shaped by as well as, simultaneously, shaping institutional practices, such as policy-making or legal judgment. In this sense, social dynamics work as bridging terms that allow relations of inequality to be just that. At the same time, they enable analysis to extend to the multiple ways in which gender, for instance, is linked to features of social life such as the spatial allocation of appropriate conduct, norms that should not be reduced to the condition of asymmetrical relations.

Social dynamics also do more than provide the supplementary or intermediate term. Social dynamics speak to the 'what' and 'how' of inequality. The tensions and interconnections flagged by the term 'the intimate/impersonal' may only partially explain *why* gender hierarchies remain. What the term does indicate, however, is a key dynamic around which gender hierarchies revolve, and through which gender relations are produced – a process far more complex than a simple binary allocation of intimate/female, impartial/male suggests. Unlike structural accounts, which declare, for instance, that patriarchy is always linked to gender, capitalism to class, my approach allows both partners – that is the social dynamics *and* relations of inequality – to slide away from each other, reform and couple in new ways. This relative independence or autonomy is important when we consider social dynamics and inequalities within alternative social spaces, where not only may both terms take on new meanings, but how they configure may also take quite different forms.

To take this further, let me introduce the two social dynamics at the centre of this discussion: the economic and sexual, chosen to highlight the spectrum of social dynamics constituting relations of inequality as well as for their capacity to illuminate the two empirical sites later discussed. After introducing them, I shall address some broader questions raised by a social dynamics approach, and then explore their intersectionality dimensions.

Economic dynamics

Economic dynamics have been so extensively discussed as production–exchange–consumption they seem almost impossible to revisit. However, since my focus is non-capitalist spaces, where commodity relations get decentred or at least re-imagined, I want to think about economic dynamics in terms of generation–access–use. This framing incorporates capitalist relations, but is slanted towards common property, welfare-distributive or gift-based modes of circulation, and the non-exhaustive, collective deployment of goods and services. I shall discuss economic dynamics later in relation to LETS, but for the purposes of advancing my conceptual discussion of intersectionality, let me provide a brief mapping of its three key terms.

In *Against the Romance of Community*, Joseph (2002: 33) uses the example of gay men creating and giving meaning to public sexual spaces to argue for a broader conception of production (also Binnie 2004). Given my focus on everyday utopias, I also take 'generation' to signify more than making tangible (or even intangible) things and wealth, to include producing meaning, sociality and affectivity – productive relations which may or may not involve payment. Things and services may be *accessed* through exchange – the conventional focus. However, access suggests acquisition can also occur through gifts, public allocation of benefits, unpaid (obligated) labour, theft and appropriation (see also Gibson-Graham 2006; Godelier 1999; Offer 1997). More generally, access, as gift scholarship has explored, recentres the fact not *all* rights of ownership are necessarily transferred. This is true for many *exchanges*, in practice. However, as a framework oriented around the paradigmatic model of sovereign owners abdicating all rights to one thing in order to gain full rights over another, exchange foregrounds a particular vision of *how* things and rights (as well as *which* things and rights) circulate (also Cooper 2007a).

To speak of use, rather than the more widely used term consumption, likewise decentres the model of the purchasing, extravagant or conventional, status-oriented consumer. Use highlights the claim – now well furrowed within consumption studies – that things are not simply used up, but used in performative ways to create (new) economic, social and cultural values as well as statuses (e.g., Crang 1996; Jackson 2004).[7] It also highlights the distinctive effort in making both thing and subject fit for use, in the absence of clear producer/consumer distinctions, and conventional economic circuits – as witnessed in many alternative community spaces. So, people use things they, individually and collectively, produce or interact as economic 'next-door neighbours' (with very truncated production to consumption chains). Indeed, *becoming* a community producer may *depend* upon processes of belonging forged through prior and ongoing histories of ritualised consumption.[8] This is apparent in alternative schools, such as A.S. Neill's Summerhill School, where identity and connection are amongst the main things used and generated.

Economic dynamics of generation–access–use underpin, mediate and provide the key terms for the socio-economic inequalities and differences encountered within the everyday utopias I studied. What I mean by this is several-fold. First, the dynamics of economic circuits (however, non-linear) encode within themselves *different* economic positions. Second, they provide key drivers in the formation of local socio-economic class relations and give content to those relations. Third, they provide an important mediation between local socio-economic relations and those relations and economic dynamics operating at other scales (and in other places). Combined, these complex connections have the potential to enhance *or* undercut *wider* inequalities. They also have the potential to enhance or undercut everyday utopias' drive towards equality, as I discuss below.

Sexual dynamics

Within the global North, desire[9] has become the self-evident truth of orientation. Rather than conduct or appearance, desire culturally functions as the directed energy that defines *what* someone is. While this could work non-hierarchically, mapping orientation as a spectrum of non-asymmetrical difference; this is currently little evident. More evident is the way that those desires, normatively authorised, are legally and politically allowed an intimacy, others are denied. In this way, intimacy provides the reward for appropriate desires. Yet it is also the space of risk and public panic – the legal, spatial and emotional angle between people that makes certain unauthorised desires and contact (boys' school homosexuality or intergenerational incest), for instance, possible. The third element, embodiment, is not simply about the need for, or centrality of, bodies within sex.[10] It is about the enfolding of the social into and through the body, whether as gender, disgust, or as other modes of social expression, like public speech. How bodies enunciate social relations provides evidence for allocation to categories of orientation; enunciation also shapes the way unequal orientations are inhabited, produced and lived out, for instance, as confident, shameful, public, secret and so on.

I suggested above that economic dynamics, within everyday utopias, may prove less linear and more compressed than the trope generation–access– use seems to imply. Sexual dynamics also take shape *differently* within different spaces. While conventionally depicted according to an authorised unidirectional flow – desire leads to bodily contact which, if successful, produces emotional intimacy – in counter-sexual spaces, this flow may be disrupted or reformed. So, in an intense, queer space such as a bathhouse, desire for the other may lead to contact which circumvents intimacy;

alternatively, spatial intimacy may be depicted as the condition for a contact which generates auto-desires, otherwise unknown or unrealised. Basically, what I want to stress at this point is that what social dynamics mean as well as the ordering of their articulation will vary by place and by time.

In the chapter's second half, I explore economic and sexual dynamics in some more detail through case-study examples of LETS and Toronto Women's Bathhouse. There, I address the way an intersectional reading complicates our understanding of the economic and sexual differences dynamics produce. However, before doing so, I want to flesh out my social dynamics framework further, drawing particular attention to questions of pluralism and change. I then turn to the contribution social dynamics make to thinking intersectionally.

While certain social dynamic articulations or constellations emerge as dominant in a given time/space, the first key feature, thrown up by discussion so far, is social dynamics' plural character – internally and externally. *Definitionally*, social dynamics' ability to support relations of inequality *depends* upon their incorporating and giving shape to a spectrum of diverse, frequently hierarchical, locations (or identities).[11] But difference and contradiction are also immanent to the elements (e.g., desire, intimacy, generation, access) through which social dynamics are forged as well as to the articulations between them. Social dynamics may *seem* to have a circuit-like quality of mutual reinforcement and iterability: so, capitalist production leads to consumption which leads to production. However, closer scrutiny reveals tensions as constitutive elements of a dynamic pull away from (as well as towards) each other.

Tensions also exist between different versions of the 'same' dynamic. Dynamics are not unified, closed structures; they also rarely fill the entirety of a social space. Within most social spaces (as well as between them) competing, or at least different, economic or sexual dynamics will exist. *How* they co-exist – whether, for instance, particular economic dynamics manage to penetrate, capture or reform each other is the stuff of politics (see also Gibson-Graham 1996, 2006). While these processes are most obviously evident within large, complex social spaces, they are also apparent in the conflicts endemic to everyday utopias, as, for instance, in the competing ways desire and embodiment are articulated together at the bathhouse or in the sharp conflicts within UK LETS between scheme and system proponents over the relationship between money, community building and trade (see Lee *et al.* 2004; North 2006).

The social and political agency involved in establishing powerful new (or revised) dynamics highlights a second issue. The relationship between social dynamics and relations of inequality is constantly changing and evolving, as activity and pressure occur at multiple points (also Yuval-Davis 2006: 200).[12] I want to stay with the question of change for a moment, while bracketing the agency involved in its pursuit, to address the *contingent* character of dynamic constellations.

Social dynamics appear to involve a limited number of central foundational elements; nevertheless, these elements are not fixed. And by this I don't just mean their internal plurality or ongoing re-articulatory processes. If one pathway to thinking about social dynamics is as a circuit, flow or constellation of discursive/material elements driving particular relations of inequalities, what stands as these key elements *may* change, in part because (but not only because) relations of inequality also change. An instance of this process is the changing status of reproduction within Britain's dominant dynamics of sexuality. Although some British scholars convincingly argue that unequal access to reproduction, and the legal regime surrounding it, continue to shore up inequalities of heterosexual and homosexual orientation,[13] today, in Britain, reproduction does not play quite the central role within hegemonic dynamics of sexuality that it did even two decades ago. This does not mean reproduction is no longer tied to power. Indeed, *new* forms of inequality sutured to a dynamics revolving around reproductive/parental status may be forming. However, in relation to the dynamics underpinning sexual orientational difference, reproductive capacity appears more loosely coupled or as an increasingly secondary element. It no longer defines, to the extent it once did, the 'lack' which instates certain desires as unnatural. Nor does reproductive access or parental status function, to the extent it once did, as a gift or entitlement meted out or withdrawn by the state from heterosexual or homosexual-identified adults, respectively.

The displacement of reproduction as a central element within a dynamics of sexuality, articulated to orientational inequalities, is even more apparent in the micro-site of Toronto Women's Bathhouse. There, dynamics of sexuality, and the relations to which they are sutured, have even less to do with parenthood or pregnancy (at least at the micro-institutionalised level). I discuss these dynamics below. However, before turning to my case studies, I want to consider how thinking about intersectionality complicates the conceptual framework offered.

Intersectional complications

Intersectionality has played an important role within legal scholarship over the past fifteen years (see especially Crenshaw 1989, 1991; Ehrenreich 2002), and as chapters in this book extensively attest, the term is used in many different ways. As a standpoint from which to do political critique, intersectionality signals multidimensional identities, the place where axes of power or systems of subordination or discrimination meet, the institutional choices of activists traversing identity boundary lines, and the discourses or regimes of institutional authority which produce, recognise (but also ignore) complex social locations. In this chapter, I complement these approaches to intersectionality by adopting a polycentric, but also *inter*-centric, account of social structure. In doing so, I bracket the terminological question of whether we should keep intersectionality – or move to alternative terms such as post-intersectionality or multidimensionality – in talking about complex inequality within social life. While the debates generating these different terms are important, in my view we need to ensure terminological differences do not override political-theoretical concerns. Here, I use intersectionality as a broad methodological orientation towards centring complex inequality. I also use it, analytically, to describe the work performed when conceptual distinctions are forded or crossed – whether this involves the identity transitions that occur when people move between (and in the process help to establish) distinct spaces, the interconnections or interface linking, for instance, mainstream capitalist dynamics to those accomplished by networks, such as LETS (see also North 2002), or the mutual constitution of sexual dynamics and a spectrum of orientations.

Yet, the intersection of *different* economic dynamics, the suturing of sexual dynamics to hierarchies of sexual orientation takes us away from the debates at the heart of this book. I therefore want to turn to intersectionality's more familiar terrain – the multiple and complex ways 'different' inequalities interrelate. I have said such a discussion needs to incorporate analysis of social dynamics as well as relations of inequality. It also needs to find a way of avoiding what Siobhán Mullally (this volume) refers to as 'add and stir'. I therefore suggest we treat intersectionality as a two-sided process. On one side is a *series* of different lenses. In each case, social life does not change but the interrelationship moving into focus does. On the other, intersectionality represents a series of conceptual travels. Here, I focus on three: categorical mobility, dynamic routing, and relational saturation.

Categorical mobility describes the journey made by inequality categories – as they detach and move from one social dynamic to another. Thus, in contrast to Fraser (1995), who distinguishes between class, gender, race and sexuality according to whether they are fundamentally organised as economic relations, cultural relations or both, I want to suggest categories can appear nomadic – changing affiliations. We can see this with the category of homosexuality, to the extent it has moved from being a sex (or third sex) – sutured to an older, prevailing gender dynamics – to being categorised primarily as an orientational minority, underpinned by a contemporary dynamics of sexuality. A second, less radical form of change, one more frequently followed in intersectional narratives, traces social categories as they weave together (or drag) accumulated baggage from one social dynamic to another, so socio-economic identities get signalled and rendered meaningful through discursive surpluses and cultural performances of sex and race (e.g., Bettie 2000; Bonnett 1998; Skeggs 1997, 2001). We can understand these processes in simple intersectional terms as the evolving, mobile creation of different relational or identity contractions. However, they also point to the importance of *mobile* social dynamics.

In relation to the latter, dynamic routing can take several conceptual forms. It can be read as a switching or meeting as different social dynamics encounter each other at particular interconnections – a process Foucault (1984: 108) describes in relation to the interchange between sexuality and alliance through the family. But social dynamics do not just encounter each other at particular terminal points. Their conceptual journey can also be read through the flattened metaphor of a railroad's constantly crossing tracks or read as a rerouting caused by signal points directing one set of tracks into another – as when sexuality gets routed through the economy in the commodification of desire, or the economy is routed through sexuality as labour relations necessitate erotic intimacy. While it is important to recognise that the economic and sexual *may* diverge as Nancy Fraser (1998: 146) argues, they may also prove so enmeshed that meaningful separation is impossible, as in the case of a sexual economy.

The intersectional lenses discussed so far focus on the power of dynamics to capture new inequalities or intersect other dynamics; the third lens focuses on the power of inequality relations to saturate or otherwise shape social dynamics. This topic has been the subject of considerable research particularly by sociologists and historians working outside the intersectionality lexicon, with scholarship ranging from analyses of how racial and gender inequalities shape economic dynamics at different, interconnecting scales to the way socio-economic inequalities structure embodied desire and intimacy (e.g., Bonnett 1998; Maynard 2004; Skeggs 2001). The power of relational inequalities to structure social dynamics invokes a range of conceptual levels – a range that sometimes gets lost. Let me briefly mention three. In the first, relational inequality shapes and fills positions within the social dynamic, so productive roles within LETS are gendered, for instance. The second concerns how relational inequalities structure the way particular dynamic terms intersect, so gender inequalities intensely influence the relationship between desire and intimacy. The third and 'deepest' level concerns how relational inequalities shape not only what dynamic terms, such as intimacy, *mean* but also what the *key* terms are constituting those dynamics dominating (and those otherwise shaping) differently scaled spaces.

The intersectional journeys mapped here are far from being intersectionality's only conceptual travels. I have focused on them, however, because they are central to the discussion of LETS and TWB that follows. But what is crucial to bear in mind, particularly to avoid the critiques made of Fraser's bivalent structure, is that identifying different intersectional relationships is the effect of viewing the social through *different* intersectional lenses and following different conceptual journeys. These intersectional relationships are not spatially and temporally separated but simultaneous, mutually formative and interlocking. Or at least they are usually.

In a complex social formation, multiple relations, effects and connections exist – indeed, constant churning throws up new material for intersectional analysis, necessitating new intersectional lenses. But are these relations and connections different when it comes to the micro-social formations of this chapter; is what gets thrown up less complex and less intense? What kinds of intersectional travels remain possible? And are these travels into or away from equality? It is to these questions that I now turn.

Local exchange trading systems

Local exchange trading systems' (LETS) development, from the 1980s onwards, needs to be situated within a broader picture of historic and contemporary attempts to introduce new monetary and economic practices (see Boyle 2002; Douthwaite 1998; Gibson-Graham 2006; Williams *et al.* 2003). Initially established in British Columbia's Courtenay, in Canada, as a way of kick-starting market relations, given a serious economic down-turn and consequence shortage of national currency, LETS subsequently spread rapidly around the globe. LETS function as local networks of multilateral exchange, oriented to neighbourly, recycled or small-scale goods and services, that sit in the interstices of the commodity economy. So, people offer a wide range of provision, including computer assistance, dog walking, baked goods, child care, car lifts, massages, cleaning, and furniture removals, all facilitated by a locally created currency, which, in the UK, exists not as coins or notes, but as debits and credits on a balance sheet maintained by each local scheme's central office.

LETS have generated an extensive literature focusing, amongst other things, on their potential to bring about greater socio-economic justice, given diverse member outlook (e.g., North 2006; Pacione 1997; Williams 1996). What I want to address here are LETS economic dynamics, their relationship to class – both the internal class positions they symbolically require and the socio-economic relations they underpin – and the way this relationship is complicated by an intersectional perspective.

LETS economic dynamics have four distinctive features. First, LETS are committed to combining generation of goods and services with the generation of sociality and friendship. Social interaction or, as it is known, 'relationship trading' reflects LETS moral character, its assumption that economic and social relations are mutually imbricated, and its ambition to build community through trade. Sociality also structures exchange, trading, and production/consumption norms themselves. What this entails varies, from an expectation that clients will chat while jobs, such as domestic cleaning, are being performed, to higher levels of courtesy and consideration towards the provider, to recognising that the work is part of a more general process of building neighbourliness (if not always friendship). Interviews I conducted in 2001–2 suggested some LETS members found sociability expectations tiresome. However, in the main, participants described not wanting to trade with those who produced or consumed services without, in turn, co-generating relationship (see also North 2006).

Second, reversing the claim that consumption/use is productive, LETS schemes have centred the *consumptive* qualities of production. While LETS encourage participants to consider other members' 'wants' in determining what to offer, many organisers saw LETS as an antidote to capitalism's alienated mode of labour. So, scheme organisers encouraged members to produce goods or services they enjoyed; in other words, to *use* the production process as a means of generating pleasure and satisfaction – even as the *hobbyfying* of LETS was seen by others as limiting its economic scope and reach.

Third, LETS' complexity comes to the fore in considering how goods and services circulate. Scholarship on LETS has generated considerable debate over whether LETS constitute a gift or exchange relationship (North 2006; see also Offer 1997). On the one hand, LETS formally require goods and services to be purchased through local currency cheque. At the same time, drawing on Zelizer's (1994) work on earmarking, the specific character of LETS currency – as a means of facilitating (and tracing) the circulation of things and labour, rather than as constituting (or representing) economic value in itself – has encouraged people to see LETS as a way of organising, symbolising and facilitating the flow of *favours* within a community. Indeed, some LETS participants refuse to take LETS payment seriously, jettisoning it altogether in multi-shot exchanges with particular trading partners or basing payment on factors other than the 'market rate' – for instance, paying a standard hourly rate, only ever paying or accepting one unit of currency, or paying more or less depending on the other person's account balance (see Aldridge *et al.* 2001; North 2006). Interpreting LETS exchange as something other than a market transaction is also strengthened by the correlation between LETS 'trade' and existing social ties. LETS may *produce* sociality, but trade is also very lumpy, largely taking place between people already known to one another, and thus conditioned by pre-existing social connection (see Aldridge and Patterson 2002; North 2006).

Fourth, the ideology and practice of many UK LETS, as evidenced by research on 1990s schemes, suggests a considerable premium was placed on locality and sustainability. While participants do not share a common politics, many identified LETS as part of a wider ecological or green practical politics concerned to reorient economies towards local production processes, particularly in relation to food. Environmental sensitivity also pervades and structures an ongoing emphasis on sustainability, angled towards reducing consumption and waste. LETS place considerable emphasis on extracting *ongoing*, non-exhaustive value from things, and much of the production process is geared towards this – whether it is selling unwanted gifts at LETS fares or offering to darn or repair torn clothing. Within LETS economies, consumption does not constitute the end of the line for things but the partial release of value prior to things' informal recommodification through subsequent LETS trades (also generally Appadurai 1986; Castree 2004). The release of value through use, then, is structured by things' longer history – the recycling that not only precedes, but is narrated as superseding, a current temporary use.

Given these features, LETS economic dynamics are interesting in several ways. Particularly relevant here is their counter-public reconfiguration of economic power. On their face, LETS' minimisation of wage differentials, the systemic rule no interest is paid on debit accounts, the encouragement to spend beyond earnings, and the fact LETS money is not intended or easily utilisable as a means of 'making money' substantiate the claim that LETS generate far less unequal networks than do mainstream economies. While a small proportion of LETS participants are businesses (including cooperatives) or public sector employers (see North 2006), LETS rarely enable surplus value to be extracted from workers or support charging users (or purchasers) a profit-making price. Most LETS workers participate in a self-employed capacity. And to the extent that LETS do establish more or less favoured producers, this mainly works in favour of those offering skilled manual trades, such as in household repairs (O'Doherty *et al.* 1999: 1642; Pacione 1997: 1195), rather than new age therapies (which are over-abundant within LETS) or more academic offerings (for which demand is low).

We might therefore read LETS as indicating how economic dynamics can create, and be organised around, relations of difference which are neither asymmetrical nor relational in capitalist terms (see Wright and Perrone 1977). Economic difference within LETS simply reflects diverse practices of generation and use. Moreover, even if unequal demand and supply of various services and things, within LETS, cause people to earn different local incomes, convertibility of UK LETS income is fairly minimal. It cannot, presently, be translated with ease into national currency, and social power within LETS schemes does not largely derive from LETS earnings. Indeed, there is not even a clear connection, within LETS, between levels of earning and spending. LETS economic power is narrow, first, in the sense of signalling intra-(rather than extra) scheme capacity; and, second, in failing to sweep from generation to use, as both the structure of LETS and the range of blockages that practically get manifested impede high account-holders from mobilising increased purchasing power.

Yet, the situation is also not as straightforward as this description suggests. While LETS may produce – as an idea and formal place within their economic circuits – positions of economic equality, the patterned micro-socio-economic relations LETS encounter, and *loosely structure*, are more complex. Four intersectionality pathways, addressing gender, community formation, economic scale, and sexual non-coherence, complicate the claim that LETS constitute an egalitarian socio-economic community network.

Gender is a major influence in the way LETS are organised and experienced as economic structures. In many ways, LETS reflect mainstream economies in this regard, although research still needs to be done to consider in more depth how and whether UK LETS skews gender differently. My own research, in conjunction with limited existing scholarship on LETS, suggests we might address the intersectional relationship between gender and LETS economic dynamics in three main ways. The first brings into focus the gendered classes LETS economic dynamics produce. This is not the more extreme form of categorical mobility in which relational categories move from one dynamic to another, but addresses how dynamics produce and get joined to classes, whose basic typology and topography comes from elsewhere. But gender does not just arrive on the conceptual scene to comprise the classes of LETS economic dynamics; it plays a far more formative role in shaping and structuring the dynamics themselves. The most obvious level on which this occurs is in shaping and filling productive roles – who does what in terms of LETS trades and how (Lee 1996: 1383). Gender inequalities also shape the relationship between generating goods and services, and access – from affecting payment rates (Aldridge *et al.* 2001) to structuring, in more complex ways, what trading and gift-giving mean, as Raddon (2003) discusses in relation to Canadian LETS.

The third dimension, the interrelationship between intimate/impersonal (or public/private) dynamics and the economic, tells us a great deal about how LETS negotiate and mediate gender inequalities. However, despite extensive LETS scholarship, there is little ethnographic research on this point. A dynamic interplay that has received more attention, also with significant implications for relations of inequality, is that between LETS economic dynamics and those of community formation. LETS emphasis on time, trust and social bonds has hindered trade between those at a physical distance (where travelling time increases), who live in neighbourhoods perceived as unsafe (or unwelcoming), or where cultural, linguistic or ethno-religious differences structure social interaction (also Aldridge and Patterson 2002: 378; Seyfang 2001). Consequently, LETS have proven far less socially diverse than the complementary logic of trading might suggest. While some LETS have been built, usually with public funds and development workers, within and for poor communities (Pacione 1997), many are organised by the well-educated (if not financially affluent). In these latter LETS, exclusions are not necessarily explicit or deliberate; however, the dynamics of community formation seem to orient members towards others like themselves (O'Doherty *et al.* 1999; Peacock 2006).

This raises a further intersectional pathway, the way economic dynamics at different scales intersect. In 1990s Britain, government policy and officials acted as intermediaries, managing LETS' place within, and signalling its relationship to, wider economic dynamics. In playing this role, government's stance towards LETS proved an uneven and contradictory one, arguably reflecting LETS ambivalent value for mainstream economies – 'retooling' the underemployed (Seyfang 2001), while simultaneously threatening, should LETS really take off, to withdraw poor prospective workers from mainstream labour (and consumption) markets.[14] Addressing government's role in this domain, I am mindful of Gibson-Graham's (1996) argument that capitalist and non-capitalist processes need to be seen as functionally separate – the welfare state, for instance, does not simply exist to shore up commodity production and markets. At the same time, government policy embeds and locates governmental agencies, as variously supportive, facilitative, regulatory, hostile and disengaged, in relation to different economic dynamics – macro and micro, hegemonic and counter-hegemonic. Thus, in Britain, local government's orientation towards community economic empowerment, and their practical support for LETS in many districts, contrasted with the less sympathetic approach of certain central governmental agencies (also Williams *et al.* 2003).

Finally, in addressing the conceptual tracks social dynamics take as they combine or get routed through each other, I want to highlight one area of (at least *attempted*) divergence. While stating that economic and sexual dynamics are heavily interconnected within global North nations has become a well-worn point, alternative social spaces provide a vantage-point from which to consider whether this is always, or necessarily, the case. LETS is interesting, in this regard, as an instance where both organisational structure and participant actions attempted to hold economic and sexual dynamics apart – most explicitly delineated by the widespread rule that sex could not be bought or gifted with local currency. The implications of this general bounding off for hierarchies of sexual orientation was apparent in interviews carried out in late 2007 involving a small cross-section of active UK members. When asked about lesbian and gay participation, several respondents replied that they had gay members. However, most indicated it was not something discussed on the grounds that it was not relevant to LETS, and all replied that *it* 'wasn't a problem'. More generally, LETS treated households as 'black boxes'. LETS exchanges were to take place *between* households, not within them. In this way, too, the primary authorised site and nexus for sexual intimacy was constituted outside of LETS sociability-based trade.

But even within LETS, the sexual and productive could not be held at arms length entirely, and sexual dynamics certainly did penetrate LETS 'relationship trading', despite disclaimers in relation to 'gay issues'. Embodied practices of desire and intimacy were evident in the way LETS economies – specifically their infrastructure of events, and practices of exchange – enabled heterosexual desires to be manifested. In the course of my research, several interviewees referred to romantic relationships or marriages arising from LETS participation.[15] More systemically, the economic and sexual meet in the very tension of their feared and risked conjoining. Thus, the prohibition on trading sex, anxieties regarding risky LETS trades, such as parents purchasing childcare,[16] reveal how sexuality's dynamics become deployed as the limit point in structuring the scope of exchange or stranger-gift relations.

Toronto Women's Bathhouse

My second site, the Toronto Women's Bathhouse (TWB), in Canada, opened in 1998 as an occasional, irregular 'counter-intimate' space within more regular male bathhouse venues (see also Belant and Warner 2002: 203).[17] Linked to other lesbian and queer community spaces, TWB also attracted bisexual, heterosexual women and trans participants attracted by the idea of a venue oriented to an adventurous, polymorphous female sexuality (Gallant and Gillis 2001; Hammers forthcoming; Nash and Bain 2007).

TWB is interesting on several counts. First, from the outset, it prioritised having volunteers who would help women learn new skills (in flirting, sexual massage, lap-dancing, g-spot discoveries and anal sex) to enhance their confidence and sexual repertoire.[18] Second, organisers worked to establish a pastoral space oriented to women's comfort and care (see Cooper 2007b; Hammers forthcoming); third, the bathhouse affirmed gender and sexual diversity, including a commitment to non-discrimination, especially (although this also proved a struggle) on grounds of trans-status and race.

As I suggested earlier, in reconfiguring the dynamics of desire–intimacy–embodiment, TWB explicitly sought to rupture more mainstream articulations, particularly the normative expectation that desire should (and was, indeed, *desired* to) produce emotional intimacy – the ostensibly special connections that lay beneath public, visible social contact – and which would produce, in return, more satisfyingly embodied materialisations of desire. While bathhouse participants did sometimes seek subsequent contact after the event, emphasis lay with the physical enactment of an autotelic desire neither authorised nor legitimated by anything beyond itself. TWB also sought to unsettle the relationship between desire and intimate, in the sense of *deeply familiar*, bodies. Emphasising exploration and adventure, as well as strongly affirming diverse, non-normative bodies and unconventional performances (Hammers forthcoming), TWB encouraged women to try something new – whether it was adopting or interacting with unfamiliar gendered/sexual forms of embodiment, such as a 'chick with a dick', or a previously untried act. Through participating, over time, women remade their own bodies as desirable (to themselves and others), drawing on unfamiliar displays (lap-dancing, stripping, intercourse), and letting unfamiliar, sometimes illegible, others access intimate body spaces in new ways in order to do so (also Nash and Bain 2007).

Yet, while conventionally normative associations between desire, emotional intimacy and embodied familiarity were unsettled through scoring new, visible, stranger-oriented pathways, sexual intimacy's *fact* was also underscored in ways that distinguished TWB from a men's bathhouse.

For many interviewees, the gendered physical intimacy and vulnerability women and trans people experienced in making their bodies sexually available represented a deeply etched aspect of being a female sexual agent, especially in a context of casual, non-committed desire. As a consequence, organisers, volunteers and even many participants put considerable energy into creating a caring, non-intimidating, educative environment. But what impact did this have on sexual hierarchies and relations of inequality? Did TWB's counter-normative sexual dynamics suture it to a sexual orientational spectrum constituted by difference rather than inequality, and how is this claim complicated by an intersectional analysis?

Just as LETS sought to realise economic differences not grounded in inequality, so TWB clearly opposed hierarchies of sexual orientation. This of course does not mean that all participants lacked conventional orientations or that they left them at the door. TWB did not have the power to establish new sexual identities from scratch any more than LETS could erase participants' wider socio-economic location. However, what I am interested in exploring here are the institutional norms and dynamics locally established.

While some heterosexual women indicated, during interviews, that the bathhouse left them feeling socially illiterate, the bathhouse did not *institutionalise* hetero/homo cleavages, except as a practical effect of excluding non-trans men from attending. What TWB did institutionalise, and participants, if unevenly, reinforced, was a different hierarchy, based on a willingness or capacity to be 'bravely', knowingly and publicly sexual. Several interviewees referred to high status participants, and the high status accorded to participants, who either engaged in theatrical sexual encounters within the bathhouse's public spaces, or through their sounds, overtures, entrances and exits made their prolific, adventurous sexual activity noticeable.

Yet, even if the bathhouse did demonstrate a hierarchy of sexual performance, does this constitute orientation? Organisers, in particular, were keen to treat sexual adventurousness as an aptitude available for all women to acquire – and indeed acquiring this aptitude was part of the bathhouse's mission. At the same time, certain sexual 'orientations' in the sense of *preferences* were recognised at TWB – particularly, fetishism, SM, exhibitionism, voyeurism, and vanilla. These, however, were not institutionally differentiated in asymmetrical ways (with perhaps the exception of vanilla which was seen by some as a lack or repressed orientation).

This illustrates, then, a point made earlier – that at particular time/spaces, social dynamics may separate from, or become far more loosely tied to, relations of inequality that they once forged or were closely coupled with, a process often accelerated by counter-hegemonic or anti-normalising projects. Alternatively, we may read relations of inequality as not separating off from particular dynamics but as becoming redefined, including in non-hierarchical ways. Indeed, in the bathhouse context, the production of orientational *difference* was, arguably, *enabled* through being played symmetrically rather than asymmetrically. In other words, the displacement of orientational inequalities by those coded in terms of sexual performance/inhibition enabled TWB to affirm, display and recognise a wider spectrum of orientations, well beyond the conventional sexualised distinctions of gender (hetero, homo, bi), age (inter-generational) and multiplicity (non-monogamous, polyamorous).

At the same time, as with LETS, this liberatory picture gets complicated once we adopt an intersectional analysis. I want to briefly consider three different intersectional lenses: cultural saturation by socio-economic class; the interplay between dynamic rerouting and particular points of interchange; and mainstream penetration of the social. My first point takes up a claim by Nash and Bain (2007) who argue, based on their research, that TWB's sexual dynamics were shaped and seasoned by an aesthetic that reflected, or more precisely was *intended* to capture (and appropriate) a particular socio-economic ethos and culture – namely of queer working-class sexuality (as against the privatised, moralistic and constrained sexuality associated with middle-class women). 'Staging the bathhouse events at what was described as a "grungier" club, used by older "street boys" and a more working-class clientele, was deliberate in terms of celebrating working-class sexuality' (Nash and Bain 2007: 55; see also Gallant and Gillis 2001: 156). This claim of a collective class performance has been contested by others (e.g., Hammers forthcoming). However, as a claim, it usefully illustrates how social forces deliberately or otherwise can seek to deploy class *culture*[19] (rather than class *relations*) to give shape to sexual dynamics: in this case to convey and accomplish a bawdy, upfront, more expressive sexuality. Less positively, cultures of whiteness were also described as pervading the bathhouse space, 'an orientation that puts certain things within reach [including]... styles, capacities, aspirations, techniques, habits' (Ahmed 2007: 154), thereby rendering TWB less conducive to women and trans people of colour despite organisers' ongoing attempts to tackle this.

The relationship between dynamics and particular group associations (if we can momentarily call culture that) coexists alongside (and of course helps to shape) a second intersectional juncture of dynamics meeting. TWB here provides an interesting contrast to LETS. I described above how LETS strove to ensure, if ultimately unsuccessfully, that sexual desire was *not* routed through local currency relations. At TWB, by contrast, we can read sexuality and economy as combining and (t)ravelling through each other. Not only did TWB's mode of embodied access through sexual exchange provide a counterpoint to the firm prohibition within LETS on transactional sex, but TWB in fact *de-authorised*, or at least temporally bracketed, conventional normative bases for sexual access, such as relationship commitment. Instead, with a far more open and partial approach to the 'property' rights sexual access makes over, the bathhouse interestingly mandated a *variety* of access routes, including request, gift and chance.

The difficulty of separating economic dynamics from sexual ones, in a context where what is primarily being generated, accessed and used are embodied desires and new forms of intimacy, does not mean a smooth monotone blending. While one intersectional lens identifies the sexual economy as a coherent entity, another identifies particular interchanges or more lumpy connections. In this respect, the comments of TWB participants regarding the erotic aura surrounding key sex producers resonates with my research findings from other sites, such as Speakers Corner and Summerhill School (Cooper 2006, 2007a). There, desire and production contracted into, and merged with, each other, as an ambivalently libidinalised desire to have and to be centred on the figure of the active, masterful creator – the brilliant, witty orator; the confident, long-standing school member – a form of inverse fetishism in which the supremely assured producer or community member stands in erotically for the *real* desired thing, namely, a more intimate relationship to the community site or its central social activity.

In addressing intersectionality through different lenses, particularly in exploring the interwoven character of TWB's sexual and economic dynamics, it is important not to forget that these dynamic connections are also shaped by the intersectionality of different scales, and of inside and out. Some of the effects of these boundary-crossing processes simply replicate more general forms of intersectional inequality – the racism, economic conditions, and gendered norms of comportment and physical capacity which structure queer women's everyday experiences. And, to the extent these operated at the bathhouse, they question the normative/cultural capacity of the bathhouse boundary to exclude wider practices of inequality (see also Nash and Bain 2007: 56; Hammers forthcoming). But the limited autonomy of the bathhouse, its capacity to exclude, also raise other, less intellectually furrowed, effects generated by intersecting scales. One relevant here concerns the power of mainstream sexual orientation categories to intrude. My research suggests that the capacity of dominant categories to structure TWB (beyond working through the identity, experience and emotional 'baggage' of participants) was limited by the fact that the bathhouse did not ally itself with mainstream policy agendas, for instance healthcare initiatives targeting 'vulnerable' sexual populations. This contrasts with the policy articulations UK LETS engaged in, as mentioned above, which brought schemes within governmental local economic strategies, involving workers, public funding, and target constituencies. At the same time, despite avoiding institutionalised connections, TWB was subject to external forces. Its sexual dynamics were also subject, if far more contingently than in the case of LETS, to the asymmetries of wider economic relations channelled through state forces' mediating role. That this had a temporal dimension was particularly evident in the shape and ethos of TWB events following the police raid for suspected liquor licence infractions on 15 September 2000 (Bain and Nash 2007; Lamble 2006). According to several interviewees, after the raid attendance shrank, particularly among participants such as sex workers, whose 'outside' occupation and precarious legal status rendered them especially vulnerable to arrest; in addition, some interviewees claimed, those attending substantially pulled back from publicly performing transgressive or legally precarious sex acts.

Conclusion

This chapter has explored social dynamics' contribution to thinking about inequality and intersectionality. In particular, it has sought to reveal something of the complicated character intersectional relations acquire once different dimensions of inequality are taken into account. With some exceptions (e.g., Anthias 2001; Yuval-Davis 2006), intersectionality scholarship has tended to focus on the interface of homologous differences within a given social space – whether of axes, groups, systems, or something else. In this chapter, rereading intersectionality as a series of lenses (rather than a single one) trained on a series of different conceptual journeys, I have bracketed the most studied homologous combination: the multidimensional subject (class) to explore other combinations and interconnections – particularly those involving different social dynamics, or involving social dynamics linked to different relations of inequality – within and across social borders and scales. My aim in doing so has been to embed intersectional concerns within a more structural, while simultaneously open and polycentric, understanding of inequality.

The benefits of a social dynamics approach to intersectionality are multiple. Amongst other things, it allows us to consider the *inter*relationship between placements within a dynamic (such as a LETS economy) *and* the hierarchical relations produced (which may involve other organising principles of inequality, including gender or sexuality). It allows us to explore how older forms of inequality may get recast as difference, while new forms of inequality arise. It allows us to see the exclusions constituted through the interweaving of different dynamic logics, such as the economic and community formation (which may be invisible if one just looks for the *presence* of multi-faceted groupings). And it allows us to follow political attempts to keep social dynamics apart.

In exploring these benefits, the chapter took alternative utopic sites as its orientation to bracket some of the well-entrenched assumptions about how intersectionality operates. My interest in focusing on utopic sites, however, was not solely for its capacity to provide a fresh empirical lens. Everyday utopias also open up the important possibility, from a social justice perspective, of social dynamics generating *non*-asymmetrical forms of difference, as I considered in relation to the class diversity produced *within* LETS circuits, and the spectrum of sexual orientations supported at TWB. However, while sites such as these two *may* be able to craft social dynamics invoking more egalitarian forms of difference, their success in *producing* (and, of course, *re*producing) relations of equality seems far less assured once an intersectional analysis is adopted.

Mainstream intersectionality approaches productively illuminate difficulties beyond the immediate reach of everyday utopia organisers – whether it is the design-based problems facing disabled queer women wishing to participate at TWB or the welfare benefits disincentives for poor women wishing to participate in LETS. Mainstream intersectionality analysis also illuminates the 'internal' challenges everyday utopias confront when women of colour identify TWB as unfriendly or non-English speaking immigrants find LETS trading off-putting. But this tends to be where much intersectionality analysis focused on groups and axes stops.

What discussion of social dynamics makes painfully evident is that the power and configurations, which prevailing dynamics take, need confronting if the inequalities these dynamics underpin or support are to be effectively tackled. TWB arguably went some way in doing this, re-imagining production–access–use in the course of establishing and maintaining a counter-normative sexual economy. Where TWB was less successful, however, was in changing the social dynamics of race that circulated despite initiatives targeted at particular, under-involved, racialised constituencies. UK LETS, by contrast, as a progressive economic initiative, showed little interest in addressing inequalities of sexual orientation – failing, for the most part, to even register that this was an issue. Yet, tackling such inequalities also requires more than strategies of recognition – to involve lesbians and gay men, for instance, as group-based categories more proactively within LETS. What also needs opening up is the interrelationship between sexual and economic dynamics to ask: what other configurations of intimacy-desire-embodiment might structure LETS dynamics of making, making available and using goods and services, other than those currently in force? How might alternative dynamic interrelationships challenge UK LETS emphasis on naturalised households, privatised intimacies, and the normative compartmentalisation of sex and economics?

Acknowledgements

I am very grateful to Kate Bedford, Brenna Bhandar, Emily Grabham, Didi Herman, Harriet Samuels and Sally Sheldon for their thought-provoking questions and comments on earlier drafts, and to Ryoko Matsuno and Achala Chandani Abeysekara for their excellent research assistance. My thanks also go to the Leverhulme Trust, Kent Law School and the AHRC Centre for Law, Gender and Sexuality for funding the research and writing of this chapter.

Bibliography

Ahmed, S. (2007) A phenomenology of whiteness. *Feminist Theory*, 8, 149–68.

Aldridge, T. and Patterson, A. (2002) LETS get real: Constraints on the development of Local Exchange Trading Schemes. *Area*, 34: 370–81.

Aldridge, T., Tooke, J., Lee, R., Leyshon, A., Thrift, N. and Williams, C. (2001) Recasting work: The example of local exchange trading systems. *Work, Employment & Society*, 15: 565–79.

Anthias, F. (2001) The material and the symbolic in theorizing social stratification: Issues of gender, ethnicity and class. *British Journal of Sociology*, 52: 367–90.

Appadurai, A. (1986) *The Social Life of Things: Commodities in Cultural Perspective*, Cambridge: Cambridge University Press.

Appleton, M. (2000) *A Freerange Childhood: Self Regulation at Summerhill*, Brandon, VT: Foundation for Educational Renewal.

Bain, A. and Nash, C. (2006) Undressing the researcher: Feminism, embodiment and sexuality at a queer bathhouse event. *Area*, 38: 99–106.

Bedford, K. (2007) *Developing Partnerships: Gender, Sexuality and the Post-Washington Consensus World Bank*, University of Minnesota Press, Minneapolis, fourthcoming (2009).

Berlant, L. and Warner, M. (2002) Sex in public, in Warner, M. (ed.) *Publics and Counterpublics*, New York: Zone Books.

Bérubé, A. (1996) The history of gay bathhouses, in Bedfellows, D. (ed.) *Policing Public Sex: Queer Politics and the Future of AIDS Activism*, Boston, MA: South End Press.

Bettie, J. (2000) Women without class: Chicas, cholas, trash and the presence/absence of class identity. *Signs*, 26: 1–35.

Binnie, J. (2004) *The Globalization of Sexuality*, London: Sage.

Bonnett, A. (1998) How the British working class became white: The symbolic (re)formation of racialised capitalism. *Journal of Historical Sociology*, 11: 316–40.

Boyle, D. (ed.) (2002) *The Money Changers: Currency Reform from Aristotle to E-Cash*, London: Earthscan Publications.

Butler, J. (1998) Merely Cultural. *New Left Review*, 227: 33–44.

Cantu, L. (2001) A place called home: A queer political economy of Mexican immigrant men's family experiences, in Bernstein, M. and Reiman, R. (eds) *Queer Families, Queer Politics: Challenging Culture and the State*, New York: Columbia University Press.

Castree, N. (2004) The geographical lives of commodities: Problems of analysis and critique. *Social and Cultural Geography*, 5: 21–35.

Coleman, S. (1997) *Stilled Tongues: From Soapbox to Soundbite*, London: Porcupine Press.

Cooper, D. (2004) *Challenging Diversity: Rethinking Equality and the Value of Difference*, Cambridge: Cambridge University Press.

Cooper, D. (2006) 'Sometimes a community and sometimes a battlefield': From the comedic public sphere to the commons of Speakers' Corner. *Environment and Planning D: Society and Space*, 24: 753–75.

Cooper, D. (2007a) Opening up ownership: Community belonging, belongings, and the productive life of property. *Law and Social Inquiry*, 32: 625–64.

Cooper, D. (2007b) 'Well, you go there to get off': Visiting feminist care ethics through a women's bathhouse. *Feminist Theory*, 8: 243–62.

Crang, P. (1996) Displacement, consumption, and identity. *Environment and Planning A*, 28: 47–67.

Crenshaw, K. (1989) Demarginalizing the intersection of race and sex: A black feminist critique of antidiscrimination doctrine, feminist theory, and antiracist politics. *University of Chicago Legal Forum*, 139–67.

Crenshaw, K. (1991) Mapping the margins: Intersectionality, identity politics, and violence against women of color. *Stanford Law Review*, 43: 1241–99.

Douthwaite, R. (1998) *Short Circuit: Strengthening Local Economics for Security in an Unstable World*, Totnes: Green Books.

Ehrenreich, N. (2002) Subordination and symbiosis: Mechanisms of mutual support between subordinating systems. *University of Missouri-Kansas City Law Review*, 71: 251–324.

Foucault, M. (1984) *The History of Sexuality, Vol. 1*, New York: Pantheon Books.

Fraser, N. (1995) From redistribution to recognition? Dilemmas of justice in a 'post-socialist' age. *New Left Review*, 212: 68–93.

Fraser, N. (1998) Heterosexism, misrecognition and capitalism: A response to Judith Butler. *New Left Review*, 228: 140–9.

Gallant, C. and Gillis, L. (2001) Pussies bite back: The story of the women's bathhouse raid. *Torquere: Journal of the Canadian Lesbian and Gay Studies Association*, 3: 152–67.

Gibson-Graham, G.K. (1996) *The End of Capitalism (As We Knew It)*, Oxford: Blackwell.

Gibson-Graham, G.K. (2006) *A Postcapitalist Politics*, Minneapolis, MN: University of Minnesota Press.

Godelier, M. (1999) *The Enigma of the Gift*, Cambridge: Polity Press.

Hammers, C. (forthcoming) Making space for an agentic sexuality?: The examination of a lesbian/queer bathhouse. *Sexualities*.

Jackson, P. (2004) Local consumption cultures in a globalizing world. *Transactions of the Institute of British Geographers*, 29: 165–78.

Joseph, M. (2002) *Against the Romance of Community*, Minnesota, MN: University of Minnesota Press.

Kwan, P. (2002) The metaphysics of metaphors: Symbiosis and the quest for meaning. *University of Missouri-Kansas City Law Review*, 71: 325–30.

Lamble, S. (2006) The politics of policing the lesbian body: Contesting moral and corporeal order in the 'Pussy Palace' bathhouse raid. *Centre of Criminology*. Toronto, University of Toronto.

Lee, R. (1996) Moral money? LETS and the social construction of local economic geographies in southeast England. *Environment and Planning A*, 28: 1377–94.

Lee, R., Leyshon, A., Aldridge, T., Tooke, J., Williams, C. and Thrift, N. (2004) Making geographies and histories? Constructing local circuits of value. *Environment and Planning D: Society and Space*, 22: 595–617.

Maynard, S. (2004) 'Without working'? Capitalism, urban culture, and gay history. *Journal of Urban History*, 30: 378–98.

Nash, C.J. and Bain, A. (2007) 'Reclaiming raunch': Spatializing queer identities at Toronto Women's Bathhouse events. *Journal of Social and Cultural Geography*, 8: 47–62.

Neill, A.S. (1937) *That Dreadful School*, London: Herbert Jenkins.

Neill, A.S. (1968) *Summerhill*, Harmondsworth: Pelican.

North, P. (2002) LETS in a cold climate: Green dollars, self-help and neoliberal welfare in New Zealand. *Policy and Politics*, 30: 483–500.

North, P. (2006) *Alternative Currency Movements as a Challenge to Globalization? A Case-Study of Manchester's Local Currency Networks*, Aldershot: Ashgate.

O'Doherty, R., Durrschmidt, J., Jowers, P. and Purdue, D.A. (1999) Local exchange and trading schemes: A useful strand of community economic development policy? *Environment and Planning A*, 31: 1639–53.

Offer, A. (1997) Between the gift and the market: The economy of regard. *Economic History Review*, 50: 450–76.

Pacione, M. (1997) Local exchange trading systems as a response to the globalisation of capitalism. *Urban Studies*, 34: 1179–97.

Peacock, M. (2006) The moral economy of parallel currencies: An analysis of local exchange trading systems. *American Journal of Economics and Sociology*, 65: 1059–83.

Raddon, M.-B. (2003) *Community and Money: Men and Women Making Change*, Montreal: Black Rose Books.

Roberts, J. (2000) The enigma of free speech: Speakers' Corner, the geography of governance and a crisis of 'rationality'. *Social and Legal Studies*, 9: 271–92.

Seyfang, G. (2001) Community currencies: Small change for a green economy. *Environment and Planning A*, 33: 975–96.

Skeggs, B. (1997) *Formations of Class and Gender: Becoming Respectable*, London: Sage.

Skeggs, B. (2001) The toilet paper: Femininity, class and mis-recognition. *Women's Studies International Forum*, 24: 295–307.

Tattelman, I. (2000) Presenting a queer (bath)house, in Boone, J., Dupis, M., Meeker, M., Quimby, K., Sarver, C., Silverman, D and Weatherson, R. (eds) *Queer Frontiers: Millennial Geographies, Genders, and Generations*, Madison, WI: University of Wisconsin Press.

Valentine, G. (2007) Theorizing and researching intersectionality: A challenge for feminist geography. *The Professional Geographer*, 59: 10–21.

Williams, C. (1995) Trading favours in Calderdale. *Town and Country Planning*, 64: 214–15.

Williams, C. (1996) The new barter economy: An appraisal of local exchange and trading systems (LETS). *Journal of Public Policy*, 16: 85–102.

Williams, C., Aldridge, T. and Tooke, J. (2003) Alternative exchange spaces, in Leyshon, A., Lee, R. and Williams, C. (eds) *Alternative Economic Spaces*, London: Sage.

Wright, E.O. and Perrone, L. (1977) Marxist class categories and income inequality. *American Sociological Review*, 42: 32–55.

Yuval-Davis, N. (2006) Intersectionality and feminist politics. *European Journal of Women's Studies*, 13: 193–209.

Zelizer, V.A. (1994) *The Social Meaning of Money: Pin Money, Paychecks, Poor Relief, and Other Currencies*, Princeton, NJ: Princeton University Press.

Notes

1   Relations of inequality refers to the complex of practices, orientations, discourses and other doings that organise, constitute and reflect systemic inequalities of power, and which structure subjectivity, agency and social location in core ways. Relations of inequality can take directly relational forms such as violence, oppression, exploitation, marginalisation, domination or operate in less directly relational ways, as where relations such as race, gender, and class structure access to resources, recognition or the terms of valuation.

2   I also draw more peripherally from field research involving two other sites: London's Speakers Corner – a counter-public space committed to a particular version of free, democratic, 'bottom-up' speech (Coleman 1997; Cooper 2006; Roberts 2000), and A.S. Neill's Summerhill School – a co-educational school, established in the 1920s in England's rural Suffolk, committed to children's rights and freedoms, and to trans-generational community governance (Appleton 2000; Cooper 2007a; Neill 1968).

3   Because writers have moved between these different accounts, and because they circulate in ways that have a power beyond the individual authors who have deployed them, I describe them here without attribution; see similarly Butler (1998: 33).

4   Scholars vary on which groups they are prepared to read in this way – the use of quotation marks signalling a discomfort about giving certain registers of inequality this a-social status.

5   Scholarship also varies in terms of whether it identifies *all* individuals as intersectionally placed or just those located at the cross-roads of vectors of disadvantage.

6   The intimate/ impersonal is a deliberate revision of the more common phrase, the public/private. It identifies a similar dynamics, but is preferable in my view as a way of characterising a key social dynamics shaping gender, within the contemporary global North.

7   The productive value that comes from *how* a site is used is particularly evident at Summerhill School. There, children's 'free' activities, including rule-breaching, were central to establishing the school's meaning and value. However, while generally interpreted positively, Neill (the then owner) did comment more ambivalently about the children's habit of swearing in front of potential parents which he remarked might jeopardise future income (see Neill 1937: 51).

8   In the case of A.S. Neill's Summerhill School, such 'consumption' included being brought before the school meeting, and fined, for breach of its rules.

9   I refer to desire rather than erotic desire because sexual orientation, in practice, is often materially sutured to a broader conception of desire (including, for instance, the desire to be looked after, to be materially secure, to have children) despite rationalisations of sexual orientation which tend to be in erotic terms.

10   And of course bodies within sex can also be virtual.

11   For instance different sexual orientations – hetero, homo, bi, SM or 'vanilla' (a term given to sexual desires and practices that do not eroticise domination, violence or things).

12   Also important to bear in mind, though not the focus of this chapter, is the extent to which identities or subjectivities vary as people move between differently configured social spaces (see also Cantu 2001; Valentine 2007).

13   My thanks to Sally Sheldon for reminding me of this point.

14   For a discussion of similar processes in the New Zealand context, see Peter North (2002).

15 I also heard occasional stories from LETS participants of receiving unwanted sexual interest.

16 In considering the intersection of economic dynamics with the sexual, we need to ask how the sexual configured within LETS – did reproduction and parenthood, for instance, remain secondary or come to constitute a more tightly and prominently coupled element?

17 Although uncommon, other sexual bathhouses for women exist, including in Halifax, Canada and Brighton, England. This relative paucity contrasts with the proliferation of men's bathhouses about which an extensive academic literature also exists, e.g., Bérubé 1996; Tattelman 2000.

18 TWB volunteers also organised workshops outside the bathhouse space to prepare women to more effectively use the bathhouse evening (Hammers forthcoming).

19 It should be noted, however, that this way of conceptualising working-class culture is not unmarked but is already saturated by other social relations, including of ethnicity.

Chapter 13

Imagining alternative universalisms

Intersectionality and the limits of liberal discourse

Lakshmi Arya

Introduction

Intersectionality as an analytical device has been used to deconstruct universal liberal discourses, of feminism and of citizenship, and their subjects. Can a narrative of intersections be used to *construct* an alternative, i.e. non-liberal, discourse of the universal, from a post-colonial perspective? This chapter attempts to do so.

Universal liberal discourses, of feminism and of citizenship, have been critiqued for presuming their subject as a site that exists prior to relations of power. Analyses of intersectionality have deconstructed, for instance, the universal feminist subject – the subject as Woman, unmarked by identifications other than gender – as the dominant subject who is enabled or *empowered* to speak due to her location in other, intersecting identifications of power, such as race, class, caste or religion. Similar critiques are also made of the site of the universal citizen-subject in Western liberal democracy. Post-structuralists have critiqued the site of the universal citizen-subject as a liberal ruse of power, which instates a dominant subject who can speak to the exclusion of others who cannot. Such critiques are transposed to the post-colonial context in contemporary India, for the Indian state is understood to be historically originally constructed on liberal discourses, derived from the colonial encounter with Britain. In this chapter, I question whether these post-structuralist critiques of liberal universalism can, in fact, be applied in the post-colonial Indian context. I argue that geo-political contexts are different and historically specific. Eurocentric models of the Western liberal state and the postmodern critiques of universalisms thereof cannot be extended to other contexts. The aim of the chapter is to posit an experience of the state and the site of the universal feminist/citizen-subject within it, which is alternative to the Western liberal model. I derive this alternative, non-liberal discourse of the universal from the history of the formation of the Indian state itself, and trace it through a narrative of intersections.

The arguments of this chapter move through three sections. Contemporary post-structuralist scholarship in India makes certain critiques of universalist discourses and their subjects. In the first section, I discuss these critiques so as to be able to draw out my points of departure from them and posit an alternative imagination of the universal in the succeeding sections. I ground my examination of these critiques in a study of the Uniform Civil Code (henceforth, UCC) debate. The controversy surrounding the UCC is about whether there should be a civil code that applies uniformly to all communities and religions in the state. This issue is of concern to feminists because civil matters such as marriage, divorce and inheritance rights that significantly affect women's lives are, at present, covered under the religious laws of various communities. The UCC debate raises questions about: (a) the subject of Indian feminism and (b) statist discourses of universal citizenship. It leads to an inquiry into the archaeology of universal, statist discourses in post-colonial India. Critics make historiographical assertions regarding both of these points, i.e. about the genesis of modern meta-narratives of the state and the consolidation of a dominant feminist subject, in the period of anti-colonial nationalism.

To review these historiographical assertions, I re-visit the historical period of anti-colonial nationalism in the second section, and draw from the archives an instance where a uniform civil legislation was enacted in colonial India. This was when the Child Marriage Restraint Act was passed in 1929 by Indian legislators, to apply equally to all communities, religions and castes in the colonial state. I look into the enactment of this legislation to examine whether there were, during this time, dominant subjects who spoke to the exclusion of others who did not. The child marriage legislation of 1929 was passed because various speaking subjects, both elite and subaltern, exceeded their supposedly primordial identifications, either of caste, class, community, or religion, to ally with other identificatory positions. Or, because identifications were multiple and intersecting.

To prove that the Child Marriage Restraint Act was not an isolated example of the excess and intersection of positions, I locate its enactment in a wider social context: in a historical time of anti-colonial nationalism, a time when other alliances were being forged between disparate elements, in a mutual agenda of anti-colonial nationalism. Through these alliances, discourses, including those of gender, transcended their erstwhile local and specific boundaries to map the contours of the nation. I argue that the site of the universal in the post-colonial nation-state derives from this history of its formation. This history challenges the notion of a dominant feminist subject or dominant citizen-subject in the creation of the post-colonial state as it witnessed the participation of both subaltern and elite elements in its constitution. Since the subaltern elements lent their agency to the post 1920s national movement under Gandhi, often redirecting and contesting it, their imaginations were included in the newly formed independent state in 1947.

This history makes the site of the universal citizen-subject in the post-colonial state different from the analogous site in the Western liberal state. In the final section, I elaborate on how this difference may be articulated by a theorization of intersectionality.

Universal discourses in post-colonial India: a liberal-colonial legacy? Historiographical reflections in the contemporary uniform civil code debate

Post-colonial feminists have employed intersectional analyses to question the universal foundations of Western feminism: to indicate that Western feminism sets up its own authorial subject, i.e. the white, upper class woman, as a universal referent who represents cultural Others by erasing the intersections of race and class in gender.[1] The post-colonial feminist intellectual, however, finds herself similarly embattled in her local contexts for the universal feminist foundations she herself has posited. I will examine this embattlement in the context of a controversy in contemporary India. This is the controversy surrounding the proposed enactment of a Uniform Civil Code (UCC) in India. The subject of Indian feminism has been critiqued in this controversy as the dominant Hindu, upper-caste, upper-class, urban woman, who speaks for and represents marginalized Others, and thereby silences them. This dominant subject, critics argue, became the norm during the period of anti-colonial nationalism itself.[2]

This critique of feminism's subject dovetails into a larger re-thinking of grand, statist discourses in post-colonial India. Post-structuralist critics see such discourses as being exclusionary, not merely of marginalized subjects, but of other epistemologies as well. Meta-narratives of the state in post-colonial India are seen as being inherently violent against non-modern, non-rational epistemologies that imagine non-universal fragments. These large narratives are viewed as a legacy of the colonial encounter with Britain and its investment in the rationalism of the European Enlightenment.[3] Thus, post-colonial–post-structuralist critics in India today emphasize the exclusionary aspects of universal meta-narratives, in terms of both subjectivity and epistemic violence, and trace their liberal genealogies to the period of anti-colonial nationalism (see Nandy 1983, Chatterjee 1986, Spivak 1985, Chakrabarty 2002).

This section will elaborate on these post-structuralist critiques and locate them in the specific example of the UCC debate. To begin with, a few words of introduction to the issue of the UCC are required. India does not have a common civil code. Civil matters such as marriage, divorce and inheritance rights are covered under the 'personal laws' of the different religious denominations, so that we have the Hindu law, the Muslim law, the Christian law, etc. These religious laws were codified during British colonial rule in

India. The colonial state codified the laws on the basis of the interpretations given by religious authorities.

The debate surrounding the Uniform Civil Code is about whether there should be a civil code that applies equally to all communities in India. I will briefly go over certain arguments on both sides of the debate. Some feminist groups have, in the past, called for replacing the religious laws with laws that are just to women. They have argued that a UCC would provide a sphere of rights to Indian women that would be alternative to the rights – or wrongs – given to them by religious laws.[4] Feminist opinion, however, has been divided.

Critics of this feminist vision of universal gender justice have pointed to the plurality of religions, castes, regions, languages and communities in India and the unequal power relations that mark these sites.[5] To elaborate, the dominant religion in India is Hinduism, and the Muslim minority is being Othered as an alien and anti-national presence by certain Hindu fundamentalist groups in contemporary India. Likewise, within Hinduism, there is a hierarchy of caste, which stratifies Hindus from the upper castes to the lowest castes (who name themselves as 'Dalit'). Given these disparities, critics see the feminist demand for a uniform civil code as an essentialism that prioritizes gender over other identifications and, in doing so, excludes other axes of power. By excluding the intersection of other axes of power in the universal foundation of gender, this feminist move allegedly hegemonizes already existing sites of dominance. Dalit feminists, for example, have made this critique of the putatively unmarked, universal claim of the subject of Indian feminist politics, a claim that renders invisible its own upper caste underpinnings in the guise of an absence of caste. As Sharmila Rege asserts:

> The upper caste status of the feminist modern is thus signified as absence of caste in claiming to represent the ideal subject of feminist politics. … The questioning and analytical gaze of the 'difference' of dalit women is therefore directed towards an interrogation of the theoretical frames of reference and the normative status of 'unmarked' feminism.
>
> (Rege 2006: 51)

The subject of Indian feminism who advocates an ideal of universal gender justice – the subject as 'Woman' unmarked by inequalities other than gender and oppressed across cultures and religions – is argued, in this critique, to be the upper-caste, Hindu, upper-class, urban woman, who suffers no inequalities other than gender. The Anveshi Law Committee,[6] in an essay on the UCC, for instance, observes:

> in the nationalist period itself, 'woman' in India had acquired the markings that made her Hindu, urban, upper-caste and middle-class. Over a period of time, through processes of consolidation, these specific

markers become invisible, and this norming of woman comes to be seen as natural. Only the normed woman can lay claim to being truly Indian.

(Anveshi Law Committee 1997: 456)

This, it may be emphasized, is a historiographical assertion, which I will address shortly, about the constitution of a dominant citizen-subject during the phase of anti-colonial nationalism itself. The subject of contemporary Indian feminism, in this post-structuralist critique of power/knowledge, is thus the woman-subject who is enabled or empowered to speak in post-colonial modern India, and, in speaking, universalizes her own limited positionality as the referent for universal female subjecthood. The ruse of the universal erases the identifications of power that produce the speaking subject of feminism, thereby hegemonizing already existing sites of dominance.

The universal feminist subject comes into being at the expense of excluded subjects who are disallowed from becoming subjects or 'speaking'.[7] And indeed, the Anveshi Law Committee's essay argues that the dominant subject of Indian feminism has maintained a hegemony within the Indian women's movement even when marginalized Others – such as Dalit and Muslim women – have raised challenges to it, by incorporating these dissensions as differences within a larger unified identity. To quote Anveshi:

The emergence in the last few decades of different social and political movements, especially the Dalit movement, has raised many questions for feminism. ... The attitude of the women's movement, normed as urban, Hindu and upper caste-class, has been to address the concerns of the Muslims or the Dalits by making some space for the Dalit woman and the Muslim woman even while insisting that their 'primary' identity is neither Dalit nor Muslim, but woman.

(Anveshi Law Committee 1997: 455–6)

This may be identified as a second historiographical statement, quite consistent with the first: if the normed[8] Indian woman, the citizen of the nation-to-be, was produced in and through the nationalist movement, Dalit and Muslim women's contestations of this norm are seen as being fairly recent.

Post-structuralist deconstruction evidently informs this critique of Indian feminism's universal subject. Anveshi locates its critique of the UCC agenda within a larger questioning of 'the notions of "democracy", "equality", "secularism" and "modernity", which are under contestation at present' (Anveshi Law Committee 1997: 455). This brings me to the second criticism that I had identified in introducing this section: that post-structuralism intersects with post-colonialism to produce a combined resistance to universal, statist discourses. Post-structuralism feeds post-colonialism to produce a unique critical position in the contemporary Indian academy: a position best articulated, at the present moment, in a school of south Asian history writing called Subaltern Studies. This position points to the epistemic violence that the universalist discourses engendered by Enlightenment rationalism enact against non-modern, non-Western epistemologies that inhabit and imagine non-universal fragments.

Scholars like Dipesh Chakrabarty suggest that such violence inheres in discourses of equal, democratic citizenship in the post-colonial Indian nation-state. The 'process of making individuals into "Indians"' (Chakrabarty 2000: 271) or equal citizens is, as Dipesh Chakrabarty argues, innately undemocratic. To enjoy the benefits that the state can distribute, to become citizens and participate in the state's grand narrative of progress, individuals have to be disciplined into the philosophies of the state. As Chakrabarty observes:

> One cannot perform effectively in the context of modern bureaucracies – and therefore one cannot access the benefits these institutions are capable of delivering – if one is not able to mobilize one's identity, personal or collective, through the languages, skills and practices that these philosophies make possible. The very idea of distributive justice requires that these languages and competencies – of citizenship, of democracy, of welfare – be made available to all classes, particularly those subordinated and oppressed. It means that when we, members of the privileged classes, write subaltern histories – whether we write them as citizens (i.e. on behalf of the idea of democratic rights) or as socialists (desiring radical social change) – a certain pedagogic drive comes into play in our writing. We write, ultimately, as part of a collective effort to teach the oppressed of today how to become the democratic subject of tomorrow.
>
> (Chakrabarty 2000: 272–3)

The pedagogic dialogue between the post-colonial elite intellectual (of Marxist or liberal persuasion), who is informed by derived universal discourses of modernity and Enlightenment rationalism, and the non-elite subaltern is, 'by its very structure', (Chakrabarty 2000: 273) undemocratic. For, as Chakrabarty goes on to say:

> a dialogue can be genuinely open only under one condition: that no party puts itself in a position where it can unilaterally decide the final outcomes of the conversation. This never happens between the 'modern' and the 'non-modern'. Because, however non-coercive the conversation between the Kantian subject (i.e. the transcendent academic observer, the knowing, judging and willing subject of modernity) and the subaltern who enters into a historical dialogue with the former from a

non-Enlightenment position, this dialogue takes place within a field of possibilities that is already structured from the very beginning in the favour of certain outcomes. ... In the pedagogic histories, it is the subaltern's relationship to the world that ultimately calls for improvement. (In the limiting case of the problem, all peasants would be educated out of their peasantness.)

(Chakrabarty 2000: 273)

The dialogue that produces citizen-subjects is violent because it involves an unlearning of the subaltern subject's native tongues, and disallows her epistemologies. It educates, for instance, the peasant to see his or her world in terms of the inequalities of class, gender and ethnicity, and unlearn the irrationalism of imagining ghosts and spirits.[9] This violence is inextricable from universal grand narratives, such as that of the state (the Marxist or liberal or feminist state), which aim to envision everyone's good through a totalitarian, monolinguistic philosophy. Subaltern narratives can disrupt this 'monomania of the imagination' (Chakrabarty 2000: 275) by contributing to the dialogue knowledge-forms that are not of wholes and totalities. Imaginations that are fragmentary and episodic:

[a] consciousness (of) the many possible worlds we inhabit, ...the possibility that these worlds may be incommensurable with each other, and hence grant our social life a constant lack of transparency with regard to any one particular way of thinking about it.

(Chakrabarty 2000: 276)

The relevance of this critique to the UCC debate is apparent, for the UCC debate is also a debate about equal citizenship for Indian women across religions and castes. The UCC can be critiqued as a grand-narrative that attempts to render 'everyone's good' transparent to a monochromic ideology tied to the state. It establishes its own fundamentalist feminist premise by assuming culture as a fundamental essence that is always-already antithetical to feminist concerns. It may be pointed out here that within Hinduism, there are communities like the Nairs in Kerala, which are matrilineal. Within India, there are 'tribal' communities like the Khasis of Meghalaya, where both lineage and property is traced through the mother. Would a Uniform Civil Code – the utopic vision of everyone's good – empower the women of these communities, or disempower them and flatten out cultural diversity?

Intersections in the Child Marriage Restraint Act 1929: the site of the universal in anti-colonial nationalism

Both the critiques that are made of universalist premises in post-colonial India that I have identified in the previous section are historiographical assertions. They point to (a) the constitution of a dominant feminist subject during the phase of anti-colonial nationalism, and (b) the derivation of positivistic meta-narratives of the state by the elite Indian intellectuals during the colonial encounter. In this section, I contest both of these historiographical teleologies by culling from the archives an instance where a uniform civil legislation was enacted in colonial India.

In 1929, the Child Marriage Restraint Act was passed to apply uniformly to all communities, castes and religions in the colonial state. Was the 'universal' in the child marriage debate an exclusionary ruse of power that benefited the dominant subjects of the nation that were being conceptualized? Were universal discourses of the nation tending to consolidate the power of dominant Hindu, upper-caste subjects as those who would inherit the nation-to-be at this historical period? I would contend that this was not so. Second, as against the argument that the post-colonial Indian state constructs and disciplines its subaltern-citizens through a pedagogic dialogue that is informed by liberal discourses of Enlightenment rationalism, I will suggest that citizens, subaltern and elite, constructed the post-colonial state in and through anti-colonial nationalism.

Through these contentions, I would delineate the difference between the post-colonial state, and the site of universal citizenship therein, from the analogous site in the Western liberal state. To elucidate the difference between the post-colonial and liberal states, it is necessary to delineate the mechanisms of Western liberalism. The liberal mechanism may be identified as exclusionary in two respects. First, the liberal state demarcates the site of its universal citizen-subject by exclusion. For the universal subject is not a pre-social, pre-discursive, transcendental – 'universal'– subject, but a subject located in sites of power, i.e. an already normed subject. Through the ruse of the universal subject, the liberal state implicitly excludes groups that deviate from the normed site of the universal. Second, as excluded groups make claims to be included in the liberal universal, the liberal state includes them and provides recognition, thereby creating neat and exclusionary positions from where excluded groups speak.[10] Thus we have 'positions' or 'categories' such as ethnic minorities, religious minorities, racial minorities, all included within a multicultural, liberal state. Both the site of the universal and its constitutive outside are therefore essential to the power of the liberal state. For the site of the universal produces the margins, and the margins are important as 'states of injury',[11] requiring the redress and recognition of the liberal state. The site of the universal excludes the margins and the margins are produced as neat and exclusionary categories that articulate their difference in order to be recognized by the liberal state.

Ironically, similar effects are seen to result from the interventions of intersectionality theory. The Western intersectionality construct first developed as a critique of gender essentialism, as an articulation of the need to recognize racialized marginalities within gender. However, in critiquing the identity politics of Woman, intersectionality theory has in turn engendered a greater proliferation of identities and multiple marginalities. Although the aim has been to comprehend the intersecting, shared experiences of marginalized populations, the political enterprise inevitably tends to speciate and distinguish 'positions' – black women, black lesbian women, Latina lesbians – as each of their experiences, or locations of intersection, is specific and historically diverse. The agenda, moreover, is to seek recognition for these identities within the law in order to secure protection against social harms and equal distribution of social benefits – or inclusion.[12] In this manner, the exclusionary mechanism of liberalism is reproduced in critical intersectionality analyses.

Was this two-fold liberal exclusion at work in the enactment of the uniform Child Marriage Restraint Act in 1929? Before I address this question, it is essential to say a few words on the issue of child marriage in colonial India. The practice of marrying children (both male and female) was prevalent in colonial India. Although this was a customary practice, it was argued to have religious sanction in the Hindu (and Muslim) scriptures. In the 1920s, a law was deliberated to fix the age at which girls could be married in India. It was proposed, moreover, that the legislation fixing the age of marriage should apply uniformly to all communities, classes, castes and religions in colonial India.[13] The universal feminist foundation that informed the desired enactment was that early marriages in India were detrimental to the health of girl children. Girls were often given in marriage before they had reached the age of puberty among both upper- and lower-caste Hindus, as well as Muslims. Consummation of such marriages was supposed to be post-puberty, but there were cases of husbands raping their immature child-wives, even to death. It was also argued that early marriages resulted in early motherhood that led to mortality of both infants and girl-wives.[14]

The impetus to save women, or rather little girls, by fixing the marriage age by a legislation applying uniformly to all communities came from the Indians themselves: therefore, it was not a civilizing/modernizing initiative of British men to save native women from the oppressions of their coloured-cultural context.[15] It came, moreover, at a time, when anti-colonial nationalism was at its peak: therefore, the agendas of gender were not subordinated to those of culture in the anti-colonial nationalism of native men and women, as some historians suggest.[16] Anti-colonial nationalism had won for Indian men the right to contest elections to the Legislative Assembly in 1919.[17] From the time of the first such popular Assembly, child marriage and age of consent had figured on the legislative agenda of the Assembly. Efforts by the Indian legislators had, in fact, failed during the tenure of first two Assemblies, because of British opposition. The British colonial government had voted with the opposition when a Bill to raise the age of consent was moved in 1922 and then again in 1925.[18] The British government aborted the final passage of the Bill as it considered its provisions far too radical and unsafe, and feared the reaction of the orthodox opposition. In 1927, Harbilas Sarda moved the Hindu Child Marriage Bill to fix the age of marriage of girls. The Bill was initially meant to apply only to the Hindu community, but in the course of debates, its scope was sought to be enlarged to include all communities and castes in India.

The native legislators who debated the Child Marriage Bill in the Legislative Assembly represented constituencies such as 'Hindu, urban', 'Hindu, rural', 'Muhammadan, urban', 'Muhammadan, rural', etc. The construction of these categories was a result of the electoral politics of liberal democracy that the colonial state introduced.[19] In addition, the colonial state produced neat positions such as the Hindu, the Muslim, and so on, through other processes of categorization such as the census as well. It also constructed certain positions as sites of injury and provided them recognition through the politics of representation in the liberal democratic electoral process. The construction of neat and essential categories is, as we have seen, an exclusionary move of the liberal state and serves its regulatory aims.

However, in the child marriage debate, there was an overstepping of this liberal construction of neat positions. Through this overstepping, there was an undoing of the liberal mechanism of the colonial state. Limits of categorization were exceeded as people professing one identification did speak *for* others, and voices were not determined by their location in social co-ordinates. Miss Khadijah Begum, a member of the All-India Women's Conference spoke for Hindu untouchables, Dr L.K. Hyder, a 'Muhammadan, rural' member of the Legislative Assembly, spoke for Hindu girls, Har Bilas Sarda spoke for both Hindu untouchables and Hindu girls, and Ramaswamy Periyar, a Dalit leader, spoke for Brahmin women and the oppressions suffered by them under upper-caste Hinduism.[20] Identificatory positions in the child marriage debate thus exceeded their social situation to intersect and overlap with other identifications. The Child Marriage Restraint Act came to be enacted as a consequence of this overlap and intersection.

This leads to the second question as to whether the site of the universal, which was being debated in the child marriage debate in 1929, was an exclusionary liberal site. Who were the speaking subjects who were mobilized at the various 'positions' in the debate and who were the subaltern subjects they silenced? When a law was proposed to apply uniformly to all communities within the emerging Indian nation, were its authors Hindu, upper-caste men and women who universalized their own subjectivity as the Indian? Did they represent and thereby silence those groups who were excluded by the dominant Hindu, upper-caste identity? It is evident from the foregoing discussion that the groups who were Others to the upper-caste Hindu identity were also speaking subjects in the child marriage debates. Muslims and Dalits were not silenced by the Hindu, upper-caste authoritative subjects. On the other hand, the Muslims and Dalits articulated positions that exhibited the same strands – reformist, anti-reformist, relativist – that the Hindu opinion did.

However, were all the speaking subjects in the emerging nation – the Muslims, Hindus and Dalits who voiced their various, intersecting opinions – essentially speaking in the same language? Was this language one that silenced those who did not speak it – those who did not organize themselves, those who did not participate in the public sphere, those who did not constitute a 'position' in the nation? Was this perhaps the difference between the speaking and the silent subjects – the essential subaltern difference? A difference not of religion or caste, but of a political vision of participation in the grand narrative of the state, the vision itself being produced by education, or intellectual hybridization. Were alternative visions and local narratives giving way to, or rather tying up, with the meta-narratives of the state in such a way that other subjectivities had to give way to that of the citizen-subject?

When alternative visions and local narratives merged with those of the nation, the agency for the merger came from one of two directions. Either those who were organized at the level of the nation went to the unorganized subalterns to elicit their responses and/or solicit their support, or the subalterns aligned with the mainstream national movement when their interests coincided mutually. An instance of the former is when the Age of Consent Committee, appointed in 1928 to enquire into the effectiveness of the age of consent law, went to the villages and spoke *to* the subaltern subjects about practices of marriage and consummation. The Report of the Committee observes:

> In every village visited, enquiries were made from among the people there as to the practices prevalent among them in regard to marriage and consummation, the evils, if any, noticed by them and the remedy proposed. Lady members made similar enquiries separately from the women gathered there. The alacrity with which in certain villages the villagers expressed their willingness for legislation to prevent early maternity was a surprise to the Committee.
>
> (Report of the Age of Consent Committee 1929: 4)

The committee's dialogue with the subaltern subjects moves from eliciting their responses to given questions, to reporting their support. The Age of Consent Committee was obviously an instrument of the state, appointed by the British Government to enquire into the existing law and suggest changes.

However, other indigenous groups with a pan-Indian organization, such as the All-India Women's Conference (AIWC),[21] also mobilized the support of local constituencies. The AIWC, for instance, localized its activities in constituencies such as Alibag, Punjab East, Punjab Central, Utkal, Bihar and Sindh.[22] The subalterns, in turn, gave their agency to the mainstream national movement when their interests intersected with those of the latter.

In fact, the merging of the local into the national was the quintessential condition of twentieth-century colonial India. This condition distinguished the twentieth century from its predecessor. Post-1920, the national movement extended its base and included the masses, under M.K. Gandhi's leadership. Religious reform movements, too, which had been discrete and regional in the nineteenth century were succeeded by organized and widespread movements in the twentieth. Likewise, movements for gender and social reform had been disparate and localized in the nineteenth century – sati in Bengal,[23] the Devadasi tradition in Mysore,[24] and so on. Each social reform body had dealt with the problems specific to its local environment, and regional variations in social conditions had kept them discrete.[25] However, in the twentieth century, age of consent and child marriage were issues dealt with at the level of the nation, and located at the universal foundation of the Indian woman, who was married as a child in all communities and castes. At the level of the nation, these issues were seen as encompassing all the communities, castes, religions and regions within the nation. The enactment of the Child Marriage Restraint Act as a uniform civil legislation in 1929 can be understood only within this historical context. It belonged to a time when local narratives were merging with the narratives of the nation and constructing the universal within it.

The site of the universal, moreover, included various positions since it was formed through their intersection. This is a very different move from universalizing the dominant Hindu subject as the national subject by muting cultural Others. The selection of the members of the Age of Consent Committee itself reflects the inclusion of the heterogeneity of castes, communities and opinions that intersected with the universal feminist foundation under-pinning the issue. The personnel of the Age of Consent Committee included a Muslim theologian, a Hindu pundit, a European woman doctor, an Indian woman, among other Muslim and Hindu lawyers and civil servants.[26] Moreover, the committee elicited the opinions of Hindu, Muslim and Dalit witnesses, region-wise, caste-wise and class-wise.[27] The identifications of Muslim, Dalit and Hindu were thus broken down to region, class and caste. In the debate on the issue several speaking subjects had a voice and their coalescence produced the site of the universal.

The post-colonial Indian state was formed through a similar coalescence of positions. The state in India emerged as a result of the anti-colonial movement. In this movement, as it took shape after 1920, 'positions' or interest groups aligned and overlapped with each other in their mutual anti-colonial agenda. For instance, peasant interests intersected with Gandhian politics, the women's organizations sought allies in the nationalist legislators, Chambers of Commerce supported the anti-colonial movement in order to protect native industries. Through this intersection, positions lost their neatness and overlapped to construct a nation-state where there had earlier been a polity of smaller, princely states.

Often, the intersecting narratives were subaltern narratives. The peasants at Kheda, the workers on the indigo plantations, the low-caste people whom Gandhi called the 'harijans', the subaltern, rural women – the anti-colonial movement under Gandhi in the 1920s was a sum total of these various subaltern interests, whose troubles were linked to the presence of the colonial state. These subaltern groups gave their agency to the national movement. They also withheld their agency and re-channelled it in different directions in order to critique native landed groups and their exploitative practices as well.[28] In this manner, the mainstream national movement was constantly challenged and forced to re-articulate itself, as the subalterns and women brought differing imaginations to the nation. The force of the national movement post-1920 came from its subalternity, its mass base and popular mobilization.

The state which emerged after colonial rule, therefore, necessarily included all the actors who had given their agency to the anti-colonial movement, who had, so to say, constituted it. The universal within the post-colonial Indian state comes from this history of the formation of the state itself. In that sense, to see discourses of the universal in India as being derived from Western liberalism is historically inaccurate. Post-structuralist critiques in the UCC debates, in fact, do lose sight of this history when they argue that the universal in India is derived from Western discourses and is thus inherently exclusionary. The post-colonial Indian state was not liberal in its formation in either of the two senses in which liberalism is critiqued: first, it did not exclude minority groups under the sign of the universal. It included the groups that had given their agency to the national movement, many of whom were subaltern groups. Second, it did not construct its citizens as neat positions requiring its recognition. On the contrary, these groups or positions constructed the state by losing their neatness and overlapping with other positions in their mutual anti-colonial agenda.

This history challenges the notion of a dominant feminist subject or dominant citizen-subject in the creation of the post-colonial state. This history is often lost in contemporary critiques of the universal in the UCC debates. It is important to retrieve this history, because it is an alternative to the histories of liberal states written in Western contexts. It is a history that speaks of an alternative experience of the state, and the universal within it. It is, finally, a history that post-colonial nation-states can perhaps contribute to Western discourses of liberalism and their critiques in contemporary post-structuralist theory.

Theorizing intersectionality, historicizing alternative universalisms

The intersection of positions and interest groups is central to my narrative of the formation of the post-colonial state, as the previous section has demonstrated. In this section, I would theorize that such intersection occurred at the limit of transcendence and difference to constitute the nation-state. I will elucidate how this theorization of intersecting positions, and the narrative of state and citizenship that it produces, differs from the discourses of citizenship within (a) historiographical narratives of the post-colonial Indian nation-state in Subaltern Studies and (b) Western liberalism and its post-structuralist critiques. Finally, I would interrogate what possibilities this theorization holds for agendas of political transformation, as compared to post-structuralist and intersectionality analyses.

Eventually, the distinction between the post-colonial state and the Western liberal state in my argument hinges on the relationship that I conceptualize between subaltern and elite elements in the formation of the Indian state. It is, therefore, essential to briefly summarize how this relationship has been theorized in other schools of south Asian historiography, and the critiques of the post-colonial nation-state that result thereof. With this end in view, I would explore the historiographies of the post-colonial Indian nation-state in *Subaltern Studies*.

The term 'subaltern' belongs to the school of South Asian history-writing called *Subaltern Studies*. How is the 'subaltern' imagined in *Subaltern Studies*? At the very inception of the series, Ranajit Guha, its editor, defined the 'subaltern', very mathematically, as those social groups and elements that represented the 'demographic difference between the total Indian population and (all those whom we have described as) the "elite"' (Guha 1982: 8), i.e. the dominant foreign and indigenous groups.

Subaltern Studies, which emerged in the early 1980s, was an attempt to write 'history from below', i.e. to relate those narratives of the subaltern domain in anti-colonial politics that elitist historiography did not. According to Guha, the historiography of Indian nationalism had been dominated by two elitist traditions: (a) the neo-colonialist, which represented Indian nationalism as a response to the ideas, institutions and resources generated by colonialism, as an enterprise wherein the native elite collaborated with colonial institutions in order to share in their rewards of wealth, power and prestige; and (b) the bourgeois-nationalist, which represented Indian nationalism as 'an idealist venture in which the indigenous elite led the people from subjugation to freedom' (Guha 1982: 2).

It must be noted that the subaltern project was sharply critical of the economistic reductionism and evolutionary teleology (i.e. the tracing of the linear progression of class consciousness, by which some resistances were found backward and others – appropriate material for historical study – more enlightened of class interest) of conventional Marxist analyses as well. The attempt was to resist the totalizing effects of this teleology, which emptied subaltern movements of their specific and local consciousnesses, practice and cultural dimensions (O'Hanlon 2000). In this, the subaltern mode was deconstructionist, one that wrote micro-histories of specific subaltern groups and their forms of resistance, traditions and subjectivities. Orthodox Marxist historiographies of colonial India, which told of peasant and labour movements, were also seen to suffer from an elitist bias, due to their focus on 'left organizational and ideological lineages' (Sarkar 2000: 302). [29]

These varieties of 'history from above' had reduced the story of Indian nationalism to an elite phenomenon and left other narratives untold – narratives of the 'contribution made by the people on their own, that is, independently of the elite to the making and development of this nationalism' (Guha 1982: 3). This last assertion contains the equation between the subaltern and elite domains in anti-colonial politics, as envisaged by Guha: an equation which, as I mentioned, is significant to this chapter, for the departure that I would like to posit from it. Guha suggests that the subaltern domain existed independently of elite politics in the history of Indian nationalism/s. This indicates a 'structural dichotomy' (Guha 1982: 6) in the anti-colonial national movement: the co-existence of two distinct domains or streams in Indian nationalism, two distinct imaginations of the nation. For Guha, this structural dichotomy points to an 'important historical truth': the 'failure of the Indian bourgeoisie to speak for the nation' (Guha 1982: 5). Or, the failure of the elite Indian leadership to incorporate the subaltern agendas in their anti-colonial politics. For, Guha argues, although the bourgeois Indian leadership tried to integrate the subaltern masses in their anti-colonial initiatives, the latter often broke away from their control, especially in movements which deviated into legal and constitutionalist compromises with the colonial state. Subaltern initiatives, on their part, were not powerful enough to get the better of this dichotomy and seize the nation – 'to develop the nationalist movement into a full-fledged struggle for national liberation' (Guha 1982: 6). To quote Guha:

> The working class was still not sufficiently mature in the objective conditions of its social being and in its consciousness as a class-for-itself, nor was it firmly allied yet with the peasantry. As a result, it could do nothing to take over and complete the mission that the bourgeoisie had failed to realize.
>
> (Guha 1982: 6)

This historiography of the subaltern-nation that 'failed to come into its own' (Guha 1982: 7) in Guha and the early volumes of *Subaltern Studies* has given way to a post-structuralist questioning of whether the subaltern can, in fact, ever imagine the nation. Or whether the subaltern and the state are essentially incommensurable. Dipesh Chakrabarty, for instance, cites Antonio Gramsci, the theorist who originally used the term 'subaltern' to this effect:

> The subaltern classes are, by definition, not united and cannot unite until they are able to become a "State". ... The history of the subaltern social groups is necessarily fragmented and episodic.
>
> (Chakrabarty 2000: 274)[30]

Chakrabarty deploys this Gramscian conceptualization to argue that the subaltern is a political position that is 'incapable of thinking the state... Once the subaltern can imagine/think the state, he transcends, theoretically speaking, the condition of subalternity' (Chakrabarty 2000: 273–4). The imagination of the state is to be brought to the subaltern by the revolutionary intellectual. The dialogue between the revolutionary intellectual and the subaltern, which seeks to produce the state, is thus necessarily pedagogic. This dialogue, as Chakrabarty suggests, is also inherently undemocratic, as it takes place 'within a field of possibilities that is already structured' – ahead of the investigation – 'in favour of certain outcomes' (Chakrabarty 2000: 273). At the conclusion of the dialogue, the subaltern would be educated out of his peasantness, his subalternity, and learn to see the world in terms of 'rational' epistemologies, grand narratives which would render everyone's good transparent to a unitary ideology. A truly democratic dialogue, on the contrary, is one wherein the elite intellectual can possibly learn from the subaltern too. And the knowledge-forms that the subaltern can offer to the dialogue are precisely the conditions of his subalternity – an imagination that is fragmented and episodic, that resists wholes and totalities, that contests monolinguistic narratives of positivistic progress tied to the state.[31]

These subaltern knowledge-forms, it is contended, can disrupt the discourses of the state in both Marxist and liberal philosophies. Since both Marxist and liberal ideologies stem from the universalistic, positivistic discourses of the European Enlightenment, the subaltern represents the epistemological movement away from Enlightenment rationalism, the trope of the 'fragment'. The subaltern in the post-colonial state has a unique significance in this movement away. In the post-colonial–post-structuralist critique of universal discourses, the subaltern combines an epistemic Otherness to Western, rational discourses with a subject-location within a post-colonial nation-state that is constructed, it is argued, on derived liberal-democratic discourses.

In this chapter, I attempt to break the post-colonial–post-structuralist critique at the hyphen by arguing that fragmentary subaltern and elite narratives intersected at the limit of transcendence and difference to constitute the state. To explain how I conceptualize this intersection, I would first inquire into tropes of transcendence in Western post-structuralist responses to liberal separation. Western post-structuralist arguments respond to liberal dichotomies by emphasizing fluidity, or the non-separability of positions, which questions the very premise of intersectionality. For instance, Judith Butler challenges the logic of exclusion or repudiation by which 'positions' emerge as neat categories that can be related, or intersected.[32] Such pluralist separation, Butler argues, is an effect of the exclusionary operations of the liberal state, which constitutes 'positions' or 'categories' by attributing a false uniformity to them. For Butler, the pluralist identifications of, say, race, class and sexuality cannot be separated, first, from the identification of gender, and second, from each other. The issue, therefore, she says is 'not one of relating race and sexuality and gender, as if they were fully separable axes of power'; but one of questioning their very 'pluralist theoretical separation... as "categories" or indeed as "positions"' (Butler 1993: 116).[33]

This theoretical position seeks to transcend the logic of repudiation which forms the basis of identity politics, by pointing to the lack of rigid boundaries that demarcate Self from Other as essential entities, or identities. As an illustration, within Butler's 'matrix of gender relations', the fluidity of identities de-centres both the phallus and the lack. Due to this fluidity of identities, power is diffuse and is continuously contested. There is no unilinearity in power relations, and relations of power are therefore too complex to be explained within the paradigms of structuralist analysis. This leads to the inevitable anxiety: on what do we base a political praxis without assuming the centricity of the dominant Other? For instance, on what do we base a feminist praxis when both the phallus and power are in pieces? Feminism as an ideology has, for long, founded itself on the received wisdom of absolute gender difference, and relations of domination and subordination.

However, the political implications of Butler's analysis for discourses of identificatory mobilization, state and citizenship are precisely these: in de-centring both dominance and its contestation, Butler's analysis enables narratives of power and resistance that are not tied to grand narratives – either of political mobilization, such as universal feminist agendas, or of dominance, such as those of the state. However, how would these alternative, localized, almost atomized, narratives of reiterated resistance contend with structural expressions of dominance such as, for instance, the state? The unison and direction of atomized narratives of resistance, on the other hand, produces collective action,[34] which sets itself up against structural inequalities. In this, it assumes the fixed stability of the dominant Other, against which it defines itself and its politics. The converse of this argument is also true: the assumption of structural inequalities in turn produces the need for collective action.

Are the only theoretical possibilities then, either to collapse distinctions into post-structuralist inseparability, or to posit the exclusionary separation of identities? I would theorize, instead, that identities negotiate at the limit of transcendence and difference. I would extrapolate from Georges Bataille's reading of the erotic tension to argue that in the politics of identity, two fundamental motivations are in conflict: what Bataille describes as the desire to recognize the Other as same and the primal motivation to resist interiorization into the Other, and the risk of subjective death that this entails.[35] This tension between differentiation and non-differentiation marks the tension between life and death itself. It is the tension between the discontinuity of life with which the individual embodied soul is invested, and the continuity which is death,[36] the final merger of the soul with the soul of the universe. In this, it is the essential human condition.

Most monistic religious philosophies see the essential human condition as the soul's aspiration to achieve continuity with the universe. The knowledge of the soul is the knowledge that all things are one. That the individual soul is one with the soul of the universe, that the individual soul *is* the soul of the universe. In certain philosophical traditions, such as that of *advaita* in Hinduism, this implies that there is no dualism, no difference between the *atman* (the individual soul) and the *brahman* (the soul of the universe). Since the *atman* is the *brahman*, it possesses the power of the universe, to make or unmake the universe. For, the universe as a manifestation that is external to the individual soul is an illusion. And when the *atman* makes or umakes the universe, it makes/unmakes not the universe, but itself.

The limit of the living condition is the boundary between the individual soul and the rest of the universe, the resistance to death, the politics of you and me. Or differentiation. The drive to repudiate transcendence and assert an autonomous difference. The tension between transcendence and difference is the essential inter-personal/inter-subjective dualistic condition. And thus it is also the intra-subjective condition, for the unstable subject who negotiates transcendence/difference with the Other emerges by incompletely quelling the Other within the self. The politics of identity is located at the tension between transcendence and difference. In unequal relations of power, the politics of identity aspires to achieve transcendence, and simultaneously to resist interiorization into the Other in its attempt to do so. For this, it needs to assume the stability of the Other.

I would theorize, therefore, that identificatory positions intersect at the precipice of transcendence and difference, as intersections in the child marriage debate exemplify. I would also extend this theorization to the relationship between subaltern and elite groups in the anti-colonial Indian national movement, and locate their negotiation at the precipice of transcendence and difference, continuity and discontinuity. This would imply that subaltern groups retained their specific and diverse agendas of resistance even while forging mutually anti-colonial alliances with the elite leadership.

That is, subaltern agendas fractured the national movement, by directing resistance at internal structural inequities, even while forging over-arching, anti-colonial alliances. Such intersections constituted the post-colonial state and the site of the universal within it. While this argument enables me to theorize an alternative discourse of universal citizenship in the post-colonial state, it also contains the seeds of envisioning a change of state, or revolution.

For, if we are to understand revolution as a change of state, then colonial India did witness a revolution, or several revolutions, that culminated in 1947. The argument of intersections is crucial to understanding this political transformation or revolution. Western post-structuralisms repudiate the logic of intersections, for their notion of fluidity challenges the premise that race, gender, class, etc. are 'pure' or distinct categories that can be intersected or related. Political transformation, within these arguments, is theorized as an ongoing process, whereby power constantly constitutes, and is constituted by, subjects. This enables localized, i.e. non-structural, narratives of agency and resistance. These are small narratives of resistance that do not produce states. Post-structuralist imaginations therefore enable small, non-statist narratives of both resistance and power. In this sense, power can be enabling. However, if we were to separate concepts of power and dominance, then how would these local, almost atomized narratives of resistance and power contend with large narratives of dominance such as, perhaps, the colonial state?

Likewise, in intersectionality analyses, the potential for political transformation is reduced to an engagement with the law, and the drive for recognition therein, of marginalized identities. The emphasis on identities fails to situate them within larger structural processes, including those of the law, through which identities and exclusions are systemically constituted, as Joanne Conaghan observes[37] (see this volume). In other words, the processes by which the law, and more importantly the state, themselves construct and perpetuate marginalities becomes sidelined in the project. An engagement with social structures, rather than with the law, requires some notion of the possibility of collective action, which the highly speciated and discrete nature of identities thwarts.

The near-liberal colonial state in India did more than merely separate identities into neat and discrete 'positions'. By separating identities, it separated narratives of resistance into piecemeal fractions. The colonial state was overthrown when piecemeal narratives of resistance were transcended, and intersected with other narratives of resistance, in collective action. What galvanized these discrete consciousnesses of resistance into collective action was the awareness of the structural inequality of colonialism. At the same time, these multifarious narratives of anti-colonial resistance also combated the structural inequalities that existed among one another.

Thus, it is at the limit of transcendence and difference that I locate the intersection of the narratives of subaltern resistance. This chapter points to a historical time when such intersections and alliances occurred, undoing the colonial-liberal division of resistance into piecemeal quarters. The intersection of elite and subaltern narratives of resistance in collective action during the anti-colonial movement produced a revolution and a state.

This narrative of intersections, resistance and revolution negotiates the gap between the liberal separation of 'positions' and the post-structuralist premise of fluidity. It conceives of alternative imaginings of the universal, other tautologies to approach the post/colonial subaltern. Of histories that contain the possibility of envisioning alternative statist discourses of citizenship and secularism, from a non-Enlightenment position. And of other ways to re-think the universal and cultural divide in gender. For debates on gender generally reach the sterile contradiction of the emancipatory potential of (Western) universal feminist discourses versus coloured-cultural oppressions. Oppression is Othered as something that occurs in the Third World, while the West becomes a sphere of post-Enlightenment universal values. Deconstructivist arguments have done much to show that cultures are seldom monolithic, and are fraught with conflicting meanings when localized, specified to region, language and community. The examples that I have already cited, of matrilineal and matriarchal communities within India, demonstrate this. The history that I have re-told provides another way out of this impasse of the transcendental Western universal and the coloured-cultural. It locates an alternative, empowering discourse of the universal in the coloured-cultural context of the Third World: it reverses tired dichotomies of West and non-West.

Acknowledgements

With thanks to Tanika Sarkar and Ratna Kapur, constant mentors both; to the Keele Law School, for providing me with many opportunities to present my work, including at the AHRC Research Centre for Law, Gender, and Sexuality's 'Theorising Intersectionality' conference (22 May 2005, Keele University), while hosting me as a Gender, Sexuality and Law visiting fellow; to Emily Grabham, Maria Drakopoulou, Stewart Motha, Jane Krishnadas, Davina Cooper and Didi Herman of the AHRC Research Centre for Law, Gender and Sexuality for stimulating conversations and feedback on earlier versions of the chapter; and to my co-panelists, audience and hosts at a very illuminating workshop, 'What's the Matter with Judith Butler: An Interdisciplinary Engagement', organized by the School of Social and Political Studies, University of Edinburgh, U.K. on 10 May 2005.

Bibliography

Primary Sources

Accessed at the National Archives of India, New Delhi and the Nehru Memorial Museum and Library, New Delhi.

Legislative Assembly Debates (1927–1929) Delhi: Government of India Press.

Papers of the All-India Women's Conference (File numbers: 59/ 201, 25/ 193, 2/1111, 8/ 825, 53/ 542, 10/ 830, 17/ 181, 37/ 419, 32/ 461, 1/ 726).

Report of the Age of Consent Committee (1929) Delhi: Government of India Press.

Sarda, H.B. (1937) *Speeches and Writings*, Ajmer: Vedic Yantralaya.

Secondary sources

Agnes, F. (1994) 'Women's movement within a secular framework: redefining the agenda', *Economic and Political Weekly* 29, 19: 1123–8.

Agnes, F. (1996) 'The hidden agenda beneath the rhetoric of women's rights' in M. Dutta, F. Agnes and N. Adarkar (eds) *The Nation, the State and Indian Identity*, Calcutta: Samya.

Anveshi Law Committee (1997) 'Is gender justice only a legal issue?: The political stakes in the UCC debate', *Economic and Political Weekly* 32, 9–10: 453–8.

Arya, L. (2006) 'The Uniform Civil Code: The politics of the universal in post-colonial India', *Feminist Legal Studies* 14: 293–328.

Bataille, G. (1962) *Death and Sensuality*, New York: Walker.

Bataille, G. (1976) 'Hemingway in the light of Hegel', *Semiotexte* 2: 1.

Benjamin, J. (1983) 'Master and slave: The fantasy of erotic domination' in A. Snitow, C. Stansell and S. Thompson (eds) *Powers of Desire: The Politics of Sexuality*, New York: Monthly Review Press.

Brown, W. (1995) *States of Injury: Of Power and Freedom in Late Modernity*, Princeton, NJ: Princeton University Press.

Butler, J. (1993) *Bodies that Matter: On the Discursive Limits of Sex*, New York and London: Routledge.

Butler, J. (1995) 'Contingent foundations: Feminism and the question of "postmodernism"' in S. Benhabib, J. Butler, D. Cornell and N. Fraser, (eds) *Feminist Contentions: A Philosophical Exchange*, New York and London: Routledge.

Chakrabarty, D. (1993) 'Marx after Marxism: Subaltern histories and the question of difference', *Polygraph* 6: 10–16

Chakrabarty, D. (2000) 'Radical histories and the question of Enlightenment rationalism: some recent critiques of *Subaltern Studies*' in V. Chaturvedi (ed.) *Mapping Subaltern Studies and the Post-colonial*, London and New York: Verso.

Chakrabarty, D. (2002) *Habitations of Modernity: Essays in the Wake of Subaltern Studies*, Delhi: Permanent Black.

Chatterjee, P. (1986) *Nationalist Thought and the Colonial World: A Derivative Discourse?*, Delhi: Oxford University Press.

Chatterjee, P. (1989) 'The nationalist resolution of the women's question' in K. Sangari and S. Vaid (eds) *Recasting Women: Essays in Colonial History*, New Delhi: Kali for Women.

Chhachhi, A., Khan, F., Navlakha, G., Sangari, K., Malik, N., Menon, R., Sarkar, T., Chakravarti, U., Butalia, U. and Hassan, Z. (1998) 'UCC and the women's movement', *Economic and Political Weekly*, 33, 9: 487–8.

Forbes, G. (1998) *The New Cambridge History of India: Women in Modern India*, Cambridge: Cambridge University Press.

Guha, R. (1982) 'On some aspects of the historiography of colonial India' in R. Guha (ed.) *Subaltern Studies: Writings on South Asian History and Society*, 1, Delhi: Oxford University Press.

Guha, R. (ed.) (1982–85) *Subaltern Studies: Writings on South Asian History and Society*, 1–4, Delhi: Oxford University Press.

Heimsath, C. (1964) *Indian Nationalism and Hindu Social Reform*, Princeton, NJ: Princeton University Press.

Hoare, Q. and Smith, G.N. (eds) (1971) *Selections from the Prison Notebooks of Antonio Gramsci*, New York: International Publishers.

Mohanty, C.T. (1984) 'Under western eyes: feminist scholarship and colonial discourses', *Boundary* 2 12, 3/13, 1.

Mukhopadhyay, M. (1998) 'Gender, state and nation: the Uniform Civil Code and the promise of equality' in *Legally Dispossessed: Gender, Identity and the Process Of Law*, Calcutta: Stree, in association with the Book Review Literary Trust.

Nandy, A. (1983) *The Intimate Enemy: Loss and Recovery of Self Under Colonialism*, Delhi: Oxford University Press.

O'Hanlon, R. (2000) 'Recovering the subject: *Subaltern Studies* and histories of resistance in colonial South Asia' in V. Chaturvedi (ed.) *Mapping Subaltern Studies and the Post-colonial*, London and New York: Verso.

Prakash, G. (1990) *Bonded Histories: Genealogies of Labour Servitude in Colonial India*, Cambridge: Cambridge University Press.

Rao, A. (ed.) (2003) *Gender and Caste: Issues in Contemporary Indian Feminism*, New Delhi: Kali for Women.

Rege, S. (2006) *Writing Caste/Writing Gender: Narrating Dalit Women's Testimonies*, New Delhi: Zubaan.

Sarkar, S. (2000) 'The decline of the subaltern in *Subaltern Studies*' in V. Chaturvedi (ed.) *Mapping Subaltern Studies and the Post-colonial*, London and New York: Verso.

Spivak, G.C. (1985) 'Can the subaltern speak? Speculations on widow-sacrifice', *Wedge* 7/8 (Winter/Spring): 120–30.

Sunder Rajan, R. (2003), 'Women between community and state: Some implications of the Uniform Civil Code debates' in *The Scandal of the State: Women, Law and Citizenship in Post-Colonial India*, Delhi: Permanent Black.

Tharu, S. and Niranjana, T. (1996), 'Problems for a contemporary theory of gender' in S. Amin and D. Chakrabarty (eds) *Subaltern Studies: Writings on South Asian History and Society*, 9, Delhi: Oxford University Press.

Vasterling, V. (2005) 'The relevance of ontology for feminist theory: A critique of Butler and Irigaray with the help of Heidegger', paper presented at the workshop, 'What's the Matter with Judith Butler?: An Interdisciplinary Engagement', 10 May, Edinburgh: University of Edinburgh.

Notes

1　For instance, see Mohanty 1984.

2　Scholarship produced from the standpoint of Dalit feminism often makes this critique of Indian feminism's subject, and not always within the context of the UCC debate. See, for instance, Rao 2003 and Rege 2006. Also, Tharu and Niranjana, in discussing the issues that confront contemporary feminist politics in India, state: 'The marking of "women" as middle class and upper caste has a long genealogy that, historically and conceptually, goes back into nationalism as well as social reform' (Tharu and Niranjana 1996: 240).

3　See Sarkar 2000 for a critical discussion of various post-structuralist positions in Indian historiography. In these postions, Sarkar observes, 'domination is conceptualized overwhelmingly in cultural, discursive terms, as the power-knowledge of the post-Enlightenment West. If at all seen as embodied in institutions, it tends to get identified uniquely with the modern bureaucratic nation-state'. Therefore, 'reified notions of "community" or "fragment" (are counterposed), alternatively or sometimes in unison, against this highly generalized category of the "modern" nation-state as the embodiment of Western cultural domination' (Sarkar 2000: 301, 307).

4　See Amrita Chhachhi et al. 1998, for a summary of these arguments. Some women's groups that advocated the UCC agenda in 1997 were the Forum Against Oppression of Women, Bombay and the Working Group on Women's Rights, New Delhi.

5　Flavia Agnes, for instance, has criticized the 'secularism' of the mainstream women's movement in India for implicitly eliding differences among women that arise from their religious and communitarian identities (Agnes 1994, 1996). See Sunder Rajan (2003) and Mukhopadhyay (1998) for a discussion of the religious, caste and communitarian issues that beset the UCC controversy and the varied responses to them.

6　This is the Law Committee of the Anveshi Research Centre for Women's Studies, established in 1985 and situated in the Osmania University campus, Hyderabad, India. The centre works in five research areas of Dalit studies, education, health, law and development, and also functions as a support group on women's issues.

7　See Butler 1995: 35–57.

8　I use the terms 'normed'/'norming' in the sense in which they are employed by Anveshi, to indicate the insidious rendering of dominant subjectivities as the invisible and implicit norm that represents marginalized Others.

9　Chakrabarty 2000: 273. Chakrabarty borrows this example of the inherently undemocratic terms of the dialogue of rational left-liberal epistemologies with the subaltern, from Gyan Prakash's book on bonded labour (Prakash 1990).

10　See Butler 1993: 116. Butler says, 'the pluralist theoretical separation (of these terms) as "categories" or indeed as "positions" is itself based on exclusionary operations that attribute a false uniformity to them and that serve the regulatory aims of the liberal state'.

11　I derive this expression from Wendy Brown. See Brown 1995.

12　See Toni Williams, this volume.

13　I refer here to the Hindu Child Marriage Bill, which was introduced in the Legislative Assembly by Harbilas Sarda in 1927. In the course of deliberations on the Bill, the Legislative Assembly considered an extension of its scope to include communities other than the Hindu as well. The Bill was passed in 1929 as the Child Marriage Restraint Act, and applied uniformly to all communities, regions and castes within the jurisdiction of British India.

14 These arguments came up repeatedly in the Legislative Assembly when the Bill was being considered therein. See the Legislative Assembly Debates 1927–29.

15 Imperial rule was often morally justified on feminist grounds as an enterprise of 'saving' native women from the barbarity of native men and their customs, as post-colonial feminists have argued. See, for instance, Spivak 1985. Spivak critiques the British abolition of the practice of sati in nineteenth century colonial India as one such civilizing mission and captures its inherent subject-object relation in the sentence, 'White men are saving brown women from brown men'.

16 Partha Chatterjee, for instance, posits that the organized nationalist movement that emerged in India in the late nineteenth–early twentieth century, subordinated gender issues to the larger concerns of anti-colonial nationalism. Or, as Chatterjee puts it, nationalism 'resolved' the women's question by subordinating it to the larger anti-colonial question. This supposedly caused a silence on questions of gender in the twentieth century, when compared to the nineteenth century, during which anti-colonial nationalism was less developed and gender was debated (Chatterjee 1998). The national proportions that the child marriage debate assumed in the twentieth century, of course, refutes this claim.

17 The Legislative Assembly was created by the Government of India Act of 1919. Women were not allowed to contest elections to the central legislature at the time of these debates.

18 The reference is to Dr Hari Singh Gour's Bill. Early in the life of the second Legislative Assembly, Dr. Hari Singh Gour introduced a Bill to raise the age of consent to 14 years in both intra- and extra-marital cases. The Bill was referred to a select committee, which reduced the age from 14 to 13 years for consent within marriage. The amended Bill was then considered by the Legislative Assembly on 19 March 1925. The Assembly carried an amendment raising the age to 16 years in extra-marital cases, by an overwhelming majority of 65 to 22, *even though* the British Government strongly opposed the amendment and voted against it. Another amendment to raise the age in intra-marital cases to 14, thereby restoring the original provision of the Bill, was also carried by a narrow majority of 45 against 43. Among the 43 who voted against the amendment were 18 official (i.e. British) members. When the time came to vote on the Bill as a whole, the motion that the amended Bill be passed was defeated by 54 votes to 36, the 54 votes including no less than 24 official members (Report of the Age of Consent Committee 1929: 11–12).

19 In 1909, when the Minto-Morley reforms first introduced liberal-democracy on a limited scale in the colonial state, the Muslims were recognized as a minority position and given separate territorial electorates where they could exclusively contest and vote in the elections. Thus, the 'Muslim' position was constructed, their identity tied to the primordial identification of religion, over and above other identifications of region, language, culture or gender, i.e. other ties with the land that they belonged to. Ten years later, the next set of reforms, popularly known as the Montagu-Chelmsford reforms, extended the system of separate electorates to other minorities as well: The Indian Christians, the Sikhs in the Punjab, the Anglo-Indians and the Europeans were now recognized as positions as well, their identities tied to primordial identifications of religion or community again.

20 Miss Khadijah Begum Ferozeuddin, in the fourth session of the AIWC on 30 December 1931, said, 'the practice of untouchability was a slur on the fair name of India …' (File no. 2/ 1111, AIWC Papers). Dr. Hyder spoke for 'the little girls who had been sent from the nuptial bed to the funeral pyre' (Legislative Assembly Debates 1929: 344). Sarda was an active member of the Arya Samaj.

The Arya Samaj, founded in 1875, was a Hindu organization, which envisioned a revival of an 'original' Vedic Hinduism in contemporary society. Yet, in a speech delivered in the Legislative Assembly on 29 January 1929, Sarda said, 'The women of India do not talk of the Sastras; they do not bother themselves about the effect of marriage on their prospects in the next world. They are practical and think of this world, and they want that their suffering in this world should come to an end' (Sarda 1937: 53 and 57). Ramaswamy Periyar started the Self-Respect Movement in south India, which mobilized the untouchable castes to contest the disabilities imposed on them by the caste system. For a fuller description of these various positions, see Arya 2006.

21   The All-India Women's Conference was one of the three 'national' women's organizations that emerged post World War I, between the years 1917–27, the other two being the Women's Indian Association and the National Council of Women in India. For a history of the AIWC, its evolving programme, organizational structure, ideologies and activities, see Forbes 1998.

22   This is derived from the report of the Secretary of the Social Section of the AIWC at the fourth session of the AIWC in 1930 (File no. 2/ 1111, AIWC Papers).

23   Sati was the rite by which a woman who had lost her husband immolated herself upon his funeral pyre. The abolition of sati was debated in nineteenth-century Bengal, and had cleft the public sphere into advocates and opponents of abolition. Raja Rammohun Roy crusaded tirelessly for the abolition, which was brought into effect in 1829, under the Governorship of Lord William Bentinck.

24   This was the tradition of dedicating virgins of the Devadasi caste to temples for the purposes of temple prostitution.

25   See Heimsath 1964.

26   See the Report of the Age of Consent Committee 1929, p. 1 for a list of the personnel of the Committee.

27   See the Report of the Age of Consent Committee 1929, Chapter IV: Provincial Conditions and Nature of Evidence, pp. 22–91. The Age of Consent Committee carried out an examination into the marriage and consummation practices of the different castes and communities within different provinces, so as to avoid making sweeping generalizations about the extent of the prevalence of these practices.

28   See *Subaltern Studies* Volumes I–IV (1982–85) for essays that discuss subaltern narratives and participation in the anti-colonial movement.

29   However, together with this critique of traditional Marxist historiography, the subaltern project still retained a commitment to 'a broad socialist and Marxian horizon' (Sarkar 2000: 300). From these beginnings of trying 'to write "better" Marxist histories', the trajectory of *Subaltern Studies* has evolved into the perception that 'a critique of this nature could hardly afford to ignore the problem of universalism/Eurocentrism that was inherent in Marxist (or for that matter) liberal thought itself' (Sarkar 2000: 302. Sarkar cites from Chakrabarty 1993, in order to sum up the transformation in the thrust of *Subaltern Studies* over the years).

30   Chakrabarty quotes from Gramsci 1971: 52, 54–5.

31   This argument is passive in Chakrabarty 2000: 274–6.

32   See Butler's discussion of identity politics in 'Political Affiliation Beyond the Logic of Repudiation', (Butler 1993: 111–18).

33   Since gender, race, sexuality and class cannot be separated from each other, each 'category' serves sufficiently as a lens of analysis for the others, and to speak of one category is also to speak of the others. To speak of gender is also, as Butler

argues, to speak of 'how the "Orient" has been figured as the veiled feminine (Lowe, Chow)', 'how the humiliations of colonial rule have been figured as emasculation (in Fanon), or racist violence as sodomization (Jan Mohammed)', and 'to what extent feminism has pillaged the 'Third World' in search of examples of female victimization that would support the thesis of a universal patriarchal subordination of women (Mohanty)' (Butler 1993: 117).

34 I am indebted to Dr Veronica Vasterling for this insight. Dr Vasterling elucidated this point in her presentation at a workshop held at the University of Edinburgh on 10 May 2005 (Vasterling 2005).

35 I am drawing here on Jessica Benjamin's re-telling of Georges Bataille. See Benjamin 1983. Benjamin refers to Bataille 1962 and 1976.

36 Ibid.

37 See Conaghan, this volume. Also, see Toni Williams. Williams's chapter in this collection illustrates (a) how intersectionality analyses that aim to explain the high incidence of crime among social groups such as Canadian aboriginal women by situating them in contexts of vulnerability that precipitate crime, are sometimes received by decision-makers to reinforce stereotypes of these groups as risky, criminal populations and (b) how such intersectionality analyses do not consider ways in which laws and prisons are themselves contexts that produce aboriginal women as 'criminal' populations.

Chapter 14

Theorising intersectionality
Identities, equality and ontology

Momin Rahman

Introduction

In this chapter I explore certain themes that arise in attempting to theorise intersectionality, focusing in particular on identity categories and related claims for equality. My central concern is the tension between the idea of universal equality and the recognition of differences that underpins intersectionality theory. However, let me begin with a brief discussion of what we mean by 'intersectionality' to contextualise these issues. It is, of course, easy to think of the concept as directing us to the specific intersections of different social inequalities, particularly focused on race, gender and class in the work of Patricia Hill Collins, who is credited with developing 'intersectionality' in the theoretical framework for her book *Black Feminist Thought* (1990/2000). Although the recognition of gender as differentiated by race has been a feature of feminist thought through the different 'waves' of feminism, particularly in the USA during the nineteenth-century campaigns against slavery (Banks, 1990), and in second wave women's liberation which engaged with black liberation politics and activism (Beal, 1970), there has been a growing critique that many feminist theories and concepts are derived from a white, middle-class experience.

Hill Collins exemplifies the latter, but it is important to understand that she and other such thinkers are not merely drawing attention to race or ethnicity as another variable which must be included in any accounting of gender divisions, but rather that the intersections of different hierarchies create qualitatively different *experiences* of being gendered and racialised. She argues for an intersectional paradigm as the only way in which to astutely understand the complexities of American black women's experiences within the specific historical context of US capitalism that structurally underpins formations of gender and race. In the second edition of her book, she reflects on the development of intersectional perspectives in the decade since the first edition, observing that by:

> rejecting additive models of oppression, race, class and gender studies have progressed considerably since the 1980s. During that decade, African-

American scholar-activists, among others, called for a new approach to analyzing Black women's experiences ... Intersectional paradigms remind us that oppression cannot be reduced to one fundamental type, and that oppressions work together in producing injustice.

(Hill Collins, 2000: 18)

In making the point that gender is experienced differently according to other dimensions of social identity, Hill Collins also argues for theoretical accounts based on researching and disseminating the experiences of those who inhabit the sites of intersection, enabling their points of view to be illuminated in order to contest established dominant perspectives. This locates her work and intersectional studies in general firmly in the feminist tradition of standpoint epistemology. This perspective takes all knowledge as relative, arguing that a group's location in social hierarchies of difference reflect divisions of power and thus affect their ability to make their knowledge (of their particular experience) both heard and taken as legitimate:

Oppressed groups are frequently placed in the situation of being listened to only if we frame our ideas in the language that is familiar to and comfortable for a dominant group. This requirement often changes the meaning of our ideas and works to elevate the ideas of dominant groups. In this volume, by placing African-American women's ideas in the center of analysis, I not only privilege those ideas, but encourage White feminists, African-American men, and all others to investigate the similarities and differences among their own standpoints and those of African-American women.

(Hill Collins, 2000: vii)

My own position in this chapter broadly follows in this tradition, particularly in the discussion of how we conceptualise the function of social identities as representations of a socially structured or *material* lived existence, and how this materiality relates to conditions of equality. However, before we get into the detail of the theoretical discussion, it is important to signpost an overarching issue in intersectionality theories, one which runs through Hill Collins' and others work, and which governs my explorations in this chapter. Whilst intersectionality is an attempt to think through lived experiences of multiple difference, it is simultaneously an attempt to locate these specific differences within social patterns of hierarchy and division. There is an inherent analytical tension in theorising intersectionality in this way, because it argues for understandings of the full diversity of experiences of those inhabiting sites of intersection *and* that we can derive some common or theoretically generalisable analytical purchase from such standpoints. As Madoo Lengermann and Niebrugge put it in their review of intersectionality theory:

This process of theory-building, research and critique has brought intersectionality theory to one of its central themes and one of the central issues confronting feminism today: how to account for the analytical principle and empirical fact of diversity among women, while at the same time holding to the valuational and political position that specific groups of women share a distinctive standpoint.

(2003: 228)

This is a crucial issue precisely because the attempt to develop standpoint knowledge from the perspective of the marginalised – black women in the context of US feminism in Hill Collins, for example – itself questions the very function of identity categories as authentic and universal representations of experience. Thus, can we really produce knowledge based on black women's experiences which is going to avoid reproducing further universal categories of identity which inevitably produce their own exclusions – black lesbians, for example – or which is going to fundamentally undermine any attempt to create common understanding of oppression across groups of white and black women? My discussion touches upon this overarching issue throughout the chapter, but we can begin by thinking of this as a major tension, illustrated broadly by the question of whether intersectional perspectives still implicitly reproduce the conceptual frameworks that they are trying to overcome, in terms of identity categories and their exclusionary and standpoint functions.

A related theme is whether intersectional perspectives reproduce an analytical emphasis on distinct vectors of oppression even as they try to work us towards an integrated understanding of how these create complex sites of social location and identity experiences. Indeed, as shown above, Hill Collins refers to the development of intersectional studies in her second edition of the book as 'race, class and gender studies' rather than as specifically 'intersectionality' studies. Of course, we need the analytical distinctions between, for example, race and gender, precisely so that we can talk of generalised, social patterns of signification and oppression, rather than disconnect, say, Muslim women's experiences from their constitution within racial, ethnic and gender hierarchies. But this means that we must tread carefully when talking of intersectionality, being particularly careful not to simply identify and categorise different variables of oppression if we want to retain the potential reach of an intersectional perspective in accessing the qualitatively different particular experience of being a woman, who is Muslim and non-white, rather than thinking simply of a woman, who suffers gendered inequalities, to which we simply add other inequalities derived from race and ethnic-religious identity.

A particular difficulty in resolving the overarching tension is the fact that the separate dimensions of oppression are often times understood through the empirical fact of the separate and exclusive *identities* which result from these hierarchies, and which have largely become the basis of political social action, and often times codified through policy and law as universal and exclusive identities – such as 'gender' and 'race'. So intersectional apprehension becomes difficult when, for example, the recent debates around Muslim women wearing the veil are thought of simply as issues of Muslim *religious* identity. An intersectional analysis would demand that we attempt to understand the standpoint of such women – somewhat apparent in some of the recent media coverage in Britain – but it would also demand that we see the complex interdependence of issues around gender, racial and ethnic inequalities that bring the tone and form of this debate into effect.[1] In reaching for such a gaze, I argue that we need to think through the social and personal functions of identity categories, and in particular how identity claims are related to two specific issues: ontology and equality.

I discuss ontology in the sense of an explanation that permits an integrated understanding of the constitution of particularised social identities and experience, thus keeping faith with the epistemological standpoint tradition in intersectionality theory but returning us to the tension between attempts to identify marginalised experience and how these illuminations may create their own exclusions. I consider whether some recent feminist deployments of the concept of *materiality* (Rahman and Witz, 2003) can help us to move towards an intersectional framework which overcomes the potential dualisms discussed above, both in reproducing exclusionary identities and distinct vectors of analysis. The discussion of materiality draws upon the longstanding debates between Marxist/socialist, radical and postmodern feminisms in their concern to understand the social ontologies of gender and sexuality as a combination of ideologically produced identity categories and socio-economic structures and, on the other hand, as lived experiences of everyday embodied interaction and identity deployment. As such, I argued that there is a commonality to these disparate theoretical perspectives centred on a conceptualisation of 'materiality' as a structurally permanent but simultaneously porous sense of the ontology of gender and sexuality.

Using this perspective, I suggest therefore that intersectionality can be understood as a concern with the sites of intersection of social hierarchies of identities, but also how the materiality of these sites is constituted through the intersection of the different realms of society. Theorising intersectionality as materiality is, by definition, a sociological task, since in both theorising and evidencing inequalities, identities and experiences, one is inevitably also engaged in theorising the ontology of these across different but intersecting realms of social structures, cultures and action, thus reaching for the sense in which intersectional experience is an instantiation of more general and structured patterns of social oppression and inequalities, or what Hill Collins refers to as the 'matrix of domination' (2000:18). Moreover, thinking about the materiality of sites of interaction directs us away from identity categories simply as reified universal markers of experience, and forces us to think of them as diverse instantiations of experience which ultimately derive from socially patterned ontological conditions.

There is a fundamentally political issue at stake in these sociological explorations, and that is the question of how such explanations of hierarchy, identity and experience provoke, suggest, and rationalise both the terms of policy remedy and the extent of their reach. My reason for raising this is because, ultimately, the political agenda behind theorising 'intersectionality' is a progressive one, concerned with questions of equality and citizenship, and so directs us to think through how the intersections of different spheres of the social intersect with separate hierarchies of difference (which themselves intersect) and how these webs of intersecting dynamics bring citizenship and equality into effect. In particular, I explore whether an intersectional analysis suggests that the condition of equal citizenship is attainable, or indeed desirable for all. In the broad democratic tradition, liberalism and equality have vied for co-existence and dominance, with the liberal emphasis on the state as a neutral guarantor and arbiter of formal rights – equality under the law – gradually being contested and reshaped by democratic impulses towards widening 'equality' to include the social and material basis of life, thus demanding a further reach for the scope of the state in ensuring equality.[2] Whilst both the actual outcomes of equality and the scope of the state are still matters of fierce contest, it is fair to say that the discourse of 'equality' has become embedded as a central, transcendent value against which we judge various experiences and conditions of social division, as well as using equality of citizenship as a goal to judge the viability of remedies for inequality. What I suggest is less certain is whether the equality we seek testifies to a universal condition of being – the traditional liberal sense of equality – or whether, when we apprehend a truly intersectional understanding of 'being' – or social ontology – a more radical theory of differentiated equality is required and therefore that intersectionality demands a shaping of equality which moves beyond liberal democratic discourses and technologies.

Identities and difference

As objects of law and social policy, different forms of inequalities are characterised as exploitative hierarchies, or at the very least, as unfair assumptions made about particular identities, thus preventing the full realisation of their potential as citizens. Anti-discrimination legislation is one keen expression of the attempt to codify and remedy the experience of oppression at both individual and social levels, making the case that people should be treated equally as *individuals* under the law, and that such anti-discrimination techniques recognise that unequal treatment derives from a generalised cultural system of beliefs about *group* identity. The overall aim is to remove entrenched patterns of signification which lead to the reinforcement of unequal treatment, unequal access to resources and opportunities. Equality, of these factors and routes, seems the logical and irrefutable political goal and indeed has been pursued for the last thirty years or so, across many western democracies, using sociologically informed explanations of gender inequalities (Banks, 1990; Dahlerup, 1990) and sexual inequalities (Altman, 1971, Richardson, 1998, 1996; Weeks, 1989) to illustrate how group identity results in individual discrimination. Thus, we can say with some certainty that movements around race, ethnicity, sexuality and gender have produced a political understanding that these identities are not somehow biological or nativist 'facts' but rather that these apparently 'natural' groupings of people have been translated into *social* identities; identities which have been the stigmatised foci of socially based oppression (Castells, 2004).

However, there has often been severe disagreement around the sociological explanations of oppression put forward, as Whelehan comments when describing the political agendas of second wave feminism:

> There was generally substantial agreement between different feminists about the main issues for feminism. However, clear splits are evident in their analysis of the roots of female oppression: while they were quite certain of the effects of female subordination, there tended to be sharp disagreements about where the origins of male power were located.
>
> (Whelehan, 1995: 14)

It is this question of explanatory power which is at the heart of both specific feminist theories, and of the debate between different feminist 'schools' of thought. The usual way of categorising feminism is to divide its strands into liberal, Marxist/socialist and radical feminisms. To this established trinity, Whelehan adds lesbian and black feminisms, alerting us to the fact that both heterosexuality and racialisation operate as hierarchies within and alongside gender and, crucially, within feminist analytics. Recognising that these categorisations are sometimes problematic in the theoretical and analytical boundaries they construct, Whelehan usefully asserts that 'All feminist positions are founded on the belief that women suffer from systematic social injustices because of their sex'(1995: 25). Just so, but reaching for an intersectional analysis moves us away from a focus on 'sex' or indeed on any unitary category of analysis, in large part driven by the recognition that, whilst women do suffer from 'systematic' socially sustained inequalities, this initial broad sociological point has too often resulted in a homogenous characterisation of women. It has resulted in the implicit abstract universalisation of women's identities and experiences, with a significant lack of nuance to differences of race/ethnicity, class and sexuality in both second wave feminism (Jackson and Scott, 1996) and lesbian and gay politics and activism (Seidman, 1996: 10–11).

Moreover, this 'universalism' has provoked a reaction from those excluded. As Butler puts it in her discussion of identity politics in the USA:

Within feminism, it seems as if there is some political necessity to speak as and for *women*, and I would not contest that necessity. Surely, that is the way representational politics operates, and in this country, lobbying efforts are virtually impossible without recourse to identity politics... But that necessity needs to be reconciled with another. The minute that the category of women is invoked as *describing* the constituency for which feminism speaks, an internal debate invariably begins over what the descriptive content of that term will be.

(Butler, 1992: 15)

The 'internal debate' over what the identity of 'women' means is a recognition that this universal identity is fundamentally problematic as a starting point for the remedial technologies of democracy and citizenship – laws which seek to ensure equality – because the subject of law becomes a generalised, or abstract grouping. For example, one of the major issues in the UK for the second wave feminist movement was women's pay, which was addressed through the Equal Pay Act of 1970, and to some further extent by the Sex Discrimination Act of 1975.[3] Thirty-five years later, the enforcement bureau for these acts – the Equal Opportunities Commission – published the *Just Pay* report, demonstrating not only that women still suffer discrimination through pay, but also that 'different' women are affected differently, especially those who are from ethnic minorities.[4]

Furthermore, there is a current recognition that combined with the intersection of class and educational levels, other intersections of race/ethnicity, culture, sexuality, may affect access to the resources of the law in remedying inequalities, and so the Gender Equality Duty Act (GED) became law in the UK in April 2007. This removes the need for individual women to sue for their rights in specific contexts, instead placing the emphasis on public authorities to demonstrate that they are pursuing and ensuring equality between genders (see Note 3):

> 30 years after the introduction of the Sex Discrimination Act [SDA], there is still discrimination. The rights of individuals do not oblige organisations to promote equality. The GED will bring about real change in the culture of organisations as the onus will be on organisations to promote equality, rather than on individuals to highlight discrimination.
>
> (www.eoc.org.uk, 26 January 2007)

There is a recognition of the limits of law as an individualised technology here, and one might even argue that this is a recognition of some difference, particularly the difference across the social resources which may limit the agency of individuals because of the structural conditions of their employment sector which may not provide the financial and professional security to sue for their rights. However, despite this advance, there is no discussion in these proposals of the complexity of the categories of gender, either in relation to each other, or, more pertinently, within the category of 'women', with only a brief consideration of discrimination against transsexuals (i.e. those who have sought reassignment to the established gender categories). This lack of complexity makes it difficult to see how the public authorities under this jurisdiction can begin to reach for ensuring gender equality which is intersectional in its form and content. For example, it is not clear that the GED would have helped the recent case of a Muslim woman teaching assistant losing her discrimination case since that judgment suggests that conceptualisations of gendered ethnicity are outwith the grasp of legal codifications based simply on gender or ethnicity or religion (see Note 1) – and it also reminds us that the bulk of equality legislation still places the duty on individuals to pursue their rights.

This brief example illustrates why there have been challenges to universalising explanations, particularly in their generalisations about identity and the authenticity of experience it presumes. Feminist challenges to the 'category of woman' are the most obvious example here, illustrated by lesbian, black, third world and postmodern feminisms, exemplified by the work of those such as Hill Collins on race (1990/2000), and Adrienne Rich on 'Compulsory Heterosexuality' (1978).[5] The challenge and promise of intersectionality is to render more complex the explanations for how individuals are discriminated against or oppressed because of the complex ways in which they belong to groups, challenging thus sociological accounts of identities which are universalist.

Implicated deeply in this critique is the exclusionary consequence of identity as a political tool – the fact that the relational nature of identity categories inevitably leads to definitions based on 'inside/outside' as Diana Fuss suggested (1991), often focusing our attention on major binary divides, such as men/women, black/white, straight/gay and codifying these through political activism and policy. However, whilst the achievement of social movements has been to show how oppression works through these divisions of dominant/oppressed identities, there has been simultaneously reification of these identity categories, often rendering invisible the perspectives and experience of those who belong, but belong in different ways. What I suggest is that this consequence of how identity functions actually *undermines* the possibilities of 'equality' as a universal condition that can be achieved. Using laws and policy to reach for an equality based on one dominant, abstract and universal version of identity and experience is necessarily going to be a partial version of the actual *lived experience* of equality because it excludes differences, excludes understandings of how those differences result from, are brought into effect by intersectionality. Thought of in this way, universal identity categories cannot provide the basis for universal outcomes of equality.

Intersectionality is therefore an urgent question if understood in terms of the challenge of difference which currently preoccupies much identity theorisation and politics. Moreover, if an intersectional perspective is demanded by difference, it is simultaneously demanded by the gaps in sociological theories that have produced universalising explanations of social relations and identities, whether of class, or patriarchy, gender or race. Sociological theorising has, perhaps necessarily, had to provide generalised explanations about the impacts of structures, cultures, action in constituting society, inequalities and identities, since attempts to theorise cannot account for every single difference without becoming particularistic. As Swingewood puts it in his comprehensive overview of sociological thought, '...society cannot be decomposed into individuals any more than "geometric surface can be decomposed into lines, or a line into a point." Knowledge of the parts can flow only from knowledge of the whole, not vice versa' (2000: 18). However, intersectionality theory presents a challenge to such versions of sociological knowledge, not because it demands particularism through methodological individualism, but because it demands that we attempt to bridge the tension between particularisms of difference and how these differences are ultimately indicative of how realms of the social and hierarchies intersect and constitute complex identities within categories of the 'oppressed'.

Furthermore, the political goal of equality becomes much more complex an issue once universal identity and experience – and the related assumed universal access to social resources – become problematised through an intersectional sociological perspective. And, I suggest, this problematisation is necessary, not only to properly achieve the sociological task of evidencing inequalities in their complex, intersecting formations, but also to resolve the attendant framing of 'equality' as a universal condition. Intersectionality demands a qualitatively different understanding of dominant, unitary categories such as gender and therefore implies potentially differentiated policies in remedying inequalities based on these categories and perhaps, ultimately, the implication of differential outcomes in terms of what constitutes 'equality'.

Equal rights, unequal ontologies

Although not termed as such, the understandings of difference and the intersections of the social have been important concerns since the beginnings of feminism in the eighteenth century and, crucially, these concerns were explored in the context of emerging discourses and practices of democracy, equality and citizenship. Beginning at the beginning – with liberal feminism – we can see its thinkers inevitably attached to democracy as the ideal system of governance, forming a significant aspect of the challenge that the development of democratic structures and principles posed to the liberal state (see Note 2). Thus, liberal feminism was, and remains, *liberal democratic* feminism, combining the aspiration of equal political participation and equality under the law (democracy) with the acceptance that this can be done through minimal formal rights, which permit integration into current systems (liberal freedom from state interference and regulation).

What I want to consider is how liberal feminism is also implicitly radical, in that it has often focused on the social ontology of gender in its emphasis on the social construction of femininity as a barrier to women's emancipation. For example, in her foundational liberal feminist text from 1792, *A Vindication of the Rights of Woman*, Mary Wollstonecraft deliberately echoes Thomas Paine's classic statement of (male) human rights, arguing that women could equally fulfil the conditions of citizenship if given equal access to education and employment. Moreover, she suggests that the contemporary social construction of femininity that identified it with supervision of the domestic realm, actively prevents middle-class women from developing their intellect:

> With respect to virtue, to use the word in a comprehensive sense, I have seen the most in low life. Many poor women maintain their children by the sweat of their brow, and keep together families that the vices of the fathers would have scattered abroad; but gentlewomen are too indolent to be actively virtuous, and are softened rather than refined by civilisation.
>
> ([1792] 1972: 16)

Her call to improve the lot of middle-class women is a challenge to both their material dependence – their lack of need for work – and to the related dominant gender framework of the time, what has been termed the 'domestic ideology' (Davidoff and Hall, 1987; Weeks, 1989). Indeed, some hundred and fifty years on from Wollstonecraft, Betty Friedan's book, *The Feminine Mystique* (1963) is another classic liberal feminist text which emphasises the limitations that domesticity places on women, similarly focusing on the plight of middle-class women in post-war America, thus demonstrating the structural permanence of the domestic ideology.

However, despite the liberalism of such arguments in arguing for changes to the law and policies which permit more women to work, it is interesting to note that these arguments also focus on dominant cultural discourses – the domestic ideology – and exhort a change in such values. The implication is that, in order to achieve 'equality' for women, even if that means merely equal opportunity under the law, you also have to inevitably engage in a rethinking of how social structures such as the division of labour and its related cultural discourse of feminine domesticity produce divisions between the genders. Remedies must therefore implicitly move beyond a traditional understanding of 'liberalism' where intervention by the state is regarded as necessary only to regulate, and in any case is ultimately distasteful because of the potential reach of state power. Rather, providing equal access, or opportunity, requires intervention, not only at the political level, but potentially also on a massive scale, both to re-order the economic and social relations that provide the basis of the domestic ideology, and to actively challenge this dominant cultural meaning system. Intersectional analysis across the social is therefore not a new concern and its purview impacts upon two related aspects of theorising intersectionalities of difference.

First, we can see that the equal rights tradition is the longest in feminism's complex history (Banks, 1990), providing the standard technique for advancing women's social position not only in liberal feminism, but also in more subsequent and radical feminisms. The common theme is that equality of citizenship becomes a condition that women – all women – can inhabit if allowed equal access to its social paths. As Phillips describes: 'Feminists looked beyond the specificities of existing culture and society (cultures and societies in which women might well appear the inferiors of men) to a more transcendent rationality and justice' (Phillips, 1993: 55). These 'transcendent' values include 'an essential human equality despite all secondary differences' (1993: 55). But this raises the second important issue: the pursuit of equality as a transcendent condition implicitly universalises that condition – it becomes, after all, transcendent precisely by ignoring differences amongst the category of identity. Thus, the question of difference is contentious because it is potentially antithetical to a universal condition of equality. Difference is therefore not only a current contention of how we think through intersections of social inequality, but has remained an unresolved theme from the early genesis of feminist thought and its engagement with questions of equality and citizenship. This inheritance directs us to the key question of whether socially significant differences have to be regarded simply as 'secondary' in their ontological contribution to a universal condition of equality.

Early liberal feminism set the tone for engagement with the discourse of equality and citizenship as a value neutral universal condition and so created a momentum within subsequent feminisms towards claims for equality, seen in manifestos from various women's and lesbian and gay liberation groups which commonly talk about equality under the law,[6] and expressed most directly in the passage of legislation during the second wave movement which attempted to outlaw discrimination. As we have seen in the example from Britain above (Gelb, 1990), many of these encompassed a universal category of gender (often codified as 'sex') which has remained to this day, despite the increasing awareness that many differences intersect to affect women in differential ways. Given the apparent antithesis between universal equality and the recognition of intersectional difference, we need to think through the implications of intersectionality as a potential rejection of universal concepts such as 'human equality' and the associated versions of 'women' and 'equality'. We should understand the emphasis on intersectional difference as a challenge to templates and technologies of liberal democracy: the abstract citizen, the individual as the fundamental political unit of participation, the lack of enabling mechanisms for participation beyond the formal 'right' to participate, the measurement of equality as a merely formal legal condition (Phillips 1993).

The implicit universalism in each of these factors is problematic precisely because it is the unequal social constitution of different identities which anchors and sustains their inequalities in the political realm. As the reports from the British government demonstrated above, the pay differentials between men and women – the main categorical division of gender – is rendered more complex when those categories are morphed into ethnic minority men and women, and more complex still when the specific ethnicities are detailed. How then, with different constitutions of the object 'identity' – thus different ontologies – can we assert a universalism of either identity or 'equality'? Properly speaking, we cannot because an intersectional perspective seems instinctively at odds with liberalism, calling as it does on a wider lens to view social inequalities and the role of the law as remedy, than liberalism admits. It challenges both the purpose of law and social policy, and thus its scope and mechanisms, but also, it fundamentally requires the admittance of socially significant differences into liberalism's apparently hallowed focus on the individual as essentially equal in the eyes of politics and the law.

However, Phillips suggests that liberalism's rejection or denial of differences is also, at one level, a profound recognition that they exist and are pertinent to determining outcomes of equality. In fact, we can understand the attempt to smooth over differences through the appeal to universal equality as a simultaneous acknowledgement that there are socially produced ontologies which are definitely unequal. Liberal, democratic, feminism could be useful here since it demands a focus on universal or transcendent values of equality, equal rights and equal citizenship – ideas which are powerful recruiters to a cause now that the discourse of human rights and equality is a globalised one (Castells, 2004). Simultaneously, the implicit suggestion in this discourse is that unequal outcomes should not be the acceptable goal or tolerable condition of our political life but that they do indeed exist. As Phillips suggests (1993), this position perhaps also allows us to discern an opening for theorising and understanding differences as the starting point for equality strategies. The trick is to extend this line of reasoning to couple the acknowledgement of difference with the appeal to equality, rather than accept the inheritance that the denial of difference is the only way to reach for equality. This presents a challenge to how we use and understand identity categories, in that we have to retain the sense of identities as legitimate markers of experience and claims to equality, whilst also pluralise the basis of that experience to include intersectional differences.

One strategy to achieving intersectional understanding of identities and experiences is to acknowledge that an intersectional perspective must also be sociologically intersectional. This immediately illustrates that identities are not solely based on one group's 'ownership' of the identity, since identities exist across the intersecting realms of the social. Identities are, by definition, representational, both in theory and in practice, and they are certainly defined by the groups claiming them (Castells 2004) – but that is not the only dimension. They are a circuit of public, collective and self representations and in this sense, they are both representations of experience and public reactions and contestations of this experience. Once we accept this empirical fact, we can begin to think through how claims for equality related to these identities are also contested, suggesting that differences in experience are already in some way the starting point for debates which inevitably contest the ontology of equality as a condition to strive for.

For example, in Britain in early 2007 we witnessed another controversy between religion and gay rights, with the Catholic Church threatening to shut down its adoption services if they were not exempted from the provisions of new equality legislation, which prohibited them from discriminating against lesbian and gay couples.[7] The line of division was not drawn over whether gays should have equal rights – not thus over the ontological existence of gays and lesbians as part of universal 'human' rights – but rather over what the ontological *experience* of equality should be: Catholics characterised the legislation as discriminating against *them* because it was insensitive to their religious moral difference, and argued that this issue should take precedence over the rights of gays and lesbians not to experience discrimination in every area of their lives.

In similar vein to the debate about the repeal of Section 28 in Britain – an infamous law which prohibited the 'intentional promotion' of homosexuality by local authorities – this issue can be read first as a tussle over how to balance rights but, I have argued, such cases are also ultimately about how the discourse of equality is now contested, and indeed deployed in different ways by opposing groups, suggesting a battle over the 'shape of equality' as an ontological resource (Rahman 2004). This is difficult terrain, since the implication is that no universal standard of equality exists and, furthermore, that claims to equality from particular oppressed groups are open to challenge from opposing groups. However, the latter is already the empirical fact, and I am not suggesting that we challenge the authenticity of identity categories as the basis for claims of oppression or equality, but rather that we understand that the ways in which identities are contested *also* indicate that equality claims are used as strategic resources to articulate lived and hoped for ontological conditions.

For example, the debate mentioned above about women who wear the veil in Britain has thrown up a complexity of intersectional issues, with many of the minority of women who have chosen the veil articulating their choice in terms of their rights to freedom of religious expression, and in part, as a strategy for avoiding some of the overt sexism and objectification that comes their way as women in Britain (see Note 1). Of course, the dominant political discourses and legal positions have not recognised either of these ontological statements, with one woman being removed from her teaching post and losing a subsequent discrimination claim, and a lack of nuance in the debates about how gender oppression and liberation are implicitly mapped onto Eastern and Western ethnicities; about the context of Islamophobia; about differences within the Muslim community along all these dimensions. Indeed, the former Prime Minister reduced the debate to 'common sense' about social interaction, with the now *de rigeur* dose of terrorist related Islamophobia thrown in (see Note 1). But thinking about the contested battle over rights as one of contest about the ontological shape of equality directs us to begin with this *function* of identity claims rather than assume the reification of identity categories.

As Motha reminds us (2007), Muslim women have claims to equality on a gendered basis which are in apparent conflict with many aspects of feminism *and* secular liberalism, but if we can realise a sense of how these are debates over the ontological condition of equality, we can perhaps begin to work through the tangle of identity, differences and equality which has so beset political strategies. We can begin to think of 'equality' less as a neutral abstract condition, and more as a contested ontological resource – a strategy for making lived experience chime better with the wishes of different groups. What I think is important to consider is that an intersectional perspective on difference can help us to work around the universalising momentum towards an undifferentiated notion of identity and equality, because it allows us to challenge the universalist assumptions around identity, which thus implicate different understandings of equality. If identity claims and reactions to them can be thought of as ontological statements about the differences of lived experience and equality, we need to theorise them intersectionally, since, as argued in the previous section, intersectional analytics are demanded by the complexities of difference. By developing intersectional analytics more fully, perhaps we can interrogate and redefine the universalism within democratic liberalism, rendering more visible the implicit recognition of difference in democratic theory in order to work towards a fulfilment of liberalism's powerful universal promise of equality.

Theorising intersectionality as materiality

In pursuing intersectionality, we see a challenge to 'equality' as a universal condition to which oppressed identities aspire; the consequence of which is that we must understand equality as a discursive political resource which is used to articulate and promote versions of lived experience or what I have termed the shape of equality. Therefore, a focus on the social ontology of lived experience is necessary to a more astute understanding of the differences within identity categories – differences in lived experience and related lived experiences of what equality would mean. Being attuned to differences necessarily demands an intersectional perspective because such analytics are grounded in the standpoint tradition, or begin with the focus on experience and knowledge of the group in question. Moreover, as with the issue of understanding equality as an ontological resource, so too is grounded experience and knowledge a question of understanding the ontological: how identities, experience and knowledge are constituted socially in their full diversity. My aim in this final section is to begin a discussion of how we might move from the intersectional combination of factors such as race, gender and class, to a consideration of whether a more condensed focus on sites of intersectionality can be achieved.

The question of the ontological is a vast one for sociology and feminism, and of course there is too much history to cover such a topic in this chapter from either literature. What I want to do is use some previous arguments developed around feminist uses of the concept of the material to illustrate contemporary concerns around ontology and work towards how we might refine intersectionality by shifting its focus somewhat to the question of what brings ontology into effect. In a recent paper, I suggested that feminist theorisations of gender and sexuality as fundamentally *social* had two purposes (Rahman and Witz, 2003). First, rendering 'naturalist' ideas as social has the effect of politicising them, making them the legitimate subject of collective social decision making and illuminating how the 'natural' is political. Second, that 'this key aim of politicisation can be understood as a focus on ontology' (2003: 244). Whilst we were discussing the ways in which the concept of the 'material' has been deployed within various feminist paradigms to characterise ontology, we also suggested that materialist (or Marxist) feminism had stretched its concept of the material in an attempt to apprehend previously under theorised aspects of ontology, such as the 'symbolic, experiential and processual aspects of the social' (2003: 244). Of course, this is the terrain that standpoint theories attempt to access, and thus, the concern with ontology here converges with the demands of intersectionality.

The key dynamic in these debates is how to retain a sense of permanence, or structural conditions, whilst similarly being attuned to the complex intersections of how the structural is lived experience, or how lived experience instantiates the structural. In its essence, the debates are about whether the insights of the more particularistic and agent focused embodiment and post-structuralist theories of gender and sexuality can be incorporated into the structuralist and deterministic bias of materialist feminism. Furthermore, this dynamic reminds us of the overarching tension in intersectionality theory, between how to account for evident diversity in particularistic experience and identity whilst retaining a sense of the social structural – or how oppressions operate in common ways across diverse identities and levels of the social. The focus on materiality is therefore keenly relevant to theorising intersectionality in that understanding sites of intersection and how diverse identities are constituted therein is precisely about understanding the materiality of these sites, both across the levels of the social and how different hierarchies operating across these levels bring complex identities and experience into effect.

In developing our concept of materiality, we suggested a common ground to a variety of these seemingly disparate theoretical perspectives drawn from materialist feminism, post-structuralism and embodiment literatures. In essence, we argued that the continuing concern to develop a fully social ontology of gender and sexuality could be discerned across the range of these perspectives as a focus on effectivity – what various materialist, symbolic or discursive, processual and praxiological factors combined across the intersecting realms of the social to constitute social ontology. We argued that the more recent term of 'materiality' evident across these literatures could be understood to denote this somewhat undefined commonality across these divergent theoretical approaches:

> If we can understand materiality as an attempt to conceptualise and interrogate elements of gendered and sexualised ontological intelligibility and process, then we can begin to understand it across a range of diverse work as an attempt to understand what effects or materialises – in the sense of bringing into being – gendered and sexualised sociality, embodiment and identity.
>
> (Rahman and Witz, 2003: 258)

A focus on 'effective materiality' allows for a more porous, more flexible starting point on understanding the complex intersectional dimensions across the social and its significant hierarchies. This flexibility is needed to theorise how the different hierarchies create different ontologies, identities and how they shape equality, because intersectional analysis requires that we reject 'additive' explanations of social inequalities, and resist any inclination to reducing oppression to 'one fundamental type' of explanatory theory (Hill Collins, 2000). Thus, I suggest that a focus on 'effective' materiality allows us to begin with the site of intersection as our empirical and analytical focus because it is theoretically and conceptually open, whilst remaining epistemologically committed to the tradition of grounded and standpoint analysis of intersectionality and, moreover, committed to theorising in a way that retains the sense of permanence of social arrangements denoted by 'materiality'.

When we begin with commitment to understanding what brings a particular inequality into effect, we explore the materiality of that situation, first and foremost with an emphasis on how the ontological is lived experience but with an overarching commitment to explaining materiality as the instantiation of structural social arrangements such as oppression. There is a subtle shift of emphasis in the focus on the lived experience of the intersection, in the sense that I am suggesting that this focus becomes a starting point, rather than pre-determined, or simply pre-judged, understandings of intersecting or interlocked social hierarchies. Moreover, this is not to dismiss or replace intersectional emphases on vectors of oppression, or interlocked hierarchies, but rather, beginning with experience allows us to think about how the ontological is the lived instantiation of intersectionality or, put another way, how we are located at the sites of intersection of vectors of oppression and inequality. Indeed, a focus on 'effective materiality' is to a large part a focus on how these more abstract patterns are instantiated within lived experience and thus how they bring that experience into effect.

I am conscious that there is little space to develop this perspective more fully in this chapter, but let me conclude with an illustration of what I mean by materiality, returning to the example of the controversy over the Muslim veil in Britain (see Note 1). I suggested that one of the missing elements from much of the discussion is any thorough, valid representation of who, how and why Muslim women choose to wear the veil, and this immediately alerts us to one aspect of the materiality of this intersectional situation that is missing: we need to have much more research on the experience of such women; how they feel that the veil is empowering – particularly in the face of claims to the contrary – how they connect their rights to equality with such a gendered garment, and how far they articulate their ethnic-religious identity in concert with their gendered, class and educational identity. The intersectionality of these issues can only be properly understood by a grounded, standpoint body of research, illuminating the effective materiality of those who wear the veil precisely by beginning with their lived experience.

However, that alone will not help us to understand the full materiality of this event, but rather we must also research what has brought the debate into effect, thus looking across the realms of the social to connect experience to the specificities of politics and culture within a historical context – the more permanent socio-economic and discursive formations which are the materiality of how specifics of the veil are brought into effect. Thus we must attend to 9/11 and Britain's alliance with the USA since then, in part creating an almost relentless focus on every aspect of British Muslim behaviour and identity, and creating a new lease of life for the uncertain multiculturalism that has characterised Britain's relationship with former colonial immigrants from south Asia (Yuval-Davis, 1997). Of course, this leads us to think about how racism operates in the UK, and how laws and policies work in relation to specific identities, and what that says about equality. For example, the Gender Equality Duty Act would not, it seems, have made it any easier for the Muslim teaching assistant who was dismissed for wearing her veil when male teachers were present, and yet, to reduce that experience to one dimension of identity – either religion or gender – is profoundly ignorant of how the veil is indeed an intersectional gendered ethnic issue. And of course, these factors may appear in any research done on Muslim women, their experience of how it is to live at the intersection of all these events, allowing us then to understand their accounts as instantiations of interlocked vectors of oppression, without reducing their standpoint to simply women or Muslims. The ultimate outcome of such research on standpoints, together with a commitment to locating the materiality of these experiences within structural frameworks, may be that we can move towards equality legislation that can be more porous to intersectionality – perhaps gender equality duties that acknowledges in subordinate clauses that religion, sexuality, disability, ethnicity may variously combine to produce gendered inequality.

Conclusion

In terms of contributing to further theorising intersectionality, I have suggested that thinking about ontology as the materiality of being helps us to reach for a better understanding of what brings particular experiences into effect. This 'effectivity' is, I argue, a subtle shift in emphasis for intersectionality, beginning at the intersection or precise experience and working outwards to more generalised and abstract analytics. This shift in emphasis allows us to rotate our initial gaze away from thinking about the interlocked or intersectional in terms of already existing and understood, discrete and distinct vectors of oppression, which has done little to challenge the momentum towards universalist categories within identity politics.

Nonetheless, we have also to admit the relevance of already existing frameworks for describing oppression, and the importance of dominant discourses such as equality and identity in furthering strategic aims and allowing the translation of intersectional ontologies into mainstream, policy fluent technologies. But, whilst we should continue to think about the importance of equality as a transcendent guiding discourse, intersectionality as a focus on the materiality of being also permits us to think about equality as a strategy, a contested version of the abstract universal condition which turns it into a resource, a way of articulating experience both lived and hoped for. The ultimate promise of intersectional analytics should be, therefore, not simply a better way to understand the myriad differences that bring particular oppressions into effect, but also to understand the different forms, the different shape of equality as lived experience, perhaps helping ultimately to shape better policy to achieve full, differentiated or *equivalent* (Cornell, 1992), equality for all.

Identity is clearly the focus of how we discuss these intersections of oppression, but there is a sense in which current controversies of difference suggest that we might move beyond identity – partly chiming with my suggestion that we need to explore the ontological purpose and deployment of identity, but also in the sense that identity politics is a curse – an inevitable playing out or self-fulfilling circuit of essentialisation, with consequently limiting results, in terms of citizenship and also, equality. But of course, the curse begins by claiming identity and that claim is irreducibly necessary to a democratic system. This ultimately relates back to my concerns to theorise intersectionality as a way of using identity politics that is not reductionist, essentialising and universalising, but expansionist, and relational. In short, theorising intersectionality in relationship to difference, may help us to explore whether a full, equal citizenship can encompass a diversity of ontological statements and conditions.

Bibliography

Altman, D. (1971). *Homosexual Oppression and Liberation*, New York: New York University Press.

Banks, O. (1990). *Faces of Feminism*, Oxford: Basil Blackwell.

Baumeister, A. (2000). *Liberalism and the Politics of Difference*, Edinburgh: Edinburgh University Press.

Beal, F.M. (1970). 'Double Jeopardy: To be Black and Female', in Morgan, R. (ed.), *Sisterhood is Powerful: An Anthology of Writings from the Women's Liberation Movement*, New York: Vintage Books.

Butler, J. (1992). 'Contingent Foundations: Feminism and the Question of "Postmodernism"', in Butler, J. and Scott, J.W. (eds), *Feminists Theorise the Political*, New York: Routledge.

Butler, J. and Scott, J.W. (eds) (1992). *Feminists Theorise the Political*, New York: Routledge.

Castells, M. (2004). *The Power of Identity* (2nd edn), Malden, MA: Blackwell.

Cornell, D. (1992). 'Gender, Sex and Equivalent Rights', in Butler, J. and Scott, J.W. (eds), *Feminists Theorise the Political*, New York: Routledge.

Dahlerup, D. (ed.) (1990). *The New Women's Movement: Feminism and Political Power in Europe and the USA*, London: Sage.

Davidoff, L. and Hall, C. (1987). *Family Fortunes: Men and Women of the English Middle Class 1780–1850*, London: Hutchinson Press.

Evans, D. (1993). *Sexual Citizenship: The Material Construction of Sexualities*, London: Routledge.

Ezekiel, J. (2006). 'French Dressing: Race, Gender and the Hijab Story', *Feminist Studies*, 32(2): 256–78.

Fraser, N. and Honneth, A. (2003). *Redistribution or Recognition?: A Political-Philosophical Exchange*, London: Verso.

Friedan, B. (1963). *The Feminine Mystique*, London: Gollancz.

Fuss, D. (1991). 'Inside/out', in Fuss, D. (ed.), *Inside Out: Lesbian Theories, Gay Theories*, New York: Routledge.

Gelb, J. (1990). 'Feminism in Britain: Politics without power?' in Dahlerup, D. (ed), *The New Women's Movement: Feminism and Political Power in Europe and the USA*, London: Sage.

Held, D. (1993). 'From City-states to a Cosmopolitan Order?', in Held, D. (ed.), *Prospects for Democracy*, Cambridge: Polity Press.

Hill Collins, P. (2000). *Black Feminist Thought: Knowledge, Consciousness and Empowerment*, 2nd edn, Boston, MA: Unwin Hyman.

Jackson, S. and Scott, S. (1996). 'Sexual Skirmishes and Feminist Factions,' in Jackson, S. and Scott, S. (eds), *Feminism and Sexuality*, Edinburgh: Edinburgh University Press.

Madoo Lengermann, P. and Niebrugge, J. (2003). 'Contemporary Feminist Theories', in Ritzer, G. (ed.) *Contemporary Sociological Theory and its Classical Roots*, New York: McGraw Hill.

Morgan, R. (ed.) (1970). *Sisterhood is Powerful: An Anthology of Writings from the Women's Liberation Movement*, New York: Vintage Books.

Motha, S. (2007). 'Veiled Women and the Affect of Religion in Democracy.' *Journal of Law and Society*, 34(1): 139–62.

Najmabadi, A. (2006). 'Gender and Secularism of Modernity: How Can a Muslim Woman be French?' *Feminist Studies*, 32(2): 239–55.

Phillips, A. (1993). *Democracy and Difference*, Oxford: Polity Press.

Phillips, A. (1995). *The Politics of Prescence*, Oxford: Clarendon Press.

Rahman, M. (2000). *Sexuality and Democracy: Identities and Strategies in Lesbian and Gay Politics,* Edinburgh: Edinburgh University Press.

Rahman, M. (2004). 'The Shape of Equality: Discursive Deployments During the Section 28 Repeal in Scotland.' *Sexualities*, 7(2): 150–66.

Rahman, M. and Witz, A. (2003). 'What Really Matters? The Elusive Quality of the Material in Feminist Thought.' *Feminist Theory*, 4(3): 243–61.

Rich, A. (1978). *Blood, Bread and Poetry*, London: Virago.

Richardson, D. (ed) (1996). *Theorising Heterosexuality: Telling it Straight*, Buckingham: Open University Press.

Richardson, D. (1998). 'Sexuality and Citizenship.' *Sociology*, 32(1): 83–100.

Schneir, M. (ed). (1972). *Feminism: The Essential Historical Writings*, New York: Vintage Books.

Seidman, S. (1996). 'Introduction', in Seidman, S (ed), *Queer Theory/Sociology*, Oxford: Blackwell.

Swingewood, A. (2000). *A Short History of Sociological Thought*, 3rd edn, Basingstoke: Macmillan.

Weeks, J. (1989). *Sex, Politics and Society*, 2nd edn, Harlow: Longman.

Whelehan, I. (1995). *Modern Feminist Thought: From the Second Wave to Post-Feminism*, New York: New York University Press.

Wollstonecraft, M. ([1792] 1972). 'A Vindication of the Rights of Woman' in M. Schneir (ed.), *Feminism: The Essential Historical Writings*, New York: Vintage Books.

Yuval-Davis, N. (1997) *Gender and Nation*, London: Sage.

Notes

1 A controversial public debate developed in the UK in autumn 2006 when the Leader of the House of Commons, Jack Straw, revealed that he asked veiled Muslim women to remove their veils when they came to see him as their constituency MP. The intersections of social interaction, ethnicity, religion, gender, terrorism and multiculturalism in this issue echoed previous debates in France (Ezekiel, 2006; Najmabadi, 2006) and sustained a lengthy discussion in British newspapers, television news and political programmes, involving politicians, Muslims and, to a lesser extent, Muslim women who actually wore the veil. See the article 'Radical Muslims must integrate, says Blair' in *The*

Guardian, 9 December 2006, p. 4, for example, and a range of opinions and some anecdotal evidence that it is young, radical Muslim women who choose the veil on http://news.bbc.co.uk/2/hi/uk_news/s413234.stm (but searching news site under 'veil and muslim women' brings up much more evidence). The debate also threw media attention on the case of a Muslim woman teaching assistant who was sacked for refusing to remove her veil when male teachers were present, and who subsequently lost her employment tribunal claiming discrimination on gender and religious grounds, although the tribunal agreed she had been 'victimised'. Also see Motha (2007) for a discussion of how veiling presents a challenge to both feminism and liberal secularism.

2 As many democratic theorists point out, contemporary democratic societies have largely developed from liberal societies, where the concern with liberty – from state interference with finances and faith – was historically more important than conditions of equality (Held, 1993). Of course, with the gradual expansion of universal suffrage and subsequent emergence of working-class political parties, concerns with social equality came to the fore, bequeathing our current democratic status quo. But the impact of liberal principles on our democratic inheritance should not be underestimated, particularly when assessing the difficulties of dealing with group identities as the basis of inequalities (Baumeister, 2000; Fraser and Honneth, 2003), and why equality has been slow to arrive, and limited in its form in the context of gender (Phillips, 1993, 1995) and sexuality (Rahman, 2000).

3 Although Gelb points out that these legislative advances in Britain were often driven by trade union movements and related groups in the Labour Party and as such 'feminists have been able to influence public policy primarily as an auxiliary resource for parliamentary actors who are responsible for initiating and passing the legislation' (1990: 116). Nonetheless, the creation of the Equal Opportunities Commission to enforce these Acts has remained an important, if under-resourced, official means of implementing the law. Indeed, their recent report – *Just Pay* – acknowledges their lack of effectiveness in ensuring equal pay and the difficulties of individuals pursuing litigation. Available from the EOC in Manchester, UK or via http://www.equalityhumanrights.com/en/Pages/search.aspx?k=just%20pay&docid=&classid=492. To some extent, this recognition has contributed to the Gender Equality Duty Act, which became law in April 2007, which places the emphasis on public authorities to demonstrate equality, rather than leaving it to individual litigation (see www.eoc.org.uk for details).

4 See the consultation and information gathering campaign, 'Moving Up?', details at www.eoc.org.uk. Current figures show that both Bangladeshi and Pakistani women (who are overwhelmingly Muslim) and Afro-Caribbean women suffer from greater pay inequalities than ethnic white women.

5 See for example, the collection of different perspectives in the collection edited by Butler and Scott, 1992; Banks, 1990 and the collection of historical writings edited by Miriam Schneir (1972), which includes transcripts of Sojourner Truth's speeches, in which she most famously raised the question – as a black, freed slave who engaged in heavy domestic labour – 'Ain't I a Woman?' – in discussion with contemporary feminist and anti-slavery campaigns of the time, which characterised femininity as somewhat too delicate for heavy labour. Jackson and Scott discuss the tensions between lesbian and heterosexual feminists in the introduction to the reader (1996).

6 See, for example, manifestos from the National Organisation of Women and more radical groups in Morgan, 1970, and the gay liberation manifesto from Britain in Evans, 1993.

7 The Catholic Church was supported by the leaders of the Church of England in this deployment of 'conscience' as a right which overrides the provisions of the Equality Act 2006. The objections are to gay and lesbian couples adopting, since they argue their faith recognises only the union between a man and woman as a proper family situation in which to place children. To some extent, they use the fact that they already consider placing children with single lesbians and gays as evidence that they are not discriminating, although it remains unclear why this policy is not also fraught with dilemmas of moral conscience. See the quality British press in January 2007 or http://news.bbc.co.uk/2/hi/uk_news/ politics/6284725.stm.

Index

ESSENTIALISM: the view that for any specific entity ~~group~~
there is a set of attributes which are necessary
to its identity & function.

LUCNA: a blank space or a missing part

TROPE: a common or overused theme or device

REIFY: to regard (something abstract) as a material
or concrete thing

UBIQUITOUS: existing or being ~~somewhere~~ everywhere at the
same time: constantly encountered:
widespread.